The Hero Succeeds

THE CHARACTER-DRIVEN GUIDE TO WRITING YOUR TV PILOT

Kam Miller

High & Low Media
Los Angeles

Ordering Information:
Special discounts are available on quantity purchases for academic use.
For more information, please send inquiries to info@highandlowmedia.com.

High & Low Media / Los Angeles
First print edition April 2016. v. 1.0

ISBN 978-0-9971880-1-1

For Robert and Sylvia Lauterborn, heroes in life and love.

Contents

Introduction: Why Me, Why Now? Why You, Why Now?...... 1

1: You're Not Selling the *Pilot*, You're Selling the *Show*............ 10

2: TV Series Treatment: Components, Questions..................... 27

3: The Hero Succeeds: Character-Driven Structure 65

4: Breakdowns: Dissection and the Anatomy of Pilots............. 92

5: The Art of the Grid: The Keys to the Kingdom 237

6: Creating Your Pilot Story Grid.. 271

7: Refining Your Pilot.. 290

8: Your Outline: Don't Skip the Outline!................................. 311

9: Your Script: Write It As Fast As You Can! 318

10: Your Second Draft: Writing Is Rewriting.......................... 343

11: Revising Your TV Series Treatment 361

12: You Succeed: Your New Life 363

Appendix.. 365

Endnotes.. 485

About the Author 499

TL;DR introduction

I'm Kam Miller. I've written and produced TV shows, and now I create and sell TV pilots to many of the industry's biggest players. All writers who want to work in TV need stellar pilots in their portfolios. *The Hero Succeeds* delivers a groundbreaking, character-driven script structure and other essential tools to create TV series that sell to Hollywood. I've helped thousands of students at top film schools launch their writing careers, and *The Hero Succeeds* can help you build or expand your TV career, too!

Why Me, Why Now? Why You, Why Now?

Welcome to *The Hero Succeeds: The Character-Driven Guide to Writing Your TV Pilot.* I'm stoked to share with you the tools and techniques that have helped me throughout my career as a TV writer and creator.

Since Aristotle first mused about a whole's beginning, middle, and end, innumerable writers have further quantified storytelling, with more-recent works focused on writing feature-film screenplays. The deceptively complex TV pilot has remained relatively unexplored territory. Now, the explosion of TV shows—a record 412 original, scripted TV series in 2015[1]—and the advent of premium cable and other TV shows with no commercial act breaks have ushered in a new era of television writing.

Television's current high profile has been driven in part by an influx of award-winning film actors and directors pursuing TV's rich story-telling and rich paydays. Today, there are more platforms and buyers for TV shows than ever before, and they all need great content. Pilot writing used to be reserved for a rarified few, but now *every* writer who wants to work in TV needs original pilots in his or her portfolio.

So why listen to me? I've been writing, pitching, selling, and developing TV pilots for years with some of the industry's biggest players. Now, *The Hero Succeeds'* character-driven structure unifies all television writing, including dramas and comedies on premium cable, basic cable, broadcast networks, and digital streaming series. *The Hero Succeeds* guides you all the way from your idea to your polished pilot script. Before we dive in, I'd like to tell you a bit about me and what sets *The Hero Succeeds* apart from some of my other favorite books about writing. I'd also like to tell you who I think *you* might be and how you can benefit from this book.

Who I am

I'm Kam Miller. I'm a working TV writer-producer and creator. I've written TV shows and features. I wrote for the long-running series *Law & Order: SVU.* Now, I primarily create, develop, sell, and write TV pilots. I have developed pilots with FOX, 20th Century Fox, CBS, CBS Television Studios, and Universal Cable Productions, among others.

How did I get here? After earning my MFA at USC and staffing on others' shows, I wrote a couple of original TV pilots that gained executives' attention and trust. On the strength of those two original pilots and my pitching skills, I landed a pilot deal with a major studio.

Since then, I've continued to work in the TV pilot world. I've sold pilots in the room. I've sold pilots months after the initial pitch. I've written spec pilots that I later sold with pitches. I've also partnered with *New York Times* bestselling authors and sold TV projects with underlying intellectual properties. I've even sold pilots over the phone.

I've continued to learn from and train with talented writers and creators. I'm a graduate of the outstanding WGA Showrunners Training Program, which is competitive and only open to WGA writers with TV projects in active development.

Through my teaching and professional programs, I've helped thousands of writers break into Hollywood. I've taught television writing at the USC School of Cinematic Arts and Boston University's Film and Television program, two top film schools.

While in graduate school, I created the highly successful USC First Pitch, the official pitch festival for the School of Cinematic Arts. As an alum, I co-created USC First Team and the Assistant Training Program for Television. I applied techniques you'll find in *The Hero Succeeds* throughout both of those successful programs.

USC First Team brought together alumni writers, directors, and producers to form teams around feature film projects. My cofounders, director Barbara Stepansky (*Ex-Best, Hurt, The Trojan Cow*) and producer Henry Lowenfels (*Visioneers, Rock the Bells*), and I shepherded these feature projects through development and took them out to the industry. Two of the USC First Team feature projects have been sold, produced, and distributed to date. One of those features, *Kelly & Cal,* won the SXSW Gamechanger Award in 2014. *Kelly & Cal,* written by Amy Lowe-Starbin and directed by Jen McGowan, stars Juliette Lewis, Jonny Weston, and Cybil Shepherd. Other First Team projects have been optioned and are in development.

Carole Kirschner (WGA Showrunners Training Program, CBS Writers Mentoring Program) and I co-created the Assistant Training Program for Television. For our pilot program, we selected recent USC writing grads and provided an intense, 40-hour training workshop about how to be a great TV assistant. We invited guest speakers from 22 current TV shows to share their insights, and we secured shadowing experiences on TV shows for all of the trainees.

All but one of our talented trainees landed TV assistant jobs that helped launch or advance their TV careers. They've now written for shows including *Sleepy Hollow, Fallen Skies, The Good Wife, Scandal, Family Guy, Dog with a Blog* and *Nicky, Ricky, Dicky & Dawn.* One of our writing grads decided to return to her successful career as an attorney.

About *The Hero Succeeds*

While I've read a ton of screenwriting books, I've never found a book that explains television writing the way I do it and teach it. Fellow TV writers and students have asked me for years, "Is there a book I can read about how *you* do this?" I decided it was time to write one. And now you hold *The Hero Succeeds* in your hands. The title stems partly from my unique character-driven story structure, which I'll share in this book, and partly from my hope for you. You're the hero of your story, and I want to help you succeed.

It's a great time to be a TV writer and content creator. The town's looking for strong voices with edge. I'll say it again: If you want to be a working TV writer today, you need kick-ass original TV pilots in your portfolio. Showrunners and TV execs almost exclusively read speculative pilots vs. specs of existing shows these days. Speculative—spec—scripts are written without a contract, and they often are used for writing samples. Spec TV pilots give showrunners and execs a clear sense of a writer's voice, dexterity, command of the page, and vision for a series.

TV pilots also can help writers attract attention and get representation. Studios and networks take notice when fresh voices generate a stellar TV series idea and pilot. For example, Mickey Fisher's career hit the stratosphere when he sold his spec pilot *Extant* to CBS with DreamWorks attached in 2013. Mickey entered his spec pilot in the TrackingB TV pilot contest and got discovered by two TV lit coordinators at WME.[2] *Extant,* starring Oscar winner Halle Berry, went straight to series and ran for two seasons on CBS.

Before you start mentally buying that house in Malibu because you hit the TV pilot lottery, understand that *writing a TV pilot is the most difficult writing in the town.* It's more difficult than writing a feature or spec-ing out an existing TV show. Pilot writers must create the infrastructure for 60 to 100+ potential TV hours. Pilot writers must launch the show's concept, characters, world of the show, story engine, and main dilemma. They need to *nail* voice and tone. Pilot writers must keep a lot of additional plates spinning while also executing all the expected and necessary screenwriting skills.

In *The Hero Succeeds,* I'm going to walk you through creating a show from an idea to a polished pilot script. I'm going to share how professional TV writers do it. I not only share with you *how* to do it, but also explain the *why,* the logic behind the various stages of creating a television show. Here are the writing assignments that build throughout *The Hero Succeeds:*

- Treatment—10-15 pages drama; 8-10 pages comedy
- Breakdown—12-15 pages drama; 8-10 pages comedy
- Grid—one page (letter or legal paper)
- Outline—12-15 pages drama; 8-10 pages comedy
- Script—60-65 pages drama; 30-56 pages comedy
- Polish—60-65 pages drama; 30-56 pages comedy

Along the way, I'm going to unravel lots of awesome TV pilots. I'll show you how the pilots were constructed so you can better construct your own pilot. Naturally, this means I'll be spoiling the hell out of some TV shows. Fair warning: You may want to watch the pilots before you read those sections. The pilots are readily available on Amazon Prime, iTunes, Netflix, Hulu, on DVD or Blu-ray, and on various other platforms. Most of these shows are designed for adult audiences, so read the advisory labels as you go, please.

When you're reading, I'll give you occasional spoiler-alert warnings. I suggest that you watch the show or film at hand before you proceed. That way you'll have it fresh in your mind as I go over it. Here are some of the great shows we'll watch, dissect, and analyze for a host of professional insights and icing-on-the-cake entertainment:

- Cinemax's *The Knick* "Method and Madness"
- Amazon's *Transparent* "Pilot"
- AMC's *The Walking Dead* "Days Gone Bye"
- Starz' *Outlander* "Sassenach"
- NBC's *Hannibal* "Apéritif"

- BBC America's *Orphan Black* "Natural Selection"
- Fox's *Empire* "Pilot"
- Fox's *Brooklyn Nine-Nine* "Pilot"
- Netflix's *Orange Is the New Black* "The Chickening"
- ABC's *Modern Family* "Pilot"
- FX's *It's Always Sunny in Philadelphia* "The Gang Gets Racist"
- Showtime's *Episodes* "Episode One"

Who you might be and how to use this book

Enough about me and the book—let's talk about *you*. Whether you're an aspiring writer, an established TV writer, a TV exec, a non-writing producer, an agent or manager, or a writing professor/instructor, I believe this book can help you make even better, logical, informed decisions about writing. It can reduce the reliance on highly subjective feelings about the crucial decisions that industry professionals make every day. *The Hero Succeeds* delivers a way to shift the conversation about writing from *feeling* like something is or isn't working in a script to *understanding* why something is or isn't working.

Aspiring TV writers

Original pilots are the gold standard in the town for writers. So, insert tiny freak-out here if you like, but you need to write a pilot. Your career may depend on it. I've helped newbie writers write their first TV scripts ever. I've helped foreign students who're unfamiliar with American television write their first Hollywood-style TV scripts. I've helped smart, creative new writers break their first TV series and finish their first pilots. Now I'm here to help you.

In *The Hero Succeeds*, you'll find hard-earned techniques that won't fail you, the mystery decoder for TV structure, and a tried-and-true method for generating TV series treatments. This book gives you the skills you need to become a professional TV writer. It employs methods we use every day, even if we aren't consciously aware of it.

If you haven't written a TV script on contract or for a show, or if you're a seat-of-the-pantser, these techniques may feel odd at first. You may be tempted to skip the breakdown, or the grid, or the outline, and jump right to the script. However, if you want to work as a professional screenwriter—television or features—you'll need to learn how to grid, outline, draft, write, and rewrite a script. Have faith. This process works. If you understand the *why* of things, it makes the *what* and *how* easier to execute. I purposely repeat certain concepts throughout the book because 1) they bear repeating, and 2) some of the concepts build as you progress through the process.

Make no mistake. Writing is hard. This is not a formula. These are simply sound writing methods, and using them will help you work smarter and write faster.

TV writers

I work with and continue to learn from amazing writers and creators who graciously share their hard-earned knowledge, wisdom, and skill. I see *The Hero Succeeds* as a way to humbly offer my own hard-earned knowledge about creating pilots to my friends, colleagues, and fellow writers. Even veterans of long-running TV shows can find writing an original pilot intimidating. Still, maybe your agent, manager, mentor, advisor, or mother told you to write a new pilot because you need it for staffing and hell, you just might sell that sucker. I hope you do. No pressure. But now what?

Staring at the blank page can feel like recreating the wheel. Writers sit down, come up with an idea, break it, and write it. Sometimes it works. Sometimes it doesn't. But each time, it's like starting from scratch. It doesn't have to be that way. *The Hero Succeeds* delivers a proven way to create pilots that sell to the town.

TV executives

I work with some incredibly smart TV execs. Knowing how to pick the winners and pass on the losers is an imprecise science, and not even the smartest, savviest execs make the right call every time. *The Hero Succeeds* offers another way to help evaluate a show's chances in a wildly competitive market. If you're among those execs who are curious about how creators come up with great TV shows and execute stellar pilots, welcome. I think you'll find some new tools and ways to assess pilots and series during their development. This book may give you new insights into why certain pilots work and how smart creators conjure those works.

Non-writing producers

Television has become *the* moneymaker in Hollywood. It's an exciting time to be in TV. Perhaps you've worked in television for decades, or maybe you've been exclusively in features but recently found TV seductive. Either way, you may want more insights to capitalize on this growing market.

Television is a writers' medium, and working with television writers requires a specific skill set. TV pilot writers create a vehicle for 60 to 100+ hours of content. The more hours of content, the more money everyone makes. You want to create binge-able content for today's television explosion? You need to be able to identify that killer new series when it crosses your path. You also need to know when pilots are well-executed, have the elements that engage audiences, and successfully set a series in motion. *The Hero Succeeds* can help you better understand the TV series creation process and make smarter, informed decisions.

Agents and managers

I work with outstanding agents and attorneys. There are some really great managers out there, too. I have such respect for the work they all do on their clients' behalf under immense pressure. I've seen their schedules. So, you're juggling a ton of calls, meetings, lunches, breakfasts, drinks—not necessarily in that order. And you've got a list of writers who need to churn out pilots for various reasons. What are the key elements you should be looking for in your clients' scripts? What's the quickest way to help your writers succeed?

The Hero Succeeds offers reps the opportunity to review writers' material more efficiently and better understand what makes pilots work. It also offers insight into ways writers can create unforgettable characters and achieve those emotionally satisfying moments. If you don't have a lot of spare time, read this book. It can help you make logical, more-objective observations about your clients' writing and make your own life easier and more productive.

TV writing instructors and professors

The Hero Succeeds follows the methods I've used successfully in my USC School of Cinematic Arts and Boston University television writing classes. I go step-by-step through the TV series creation process. This book focuses on current television shows and covers both drama and comedy pilot writing.

Welcome, all. Let's create some stellar television!

CHAPTER 1

TL;DR chapter 1

TV pilot writers must develop a show idea that can sustain 60-100 hours of content. The story engine is the element of the show's concept that generates stories. Don't let research turn into procrastination. Ride-alongs rock. TV execs may shy away from shows about high school, college, families, relationships, newsrooms, and anthologies. Assignment: Research an arena that fascinates you.

You're Not Selling the *Pilot*, You're Selling the *Show*

In this chapter, you'll find:

- the nuts and bolts of idea creation for a TV pilot;
- TV show research tips;
- three vital TV show components;
- caveats about certain types of shows; and
- an assignment to research an arena that fascinates you.

Greetings, fellow television writer! Yeah, you! Why not you? I was you. And I'm still you. I love television and movies. I consume tons of entertainment content. I watch everything from *True Detective* to *The Vampire Diaries,* from *The Vikings* to *Jane the Virgin.* I watch all the Oscar fodder and the big tentpole franchise movies. And I write. I write a lot. And I get paid to write.

Working in Hollywood is one of the greatest jobs on the planet. We get to play all day. Yes, it is work. Yes, we have pressure. But let's not kid ourselves—the fate of the world does not rest on our shoulders. So if you like TV and like to write and create content, we're kindred spirits and you're in the right place.

* * *

Let's start with a blinding flash of the obvious: Coming up with a great TV series idea is crucial to creating an undeniable series. Still, many people are surprised to hear that TV writers don't pitch our pilot story when we pitch TV shows. We pitch the *show*. TV executives are less concerned about a pilot story and more concerned about having a show.

All too often a writer comes up with a mind-blowing pilot. Unfortunately, that pilot story is all the writer has. There's no show after the pilot. In other words, it's essentially a feature or short film. Not surprisingly, this is a problem that feature writers often face when they transition from features to television. A feature only has to work for two hours. Pilots need to launch a *series* with multiple seasons and many hours of content.

So, TV writers must be idea machines. We need to come up with new ideas every year, season, month, week. We face the blank page. We catalyze a whole project. We write it, and through production we make it come to life. Where do great ideas come from? In this chapter, you learn to cultivate an idea and develop it into a TV show.

How do I know if there is a TV show in a given idea? I know if the writer has an interesting, immersive world, compelling characters, and a strong story engine, we can make a show out of the idea. If we have a show, we can create the pilot story. Before you start breaking your pilot story, you have to break the TV series idea. Great shows can come from unconventional ideas. And more often than not, when a writer has a unique idea, non-writers can be quick to say, 'That's not a show." Primarily, it's because they don't see it immediately. Seeing a show immediately can be great. But so can *not* seeing the show immediately.

As a pilot writer myself, I'm open to experimentation. Every idea I've ever been urged *not* to write and I've written anyway—those are the pilots everyone has wanted to read. Making sure there's a show in an idea—that's the key.

From inkling to idea

You may be asking, "But how do *you* come up with the initial idea?" As writers, we get to learn about other people and live their lives vicariously through our writing. One day we're cops. The next day we're rocket scientists. The day after we're football coaches. We can delve into any world we choose.

So the first thing I do when I'm developing a new show is find an arena that interests me. This could be marine biology, astrophysics, or psychology. For you it may be a sport, or role-playing games, or some particular profession. I find an arena that catches my attention, and I research it. I'll read books, articles, and blogs on the subject. I'll interview experts. I'll go on ride-alongs. What I *don't* do, I don't create the show before I do my research. The research informs the story engine, the world of the show, and the characters. (I'll address these terms later in the chapter.) The research tells me what the show can be.

I find the best shows hit on the *truth*. Each show has its version of the truth. The truth of *Scandal* is different from the truth of *True Detective*. Think about *Mad Men*. Having the appropriate period cocktail glasses for all of those Old Fashions contributed to the veracity of the show. If Don Draper was slamming Red Bulls and vodka, *Mad Men* wouldn't have been Matt Weiner's *Mad Men*. Take *Game of Thrones*. If the Dothraki were riding ATVs, it wouldn't be George R.R. Martin's *Game of Thrones*. George created a very specific truth for his fantasy world.

I may take dramatic license with an idea. However, I find leaning on the truth in the show's real-world iteration makes the show stronger. Doing research helps cement the world of the show in my mind. It also introduces you to incredible characters.

How do you research an idea?

During my research phase, I don't encumber myself or the project with story or characters. I let the story and characters come to me through the research. I've found that simply being open to possibilities yields the most interesting, exciting shows. What happens in real life often exceeds one's own imagination.

Let's say you're writing about a master criminal. Unless you *are* a master criminal, you likely will not think like a master criminal. If you research master criminals, you'll discover unique elements about their lives as well as commonalities. Usually, different professions attract different personality types. Being a master criminal probably lends itself to a fascinating personality type.

During my research, I discover all kinds of quirky, fascinating info that informs me about the people who inhabit this world. You may wonder what happens if I do a bunch of research and find there *isn't* a show in the arena. Weirdly, this has never happened to me. I believe learning, just for the sake of learning, has value. Everything I've ever researched keeps coming back up in future work. You'll be surprised how often you rely on info you researched for previous projects.

One of my friends, Paul Grellong (*Law & Order: SVU, Scorpion*), wrote a terrific pilot called *Roast*. It's about a family caught up in the seedy underbelly of the coffee trade. Yes, you read that right—his pilot is about coffee. Paul was fascinated by coffee, including the growing and distribution of coffee. I don't even drink coffee, yet I found *Roast* riveting. Paul infused *Roast* with the truth about the coffee trade and created compelling characters. Paul's unique take on an unfamiliar world underlying a very familiar part of our daily lives makes his original pilot stand out.

Ride-alongs are interview/shadowing experiences with cops, firefighters, and other specialists. Typically, a writer accompanies a specialist during his or her activities through the day or night. Ride-alongs are invaluable experiences that can generate lots of questions and fodder for stories. It's the details that make writing rich and help readers/viewers suspend their disbelief. You may be surprised how open experts and specialists are to interviews and ride-alongs.

What happens if research turns into procrastination?

When do you know it's time to write? Once I'm on the trail of a good topic, I'm avid. I'm obsessive. I constantly think and talk about it with my wonderfully patient husband. Once I start seeing commonalities, the puzzle pieces start falling into place.

Again, you need a fascinating world of the show, compelling characters, and a strong story engine. As I research, I ask these three questions:

1) What's the world of this arena?

2) What are the types of people inhabiting this world?

3) How do new people intersect with people who live in this world?

Answering these questions feeds directly into the story engine, the world of the show, and the characters. I'll talk more about these important components in this chapter and the next chapter. Once I realize I have the beginnings of these components, I start formulating the show.

Essentially, my approach allows you to start working on the idea when you start researching. You'll pour the information into the show treatment almost immediately. That way, you aren't procrastinating; you're building.

In today's television landscape, studios and networks are looking for edgy, noisy shows. This means they are looking for shows that stand out against the barrage of other television content and competing diversions such as videogames.

One great example of edgy and noisy is Amazon's *Transparent.* In *Transparent,* Jeffery Tambor stars as a professor and father who is transitioning into a woman. Jeffery's character has three adult children who all have their own secret lives. There is something very important to notice in that description of *Transparent*; it focuses on the *characters.* I'll discuss *Transparent* more in the next chapter.

All great story comes from characters. If you think about the TV shows, movies, books, and comics you love, you'll likely think of the main characters first. For example, Sherlock Holmes, Liz Lemon, Archie Bunker, Olivia Pope, Big Bird, Khaleesi Daenerys Targaryen, Tony Soprano, Alicia Florrick, Dexter Morgan, Buffy the Vampire Slayer, Don Draper, Sarah Manning, Walter White, Lorelei Gilmore, and, of course, Olivia Benson. In television, having great characters trumps high concept every time.

Consider *Modern Family*. The concept isn't earth-shattering. *Modern Family* is about three different yet related families in the Los Angeles area. The brilliance of *Modern Family* lies in its characters, not in its concept. When you're thinking about your own original TV series, try to focus on the characters first.

What is unique about these characters? What do they want? And why should we watch them want it? *Breaking Bad*'s concept was very straightforward. Here's the logline: Terminally-ill high school chemistry teacher Walter White wants to take care of his family, even after his death, so he uses his insane chemistry skills to cook meth and make money fast. The concept of *Breaking Bad* involves Walter White, his want, and his plan or decision.

Understanding the meth trade, including the cooking process, was essential to the show's veracity. Vince Gilligan needed to know a lot about meth and chemistry to take viewers into the world of the meth trade. He also needed to understand the mentality of a high-school chemistry teacher and someone who was terminally ill.

It could be tempting to just make up information about a high-school chemistry teacher and a patient with terminal cancer. Most of us have been to high school, and most of us have seen cancer patients portrayed on television and in films. If I were delving into these two areas, I would interview people who have experienced them firsthand. I'm sure there are things I don't know about high-school teachers and cancer patients. Again, it's the details that help your audience suspend disbelief. The accurate portrayal of characters also draws viewers into your show.

Story engine

A television series is designed to be just that—a series. By its nature, you need to come up with story after story. You need a strong *story engine.* The story engine is the element of the show's concept that generates stories. The story engine depends on the characters and how they intervene in other people's lives.

Often the story engine depends on your characters' professions. For example, police, lawyers, and doctors have a license to intervene in other people's lives. A cop can arrest a criminal or protect an innocent citizen. A lawyer can defend or prosecute a defendant. A doctor can heal a patient. Cop, lawyer, and doctor shows inherently have strong story engines, which is why there are a lot of cop, lawyer, and doctor shows. Stories get generated through the characters' professions. Each week there is a new case, new criminal, new patient, new defendant.

These aren't the only professions that lend themselves to story generation. In *Friday Night Lights,* the coach and his guidance-counselor wife, Mrs. Coach, intervened in students' lives. Their interventions generated stories. In *Six Feet Under,* the family mortuary business brought new people into the Fisher family's lives. A strong story engine also might be something that brings new characters into your characters' world. For example, in *Game of Thrones,* the various characters vying for power bring them into each others' spheres. In *Lost,* the shared desire to survive and get off the island pulled the characters into each others' lives. In *Glee,* the characters' desire to be accepted (and make it to regionals) pulled them into other characters' lives.

If the story engine is weak or non-existent, you don't have a show. You can have a great story without a story engine. That great story might be a feature, novel, or short story. However, a television series needs a potent story engine.

Again, story engine is the component of your show that generates story. It deals with the characters' professions or a unified goal that brings the characters together and gives them license to intervene in new characters' lives.

World of the show

The audience wants to know what to expect when your show comes on the air. Is this a world with dragons, mammoths, three-eyed ravens, and sprites that shoot light spears? Is this a post-Katrina New Orleans, where long-time residents are uprooted from their mold-ridden homes, jazz musicians play gigs in the bars and on the streets to make ends meet, and cops lie about the whereabouts of citizens displaced during the storm? Is this a world of a motorcycle gang? Are we going to be spending time on the road, in the gang's clubhouse, and in prison? Is this a post-apocalyptic America where uninfected humans fight to survive an onslaught of zombies? Is this a world with vampires, werewolves, witches, and *doppelgängers*? What can we expect from your show each week?

Audiences want to be immersed in a world. They want the world to feel as realistic as possible so they can escape their own daily lives. Audiences want to live vicariously through your characters. They want to live in *your* world for a while. To get audiences to commit to your show, they need to feel that you've captured the world completely, that there is no camera.

The world also will help you convey the vibe of your show. Will it be gritty-realistic like *The Wire*? Will it be over-the-top grotesquely artistic like *Hannibal*? Will it be pretty, playful, and punctuated by pastels like *Jane the Virgin*? Will it be fast-paced with bold colors set against stark blacks and whites like *Scandal*?

Is your show based on a real-life event or person like *Scandal*? Is your show full of imaginary creatures and characters from fairy tales like *Once Upon a Time*? Is your show set in a specific time period like *The Americans, Halt and Catch Fire,* or *Turn*? Wherever you're setting your show, you want to fully realize the unique world of your series.

Characters

Warriors, peace keepers, narcissists, optimists—what types of people are drawn to the world of your show? If you're writing about FBI recruits, research the type of people who want to be FBI agents. What personality traits do they share? What are their families like? What types of people do the FBI recruit? What is the FBI looking for in a recruit?

How do people in the world of your show see their world? If you're writing about New York real-estate agents, how do they relate to the world? Imagine if they were real-estate agents in the rural South? Would your characters be different?

As you determine the types of people drawn to the world of your show, you'll start to understand the characters who need to inhabit your show. David Simon's *The Wire* on HBO is one the best examples of understanding the characters who need to inhabit a show. From McNulty to Bunk to Stringer Bell to Avon Barksdale, David Simon understood the people drawn to be Baltimore murder police and drug dealers.

Simon did the same thing with *Treme*, another HBO show. From Davis McAlary to Antoine Baptiste to LaDonna Baptiste-Williams to Toni Bernette, Simon explored the people and art of New Orleans. In both series, he featured the *cities* as characters, imbuing them with their own vibe and tonal outlook. He populated them with the types of people he met while researching, studying, and living in these cities.

We'll dig deeper into your characters in the next chapter. First, look at the world of your show and figure out who needs to populate it. Let's take a beat to address some common advice that well-meaning people give writers: "Write what you know."

Don't let yourself be limited to what you know *now*! I can honestly say I'm not a serial killer; a New York police detective; an Oregon doctor; a D.C. psychologist; a Jesuit priest; a time-traveling lover; an assistant district attorney; a bank robber; an alien; an immortal; or an Army officer, but I have written about all of these characters. I believe writing is getting to know about things you want to write. Being intellectually curious is a writer's greatest asset.

* * *

While you're considering your arena to research, let's cover several potential pilot arenas that may seem like slam dunks but have some inherent problems.

High school/college shows

A lot of young writers feel comfortable writing about high school and college because they have experienced both. Translation: There are a *lot* of spec pilots about high school and college. The first and most difficult problem is: The show is based in high school or college.

High school and college have short expiration dates. Granted, some people go to college longer than others, but generally high school and college last around four years each. As a television show creator, you want to create a show that can go on for five, seven, even ten years or more. The more years you can get out of a show, the more successful the show is. Look at *Grey's Anatomy*; at the time of this printing, it is preparing for its 13th season. *Law & Order: SVU* is in its 17th season.

Studio and network executives are wary of shows set in high school or college, because these shows have a biological clock. The characters age out of the show and graduate. And the story engines tend to be weak.

Take Ryan Murphy's *Glee* as a case study. The highly popular show started to falter when Rachel, Finn, Kurt, and Santana graduated. The core leads of the show were no longer in high school. The show had to evolve into a high school *and* a New York City show. This meant the show needed to make new sets for the New York City scenes. It had to create the world of NYC and integrate it with the high-school scenes. Plus, new cast members needed to fill those empty high-school slots. The audience needed to fall in love with new cast members *and* sign on for a completely different show from the one they were promised in the pilot. The promise of the pilot was a show about outcast characters who are united in song and personal expression. Eventually, the show became about making your dreams come true in New York and dealing with the ups-and-downs of an aspiring artist's life. It's a different show.

Glee became a bit of a mash-up mess. It didn't work as well as it had in previous high-profile seasons. Unfortunately, the audience didn't want to invest in the new high-school characters; they wanted to stick with the high-school grads they had grown to love. The attraction of the outcasts overcoming their alienation through song had been played out when Rachel, Finn, Kurt, and Santana graduated from the high school where the alienation took place. As a result, *Glee*'s ratings fell and never rebounded.

New cast members and new sets increased the show's budget. At a time when the studio and network had to spend more, the ratings dropped and the show lost viewers.[3] For all these reasons, studio and network executives tend to be skeptical of shows set in high school and college.

Family shows

Family shows are a staple of television, right? Well, yes, but.... Family shows tend to have weak story engines. Think about it. If the story engine is how your characters intervene in new characters' lives, how do family shows pull new characters into their stories every week? If you have a family whose members don't have jobs that allow them to intercede in others lives, where do you get your 30th story? What's episode 44? Some TV executives instinctively cringe at family shows. They might ask, "Could they *be* a family of doctors?" or "Could they *be* a Russian sleeper cell in the 80s and they've just been activated?"

A show like *Parenthood* could be a tough sell today, despite having Imagine's Ron Howard and Brian Grazer and *Friday Night Lights* EP Jason Katims behind it. Throughout its run, *Parenthood*'s ratings kept it on the bubble. In an interview with Mashable, NBC President Bob Greenblatt talked about *Parenthood* and the future of family drama at the network. "We had one of the best [family dramas] on for years, and so many people didn't watch it," Greenblatt said. "I can't say one of the goals is to put on a family drama."[4]

However, *combining* the family drama with strong story engine can help get buyers interested. Fox's *Empire* is King Lear set in a hip-hop music and entertainment company. It combines a high-stakes family drama with a legit music business that was founded with drug money and criminal endeavors. The music business and crime are story engines. *Empire* premiered with 9.8 million viewers with a 3.7 rating in the coveted 18-49 demographic.[5] Its popularity grew; for its freshman season finale, the drama drew 16.7 million viewers and a 6.5 in the 18-49 demo.[6] It's still doing well in its second season.

The final season for FX's *Sons of Anarchy,* another family drama married to a stronger story engine, delivered the network's all-time high ratings. The seventh season of "Hamlet set in an motorcycle gang" drew an average total viewership of 7.54 million and 5 million among adults 18-49, making that season the most watched in the network's history.[7] Combining the high-stakes family drama in the criminal enterprise of the Sons of Anarchy Motorcycle Club made *Sons of Anarchy* more attractive. Crime is a popular story engine that helps core characters intersect with new ones.

Family comedies do tend to fare better than family dramas. ABC has hit the sweet spot with family comedies lately, building an impressive list of sitcoms that includes *Modern Family, black-ish, Fresh Off the Boat, The Middle, The Goldbergs,* and *Last Man Standing.* Each of the ABC sitcoms offers a unique perspective on the families. They also hone *complementary character traits,* which I'll talk about in the next chapter.

CBS has had some difficulty with their recent family sitcoms. *The Millers* and *The McCarthys* didn't survive the 2014-15 season. Only *Mom* starring Allison Janney and Anna Farris was renewed to the 2015-16 season. With ratings giant *The Big Bang Theory* along with solid performers *2 Broke Girls, Mike and Molly* and freshman *The Odd Couple, The Millers* and *The McCarthys* had tough competition at the Eye.[8] On other networks, both of these show's ratings would have been seen as solid performers and likely would have gone on to subsequent seasons.

The takeaway: Family dramas work best when combined with a stronger story engine. Family comedies benefit from a unique-but-relatable perspective.

Relationship shows

As with family shows, TV execs may hesitate a little when writers pitch a purely relationship-driven show. As a story engine, relationships are limited. While looking for love does have characters intersect with new characters, the number of new characters are limited. So is the agency of the main characters to intervene in new characters' lives.

For dramas, relationship shows lean toward soapy drama. ABC's *Nashville,* like Fox's *Empire,* has elements of a family drama set in the music business. However, unlike *Empire, Nashville* hasn't been able to convert in the ratings quite as well. Still, *Nashville* has other attractive aspects that keep it on the air, including cross-platform marketability. Both *Nashville* and *Empire* have life beyond the episode model. They sell music on iTunes. They have the promise of concerts and music tours. ABC has aired several specials called *Nashville: On the Record* that feature the cast of *Nashville* performing various songs before a live audience. *Empire* and *Nashville* both also offer t-shirts, totes, and tchotchkes.

A CW relationship dramedy that has garnered a lot of attention and awards is *Jane the Virgin. Jane the Virgin* is adapted from a Venezuelan telenovela, *Juana la Virgen.*[9] It has family-drama, crime, and police elements along with relationship issues. These other elements strengthen the story engine and allow the show maneuverability. Broad, over-the-top, yet sweet and heartfelt, *Jane the Virgin* has charmed the critics but hasn't delivered stellar ratings.[10] However, it's on the CW, which has a reputation for giving shows breathing room to find their audience and grow their ratings.

Relationship comedies are suffering a massive heartache of late. The 2014-2015 season was supposed to be the year of the rom-com sitcom.

However, most of the rom-com sitcoms failed. *Marry Me, Selfie, A to Z, Manhattan Love Story,* and *Weird Loners* didn't make it past a first season.[11] Even *The Mindy Project,* which was in its third season, got the break-up text from Fox. Poised to push through to syndication, *The Mindy Project* seemed like it would make it another season. However with Universal Television as its studio, it lacked vertical integration. That variable coupled with *Mindy*'s poor ratings put the show on The Cancel Bear's dinner plate. Fox likely wanted that time slot back to plug in a new show developed with its sister studios. Hulu picked up *The Mindy Project,* so the show got 26 episodes for its fourth season.[12]

News shows

News-based scripted shows have been tried and tried again, but they often fail to attract audiences despite being well executed. Aaron Sorkin's *Newsroom* and *Sports Night* both struggled to gain viewers.[13] Fox's *Back to You,* created by *Modern Family*'s Christopher Lloyd and Steven Levitan and starring Kelsey Grammar and Patricia Heaton as Pittsburgh news co-anchors, was cancelled after one season.[14]

At first blush, journalism seems like it could be a strong story engine. Each week, reporters have to get new stories. However, while reporters do meddle in other people's lives, a reporter doesn't have *license* to intervene in someone else's life. A reporter can't arrest, prosecute, or heal someone. A character's agency completes the story engine, and that gives the stories satisfying emotional stakes and resolution. Without character agency, the stories fall flat.

The news-oriented scripted shows' limited appeal may have to do with viewers' constant contact with actual news outlets. With the 24/7 news cycle, viewers may have news fatigue. Another reason audiences may tune out of drama and sitcom news-related shows: *Faux* news comedy shows may have successfully attracted the niche audiences interested in news-related shows. *The Daily Show with Jon Stewart,* (now *The Daily Show with Trevor Noah), Last Week Tonight with John Oliver,* and

The Nightly Show with Larry Wilmore have largely replaced the traditional comedy variety shows.

Anthology

With *American Horror Story, True Detective,* and *Fargo,* we're experiencing a resurgence of the anthology show. Despite some critical acclaim, none of these shows has been a ratings hit.[15] Reinventing the show each season may contribute to the lower ratings. Audiences hook into characters and ongoing stories. When everything resets, that gives the audience an opportunity to drop the show from its must-see list.

Writing a spec pilot for your own anthology show would be a risky endeavor. With a spec pilot, you want to demonstrate an understanding of television and a mastery of skills. One of those skills is the ability to create long-arc storytelling. You want to demonstrate you can attract an audience and keep it. You want to present yourself as a creator who can develop properties that will live for multiple seasons without audience attrition.

The 'I'm-NOT-going-to-do-it-like-X' trap

Some writers handicap themselves because they want to defy the system. They want to do things their way, which is great. However, they often don't understand *why* professional TV writers rely on certain character and storytelling devices or why professional TV writers leave doors open for the future.

Yes, you should strive to be different, fresh, original, new, unique. However, screwball comedies work because of the chemistry between the characters. A screwball comedy features two main characters who are opposites. *2 Broke Girls* an example of a screwball comedy. Screwball comedies work precisely *because* the two characters are opposites. If you buck the convention by creating a show with two characters who see eye to eye, it may not deliver the laughs.

If you're resisting a technique or convention simply because other shows do it, take a step back. Evaluate *why* other shows do whatever it is you're trying to avoid. Consider the idea that these creators have used a technique that works because, well, it works. If you're going to do something different, fine. But don't be different just to be different. Be smart. Think about why these other creators have relied on a convention or technique, what purpose it serves, and then figure out another way to achieve the same goal.

Assignment

Okay, let's get started! Research an arena—that is, a topic, profession, world, etc.—that fascinates you. As you're researching, ask yourself these three questions:

1) What's the world of this arena?
2) What are the types of people inhabiting this world?
3) How do new people intersect with people who live in this world?

Document the details of the world. Be sure to capture your sources digitally or in a notebook, because you may need to go back to those sources in the future. When you've decided on an arena that has interesting answers for those three questions, start boiling down that arena down to a TV series idea. Focus on the world of the show, possible characters, and story engine.

* * *

When you've completed your initial research, you may be thinking: How do I know if I have a viable idea for a TV series? At this point, it's not about right or wrong. There's no particular litmus test for TV series ideas. It's more of a gut check. Early on, I might be the *only* person who can see it, but I know I've got a show on my hands. It's usually when I can answer unreservedly "yes" to all of these questions:

1) Do you see a compelling main character? If yes, then without worrying about whether it's right or wrong, write a quick thumbnail sketch of your main character. What is your gut telling you about your main character?

2) Are you fascinated with this world? If yes, then write a few paragraphs about why this world still fascinates you.

3) Does it seem like the world will open up and get bigger as the series progresses? If so, then without bogging yourself down, write some of the possibilities you see for the series. What might happen to your main character in this world?

4) Do you get the impression there are *seasons* of stories to tell with your main character? If you do, then without censoring yourself, write as many ideas for stories as you can.

CHAPTER 2

TL;DR chapter 2

Assembling the ten essential TV show components of your series idea will help you solidify your series and pitch it to others. Answering the six big questions about your TV series idea will help you understand the intangibles of your idea. Assignment: Write your TV series treatment.

TV Series Treatment: Components, Questions

In this chapter, you'll find:

- ten essential TV series treatment components;
- six big questions about your TV series idea; and
- your TV series treatment assignment.

One of the biggest myths about Hollywood is that Hollywood buys ideas. Hollywood doesn't buy ideas; it buys the *execution* of ideas. You can have a great idea, but if you can't execute, it doesn't matter. Hollywood always wants excellent execution. Some ideas are high concept—*Game of Thrones, Sleepy Hollow, Gotham, Marvel's Agents of S.H.I.E.L.D., The Last Ship, Fallen Skies, The Strain,* and *Daredevil,* among others. Hollywood execs might buy into these ideas, but they also will be looking for writers they know can execute them.

Crystallizing your TV series into a treatment will help clarify execution for you. It will help you write your original pilot. It'll also help you when you pitch your series.

You'll need to write a TV series treatment that not only captures your show, but also captures your voice and excitement for your project. Hollywood wants to hear and read projects writers are passionate about. It doesn't want a dry interpretation of your stellar idea. Imbue your writing with your voice. Know this: You must captivate your audience every time you string words together. This is true for your treatments, outlines, and scripts.

The TV series treatment

You researched your arena. You've answered the three questions about the world of the show, characters, and a strong story engine. Now it's time to distill your brand-new show into a treatment. Here are the 10 components you'll need:

1) Title
2) Type of show
3) Idea
4) Logline
5) World of the show
6) Characters
7) Story engine
8) Themes
9) Tone
10) Season arcs or possible episodes

Your treatment likely will weigh in at around 10-15 pages for a drama and 8-10 pages for a sitcom. By the way, don't confuse a treatment with a show bible. Bibles can run 70-100 pages. You may need to write a bible for your show if you're writing a fantasy or sci-fi drama that requires a lot of world building, but it's too early for it now. Plus, show bibles are part of the WGA minimum basic agreement.[16] The creator should get *paid* to write a bible. In other words, bibles are often written after the show sells. Sometimes they are written in conjunction with the writers room. Right now we're focused on capturing the major components of your show. Let's do this treatment thing.

Title

Create a title for your project immediately. It doesn't have to be perfect. It can be a working title. Even a lackluster title can get people charged up about your show. Suddenly, your show goes from an untitled project to *Mad Men, The Good Wife, Lost, Nashville, The Flash, Breaking Bad, Game of Thrones, The Knick*. If you're not happy with your working title, the perfect title might present itself during the development of the series or the writing of the pilot. Your friends might get so excited about your project that they come up with alternative titles. Giving your project even a working title makes it *real*.

Type of show

You'll need to decide if you're writing a drama or a comedy. For sitcoms, there are single-camera and multi-camera comedies. Single-camera comedies are quite popular now. *Modern Family, Brooklyn Nine-Nine, The Mindy Project, Transparent, Veep, Silicon Valley*, and *New Girl* are examples of single-camera comedies. This style of comedy relates to how the show is shot.

Single-camera comedies look more like movies or dramas. The narrative is told through camera angles. Single-camera comedy is a misnomer, in that there may be more than one camera on set. However, the setup makes it appear that production is shooting with one camera. The camera's POV is part of the storytelling. Single-camera comedies are shot without a studio audience, and they have the flexibility to shoot on location.

Multi-camera comedies have fallen out of favor in some circles. However, CBS still has several multi-cam comedies, like *The Big Bang Theory, Mike and Molly, 2 Broke Girls*, and *Mom*. CBS rules the ratings with their multi-cams, and it likely will continue to produce multi-cam comedies. (CBS also launched single-cam comedies *Life in Pieces* and *Angel from Hell* in 2015.)

The multi-cam set-up refers to a style of shooting that requires multiple cameras on a soundstage to shoot the show as if it were a play. Multi-cam comedies are generally shot before a live audience. The play-like nature of the action and the way the show is shot gives the television viewing audience the feeling they are in the studio audience, too.

In the United States, we don't define dramas by the shooting style. There is no such beast, really, as a single-cam drama or a multi-cam drama. All dramas are shot without studio audiences and have the flexibility to shoot on location. There is a hybrid of single-camera comedy and drama called dramedy. Dramedies are one-hour shows with comedic elements; *Orange Is the New Black, Jane the Virgin,* and *iZombie* are examples. Dramedies are shot without a studio audience and may shoot on location.

When you decide on the general type of show—single or multi-cam sitcom, drama, or dramedy—you'll need to decide on the type of storytelling you want to do with this show. The main types of storytelling include: character-centric; serialized; procedural; and stand-alone. (I cover the details of each sort in chapter 6.) I like to add other storytelling styles, which can include sci-fi; workplace; family; fantasy; period or historical; musical; animated; soap opera; medical; legal; police; or anthology.

Being specific about the type of show you want to make will help your audience, readers, studio and network executives, and producers sign on for your vision. It could be a single-cam family comedy like *black-ish,* a period family-centric drama like *Downton Abbey,* a period family spy drama like *The Americans,* a soapy political thriller like *Scandal,* a fantasy drama like *Game of Thrones,* a multi-camera workplace comedy like *2 Broke Girls,* a single-cam relationship ensemble comedy like *New Girl,* a single-cam post-apocalyptic relationship comedy like *The Last Man on Earth,* a supernatural coming-of-age drama like *The Vampire Diaries,* and so on.

Idea

Your idea can be high concept or complex concept. A high-concept idea generally has mass appeal. The potential for a high-concept idea should be obvious to buyers and viewers. Let's compare an example of each type of idea.

Fox's *Gotham* is high concept. *Gotham* is a superhero drama about future police commissioner Jim Gordon as a young detective and the evolution of Gotham City's villains who will one day face Batman.

Batman as a character, a movie franchise, and a TV series has been wildly popular and lucrative. Yet a unique take on Batman that might make it a breakout hit on television hadn't come to fruition recently until Fox launched *Gotham*.

The idea of the years leading up to the emergence of Batman had immediate appeal. Plus, the ability to explore the backstories of the Penguin, Catwoman, Riddler, and other Batman villains was enticing. Their criminal enterprises lend themselves to a strong story engine. Centering the show on a young Detective Jim Gordon further strengthened the show's story engine. There has always been a vital connection between Gordon and Batman/Bruce Wayne, so that part seemed a natural fit. There was a built-in audience for this show.

A complex-concept idea generally has niche appeal, and the apparent potential for the idea can run from less-than-obvious to minimal. HBO's *The Wire* is a complex-concept idea. *The Wire* is a character-driven procedural drama about the flawed Baltimore Police Department and Detective Jimmy McNulty, who tries to maintain order in the corrupt city. *The Wire* was pitched and set up on the strength of David Simon's novel *Homicide: A Year on the Killing Streets* as well as his work on *Homicide: Life on the Street*. HBO wanted his complex, nuanced look at cops and criminals in a major metropolitan area.

The Wire and *Gotham* are similar in that the cities themselves are characters. Both have law enforcement at their centers. Both look at the inner workings of criminal organizations. However, this is where they diverge. *The Wire* takes a novelistic and nuanced approach to law enforcement. The cops are flawed—some perhaps as much as the criminals. Detective McNulty, who likely would be considered the lead for this ensemble cast, is a self-sabotaging, womanizing alcoholic. *The Wire* explores the complex, symbiotic relationship between the police and criminals. Where *Gotham* is essentially black and white, *The Wire* is gray.

Sometimes I hear that high-concept ideas are defined by the fact that they can be pitched succinctly. I believe both high-concept *and* complex-concept ideas can be pitched succinctly—so should your agent. As you've seen above, both high-concept and complex-concept ideas can to be distilled to a logline sentence. When you write a pilot, your agent will ask you for a logline. Why? Your agent must pitch your idea succinctly to other agents and reps, studio and network executives, and producers. Regardless of the type of idea, you'll need a logline.

Logline

The logline of your show is one sentence that identifies the main character, the obstacle for the main character, and the main storyline for the series. In other words, a good logline will answer the following questions:

1) Who is your main character?
2) What is the main storyline for your series? and
3) What is the main obstacle for your main character?

A logline should be one sentence with 30 words or fewer. Your goal is *simplicity*. This may be difficult because you're very close to the material and have all the complexities of the world and characters in your mind. However, you need to simplify your idea to its bare bones for the logline. You're trying to communicate your TV series idea clearly and succinctly so studio and network executives can get on board with it.

* * *

Let's look at the loglines for *Gotham* and *The Wire* again.

> *Gotham* is a superhero drama about future police commissioner Jim Gordon as a young detective and the evolution of Gotham City's villains who will one day face Batman.

> *The Wire* is a character-driven procedural drama about the flawed Baltimore Police Department and Detective Jimmy McNulty, who tries to maintain order in the corrupt city.

The Wire is perhaps one of the best dramas in the history of television. However, it doesn't have an obvious strong hook. It's been described as cerebral, aloof, nuanced. It didn't garner high ratings. It doesn't have obvious mass appeal. The reader, audience, agent, executive, or producer gets this vibe in the logline.

Gotham is in its second season. It has a strong hook. You can see the appeal of this high-concept show in the logline. However, it's only been doing OK in the ratings. The first season finale brought in a 1.7 rating in the 18-49 demo with 4.9 million viewers.[17] The show slid in the second season. But Fox is betting on the world of the show's mass appeal and the synergistic marketability with the *Batman v Superman: Dawn of Justice* feature film coming out in 2016.

As you can see, both shows can be distilled to a logline and pitched succinctly. High concept doesn't always deliver massive ratings. Complex concepts can have enduring effects on the industry. Both types of ideas have a home in Hollywood.

World of the show

I discussed the world of the show in the first chapter. Now you need to drill down and define *your* world of the show. For example, *Game of Thrones* has magic, dragons, mammoths, and giants in its world, all great elements. We also need to understand this is a world like medieval Europe. It's based, in part, on the War of the Roses.[18] There are seven kingdoms in *GoT*. The seven kingdoms are vying for the Iron Throne.

World of the show is where the writer would tell us about the seven kingdoms. We'd learn about the North and the Wall. We'd get background on Westeros and Essos. We'd understand that a decade-long summer is ending and a decade-long winter coming.[19] Winter means war with a magical, undead army of White Walkers as well as famine.

The writer would explain the levels of technology and industry. The writer would explain in general the rivalries among the various families and houses. We would learn about the locations of various kingdoms and where the families are located. In other words, this is where the writer defines the nitty-gritty of world-building.

The world of the show may be less involved for a different show. It may be as simple as defining a city, a setting. For example, *Friday Night Lights* is set in Dillon, Texas—a tight-knit, modern-day, rural community. Football rules Dillon and it's football season. The writer might write a bit about the mom-and-pop businesses, Dillon High School, and small-town life.

Executives and producers want to get a feel for the world of the show. They want to imagine what sets the show will need, where the show might be shot, and whether special effects will be needed. They want to know where the writer is going to take them every week—Westeros, Dillon, or elsewhere in the writer's vivid imagination. The more specific you are, the better others can see your vision.

Characters

Creating three-dimensional characters will make or break your show. While we've touched on concept, TV shows are *not* about concept; they're about characters. Everything good—drama, comedy, devotion, engagement, commitment, *everything*—comes from characters. A concept can be mind-blowing, but it doesn't mean anything to the audience without characters.

Many, many TV shows have failed because they were concept-oriented vs. character-driven. Both *Gotham* and *Marvel's Agents of S.H.I.E.L.D.* are struggling in the ratings despite the pre-sold worlds of the shows and high concepts.[20] One of the major complaints about both shows has been that they're missing their signature characters. *Gotham* is *Batman* without Batman. *Marvel's Agents of S.H.I.E.L.D.*. is *The Avengers* without the Avengers.

It doesn't matter if the show is an adrenaline action thriller or a quiet family drama; the audience hooks into the characters. That's why all TV shows should be character-driven. You want your audience to invite your characters into their homes week after week. You want your fans to get obsessed with your characters. These characters become like friends. They're familiar and comforting. It may seem bizarre, but our characters can affect people's daily lives. Sometimes it bothers actors when people come to believe they actually *are* the characters they play. However, sometimes a fictional character can be a lifeline for a person going through a traumatic time.

I've seen firsthand the positive effect that Mariska Hargitay, who plays Olivia Benson on *Law & Order: Special Victims Unit*, has had on rape and domestic-violence survivors. After landing the role of an SVU detective, Mariska received letters from fans who said they had finally found the courage to admit they had been sexually assaulted.[21] These survivors felt empowered to trust Mariska via Olivia Benson, a character who finds justice for sexual assault survivors week-in and week-out. In real life, Mariska founded the Joyful Heart Foundation so she could help survivors of sexual assault, domestic violence, and child abuse in a tangible way.

As you're creating your characters and shows, imagine your fans. All of your choices will be important to them. All of the nuances you put into your characters will be appreciated. Understand that you may be changing lives, even changing society in some significant way. Your characters are ambassadors to your audience. They need to be unforgettable, distinct, well-defined, and three-dimensional.

In his 1946 book *The Art of Dramatic Writing*, playwright Lajos Egri suggested a powerful tool—the character bones structure—to create three-dimensional characters.[22] In Egri's character-bones structure, he divides the character bio into three sections: physiology, psychology, and sociology. By addressing the attributes under these categories, you'll flesh out your own characters. You should use complete sentences and infuse your characters' bios with your voice. *Simple lists of attributes fail to fully define your characters.* Writing complete sentences makes you construct the hows and whys of the attribute. *Why* is this person like this? *How* did the person become like this?

For example, let's look at a major physical attribute of *House, M.D.*'s title character, Gregory House. Try to expunge the phenomenal Hugh Laurie as House from your mind, because character bios are written for characters who haven't been cast yet. The character of Gregory House, M.D., walks with a cane and a limp because he suffered a leg infarction—an ischemic event that caused death to muscle tissue in his right quadriceps muscle. While this injury happened years ago, it continues to cause him severe physical pain. House takes and abuses Vicodin for his leg pain.

For the character of House, a character bio would note a limp and the related Vicodin abuse. Creator David Shore modeled House on Sir Arthur Conan Doyle's character Sherlock Holmes, who was addicted to cocaine and also dabbled in morphine.[23] House needs a razor-sharp intellect and incurable curiosity. Likely, the actor himself would need a keen mind and an intense gaze.

Hugh Laurie won the role and inhabited the House character for eight seasons. He was nominated for six Primetime Emmys as lead actor.[24] Clearly, he was the best actor for the role, right? Except *House, MD* creator David Shore said he didn't immediately see Hugh Laurie as House when he was casting the role. He considered other actors, including Dennis Leary, Rob Morrow, and Patrick Dempsey. In fact, Gary Sinise was offered the role of House, but he wound up joining *CSI: NY*.[25]

In an *Entertainment Weekly* interview, David Shore said he had been familiar with Hugh Laurie's comedic work. "But honest-to-God, I never thought he'd be right for this role," he said.[26] Obviously, David was pleasantly surprised.

So when you're picturing your own characters, it's good to be specific enough to write them, but always remember you want the best actor to embody them. The best actor may surprise you and look completely different from your imagination. One of the most exciting aspects of making television and films is working with the actors. They bring something unique and personal to the part. They may challenge your preconceived notions about the part. They make a "part" whole.

In these nascent stages of series creation, let your imagination run wild. If you see a character in a super-specific way, use that vision to shape the character. If you see a specific actor or type of actor, use that knowledge to help you flesh out the character. Do whatever you need to do to help you write the three-dimensional character bios. Just remember, if you're lucky enough to get to casting, you should be open to suggestions. Details like "blue eyes and dimples" need to fall by the wayside because a stellar actor with dark eyes may just bring that character to life and keep you on the air for a decade.

* * *

Here are Lajos Egri's attributes for his character-bone structure.[27] As you write your character bios, remember to write in complete sentences in your voice. You'll want to cover all three areas as comprehensively as you can. You'll find sample character bios in *The Hero Succeeds* appendix.

Lajos Egri's Character Bone Structure

Physiology
Physical description
Gifts/talents
Defects

Sociology
Class
Occupation (type, hours, difficulty, attitude)
Education (aptitudes, weaknesses)
Home life (parents, siblings, relationships)
Religion
Race
Nationality
Prejudices
Place in community (friends, enemies, popularity, attitude)

Psychology
Sex life, morals
Point of view
Ambition
Frustrations
Disappointments
Temperament (breezy, pessimistic, extrovert/introvert)
Who is he/she? To him/herself? To others?
Attitude toward life (resigned, militant, positive/negative)
Complexes, obsessions, inhibitions, fears
Abilities, talents, IQ
Qualities (taste, judgment, imagination)
Hobbies, amusements

Show premise

In addition to Lajos Egri's suggestions, I recommend that you think about your show's premise. Often your show's premise conveys a central *theme*. Is there something about your show premise that relates to the characters? For example, *Lost*'s premise involved characters who were physically, psychologically, and emotionally lost. If you were writing character bios for *Lost*, you would need to include how each character was physically, psychologically, and emotionally lost.

Signature trait

Some shows feature main characters with a signature trait. This trait is something the audience loves. Every week the audience tunes in to see this character use his traits. Two shows titled for their singular characters are NBC's *Hannibal* and BBC's *Sherlock*. These shows provide excellent examples of characters with signature traits.

Hannibal Lecter is a brilliant psychiatrist who also is a psychopath, serial killer, and cannibal. He manipulates everyone around him, pushing them to their darkest selves. Audiences tune in to see how far Hannibal can drive others to commit dark acts. They also delight and disgust in Hannibal's culinary skills.

Sherlock is a brilliant consulting detective who also is a cold, technologically adroit, possibly Aspergerian genius. Sherlock speaks at the speed of thought, and he can deduce a person's life nearly as fast as a neuron fires. Audiences marvel at Sherlock's superpower intellect.

While creating your main characters ask yourself: What is your main character's signature trait? What does he or she do every week that viewers love? Not all main characters will have a signature trait, but it's something you should explore.

Comedic negative and complementary character traits

It may seem to follow that comedy in sitcoms comes from the situation. They're called situation comedies, after all. Some writers believe if they come up with funny, wacky situations, hilarity will ensue. However, a situation isn't funny in a vacuum. For example, sitcom settings like a start-up business incubator (*Silicon Valley*) aren't inherently funny, nor are apartments (*The Big Bang Theory, New Girl, Friends, The B in Apartment 23, and many more*), hospitals (*Scrubs, Children's Hospital, Getting On, Nurse Jackie*), or restaurants (*2 Broke Girls, Happy Days, Friends'* Central Perk, *Seinfeld*'s Monk's restaurant). It's the *characters* who populate these settings that generate the humor.

Comedy comes from character. Focus on creating characters who give you the greatest opportunity for humor. To do this, you should consider creating characters with complementary character traits. For a long time, comedy writers have emphasized negative character traits. How long? Try back to Aristotle again. In his posthumously published 1976 book *On the Comic and Laughter,* Vladimir Propp attributes to Aristotle the idea of negative character traits. Propp notes the main Aristotelian technique for portraying comic characters is an imitation of men worse than the average. Propp suggests that the "exaggeration of negative traits draw the reader or spectator's attention to them" and is required in order to create comedic characters.[28]

Throughout our comparatively recent TV history, negative or bad character traits *have* lent themselves to good comedy. For instance, *It's Always Sunny in Philadelphia* is about five depraved underachievers who run a bar and constantly try to take advantage of each other. *Sunny* was created by one of the leads, Rob McElhenney, with help from fellow cast members Charlie Day and Glenn Howerton.

Curb Your Enthusiasm features a fictionalized version of TV writer and producer Larry David, who follows his own neurotic, bent moral code and foists his iconoclastic views on those around him and society at large. Similarly in *Maron,* comic Marc Maron plays a fictionalized version of himself. *Maron*'s twice-divorced, recovering-alcoholic title character grapples with anger issues and neuroses while trying to turn his life around by starting a podcast, *WTF,* in his garage. It's important to note the creators of these shows are poking fun at themselves.

There has been an evolution in comedy, a softening trend. Comedy still comes from character. However, some comedy can stem from *complementary* character traits rather than negative or bad character traits. Complementary character traits leave room for softer, sweeter characters. The audience may more readily identify with these characters as opposed to characters with negative character traits. While the main characters on *It's Always Sunny in Philadelphia, Curb Your Enthusiasm,* and *Maron* are funny, they aren't easily relatable. Most of the audience will not see themselves as neurotic know-it-alls or part of a gang of despicable, selfish people.

It's this focus on more-relatable, softer characters that drives most broadcast network comedies today. The combination of flawed but well-meaning characters create the funny. Comedies like *New Girl, Brooklyn Nine-Nine, The Mindy Project, The Big Bang Theory,* and *Modern Family* focus on groups of endearing characters.

* * *

Let's take a closer look at *Modern Family.* It's a symphony of complementary characters. The show's concept itself is simple. *Modern Family* is about three related families in Los Angeles. That's it. That's the situation. It's the characters that make this show. Here's exactly how Steven Levitan and Christopher Lloyd described the main characters in the *Modern Family* pilot (originally titled *My American Family*).[29]

Characters:

The Dunphy Family

Claire – Late 30s, uptight suburban mom, tries to make every day special for her kids, needs control.

Phil – Late 30s, real estate agent, upbeat, goofy, thinks he's cooler than he is.

Haley – 16, social, fashion-conscious, rebellious, has a wild streak.

Alex – 13, (girl), smart, cynical, insightful for her age.

Luke – 10, immature, simple, not the brightest bulb.

The Pritchett-Delgado Family

Jay – 60s, successful businessman, divorced. Recently married Gloria, struggles to stay "young" for her.
Gloria – 30s, Hispanic, beautiful strong, quick-tempered. Protective mother. Divorced six years ago.
Manny – 12ish, Gloria's son – Jay's stepson. Old soul, sensitive, passionate, a young romantic.

Mitchell & Cameron's Family

Mitchell –Mid-to-late 30s, dentist, gay, emotionally restrained, worrier.
Cameron – Mid-30s, gay, free with emotions, lives in the moment, surprisingly strong.
Lily – Baby girl, adopted from Vietnam.

Steven and Christopher described each one of these character's personalities in a very positive way. They changed Mitchell's profession from dentist to lawyer, which does seems to suit him better. The striking aspect is all of these characters could be in your family. All of us know people like at least some of these characters.

Each of the characters in *Modern Family* complement other characters. Jay is a gruff but loving parent. Gloria is a permissive, supportive, and loving parent. When Manny brings them an issue, the way they approach the issue is completely different. They clash, but for the right reasons. Steven and Christopher created multiple complementary comedic character pairings for *Modern Family.* You can pair any of the characters and find humor.

Having distinct, different points of view for your characters will help them create conflict and humor. It's also helpful if these points of view have validity. If the audience can see one character's point of view as well as the other character's point of view, the audience will be more engaged. As you're creating your characters, think about who you'll pair and how those characters see the world differently. If you develop distinct, well-defined, three-dimensional characters who have complementary character traits with other characters on your show, you can put them in almost any situation and find the funny.

Focusing on complementary character traits often takes the mean streak out of the comedy. Sure, there's an audience for the mean-spirited humor, but some viewers do seem to prefer well-meaning characters who have different points of view.

Spoiler alert! You may want to check out *Star Trek: The Next Generation*'s season three finale and season four premiere, "The Best of Both Worlds Parts 1 and 2."

Creator as collaborator

The concepts of show creator and showrunner have leaked into pop culture. A lot of people misunderstand the roles of show creator and showrunner. The show creator and showrunner may or may not be the same person. The creator breaks the TV series idea and creates the characters, world of the show, and tone. The creator is the voice of the show. The showrunner makes sure the show stays on track production-wise. She minds the budgets; works with stars' agents, managers, and other handlers; and wrangles the multitude of challenges that arise every day.

Both positions make a lot of decisions—about 867 decisions per hour sounds about right. Taking on both roles of creator and showrunner may sound awesome, powerful, ego-boosting. The idea of being the 800-pound gorilla can be intoxicating for some people.

However, if you're a brand new creator and your show crashes and burns, you may never—never—get the opportunity to create a show again. So having a showrunner partner can be a fantastic option. The creator and showrunner can have a wonderful symbiotic relationship. Both want to make sure the show succeeds. Both have specific duties to promote the success of the show. As partners, the creator and showrunner are collaborators. We collaborate with each other. As creators, the first people we have the fortune of collaborating with are our characters.

If you create three-dimensional characters, they will help you figure out where the story is going. Here's one example. In June 2015, *The Hollywood Reporter* featured an admiring 25th-anniversary retrospective about *Star Trek: The Next Generation*'s pivotal story arc, "The Best of Both Worlds Part 1 and Part 2." [41] Executive producer Michael Piller, who was also the showrunner and creator of *Star Trek: Deep Space Nine, Star Trek: Voyager,* and *The Dead Zone,* wrote this arc with actor Patrick Stewart at its center. The article examined how Michael wrote himself into a corner and changed the course of the show forever.

In the story, USS Enterprise Captain Jean-Luc Picard gets captured by the indomitable alien species the Borg and turned into a Borg himself. At the end of season 3, the Enterprise crew prepare to fire their arsenal on the Borg ship where their captain is being held. In other words, they're about to blow up their own captain to save themselves and warn the Federation, and the show appears ready to kill off one of its lead characters. That's a pickle.

Evidently, Michael wrote Part 1 and its cliffhanger without knowing how the hell he was going to save Captain Picard and the Enterprise from the Borg. Sadly, Michael Piller had died in 2005 after a battle with cancer. But Ben Robinson, author of *The Official Star Trek Fact Files,* shared some insights from an earlier interview with Michael Piller about his experience writing himself into a cliffhanger corner.

> ...[E]ssentially I started writing without knowing [the solution]. I figured I'd work it out when I actually got to the scene itself where I had written 'The crew figures out how to beat the Borg,'" Michael said. "What happens when you really are involved with your characters and you are inside their heads, is that they become collaborators in a sense. Those characters had to figure out some way to defeat the Borg, and I was one of a group of people who were working on the problem. I worked on it with Data and Riker and Guinan and the whole group.

> How to defeat the Borg became clear to me in the very moment that it became clear to the crew. The hive mentality that was [the Borg's] strength was also its weakness. It really almost was dictated to me by the crew of the USS Enterprise.[42]
>
> —Michael Piller interview by Ben Robinson

Exactly. We're collaborators. We're custodians of the characters. It's their show, not ours. That's why they're the most important asset you have. Not only will your audience fall in love with your characters, but the characters will help you when you need that story fix. They will work with you to tell their stories.

In the next chapter, I'm going to share details about the character-driven story structure. With character-driven structure, your story solutions come from the characters and help you to create emotionally engaging and satisfying stories.

Story engine

As you may recall from the first chapter, the story engine is the element of the show's concept that generates stories. Your story engine keeps your show going for years. It gives your show the juice to make stories season after season. It also gives the network and studio confidence your TV series will go the distance. You want the strongest story engine possible for your show, because you want your show to be on the air for five, seven, 10, 15 seasons and beyond.

The story engine often deals with your main character's profession, something that gives your character a license to intervene in new characters' lives. For example, *Law & Order: SVU*'s Detective Olivia Benson has a license to intervene in other characters' lives because she is a cop. It's her job to solve crimes and to help get justice for victims. She has to find the bad guy and get the evidence to convict the bad guy. She is willing to plow into anyone's life necessary to convict a murderer, rapist, pedophile, all-around scumbag.

Master of Sex's Dr. William Masters has a license to intervene in his patients' lives because he is a fertility doctor, obstetrician, and trail-blazing sex researcher. Couples who are having trouble conceiving come to Dr. Masters for a miracle. Women come to Dr. Masters to make sure their deliveries are successful and their babies are healthy. Dr. Masters recruits subjects for his sex studies because he believes his findings will help everyone. Everyone has sex. Dr. Masters wants to understand the physiological process of sex so more people are satisfied with their sex lives. Dr. Masters' work has an effect on mankind.

The Good Wife's Alicia Florrick has a license to intervene in other people's lives because she is an attorney. People come to Alicia when they have been accused of a crime and need someone to defend them. Alicia also is a partner in a law firm. She and her partners determine the fates of their employees and clients. Politics pulls Alicia into other characters' lives as well. Alicia's husband is the Illinois governor. By extension, Alicia has responsibilities to the citizens of Illinois. She often makes public appearances and statements. She also ran for the state's attorney general office. Through her own campaign, she was drawn into new spheres of influence.

The story engine can also be a unifying desire or dilemma that pulls other characters into your main character's life. For example, on *The Walking Dead,* the characters' desire to survive a zombie apocalypse pulls them into each other's lives. It requires them to interact, make decisions together, and form alliances.

In *Orange Is the New Black,* the characters' situation—incarceration—forces them into each other's lives. They have arguments, rivalries, and alliances that help them cope with imprisonment.

On *Lost,* the survivors of Oceanic flight 815 must cooperate to survive on this mysterious, supernatural island. They vie for control of the supplies, the group, and their destinies. Eventually, they must unite against "The Others" and the world at large.

Story can come from characters having to work together or fight each other. Any story device that pulls new characters into your characters' lives can generate story. When a character has agency to interfere or intervene in new or other characters' lives, you can create story. You need to maximize the story engine or engines in your show. By maximizing the story engine, you increase the chance of your show's survival.

Themes

Themes elevate your show from something cool to something meaningful. Your theme is the central idea of exploration for your show.

I suggest exploring universal themes. Universal themes are ideas that tend to be relatable to everyone. For example, the idea that "we all want unconditional love" could be a universal theme. "Parents want a better life for their children" could be a universal theme. Some writers break themes into one- or two-word ideas like love, unconditional love, sibling rivalry, letting go, *carpe diem*, acceptance, and so on.

Do what works best for you. I find both approaches useful. Once you hit on a theme, I suggest free associating with that theme before breaking your story. Free association is a technique popularized in psychotherapy by Sigmund Freud. It was a way to discover associations among ideas in a person's mind. Basically, you think about an idea or theme and write down whatever pops into your mind. Draw from your life experiences. What happened to you when you wanted unconditional love or had a sibling rivalry? What did you feel when you had to let someone go from your life or let go of a grudge? When you open your mind and heart to the writing process, you'll find beautiful, relatable characters and scenes that resonate with your audience. That's what you want.

A theme should not be confused with a thesis. A thesis is an idea the writer sets out to prove to the audience. "Guns should be banned" could be a thesis. "Everyone should be treated equally" could be a thesis. While these ideas are interesting, writing a piece of fiction to prove a thesis tends to fail as art. When writers set out to prove a social or political point with their writing, all of their characters, character decisions, world of the show, world decisions, everything about the work is manipulated to come to the inevitable conclusion that proves the writer's point. The problem with manufacturing storylines to prove a point is not trusting your audience's intelligence.

Today's audiences are very savvy. We can see manipulation ten steps down the line. We sense what the writer wants us to believe, and we rebel. We rebel against writing that preaches to us even if we happen to agree with the message. We don't like being told what to think. But we love being challenged. We love thought-provoking stories.

Tone

New writers and pros often struggle with tone. It's one of the most difficult components to nail down. Tone can't be described by adjectives only. "Young, hip, hot" is not a show tone. It could be the tone of a print ad, fashion trend, or a storefront, but it means nothing to TV executives. What is tone exactly? That's an excellent question.

In television, tone refers to the vibe of the show. Is the show dark and gritty? Is the show blue skies? Is the show snarky or sincere? In television, tone and mood are so closely related as to be indistinguishable. When an executive asks about the tone of your show, she wants to know what the audience is signing on for. How will the audience *feel* while watching the show? Often executives will want tonal references to other shows or films.

For many seasons, the USA Network made predominately "blue skies" shows. *Burn Notice, Royal Pains,* and *Psych* were light in tone. They were pleasant, enjoyable, breezy. When audiences thought of USA shows, they were primed to think the skies are clear and blue and all is well.

Currently, the USA Network has grayer skies, but it took them several seasons to get there. *Dig, Complications, Graceland,* and *Mr. Robot* are more serious than past USA shows. They deal with more-complicated subject matter. For example, *Dig* is about an FBI agent stationed in Jerusalem. When this agent investigates the murder of a young American, he uncovers a centuries old conspiracy that could change the course of human history. That's not very blue sky. There's a bit of *Da Vinci Code*-ish conspiracy mixed with *Orphan Black* thriller and action.

Skies got very gray with USA's *Mr. Robot.* It's not about an android or a robot. It's actually about Elliot, a cyber-security tech by day and a hacker vigilante by night. In the pilot episode, Elliot faces off with a pedophile, snorts morphine and Molly, has random sex, hacks his friends' and psychologist's personal accounts, and faces a *Fight Club*-like decision about a financial meltdown. Did I mention he's delusional and neurotic? Skies got *Take Shelter*-gray at USA.

Using other television shows and films as touchstones does help convey tone. Executives generally will ask about tone, and they appreciate the shorthand of other works. While inside the industry we knew what "blue skies" meant, we also had *Psych, Monk,* and *Burn Notice* as touchstones. For several seasons, USA had been trying to change its tone. USA execs used the term "grayer skies." But either the pitch would be too dark or still too "blue skies." Trying to hit a sweet spot somewhere in between was challenging.

As the USA Network redefines itself, there have been some adjustments for them and their audience. *Dig*'s first season ratings were anemic. It averaged 0.32 in the demo with 1.21 million viewers.[30] *Complications,* a dark drama about a doctor, premiered with 0.41 in the demo and 1.9 million viewers.[31] USA cancelled a previous dark drama about a doctor, *Rush,* due to low ratings. It averaged a 0.4 in the demo with 1.65 million viewers for its first season.[32] As USA moves in this new direction, it will take time for them to draw new viewers and for loyal viewers to get used to the tonal shift.

USA does seems to have found the right shade of gray with the terrific *Mr. Robot.* In fact, the network picked up the *second* season of the series before the pilot aired because of its thunderous online reception. *Mr. Robot*'s series premiere garnered about 3 million views across multiple non-linear platforms. Its second episode averaged 1.11 million viewers in the 18-49 demo with 3.2 million overall.[33]

As you are deciding on a tone for your show, think about other TV series and films that have a similar tone. What aspects of these shows are similar to your new show?

Resist the this-meets-that convention! It's *Game of Thrones* meets *The Office*. It's *The Big Bang Theory* meets *The Sopranos*. It's hard not to respond to a "meets" construction with a "huh?" followed by a "meh." The "this-meets-that" construction can be completely clear to the writer. But to the reader or listener, it can be entirely opaque. Is it dragons in a paper-products business? Is it nerds who become mafia dons? What are we watching?

Try this construction instead: My show has the political machinations of the seven kingdoms vying for the Iron Throne set in a modern, mundane setting like the company Dunder Mifflin from *The Office*. *Ohhh, tell me more.* The listener might not totally get your idea, but drawing out the aspect that makes you think of a particular show can help the listener stay on board with you. Here's another construction: My show is a family drama in the vein of *The Sopranos* where the patriarch is a Caltech theoretical physicist with Aspergerian tendencies like Sheldon from *The Big Bang Theory*. *Ohhh, tell me more.*

Highlight the elements from shows that give listener a feel for the tone of your show. It has the grittiness of *Sons of Anarchy*. It has the soapy drama of *Scandal*. It has the exuberance of *The Unbreakable Kimmy Schmidt*. This will help the reader or listener zero in on the elements that mirror your show.

Season arcs or possible episodes

If your show is serialized, meaning that each week the characters change and their stories are affected by previous episodes, then you need to plan at least three seasons of the main character's arc. We call this "arcing out a season."

For example, *Scandal* is a serialized show. Each week, the characters and their stories are affected by the events in the episodes. To arc out three seasons, you'll need to decide where your main character begins for season one. What is the main dilemma your character faces in season one? You want to hook into the emotional journey of your characters.

You'll track the main events, along with their emotional consequences, of season one. These events will correlate with big episodes. These episodes likely will present increasing obstacles. Then you'll tell us how your main character resolves the season-one dilemma and how that catapults the main character into an even bigger dilemma for season two. Probably your main character will face the greatest dilemma of her life at the end of season one.

For season two, having faced the greatest dilemma of your main character's life, where is she? Is she a broken woman? Is she pitted against a rival? Where is she and what is her new dilemma as a result of season one? Then you'll track the major events, along with their emotional consequences, of season two. Again, these will be big episodes. At the end of season two, how does your main character resolve the main dilemma of season two and how does that catapult her into season three? Generally, the end of season two will be even worse for your main character than the end of season one.

The end of season two will catapult your main character into season three. You'll arc out the main dilemma of season three. You'll give major events for the season three. At the end of season three, your main character will face an even greater dilemma, which will catapult her into season four.

Professional TV writers use a trick when arcing out a season. We structure seasons the way we structure one episode of television. We create a narrative that has a beginning, middle, and end. Structuring seasons with all the character-driven landmarks of a great story gives the overall season that satisfying storytelling feel. Your audience, executives, and producers will feel like they're in the hands of a master storyteller. And that's what they want. They want you to guide them through a satisfying entertainment experience. As I mentioned, I'll cover character-driven structure in chapter three.

* * *

For non-serialized dramas and comedies, you'll need to include 10 loglines for possible episodes. An example of a non-serialized comedy is *Modern Family*. While it has some life events—Haley graduating from high school, Jay and Gloria having a baby—the show is minimally affected by serialized storytelling elements. The *NCIS*, *CSI*, and *Law & Order* franchises tend not to be affected much by serialized storytelling elements. They tend to do stand-alone episodes, which is why they translate into syndication so well. You can sit down and watch almost any episode of *Modern Family*, *The Big Bang Theory*, and the *NCISs*, *CSIs*, and *Law & Orders* without having to know what happened "previously on." Creating a strong list of compelling stand-alone episodes will help sell the idea of your show.

Networks and number of episodes

You're going to want to consider what network or type of network that would be interested in your show. For example, if you are writing for the broadcast networks—ABC, CBS, CW, FOX, or NBC—you'll need to consider standards and practice (S&P). S&P determines the content and levels of profanity, sex, and violence allowed in your show. If you're writing for broadcast, you'll need to curb these elements.

Broadcast also tends to do longer seasons—usually 22 episodes. If your show could go to basic cable, you'll also have limitations on language, sex, and violence. Basic cable tends to do 10-13 episode seasons. If your show could go to premium cable, all bets are off on language, sex, and violence. Premium cable tends to do 8-10 episode seasons.

A surprising number of writers say they only want to write for HBO. That's a way to go. However, if your pilot can only go to one buyer in the town and that one buyer doesn't buy a lot of new shows—especially original, spec shows—well, if HBO says "no," you're done. That's it. If your show could go to several buyers and translate to different networks, it's a smarter choice. You broaden the base of your appeal.

You demonstrate to the town that you understand television and the TV business. Plus, you give yourself more options.

Broadcast gives the writer the option of a 13-episode pickup with the possibility of a back nine. This could mean 22 episodes of a show. This means a lot more money and a lot more work. Basic cable offers a 10-13 episode pickup, which is a few months' work. Basic cable pays less than broadcast. Be aware that some cable contracts hold writers for several months without a subsequent season pickup. Cable writers can remain in limbo waiting to hear if they're going to have work for the next year. Premium cable likes to go with shorter seasons, 8-10 episodes, which is less work than broadcast or basic cable. Those writers often only learn about a subsequent season pickup after the season premiere.

For the content of your original pilot, you need to figure out what networks might be interested in your show and how many episodes constitute a season. This will determine the levels of profanity, sex, and violence in your pilot and series. It will also affect how you arc out your seasons.

* * *

The big questions

Okay, so that covers the 10 essential components. Nothing to it, right? Flesh out these components and you have your treatment. I suggest that you answer the following six big questions, too. The answers to these questions will give you insights into the marketability of your show and your investment of time and energy in it.

Why is your show relevant now?

Shows should be fresh, vision-forward, and cutting edge. The audience should believe your show should be on the air right now because of a specific need in society. Your show should fit in today's world and inform audiences about their lives. Even if your show is a period piece, it should be relevant for today's audiences.

Orange Is the New Black is a great example of fresh, vision-forward, and cutting edge. It features mostly women actors from diverse backgrounds, which is very unusual in Hollywood. It delves into the various characters' backgrounds through character-driven flashbacks. The writers have taken a modern approach to the structure of the flashbacks.

We used to bookend flashbacks within a present scene. We would begin with the featured character before we went into that character's flashback, then we would come back to the featured character in the present just where we interrupted the scene. *OITNB* usually does away with one of the bracket scenes to their flashbacks. The writers might start the show in a flashback so there is no beginning present scene. After the opening flashback, the writers will take the audience into a present scene with the featured character.

The *OITNB* writers also do the reverse. They may begin with a present scene of the featured character, then flash back to the character's life before prison. When the flashback ends, the writers often pick up with another character's storyline. The writers assume the audience will be able to follow the action because most of the present scenes take place in prison. Almost any time a featured character is outside of the prison and dressed in regular clothes, not the orange or tan prison wear, she is in flashback.

When writers are pitching shows, executives often are thinking, What does the audience want right now because of the political and social climate? Post 9-11, ripples went through Hollywood as the country recovered from the attacks. Creators, studios, and networks wondered, "What does America want to watch right now?" Market research that gauged Americans' responses to dark times all the way back to World War I helped shape TV buying patterns in the town. "Blue skies" was a catch phrase. The prevailing thought was that audiences wanted to see shows and films that showed everything was going to be all right in the world. Basically, if a writer had a darker-toned show then, he had to wait to pitch it. After a couple of buying cycles and some distance, the town was open to darker shows again.

Everything is cyclical in Hollywood, especially TV show buying. One pilot pitching season will be all about single-camera comedies or serialized dramas. For a while, reality shows ruled and scripted creators feared no one would ever want to buy their shows again. However, right now reality shows are waning and scripted shows rule. It's always good to remember—everything is cyclical. Just because the buying patterns for this season focus on something you don't write, it doesn't mean next season will be the same.

Writers shouldn't try to chase the market. For a while, industry reps were all about writers finding that next *Twilight*. Let's call that the vampire boom. For some writers, it was tempting to create or search for underlying properties that had vampires. Vampires who lived, died, and loved. Vampires who struggled with their identities. Vampires who went to high school and private academies. Vampires who solved crime at night. Several vampire shows launched, including HBO's breakout hit *True Blood*. *True Blood* was developed by one of my favorite showrunners, Alan Ball, and was based on my friend Charlaine Harris' Southern Vampire Mystery novels. It was about a telepathic waitress, Sookie Stackhouse, and her recently out-of-the-coffin vampire lovers, Bill Compton and Eric Northman. It was tempting to chase that vampire rabbit, but the truth is, if you weren't a vampire lover before the vampire boom, if you weren't tapped into that zeitgeist before everything hit, you were too late.

Follow *your* truth. Follow your interests. You have to love your show into being. It doesn't matter who you are. You'll put barrels of sweat equity into a show before it ever has a chance to hit. When creators compare a TV show's creation to the birth of a baby, they mean it. You must have the passion, drive, and desire long before you'll ever see an actual screaming, bawling baby. You'll gestate this idea for a long time. You'll talk about it. You'll get other people excited about it. And you might find your friends don't really care. You might find your agent can't see this beautiful offspring you describe so lovingly. You might find your parents think this is a bad idea. You might doubt your own ability to make this show come to life, for you to parent it after its naked form appears in our cold, cruel world.

Still, that's the gig. Once you've felt the true love of TV series creation, you're hooked. No matter how many times you say, "I'll never do that again," the moment a new idea sparks you're in love again; you're pregnant with promise.

However, it's important to remember—we create shows for audiences. We don't create shows for ourselves. We create our shows, our art, to be experienced by other people. Those people are your fans. You have fans. They might not know it yet, but once they're drawn into your characters' lives and the world of your show, they're hooked. They see what you see. They share the love you've been feeling for your project. For a creator, this validation can be wonderful and overwhelming. Suddenly, something that was inside your head is playing in the street.

It is important to think about your audience while creating a show. As you consider your show, it should have more heft than cool factor. It should fill a specific need in society. The show can still be cool, but too often creators focus solely on the "wouldn't it be cool if..." part of a show. You need to focus on what are you trying to *say* with your show. What will your fans relate to in your show? Cool only goes so far. You want your show to resonate with audiences. Your show needs to speak to your audiences' souls.

How is your show different from other TV shows?

Buyers are looking for shows they don't have. They're looking for shows their competitors don't have. Different can be expressed in format, like *24* or *The Wire*. Different can apply to subject matter, like *Sons of Anarchy* or *Mad Men*. It can be both, as in the case of *Game of Thrones* or *Treme*. It can be a unique take on source material like *Bates Motel* or *Once Upon a Time*.

Think about how your show is different from other shows. You might want to explore a world that isn't well known. You might want to take a character on a journey you haven't seen recently. You might want to break with usual television format like *24* did with its real-time element.

If you are going to break format, please understand this doesn't mean you can create hour-and-a-half episode shows or 15-minute shows for the big studio and network buyers. The format breaking should be within the confines of the usual 30-minute sitcom and 60-minute drama/dramedy format. Also, breaking format should be done for a smart reason. The series *24* wanted to create an adrenaline-fueled dramatic television show. They wanted that hour of television to keep the audience on the edge of their seats. They created a compelling character in Jack Bauer and delivered hard-driving action. Their decision to break format had style and substance.

You may think you've come up with a show idea that no one has ever tried before. I'd announce that breakthrough cautiously if I were you. Just because you aren't familiar with a show in the world you want to explore doesn't mean no one has developed a similar idea.

Consider this. Every pilot pitching season, the broadcast networks hear approximately 400 full-on, in person pitches. Each network—ABC, CBS, CW, FOX, NBC—hears 400 pitches and around 500 soft pitches.[34] Soft pitches are loglines or synopses from agents. That's 2,000 to 2,500 TV series ideas in a given season. Of those pitches, each network buys and develops around 70 pilot scripts. Of those 70 pilot scripts, each network puts 10-12 to pilot. Of the 10-12 produced pilots, the network will put approximately four to series. Of the four, maybe one of those new shows will be a hit.[35] So, it's likely someone has come before you and developed a show in your arena.

If you say, "No one has ever done a show about massage parlors before," you've just thrown down the gauntlet. You've dared the executive to think about everything that's ever been pitched and/or developed in the past and prove you wrong. You don't want the people you're pitching to be on the defensive and not paying attention to your pitch. As for TV shows about massage parlors, Lifetime's *The Client List* starring Jennifer Love-Hewitt springs to mind.

How does your show push the envelope? How is it edgy?

Buyers, readers, and audiences want to be wowed. They want something they can't stop thinking about. And while everything in television is cyclical, I think we are entering a phase of television that is unique. There are more television content buyers in the town than there have been in the history of television. While people outside of Hollywood may continue to think of the town as feature-film oriented, insiders know television is the dominant force.

In recent years, we've seen a mass exodus of creators from film to television. They've justified their forays in television because television has "just gotten better." Filmmakers often say television "is doing edgier character-driven work now." We've *been* doing that.

The real reason filmmakers are getting into television is money. We have money. We have great development cycles. We have a sense of near-immediate gratification. We can create, sell, write, and produce a television show in less than a year. Most feature films take an average of seven years to produce. And there are so many sticking points, so many frustrations in those seven years that television looks like a vacation in Fiji. And while there *are* frustrations in television, we do have it good. It is awesome to work in television. We get to create and get paid well. We get to work with top talent. As writers, we have more control over the process and end product than in films. What could be better than that?

However, with so many buyers, creators must create edgy, noisy shows. We need to be edgy and noisy to attract an audience. The audience has so many choices that if your show isn't edgy and noisy, they may never know it exists. You could have a great show that goes unwatched.

What is edgy and noisy? Good question. Hollywood is always looking for edge. Think the opposite of safe. Think cutting edge, *bleeding* edge. While writers can't chase the market, they do have to think ahead—way ahead. Plus, they have to make creative choices for their characters that are out there, risky, risqué, fresh. Your audience should say, "Wow, I've gotta see more."

In chapter 1, I mentioned Amazon's *Transparent* as a great example of edgy and noisy. The idea of a mild-mannered professor and father deciding later in life to make a transition to a woman is fresh. And it's authentic. Creator Jill Soloway's parent made this transition.[36] Jill can show audiences a bit of what it's really like to go through this transformation as a family. Plus, all of her characters have flaws and secrets. The adult children of the main character are going through their own transitions. The thematic unity of this show elevates it. At its heart, the show is about family and acceptance. Everyone has a family, and everyone wants to be accepted. These universal themes shot through the prism of a unique topic make the show resonate with audiences.

Another example of edgy and noisy is Cinemax's *The Knick*. After saying, "Movies don't matter anymore" and retiring from filmmaking, Steven Soderbergh has joined the television community as executive producer, director, and director of photography (under pseudonym Peter Andrews) of *The Knick*.[37]

Starring Clive Owen, *The Knick* chronicles the life of a fictional star surgeon and cocaine addict at New York's Knickerbocker Hospital in 1900. Setting the show at the turn of the 20th century, a time when medical pioneers believed themselves on the cutting edge of medicine, gives the show relevance to today's audiences. We see how barbaric medical practices were in the past, yet how advanced the people at the time believed their medicine was. It's difficult not to compare then to now. The character of Dr. John Thackery pushes the envelope because we know now how dangerous and addictive cocaine is. We know a surgeon should not cut someone open while high. Yet at the time, cocaine was seen as a miracle drug available by prescription. It helped the pioneers stay up for days, perform under stressful conditions, and face defeat in the surgical theater repeatedly. The surgical scenes are intense and often gruesome. *The Knick* provides shock and awe as well as a reflection on our society.

Still, even with stellar performances, edgy premises, compelling characters, *Transparent* and *The Knick* haven't been noisy enough to break through to the average viewer. Amazon hasn't revealed its viewership numbers. The online shopping-cum-video-streaming service points to *Transparent*'s perch atop its Prime Instant Video ratings, but those ratings aren't quantified.

The Internet Movie Database, IMDb, collects user ratings for various shows. *Transparent* has a total of 7,792 user-rating votes. Comparatively, Netflix's *Orange Is the New Black* has accumulated 141,558 user-rating votes. *House of Cards* has collected a whopping 222,212 user rating votes. Still, these numbers are far below the usual viewership numbers for shows we'd call hits.

The Knick drew 1.7 million viewers with a Cinemax and HBO combined premiere.[38] However, it garnered only 413,000 viewers with its Cinemax-only season-one finale. Cinemax's *Banshee* is probably one of the edgy, noisy winners in recent history. The *Banshee* season 2 finale demolished Cinemax's ratings record (591,000 viewers) when it drew 733,000 viewers for the 10 p.m. airing. When the 11 p.m. airing was factored in, *Banshee* scored 968,000 viewers for the finale.[39] Their season three numbers weren't quite up to this level, with an average of 580,000 viewers for the season.[40] Still, Cinemax renewed the crime-action drama for a fourth and final season.

As you can see, you need to push the envelope to grab viewers' attention. With the fragmentation of television, viewers have so many more choices clamoring for their attention. Your show needs to stand out against the crowd.

What did you discover through real-world research about your idea? How did you incorporate it into your show?

Many writers believe they should make up ideas whole cloth from their minds. However, research will add an extra dimension to your project. When you can pull from real-world experiences, you'll enrich the story and characters, making them feel more substantial and relatable. Research convinces executives you're passionate about the subject matter and that you have answers. They want you to have answers. That's what you're getting paid for. Also, audiences want to be immersed in unfamiliar worlds. Research will help you get the details correct.

What other art has influenced your TV series idea?

You are an artist. We expect you to be interested in other art. This could include other television series, films, paintings, poems, novels, music, any other art form. Understanding your influences can help us understand what you are trying to accomplish in your TV series. We want to know *how* this art influenced you. This can help us understand you, too. Artistic touchstones can help guide you as you develop your series and help you describe your series to other people.

Why are you the only person who can create this TV series?

This is probably the most important question you can ask yourself during development. You need to have a compelling reason to develop this pilot. You need to know why you have to write this project, why you are willing to work on this project for the next five years, even if you aren't getting paid, and why you and only you can create this particular take.

This can be one of the most difficult questions to answer. Relying on sheer personal experience can be a slippery slope. *I'm the only person who can create this show because I experienced X.* You could be interested in a fascinating arena, but you don't own the arena just because you worked at a dog park, zoo, hospital, etc. Let's say you have a fascinating arena, but you don't convince studio and network executives that you have a unique vision for a show in this arena *and* can execute it. They could easily turn to someone they trust and ask for a take in the arena you pitched. Sounds cut-throat, right? Well, it is.

Studio and network executives meet literally thousands of writers. Of those thousands of writers, there are ER doctors, former special warfare military officers, former White House speech writers, white-hat hackers, comic-book creators, videogame programmers, former cops, and former Manhattan assistant district attorneys. You name it, and they're your competition.

Studio and network executives know many writers they already trust who probably can create a show in that arena. You need a compelling reason why *you* are the perfect writer for this show. What makes your take special? What will make it resonate with executives in a room and an audience at home?

I like to think about this question in this way: "Why me? Why this?" I think about why I'm fascinated with this idea. What do I see that is unique to me? What do I bring out of this idea that is uniquely me? You want someone to buy into your series sight unseen. You want them to believe you *have to* create this show. It will always connect to your passion.

Whatever you write, be passionate. In Hollywood, we're suckers for passion and intelligence. Put these two elements together, and you've got what you need to convince others to follow your vision.

Assignment

Now it's time to write *your* TV series treatment. There are sample treatments in the appendix. Create a document with a section for each of these ten components:

1) Title
2) Type of show
3) Idea
4) Logline
5) World of the show
6) Characters
7) Story engine
8) Themes
9) Tone
10) Season arcs or possible episodes.

As you look at the information you gathered from your chapter 1 assignment, start filling in any details you have for world of the show, characters, and story engine. As you refine your show, focus on the characters and use Egri's character bones structure. Write your character bios in complete sentences and infuse your bios with your voice.

Make sure you give your project a title, even if it's just a working title. Be specific about the type of show you want to make. Boil your logline down to 30 words or fewer. Try to find a universal theme for your show. Clarify tone by referring to other TV shows or films. Choose a strong story engine or engines. Resist thinking story will come from relationships.

Clarify the world of your show by describing where your characters will spend the most time. Think about the standing sets you'll need and describe them. For example, *It's Always Sunny in Philadelphia* is set in Philadelphia. However, the gang spends most of their time in Paddy's

Bar, various characters' apartments, and the coffee shop. Philadelphia itself isn't an especially important part of the show. Make sure you convey what locations you'll show audiences each week.

After you've nailed down your series idea, logline, story engine, world of the show, and characters, tackle your season arcs or possible episodes. If you have a serialized show, arc out at least three seasons. If you have a show with stand-alone episodes, include ten possible amazing episodes.

* * *

After you've completed the 10 components, answer the big questions:

1) Why is your show relevant now?

2) How is your show different from other TV shows?

3) How does your show push the envelope? How is it edgy?

4) What did you discover through real-world research about your television show idea? And how did you incorporate that info into your show?

5) What other art has influenced your TV series idea?

6) Why are you the only person who can create this TV series?

When you have all of these elements, you'll be prepared to discuss your show with agents, managers, producers, and execs. This is a living document. Things may change as you move forward with the process. However, sometimes the creator sees things so clearly from the beginning she knows exactly the series she wants to create. Whatever you do, have fun bringing your vision to the world.

CHAPTER 3

TL;DR chapter 3

Broadcast networks added *more* commercial breaks to TV shows just as premium-cable shows with *no* commercial act breaks exploded, so we ushered in a new era of television writing. Character-driven structure unifies drama and comedy television writing, including premium cable, basic cable, broadcast network, streaming, and on-demand platforms. Assignment: Write character-driven landmarks for your pilot.

The Hero Succeeds: Character-Driven Structure

In this chapter, you'll find:

- the logic and landmarks of character-driven structure;
- a breakdown of *Raiders of the Lost Ark;*
- a breakdown of *The Knick* for comparison; and
- your character-driven landmark assignment.

I mentioned Aristotle and his beginning, middle, and end in the introduction. More recently, contemporary writers have written volumes about feature-film screenwriting. They're framed with formulas, paradigms, steps, and beat sheets. Many of those books' authors have focused on plot and called for various plot points to appear on specific pages of feature-film scripts.

The Hero Succeeds takes a different approach. The character-driven structure unifies drama and comedy TV writing *with and without commercial act breaks* across premium cable, basic cable, broadcast network, streaming, and on-demand platforms.

Most professional television writers know TV structure because they've broken and written dozens, even hundreds of episodes of television. TV structure eventually becomes ingrained in them. They instinctively understand this structure. It's a skill that gets passed on in the writers room, but generally not written down, analyzed or studied. The pace in TV demands fast writing. We learn how to do it, then we crank out episodes.

Sometimes episodes work. Sometimes they don't. We've all seen examples of both. When I started my career, I wanted to better understand the difference between stellar TV and episodes that fell short. So I took what I was learning in the TV trenches and combined it with the results of systematically breaking down all kinds of TV. I explored ways to streamline the writing process, to strip it down and make it faster, more efficient. What I found was an inherent structure based on character. The common denominator of all well-structured television is *character-driven structure.* This story structure focuses on your main character, your hero, and her journey through the episode.

Character-driven structure is not a formula

The Hero Succeeds' character-driven structure is not a formula. It's not warmed-over Jung or Joseph Campbell, or paradigms, or beat sheets, or rising action. It not a plug-scene-in-here approach to writing. Rather, it's a flexible guide that helps writers create three-dimensional characters from whence all good things—including plot and satisfying story shapes—flow. The best way for me to explain how character-driven structure works is to start with the familiar three-act structure.

Three-act structure

Three-act structure harkens all the way back to Aristotle—335 B.C.E. In his work *Poetics,* Aristotle didn't refer to acts *per se,* but he proposed the very simple idea that "A whole...has a beginning and middle and end."[43] In other words, stories have a beginning, middle, and end. Boy meets girl. Boy loses girl. Boy gets girl. Simple, right? This is a simple story told with a beginning, middle, and end, or for our purposes, act one, act two, and act three.

It might seem that a three-act story would be divided into three equal parts. However, it's a bit more complex because the parts aren't equal in length. Act two, the middle part, clocks in at twice as long as act one or act three. The story evolves into something like this (and feel free to switch up the sexes any way you like): Boy meets girl. Boy wants girl. Boy gets and loses girl. Boy wins girl back. While we call it three-act structure, and there *are* three acts, I just listed *four* structural elements in a story. That's because three-act structure divides the story into *fourths.* I'll annotate three-act structure in feature films for the sake of familiarity, then I'll bridge this concept to television.

A feature-length screenplay can be divided into fourths. The first act is one-fourth of the entire script. The second act is two-fourths or a half of the script. The third act is the final fourth of the script. As a rule of thumb, one page of a screenplay equals one minute of screen time for films, a little less for TV. So, the first act of a two-hour film is approximately the first 30 script pages. The second act consists of the next two-fourths of the script or the next 60 pages. And the third act is the final 30 pages. It's all neatly charted in Figure 3.1.

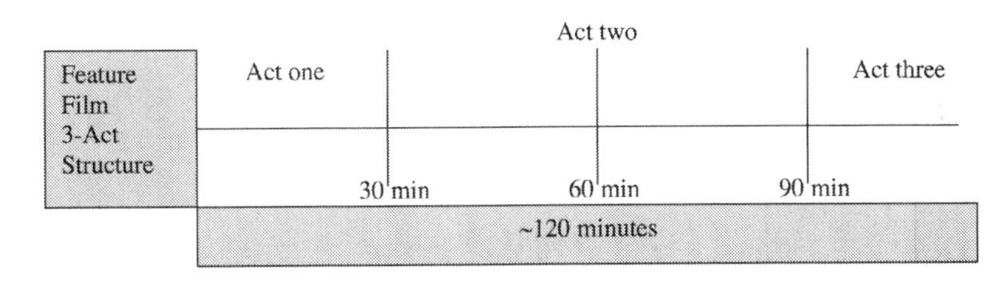

Figure 3.1: Feature-film script divided into 30/60/30 pages using traditional three-act structure. Image by Kam Miller.

What about films with running times less than two hours? The writer would simply divide the script into fourths. For example, a 90-minute screenplay yields approximately a 22.5-page first act, a 45-page second act, and a 22.5-page third act. These numbers are approximate.

For those of you who may be a little math-phobic, please stick with me on this. This bit is important. These divisions—first act, second act, and third act—delineate the beginning, middle, and end to your story.

More importantly, there are landmarks within these divisions that help shape your story. These character-driven landmarks will help you structure your story and give your audience a satisfying viewing experience. Associating these landmarks with pivotal character scenes—whether you're writing an action-adventure or cerebral-thriller or slapstick comedy—will help you deliver an engaging, compelling experience for your audience.

Before we get into the details, just remember this: Character-driven structure works because *all good things come from character.* Every meaningful moment in your story will come directly from character. Your story will come directly from your characters. In other words, the story structure becomes your character arc. They're inextricably wedded, so story, character, and that four-letter word—plot—are not separate entities that you have to achieve or juggle. *They're the same thing.* Character becomes story. You don't have to worry about internal and external forces, rising action, or other nebulous, confusing writing concepts. Suddenly, your life gets a whole lot simpler. All you have to focus on is character. Let me show you how character-driven structure works using a more-familiar platform: feature-film structure.

Feature-film structure to television-show structure

In feature-film structure, there are several conventional storytelling landmarks within the three-act structure. These landmarks include the point of attack; end of first act; mid-point; end of the second act; and third-act climax.

Having a series of smaller, interim goals or landmarks during the writing helps guide the writer and makes the writing easier. If the writer works toward these landmarks, the writing will be divided into smaller goals and the script ultimately will fit three-act structure.

In a two-hour movie, the point of attack typically happens around the ten-minute or ten-page mark. The end of the first act happens around 30 minutes into the film. The mid-point of a two-hour film happens around 60 minutes or 60 pages into the script. This is halfway through the film. The end of the second act occurs around the 90-minute or 90-page mark. The final 30 pages are the third act. The climax happens around the 105-minute or 105-page mark. Again, if the film is shorter, these landmarks happen sooner. Figure 3.2 graphs the feature-film structure using the conventional landmarks.

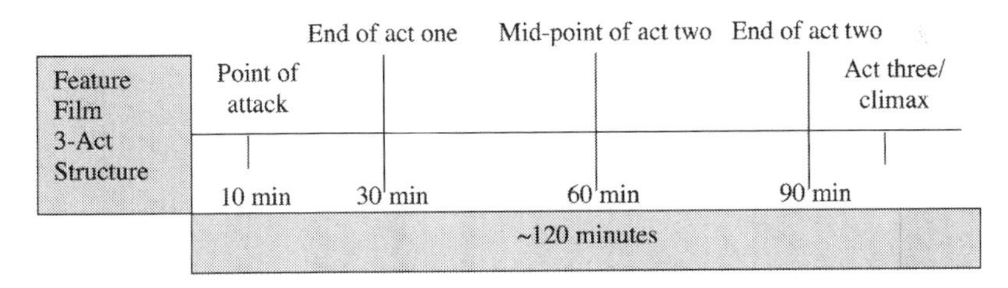

Figure 3.2: Feature-film script with conventional landmarks in traditional three-act structure. Image by Kam Miller.

This next bit is important. In television, shows are divided into acts depending on the commercial breaks. Every time there is a commercial break, we say it's an act break. Broadcast and basic cable added more commercials in recent years. (More on that in chapter 5). So today's TV shows could easily have what we call a teaser-and-four-act structure, a teaser-and-five-act or teaser-and-six-act structure, a (nod to Shakespeare) five-act structure or even a six-act structure. There are cold opens and tags in the structural mix, too, and shows with *no* commercial act breaks. However, regardless of the television nomenclature, *all TV shows still follow character-driven structure.* Let me show you.

Let's start with the easiest comparison: a three-act feature film to a teaser-and-four-act TV show. In television, the point of attack happens in the teaser. The end of act one happens at the end of act one. Here's where things get a little tricky. Remember when I said features are divided into fourths? In television the mid-point of the show happens at the end of act two. This is half-way through a four-act show. In television, the next act is act three. The landmark that generally embodies the end of act two happens at the end of act three in a television show. The act-three climax happens in act four for TV.

Take a look at these two graphs. The first graph is the feature-film landmark graph we just reviewed. The second graph represents a teaser-and-four-act television structure. See how nicely these landmarks line up on the two graphs!

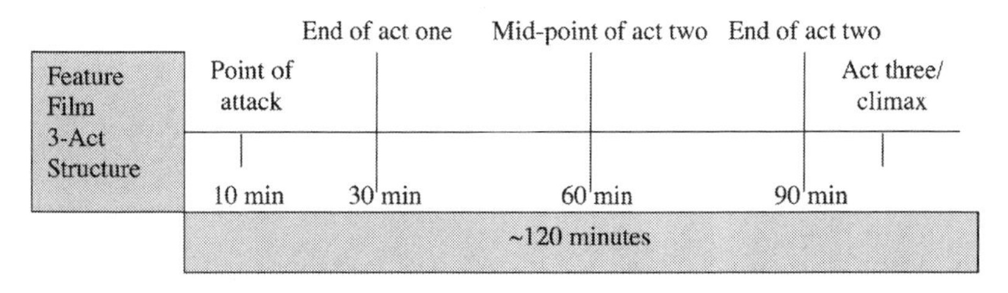

Figure 3.2: Feature-film script with conventional landmarks in traditional three-act structure. Image by Kam Miller.

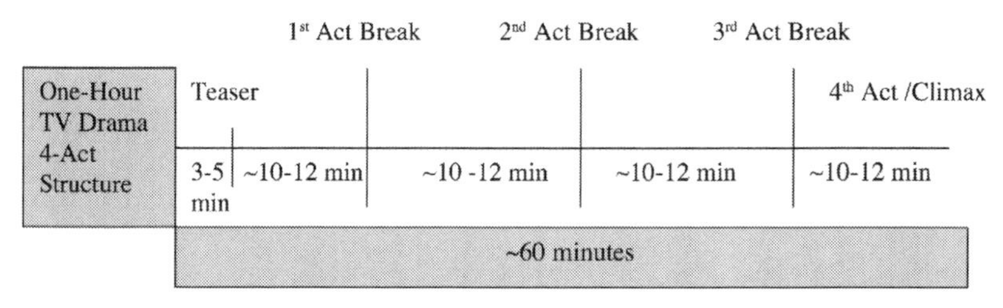

Figure 3.3: TV script with conventional landmarks in teaser-and-four-act structure. Image by Kam Miller.

Character-driven structure

These writing landmarks mean more than just page numbers or screen time. They have story meanings. In character-driven structure, these landmarks relate to the character journey. Remember, all good things come from character.

If you focus these landmarks on the character, you'll automatically create the character arc of your story. What's more, you'll create a story that is structurally sound, has shape, and is emotionally satisfying to your audience. Plus, you won't have to think about plot ever again. Say what now? That's right. Your story comes from character, so your character arc becomes your story. You don't have to think about plotting your story and arcing your characters. You'll automatically have an arc for your character within your very satisfying, structurally sound story.

Here are the landmarks of character-driven structure in **bold**. The **point of attack** is the first whiff of the problem your main character will face. It's not the whole problem. It's just a whiff of the problem. At the end of the first act, your **hero is committed** to your story. Until that point, the hero could go back to his old job, old relationship, old apartment, whatever. After the end of the first act, he is committed to the journey of the story. At the mid-point of your story, your **hero succeeds—almost**. In other words, your audience gets a glimpse at your hero succeeding, then that success gets snatched away. In a romantic comedy, the heroine kisses her crush and there are sparks, but then she learns her crush just got engaged. The audience sees for a moment how good these two people could be together, then they realize something stands in their way. *It's not "the hero fails"!*

Historically, the end of the second act has many names. Some call it the all-hope-is-lost moment or the deepest-darkest moment. In character-driven structure, it's called the **emotional squeeze**, because it encapsulates the meaning of the landmark as it relates to your character.
At the end of the second act, your main character will face her greatest emotional dilemma. She'll be squeezed or pressured by the main forces in her life. She'll have to make a tough decision between two bad

options. This is where she demonstrates that she has changed as a character.

The third-act climax often occurs when the conflict of the story reaches its peak. The climax might be when your hero finally fights the bad guy. Or your hero might run through the rain, an airport, or New York City and finally declare his love for his crush. This landmark is the **hero succeeds** moment. We see the hero use what he has learned from the story and succeed in his mission. Every moment of your hero's story up this point has prepared him to succeed in a unique way.

Often when the hero succeeds, there is a emotional surprise for your character. This is the **emotional twist**. For example, in *Star Wars,* Han Solo changing his mind and coming back to help the rebels destroy the Death Star is an emotional twist, as is Luke Skywalker foregoing the technological advances of his X-wing fighter's targeting system and using the Force to save the day. The hero succeeds, with a twist.

After the hero succeeds, the story ends in a resolution. The resolution is the **hero's new life**. This landmark serves two purposes. One, it allows your audience to understand how your character's life has been affected by his journey, how his life has changed. Two, it allows your audience to process the story and its meaning. This moment in the storytelling also is called the denouement. The denouement is when the storylines come together and are resolved.

It is important to remember it's not just about your story or you; you need to take care of the audience. We make art to be shared with an audience. We have a responsibility to them. They've just gone on a journey with your characters. They may have been changed by your characters and your storytelling. You need to give them a moment to process your story before you send them into the harsh light of day or on to the next TV episode.

* * *

Character-driven landmark overview

Point of attack: The first whiff of the problem your main character will face.

Hero committed: At the end of your first act, your main character commits to the story. Until this point, your main character could turn around and go back to his old life. After he is committed, he must attempt to accomplish his goal.

Hero succeeds—almost: At the midpoint of your story, your hero has some success. However, this success is short-lived. Something or someone snatches the success away from your hero. This landmark is very important for your audience. Your audience needs to see what success looks like—*it's not "the hero fails."* Your audience needs to see your hero *can* be successful.

Emotional squeeze: At the end of the second act, your hero is squeezed emotionally. Under pressure, he must make a difficult decision, often between two bad options. Your hero's decision will demonstrate that he has changed because of his experiences in your story.

Hero succeeds: In the third act, your hero will face his greatest challenge. Within that challenge, there may be an unexpected twist or change in story direction that neither the character nor the audience anticipated. Now a changed person, your hero uses everything he has learned from your story to finally succeed.

Hero's new life: At the end of your story, your hero now has a new life because of his story experiences. In the resolution, your hero demonstrates his new direction in life.

* * *

Let's break down a familiar classic feature film, *Raiders of the Lost Ark,* to illuminate character-driven structure, then demonstrate how it matches up perfectly with a modern TV pilot.

Raiders of the Lost Ark is one of the best-structured films in cinematic history. On its surface, it seems like a fun action movie with a great character at its center. However, *Raiders* is much more. Its iconic character, adventurer-archaeologist Indiana Jones, goes through a spiritual and emotional transformation as he treks across the globe in search of the lost Ark of the Covenant. More than 30 years later, *Raiders* continues to sell out theaters and festival screenings. And that's what you want. You want people to connect with your characters and their story arcs.

Figure 3.4: Sold-out *Raiders of the Lost Ark* Cinespia event in Los Angeles July 3, 2014. Photo by Kelly Lee Barrett courtesy of Cinespia.

Spoiler alert! Watch *Raiders of the Lost Ark,* then come back to see why this classic film works because of its character-driven structure.

Raiders of the Lost Ark

Script by Lawrence Kasdan with story by George Lucas.

Figure 3.5: *Raiders of the Lost Ark* point of attack.

Point of attack

The audience hears about the lost Ark of the Covenant for the first time when archaeologist Indiana Jones receives a visit from two Army intelligence agents. They tell Indy that the Nazis are obsessed with the occult and are searching for his former mentor, Abner Ravenwood. Based on an intercepted Nazi message that mentions Ravenwood and Tanis, Indy concludes the Nazis have found Tanis, an ancient Egyptian city believed to be the resting place for the lost Ark of the Covenant.

Ravenwood, an expert on the ark, had collected the headpiece to the Staff of Ra. According to lore, the headpiece of the Staff of Ra would help locate the Well of the Souls, believed to be the last known location of the lost ark. The Nazis want the ark because Hitler believes that any army with the ark in its possession would be invincible. Indy suggests that the agents ask Abner for help. They tell him his mentor is missing.

The moment Indiana Jones learns his mentor is missing, he becomes emotionally invested in the search. He has a personal connection to the problem. This is the **point of attack**. It's the first whiff of the problem. This is the first indication that Indy will eventually seek the lost ark. However, first he must find Abner and the headpiece of the Staff of Ra.

After dodging a massive rolling boulder and running from the Peruvian Hovitos in the teaser, this point of attack may seem rather tame. It almost seems mundane. It's an expositional scene where the Army agents and audience learn about the lost ark. However, it is a crucial moment for Indiana Jones as a character. It helps establish Indy's dismissal of the supernatural. It shows his secular, academic attitude toward a religious artifact and the mythology that surrounds it.

In the next scene, Indy even tells his friend Brody that he doesn't believe in superstitious mumbo-jumbo. This is essential to his character arc. Marion Ravenwood's name also comes up. Indy hints at their previous romantic involvement. This is the **point of attack for the Marion storyline.** Indy's desire for the ark and his desire for Marion compete during the second act.

Figure 3.6: *Raiders of the Lost Ark* hero committed.

Hero committed

Near the end of the first act, Indy has traveled to Nepal and found Abner's daughter, Marion. They allude to a previous romantic relationship. Marion's still wounded by this relationship. Marion tells Indy that Abner is dead. Indy wants the headpiece to the Staff of Ra. Marion tells him to come back tomorrow.

Shortly thereafter, Nazis show up and want to torture Marion for the whereabouts of the headpiece. Indy comes to save Marion. A shootout and blazing fight sequence result in Marion losing everything she owns, with the exception of the headpiece of the Staff of Ra.

Standing outside her burning bar, Marion brandishes the headpiece and informs Indy, "I'm your goddamn partner!" At that moment, Indy is committed to finding the ark—with Marion. The marriage of these two storylines is essential to the rest of the story.

Figure 3.7: *Raiders of the Lost Ark* hero succeeds—almost.

Hero succeeds—almost

There are two **hero succeeds—almost** moments in the film. The first one centers on the Marion storyline. Indy believes Marion has been killed in an explosion. However, after Indy finds the true location of the ark and is preparing to excavate it, he finds Marion tied up in the tent of his rival and Nazi conspirator, René Belloq. Overjoyed, Indy kisses Marion. Marion wants him to cut her lose. But Indy realizes if he releases Marion, the Nazis will know he is in the camp and will search for him and Marion. If he frees Marion now, Indy can't get the ark. Indy succeeds in finding Marion, yet he can't quite save her now because he wants the ark more. This first **hero succeeds—almost** moment is the lesser one, but it's still important. Throughout the film, the ark and Marion storylines are intertwined. Consistently, Indy must choose between the ark and Marion.

At the true midpoint of the film, Indy and Sallah, his friend and expert digger, have excavated and opened the roof high above an ancient burial chamber. While avoiding thousands of snakes in the chamber, they heft the Ark of the Covenant out of its protective crypt. The audience sees the glorious golden ark for the first time.

Indy and Sallah stow the ark in a wooden crate. Their crew lifts the crate through the ancient burial chamber's ceiling with thick ropes. Sallah ascends the rope next. Indy fends off snakes with a dying torch.

As Indy prepares to climb out, the rope suddenly slips through the ceiling and coils onto the burial chamber's floor. Belloq appears in the ceiling aperture. He takes the ark away from Indy and announces his plans to seal Indy in the chamber, effectively killing him. The Nazis throw Marion into the chamber. Indy and Marion watch as the heavy stone slab slides into place, cutting them off from the outside world. **The audience sees Indy succeed, then watches Belloq snatch success away from him.** Indy also has found but not saved Marion. They are both doomed, or so it would seem.

Of course, Indy and Marion do escape, and Indy begins an arduous, thrilling chase to recover the ark.

Figure 3.8: *Raiders of the Lost Ark* emotional squeeze.

Emotional squeeze

After the Nazis seize the ark and Marion from a tramp steamer, Indy hitches a ride atop the Nazi's U-boat. Once the sub docks at a nearby island in the Aegean Sea, Indy poses as a Nazi solider until he can get the upper hand. At the end of the second act, Indy seizes his opportunity. He seeks higher ground with a bazooka. Indy threatens to blow up the ark if Belloq doesn't give him Marion. "All I want is the girl," Indy says.

However, Belloq knows Indy better than Indy knows himself. Belloq calls Indy's bluff and tells him to blow up the ark. Indy must choose between destroying the ark or surrendering. He has to make a choice between two bad options. Indy surrenders. Indy can't bring himself to destroy the ark. Indy is being squeezed by the forces in his life.

Figure 3.9: *Raiders of the Lost Ark* hero succeeds.

Hero succeeds

Indy and Marion stand bound together as Belloq performs a mystical open-air ritual and opens the ark. Suddenly, the electrical equipment fails. Indy realizes something supernatural is about to happen. He has come to believe the ark is more than a container for stone tablets. He believes it is other-worldly. He has gone from a man who doesn't buy superstitious mumbo-jumbo to an absolute believer.

In one of the greatest magic tricks in cinema history, Indy tells Marion to shut her eyes. "Don't look at it, Marion," Indy says. He knows if you look upon God you will perish. However, we the audience can't look away. We see what our hero doesn't.

The supernatural provides the emotional twist. Angelic ghosts float out of the ark. Belloq says, "It's beautiful." No matter how enticing it might be to open their eyes, Indy is adamant that Marion not look. And boy, is he right. The ghosts turn hideous. Through supernatural torture the Nazis and Belloq die horribly. Having respected the wrath of God, Indy and Marion are alive, the firestorm having freed them from their bonds. **The hero succeeds.** Indy's newfound belief in the other-worldly is an **emotional twist** for his character. At the beginning of the film, he didn't believe in supernatural nonsense, but by the climax, Indy believes. He succeeds in saving Marion from the ark and the ark from the Nazis.

Figure 3.10: *Raiders of the Lost Ark* hero's new life.

Hero's new life

At the end of the film, the Army Intelligence agents have gained custody of the ark. Indy wants to know what they have done with it. The agents are evasive. Indy warns the agents that they are dealing with unspeakable power. Still, the agents refuse to tell Indy anything more about it.

While Indy *loses* the ark (again), he has Marion on his arm (thanks to Marcia Lucas) [44] and has gained knowledge of the supernatural—faith, even. He knows there are supernatural objects that have survived for millennia. These objects must be respected for their power, not just their link to the past. Indy now values Marion. He has come to respect her in the now and not as someone he left in the past. This is **Indy's new life**.

Character-driven structure gives emotional meaning to your story. In *Raiders of the Lost Ark*, it elevates a popcorn action film to a character journey that still resonates with audiences decades later. Together, George Lucas, Lawrence Kasdan and director Steven Spielberg created an exceptional, enduring film.

* * *

Now that you've seen a big-screen version of the character-driven story structure, let me show you how it relates to modern television by applying it to the pilot for Cinemax's *The Knick*.

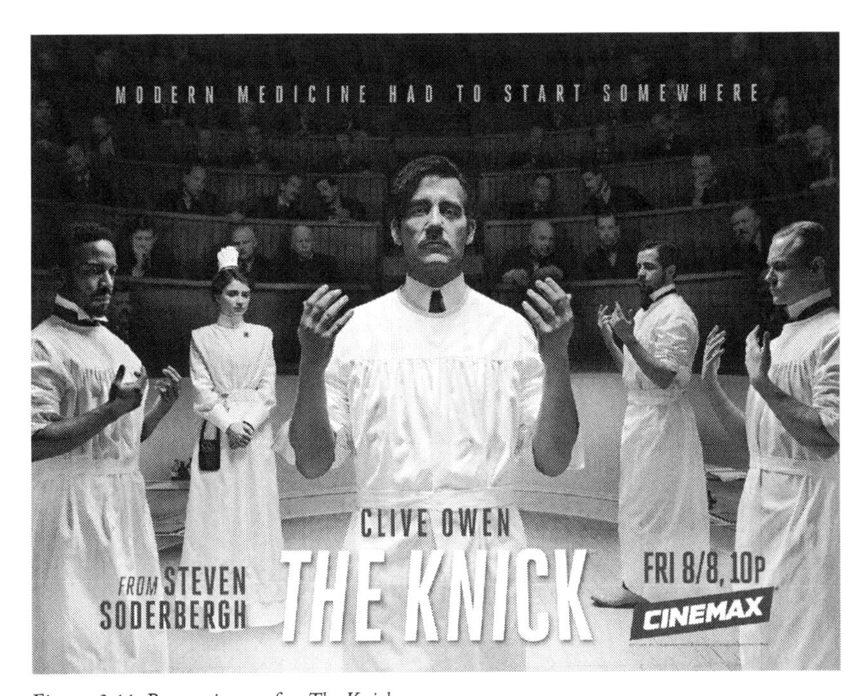

Figure 3.11: Promo image for *The Knick*.

The Knick sets a medical drama in New York City during 1900. It highlights the to-our-eyes barbaric medical practices that were thought ground-breaking and ultra-modern at the time. The central character, surgeon Dr. John Thackery, self-administers injections of cocaine before performing surgeries. He is seen by his peers as a maverick and visionary. The show examines the social issues of the time. Thackery opposes the hiring of a new surgeon, Dr. Algernon Edwards, who is a well-trained black doctor, because no patient would want to be seen by a "Negro doctor."

The spectacle of the surgeries, many of which are performed in a gallery before an audience of doctors, are gruesome and graphic. The performance-art nature of the procedures provides added tension to the scenes, as does the addictive mindset of Dr. Thackery himself.

Spoiler alert! Watch the pilot for Cinemax's *The Knick* then come back to see why this show works because of its character-driven structure.

Cinemax's *The Knick*

"Method and Madness" pilot by Jack Amiel and Michael Begler.

Figure 3.12: *The Knick* pilot point of attack.

Point of attack

In television, the point of attack generally happens in the teaser. *The Knick*'s **point of attack** happens at the very beginning of the show. Dr. John Thackery wakes up in a Chinatown opium den. This is the first whiff of the problem Thackery will face. As he hires a horse-drawn carriage to take him to The Knickerbocker hospital, Thackery specifically asks for a route that will require the carriage to wait at the trolley car tracks. As the trolley passes, Thackery slips off one of his signature white leather shoes, slides out a syringe kit from his medical bag, and injects himself in the foot with cocaine. Anyone who has to go through such machinations before work has a problem. Thackery's addiction will be a problem in the pilot and throughout the series.

Figure 3.13: *The Knick* pilot hero committed.

Hero committed

The **hero committed** moment occurs when Thackery accepts the chief of surgery position now open due to the suicide of his mentor, Dr. J. M. Christiansen. Thackery accepts this position, but he is adamant that the position of deputy chief go to Dr. Everett Gallinger. This is a brilliant piece of writing by Jack Amiel and Michael Begler. Jack and Michael have committed John Thackery to the season with his acceptance of the chief of surgery position. At the same time, they make clear a significant obstacle for the pilot episode. Thackery must fight to keep Dr. Gallinger as the deputy chief rather than powerful board member Cornelia Robertson's choice, Dr. Algernon Edwards.

Figure 3.14: *The Knick* pilot hero succeeds—almost.

Hero succeeds—almost

Thackery smelts a strange, new surgical instrument in the basement of the Knick. This gives the audience some insight into the way doctors approached their jobs at the time. They were part innovators and part practitioners. We have no idea what the device will be used for, so it's intriguing.

In the coal dust filled basement, Thackery meets Dr. Algernon Edwards, who is different from what John expected. While being a highly qualified Harvard-trained surgeon, Dr. Edwards also is black. Thackery's prejudices are clear from the start. Thackery didn't want Edwards before he found out the physician was black; he definitely doesn't want him now.

Thackery successfully gets his point across to Edwards. The **hero succeeds, or so he thinks**. When Cornelia Robertson finds out Thackery has dismissed Edwards and confronts him, Thackery tells her that hiring a "Negro" doctor won't help The Knick, and that he doesn't want to work with Dr. Edwards. In a completely arrogant and self-sabotaging move, Thackery suggests that she and her father find another hobby for their money. She calls his bluff and withdraws the funding for the electrification of the Knick.

If Thackery wants to stay in the dark ages, Cornelia Robertson is more than happy to oblige him. However, the Knick is in such dire straits, they can't afford to run without the Robertsons' donations. Herman Barrow, the hospital administrator, tells Thackery that Dr. Edwards *will* be hired.

Figure 3.15: *The Knick* pilot emotional squeeze.

Emotional squeeze

The **emotional squeeze** happens when Thackery has decided to go the night without cocaine. A patient at the Knick needs an emergency surgery and Thackery's expertise. After arguing with Dr. Edwards, Dr. Gallinger tells Nurse Lucy Elkins to find Dr. Thackery. Elkins goes to Thackery's brownstone.

After there is no answer at the door, Elkins climbs through an open window. She finds Thackery bedridden in full withdrawal. He wants her to leave him alone. And perhaps, if Thackery could kick his habit, it would be best for everyone involved. But Elkins tells him of the patient. Thackery has a choice. Does he continue feeling excruciating pain and misery as he withdraws from cocaine, or does he succumb to his addiction, an addiction that contributed to the suicide of his mentor?

Thackery feels the pressure of his new position, his oath, and his drive for fame. He also feels the pressure of his addiction. He decides to take the cocaine and do the surgery. However, he can't inject himself because he has the shakes. He orders Elkins to inject him, but she can't find a vein. Finally, Thackery decides to reveal his addiction and be entirely vulnerable. He opens his fly and tells her to inject the liquid cocaine in the urethral vein on the underside of his penis.

This is one hell of an emotional squeeze.

Figure 3.16: *The Knick* pilot hero succeeds.

Hero succeeds

John Thackery arrives in the surgical theater feeling invigorated. After the cocaine injection, he is himself again. We the audience knows he is high as he approaches this tricky surgery. We've already seen one patient die on the table.

Dr. Edwards and Dr. Gallinger squabble. Thackery tells Edwards that he didn't hire him and he doesn't want him. Edwards says he will resign after the surgery.

The patient can't be put under anesthesia because he has bronchitis, so Thackery suggests they inject cocaine into his spinal canal to numb him from the chest down. Essentially, Thackery wants to do an epidural in the thoracic vertebrae. This has only been attempted once before—on a Labrador Retriever. There isn't a day that goes by when he doesn't miss that dog, Thackery says.

Thackery successfully numbs the patient, who remains awake for the surgery. Then he asks Edwards to retrieve an instrument that has been sterilized. It's the device Thackery was smelting when he met Edwards. Thackery uses the device to help rejoin the patient's intestine after he excises 12 inches of the man's bowel. The **hero succeeds.**

Impressed by Thackery's expertise, Edwards retracts his previous statement. He says he will stay at the Knick until Thackery has nothing left to teach him.

Figure 3.17: *The Knick* pilot hero's new life.

Hero's new life

At the end of the day, Thackery packs up his medical bag and leaves the Knick. The electricians are back and installing the electrical lighting.

Thackery hires a carriage to take him to Chinatown, so he is going back to the opium den. He embraces his addiction and the life he has been leading.

The electricians turn on the lights, which are glorious, modern. Welcome to the 20th century. This is Thackery's new life. The frontiers of science await him.

* * *

Jack Amiel and Michael Begler bring us into *The Knick* and the world of John Thackery. They put Thackery on a specific character arc, not only for the pilot, but also for the series. Thackery gets thrust into the role of chief of surgery after his mentor commits suicide. He boldly pushes forward, barely considering the reasons his mentor felt so hopeless. Yet alone in his home, he remembers being in awe of his mentor, who had the stamina to work through the night. His mentor credited his stamina on his insatiable desire for fame—and on liquid cocaine. It was Thackery's mentor who got him hooked on cocaine.

Thackery's work and future fame are inextricably linked to cocaine. Also, the permission he had received from his mentor makes him feel like using cocaine is akin to using a new technology. It's using medicine to create medical breakthroughs. In that moment, we can forgive Thackery his addiction, but we also see it'll be his undoing.

While there are some fascinating and stomach-churning cases, the show remains firmly affixed to the characters. Thackery's addiction, arrogance, and self-delusion are the focus of the series, as are the effects of Thackery's psyche on everyone around him.

* * *

This is not a formula

Character-driven structure is not a formula. It is not a plug-scene-in-here approach to writing. It's a guide. You create your characters. Your story comes from your characters. Character-driven structure merely helps you shape your hero's character arc. As you'll see from studying professional writers' TV pilots, *how* the hero succeeds remains as varied as the heroes themselves.

Assignment

It's time to identify the character-driven landmarks for your pilot. Think of the central challenge for your main character. Develop your rough draft of character-driven landmarks for your hero: point of attack; hero committed; hero succeeds—almost; emotional squeeze; hero succeeds; and hero's new life. Here's a sample of the character-driven landmarks from the pilot for *The Knick*.

Character-driven structure landmarks

The Knick
"Method and Madness" by Jack Amiel and Michael Begler
Point of attack: After waking up in an opium den, Dr. John Thackery shoots up cocaine on his way to work.
Hero committed: Dr. Thackery accepts the role of chief of surgery. He wants Dr. Gallinger to be his deputy chief of surgery against the wishes of the powerful Robertson family.
Hero succeeds—almost: Thackery refuses to hire Dr. Algernon Edwards because Edwards is black. The Robertsons pull their funding from the financially strapped Knick.

Emotional squeeze: Dr. Thackery must decide between continuing to detox from cocaine or asking Nurse Lucy Elkins to inject him in his urethral vein. He decides to get the injection so he can perform the emergency surgery.
Hero succeeds: Dr. Thackery successfully performs an experimental surgery and wins over Dr. Algernon Edwards.
Hero's new life: As the Robertsons' electricians install electric lights in the Knick, Dr. Thackery grabs his medical bag and heads back to the opium den.

CHAPTER 4

TL;DR chapter 4

Ripping apart existing pilots and other TV episodes will help you reverse-engineer outlines. Deconstructing pilots and creating reverse-engineered outlines can help you understand story structure, pacing, story momentum, and scene structure more intuitively than just watching TV. Assignment: Break down a pilot that's similar in structure to your show.

Breakdowns: Dissection and the Anatomy of Pilots

In this chapter, we'll break down and analyze the following drama and comedy pilots:

- NBC's *Hannibal* "Apéritif";
- BBC America's *Orphan Black* "Natural Selection";
- Fox's *Empire* "Pilot";
- ABC's *Modern Family* "Pilot"; and
- FX's *It's Always Sunny in Philadelphia*'s "The Gang Gets Racist."

I watch a lot of television. A *lot.* It's what I do for a living. It's awesome. However, merely watching TV doesn't reveal the underpinnings of television writing and story structure. Gaining that understanding requires active engagement and critical viewing and thinking. One of the best ways to improve your TV writing is to deconstruct episodes.

Breaking down episodes helps you work smarter by systematically planning your episode vs. winging it, or pants-ing it. Understanding the structure helps you avoid having to fix major issues in your rewrites. Spending the time to plan your story before jumping into your script will help you deliver a more cohesive, logical, and emotionally satisfying script. Also, when you use the character-driven structure, you'll know your story will be structurally sound. You'll *know* it works and be confident about your story, as opposed to *feeling* like it works.

It may be tempting to read the examples I've provided, think you understand the concepts, and skip the exercise of breaking down other TV episodes on your own. You would be shorting yourself. When you break down episodes yourself and make the decisions about the scenes and structure, you'll get better at creating and assembling character-driven stories from your own imagination.

* * *

Show breakdowns

A TV show breakdown is a scene-by-scene, moment-by moment synopsis of an episode. Breakdowns deconstruct episodes and break them down to their smallest, most-important parts. To deconstruct a show, watch a show and write down all the scene headings and the basic *beats* of each scene. The scene beats are what happens in a scene. Track the "in" and "out" or start and end times of the scenes. Timing the scenes helps you understand the pacing of the show.

Yes, I know this seems tedious. It is. I broke down five pilots for you in this chapter, so I know exactly how labor intensive this exercise is. But think of it as reverse-engineering an outline—the blueprint for the script. Having a blueprint of the script will help you understand the infrastructure of the show. You'll get *why* the show and the writing work. You'll glean lessons from professional writers who have cracked the code for their shows.

Spoiler alert! Watch *Hannibal*'s "Apéritif," then come back to discover why this procedural-with-character show works because of its character-driven structure. **Fair warning, *Hannibal* delves into dark, violent themes, and some of the images are disturbing.**

Let's dissect the pilot for *Hannibal,* a critically hailed show that ran for three seasons on NBC. *Hannibal* is a reimagining of author Thomas Harris's characters Hannibal Lecter and Will Graham. Bryan Fuller, the creator of the *Hannibal* TV series, and his fellow *Hannibal* writers carefully chart Will and Hannibal's codependent, near-symbiotic relationship. They delve into the twisted psychological underpinnings of the FBI special investigator and the scarily intelligent psychopath psychiatrist serial killer. The show balances highly artistic, macabre visuals with compelling character work. They have elevated the show beyond serial-killer-of-the-week fare to a thought-provoking, probing ensemble character piece.

While *Hannibal* was on a broadcast network, its leanings are more cable. The FBI procedural/character drama combines fantasy and dream elements, gorgeously grotesque crime scenes, penetrating psychological thrills, and gallows humor. Here's a look at its pilot, "Aperitif."

Note: The scene "in" and "out" times might vary a bit depending on the viewer used. You'll find *my italicized notes* occasionally throughout the breakdown. I have **bolded** the character-driven landmark scenes, and they each are illustrated with a frame or two from the landmark scene.

Hannibal "Apéritif" by Bryan Fuller; breakdown by Kam Miller

1. EXT. MARLOW HOUSE – NIGHT (00:00–00:08)
CRIME SCENE TECHNICIANS and POLICE OFFICERS work a crime scene. Everyone walks with purpose. Everyone has a part to play. An undercurrent of urgency runs through their actions.

2. INT. MARLOW HOUSE – NIGHT (00:09–1:09)
A pool of blood glistens on a hardwood floor. Blood spatter covers a security alarm interface on a wall. A man's body is put into a body bag. This was MR. MARLOW. A woman, MRS. MARLOW, lies in a pool of blood.

WILL GRAHAM (30s, intelligent, thoughtful, perhaps fragile) watches, taking it all in. Eerily calm, Will seems to be apart from the industry around him. He has a secret. He closes his eyes and the scene is bathed in a golden light. The sound of Will's heartbeat plays under. We're going into Will's mind.

Over BLACK, a golden light bar metronome swipes the frame. FRUM. FRUM.

BACK WITH WILL – Still bathed in the warm light, Will looks over the scene. The light bar metronome swipes the scene, erasing the crime scene techs and cops. Will walks up to the woman's body in the pool of blood. The light bar erases the pool of blood, then her body. Will is decriminalizing the scene in his mind. Will sees another blood pool recede. The blood spatter on the wall and security system interface lifts off in reverse.

Will walks backward out the front door.

3. EXT. MARLOW HOUSE – CONTINUOUS (01:10–01:31)
Will walks backward through the front door. The door closes and is whole and secure. Will walks backward through the phalanx of cops, crime scene techs, FBI agents, and emergency personnel. Ambulance and cop car lights strobe. However, the people are frozen in place.

As Will steps past them, they disappear.
(01:32-01:45)

Now Will stands in front of the house as it was before the crime. It's an average house in an average neighborhood. Will blinks. Now he sees Mrs. Marlow, alive, through the front window. With speed and ferocity, Will approaches the front door and kicks the door open. It slams against the wall.

4. INT. MARLOW HOUSE – CONTINUOUS (01:46-03:01)
Out of nowhere, Will has a gun. He aims and shoots MR. MARLOW, who is coming down the stairs. In a dispassionate tone, Will explains what he is doing while he is doing it. Clearly, he is reliving or imagining the crime, saying, "This is my design."

Will shoots MRS. MARLOW, who is desperately trying to get help at the wall security alarm interface. Her blood spatters on the device. She falls to the floor. Will explains what is happening. He pushes the buttons on the security wall device to shut off the alarm. He realizes the security company would call the Marlows through the alarm interface. He turns...
(03:01–03:24)

...Will is out of the warm light and into the cold harsh light of the active crime scene. Techs and cops work around him, but Will still seems separate from them, not one of their ilk. Will asks for the incident report. A cop gives it to him. (03:03) Will reads that tonight's call was marked as a false alarm and that there was a false alarm last week. He realizes the killer tapped their phone.

5. EXT. MARLOW HOUSE – NIGHT (03:25–03:27)
A PHONE SERVICE MAN is at the top of a telephone pole. He confirms the Marlow's phone was tapped.

6. INT. MARLOW HOUSE – RESUME (03:28–4:11)
Will says the killer recorded Mrs. Marlow's conversation with the security company during last week's "false alarm." The killer played the recording of Mrs. Marlow's voice to the security box interface. Her voice answers the security company man's questions. The security company is satisfied everything's fine at the Marlow's house; the killer gets off the phone with them. Will says, "This is when it gets truly horrifying for Mrs. Marlow."

Figure 4.1: *Hannibal* pilot point of attack.

7. INT. FBI ACADEMY – CLASSROOM – DAY (4:12–5:50)
Will is teaching a class about the Marlow murders. "Everyone has thought about killing someone..." He wants his students to think about killing Mrs. Marlow.
Point of attack

(04:28–Hannibal title)
Will wants his students to tell him what *their* design is. Who they really are.

> *Note: Bryan Fuller wrote in great detail about his vision for Will's process. The light bar, the sound effects, the warm light bathing the scene—these are all in his pilot script. Bryan takes us into Will's mind with visual and sound effects. We spend four minutes going into Will's mind. As Bryan introduces us to Will Graham and achieves interest, sympathy, empathy for his main character, he also takes us into the vibe of the show. (I'll discuss character introductions in greater detail in chapters 7 and 9.) We're going to travel fluidly between reality and imagination. We're going to go into the dark, disturbing minds of cold-blooded killers. And, as Will notes, this is when it gets truly horrifying, because we the audience haven't seen anything close to the grotesque things we will see. We're going to be awed by the vivid beauty of death. We're going to be seduced by serial killers with grotesque stagecraft. This will be outsider art taken to the extreme.*

JACK CRAWFORD, head of the FBI's Behavioral Science Unit, wants Will to help him. Formidable, intelligent, and driven, Jack pushes Will's buttons. He knows Will has psychological issues. He knows Will has trouble being social. Will says he is closer to Asperger's and autistics than narcissistic psychopaths. But Jack knows Will can empathize with narcissistic psychopaths. Will attributes his ability to an active imagination. Jack wants to borrow Will's imagination.

8. EXT./INT. FBI ACADEMY – DAY (05:51–06:24)
Jack tells Will that eight girls have been kidnapped over the past eight months. One was abducted three minutes before Jack went into Will's class. Will realizes they haven't found any bodies and that they were abducted from somewhere else, not where the FBI believes they were abducted.

9. INT. FBI HEADQUARTERS – JACK'S OFFICE – DAY (06:25–08:05)
Jack shows Will a corkboard with the girls' photos and a map. The eighth girl is Elise Nichols. She was supposed to come home from college and house-sit for her parents. She was supposed to feed the cat. Will surmises the other seven girls are dead because the killer got himself a new girl. Jack notes the girls fit a type. Will says it's not about all of these girls. It's about one girl. The killer's golden ticket.

> *Note: When Hugh Dancy as Will mounts Elise Nichols' photo to the corkboard, he sticks the push pin through Elise Nichols' head. This was a choice by the actor. Most of us would stick the pin closer to the edge of the photograph, careful not to mar it. Hugh as Will has a disregard for her image. He thinks nothing of penetrating her mind. He also may think nothing of imagining her murder in great detail. She is a victim to Will. The real focus for Will is the killer.*

Jack wants Will to get close to this case. Will refuses. He says Heimlich at Harvard and Blum at Georgetown do what he does. But Jack disagrees. Will has a very specific way of thinking. Will says the evidence explains the leaps he makes. Jack wants him. Working the case might require Will to be sociable, which is uncomfortable for Will.

> *Note: Bryan Fuller only spends a little more than two minutes getting Will into the case.*

10. EXT. DULUTH – NICHOLS HOUSE – NIGHT – ESTABLISHING – TIME LAPSE (08:06–08:09)
The Nichols house is an unassuming two-story brick Victorian.

11. INT. NICHOLS HOUSE – NIGHT (8:10—10:04)
Jack talks with Elise Nichols' parents while Will cases the place. MR. NICHOLS is in denial. MRS. NICHOLS is more realistic. They want to know if Elise could still be alive. Jack says they just don't know. Will wants to know how the cat was when they came home. Elise was supposed to feed it. Was the cat acting weird? The parents didn't notice. (09:24)

Jack talks with Will alone. Will explains that Elise was taken from her parent's home. Jack immediately calls an Evidence Response Team to the home. The Nichols house is a crime scene.

Will wants to see Elise's room. The Nichols say the police were up there this morning.

> *Note: At the beginning of the scene, Jack Crawford closes and opens his eyes; it's similar to what Will does when he is imagining a crime. This may be a nod to the idea that* this *is Jack's design. He wants Will on this case. He has set things in motion. He is the architect of everything that will come after this event.*

12. INT. NICHOLS HOUSE – HALLWAY – NIGHT (10:05–10:30)
Mr. Nichols leads Will to Elise's room. He asks Mr. Nichols not to touch anything. Mr. Nichols says they've been in and out of the room all day. Will says Mr. Nichols can hold the cat if it's easier.

> *Note: Will's suggestion to hold the cat is his awkward attempt to offer Mr. Nichols comfort. Will prefers the company and comfort of dogs. Will understands their motives, their inclinations. Unlike people, dogs don't challenge your intellect. They don't manipulate. They aren't passive aggressive. The relationship dynamics between human and dog are fundamental. They're easy to understand and manage. Will needs that in his life. And maybe Mr. Nichols, who is in massive denial, needs that as well. Will can't give it to him. Perhaps the cat can—at least, that might be what Will thinks. Holding the cat also keeps Mr. Nichols' hands occupied.*

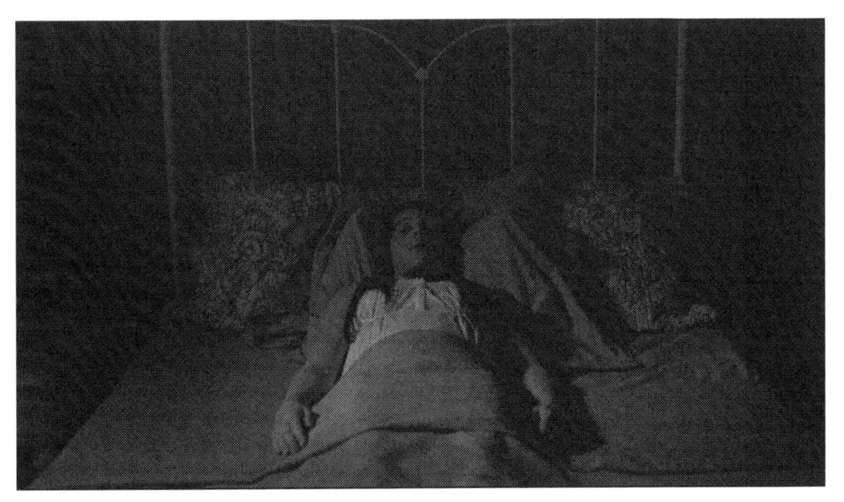

Figure 4.2: *Hannibal* pilot hero committed.

13. INT. NICHOLS HOUSE – ELISE'S ROOM – CONTINUOUS (10:31–10:49)
Will opens the door. Elise's body is in the bed. Elise looks peaceful, as if she is just sleeping. Will pushes Mr. Nichols out of the bedroom. Hero committed

END OF ACT ONE

ACT TWO

14. INT./EXT. NICHOLS HOUSE – ELISE'S ROOM – NIGHT (10:51–13:36)
Jack leaves Will in Elise's room to do his thing. Will looks outside at the emergency personnel. The light bar metronome sweeps across the scene and Elise's body moves. It sweeps again and it erases her wounds. Bathed in warm light, Will imagines Elise sleeping. He jumps on top of her and strangles her. It's violent, visceral.

(12:14) A voice interrupts him. Will is jarred out of his imagination by the intrusion. DR. BEVERLY KATZ recognizes Will. She has found antler velvet in two of Elise's wounds. She questions him about being an FBI agent. Will says he is a special investigator. The FBI screening test detects instability. She asks him if he is unstable. Jack comes in and tells Beverly that she is not supposed to be in the room with Will. Other FBI techs, JIMMY PRICE and BRIAN ZELLER, come in.

Will reveals that antler velvet is rich in nutrients. It actually promotes healing. The killer might have put it in there on purpose. The killer was trying to undo what he did to her. This was an apology.

Will wants aspirin.

> *Note: Will asking for aspirin is significant to his arc. Here it helps us understand the toll that getting into the killer's mind takes on him.*

15. INT. AIRPLANE – NIGHT (13:33–13:39)
Exhausted, Will dry swallows aspirin. Visiting crime scenes and getting into the killer's mind drains Will physically and psychologically.

16. INT. CAR – MOVING – NIGHT (13:40–13:46)
Will sees a stray dog running down the road. He drives next to the dog and says hello.

17. EXT. ROAD – NIGHT (13:47–14:04)
Despite his exhaustion, Will has pulled his car across the road.
He engages the dog, but the dog is scared.

18. INT. CAR – MOVING – NIGHT (14:05–14:07)
Will drives.

19. EXT. ROAD – NIGHT (14:08–14:21)
Will sits in the back of his car with the hatch open. He clearly went home and got dog treats to entice this stray to trust him. He gives dog treats to the scared dog.

20. EXT. WILL'S HOUSE – PORCH – NIGHT (14:22–14:55)
Will bathes the dog. He blow dries the dog. He introduces the dog to his five other dogs. Will has a soft spot for strays, but with a mere hiss, Will can silence his pack. Here he is alpha.

Note: Bryan Fuller spends about a minute and 10 seconds establishing Will's home life. In that brief time, Will adopts Winston. This softens Will in the viewer's mind. We just saw Will strangle Elise Nichols in her bed, after all. I think Bryan and the development execs wanted to make sure the audience separated Will from the real killer. Having Will adopt Winston helps us see him as a compassionate, gentle soul.

21. EXT. WILL'S HOUSE – NIGHT – TIME LAPSE (14:56–14:59)
Clouds fly across the night sky above Will's farmhouse.

22. INT. WILL'S HOUSE – NIGHT (15:00–15:56)
Will sleeps. His pack of hounds sleeps peacefully next to the space heater on the hearth. Will opens his eyes as if some sense tickled the back of his mind. Hesitantly, Will turns his head. Beside him in his bed is Elise Nichols. As Will fully turns toward her, we see a blood stain on the sheet above her abdomen. As Will reaches for her, Elise rises into the air, eluding his grasp. The sheet falls. Her nightgown becomes drenched in her blood. She rises into the blackness too complete to be just night. It is death. (15:34)

Will jolts awake, drenched in sweat. No one is in bed with him. Clearly, he was dreaming.

Time cut: He covers his bed with a towel and lies down on it. Then he covers himself with another towel. Waking in a cold sweat must be a common occurrence. He has a system for dealing with it.

Note: Will's dream of Elise Nichols' body in bed with him is almost rudimentary compared with the dream imagery that will follow in coming episodes. Bryan Fuller is smart to ease the audience into the idea of Will's metaphorical dreams by giving them something easy to understand. Had Bryan started with a more-complex metaphor, he likely would have lost some of his audience. Also, Bryan takes us fluidly from reality into the dream world. Will really is sleeping in his bed. The dogs really are sleeping next to the space heater. Then—BAM—we're in Will's dream. There is no light metronome or other bridge to alert us to this dream transition. Bryan wants us in Will's mind. He does this quite deftly. Again, all of this is written in the script. Director David Slade does a great job executing Bryan's vision.

END OF ACT TWO

ACT THREE

23. INT. FBI HEADQUARTERS - JACK'S OFFICE - DAY (15:57-16:05)
Jack punches the corkboard in frustration.

24. INT. FBI HEADQUARTERS - MEN'S ROOM - DAY (16:06–18:03)
Will immerses his face in water. He imagines the water filling with blood. When Will emerges from the basin, his face dips water, not blood. Jack comes in—hot and aggressive. Jack confronts Will. Jack knows Will knows more than he is telling. Jack wants to know what Will is holding back.

Will is confused by the killer because the killer is a sensitive psychopath. He'll take another girl soon.

Note: We understand the emotional logic of this bathroom scene because Bryan Fuller shows us Jack Crawford's frustration in the previous moment. He also shows us Will's break with reality as he imagines the wash basin filling with blood. The audience tracks emotional logic. Characters need to act in a way that is consistent with emotional logic. If characters don't act in an emotionally logical way, it breaks the suspension of disbelief contract we have with the audience. We promise to present a story that follows story logic and emotional logic for the world of our show. Audiences will buy into a certain suspension of disbelief.

In Hannibal, *the audience buys into the world of brilliant, artistic serial killers and intuitive, psychologically crippled FBI special investigators. We'll accept the impossibly elaborate crime scenes and the almost surreal killing rooms if everything else makes sense. We have to understand and believe Will and Jack's emotional states. We have to believe their motivations. If we do, we'll come along for the ride of the show.*

ALSO NOTE: This scene is almost exactly two minutes long, about the average length of most long scenes for today's shows.

ALSO, ALSO NOTE: It is not a coincidence that the accent color of this men's room is red, bright arterial blood red. The production design for Hannibal *is amazing. They imbue scenes with subtle and not-so-subtle hints of the characters' emotional states. Also, they are ramping up their influence and signature as the show progresses. The Marlow crime scene looked like many crime scenes on television. The main visual elements, the blood spatter, blood pools, red door, yellow walls, etc., don't play as abstract as future crime scenes do. Again, the show is easing audiences into the world of the show. Production design helps tremendously.*

ALSO, ALSO, ALSO NOTE: If you can have Laurence Fishburne in your show, jump at the chance. One of the best lines in this entire pilot is Jack Crawford yelling at that poor unsuspecting agent and telling him to use the ladies' room.

25. INT. FBI HEADQUARTERS – CRIME LAB – DAY (18:04–18:23)
Dr. Katz scrapes a metal filing off Elise Nichols' nightgown.

26. INT./EXT. FACTORY – DAY (18:24–18:43)
CLOSE ON machinery carving grooves into metal. The metal shavings fall off, forgotten. FACTORY WORKERS work. A car pulls up outside. A GIRL who looks like Elise gets out of the car. She slings a large lunch

cooler over her shoulder and waves at a FACTORY WORKER, who is out of focus.

27. EXT. FBI ACADEMY – DAY (18:44–20:08)
Jack talks with DR. ALANA BLUM (early 30s, pretty, smart, diplomatic). Alana says she has been as honest with Will Graham as she has with any patient. Jack says she has been observing Will while she has been guest lecturing at the FBI Academy. He wants her to do a study on Will Graham. Jack has already asked her to profile Will and she said "no." Alana wants to be Will's friend. Alana and Jack agree that Will Graham deals with huge amounts of fear. Alana says she wouldn't put Will in the field. Jack tells her Will is already out there. Alana wants Jack to promise not to let Will get too close. Jack promises.

> *Note: This scene works on the text* and *subtext level. We glean a lot of what Alana means from what she doesn't say. She has a more than a professional interest in Will. That interest is more than friendship. Jack says Will is already out there. Will is already too far out there. Jack doesn't know how far yet. Jack feels like he can cover Will 80 percent, but from what we know about Will, we gather Jack can't cover him at all. Jack can't protect Will from Will's own mind. Jack feels the instinct to protect Will, but the very thing he needs from Will—his mind—is the very thing that is at risk.*
>
> *ALSO NOTE: Alana is wearing a red skirt and a red patterned blouse. The use of the color red here is not a coincidence, either. The costume designer is hinting at the relationship Alana and Will may have. Blood may bring them together. Red is not only the color of blood, but also the color of love and romance.*

28. INT. FBI HEADQUARTERS – CRIME LAB – DAY (20:09–21:41)
Jimmy Price, Brian Zeller, and Beverly Katz go over Elise Nichols' body. Will stands in the background, not making eye contact. Jimmy, Brian, and Beverly talk about the lack of evidence that they've found. Will suggests they look for tool workers. Then Will glances at Elise Nichols' body. He focuses on it and the deep black of the body bag.

The BLACK of the body bag eclipses the frame. From the blackness, Elise Nichols' body glides forward. Her head slumped, her arms and legs dangling limply, Elise is vertical in the frame. Suddenly, antlers piece through her from back to front. Her white nightgown becomes soaked with blood. Miraculously, Elise lifts her head, as if the goring healed her.

Will realizes Elise was mounted on the deer antlers and she may have been bled. The techs note that her liver was removed and put back in. They wonder why.

Figure 4.3: *Hannibal* pilot hero succeeds—almost.

With a nauseated quiver in his voice, Will says, "There was something wrong with the meat." The techs confirm Elise had liver cancer. Will says the killer is eating them. Will smiles slightly, self-satisfied, but is that satisfaction really for himself or the killer?

Figure 4.4: *Hannibal* pilot hero succeeds—almost.

Figure 4.5: *Hannibal* pilot hero succeeds—almost.

29. INT. HANNIBAL LECTER'S HOUSE - DINING ROOM - SAME (21:42–22:15)

HANNIBAL LECTER (late 30s, early 40s, sophisticated, erudite, predatory) sits at a glossy dining table. He delicately chooses a slice of meat from a sumptuously displayed dish. He places the meat on his

plate. He slices a tender piece and spears it with his fork. He lifts the meat to his mouth and savors the unknown delight.
Hero succeeds—almost

> *Note: The lighting of Hannibal Lecter hints at his sinister nature. He is lit from above, which puts his eyes in shadow. His eyes are dark, sunken pits. The light highlights his bone structure, making him appear skull-like. Will, on the other hand, has been lit from the front. When in real life, Will has been lit coolly. When in Will's imagination, he is lit warmly. We've seen his tortured, restless eyes that don't like to make contact with others. We've seen his pained expressions. We've seen him become the killer in brief moments. Will's face has been open to us. We've been able to study him in great detail. Hannibal, on the other hand, is more elusive.*

END OF ACT THREE

ACT FOUR

30. INT. HANNIBAL LECTER'S HOUSE - OFFICE - DAY (22:18–23:22)
Hannibal counsels a patient, FRANKLYN, who is crying, distressed. Hannibal seems rather cold, unfeeling, removed from Franklyn. It appears to be his clinical detachment, but it's actually his disgust for Franklyn and Franklyn's demeanor. Franklyn has anxiety issues. Hannibal wants Franklyn to convince himself there isn't a lion that wants to eat him in the room.

31. INT. HANNIBAL LECTER'S HOUSE - PRIVATE EXIT - DAY (23:23–23:52)
Jack greets Hannibal as Hannibal's patient, Franklyn, is leaving. Hannibal is displeased to see FBI Special Agent Jack Crawford waiting for him in the wrong area. Jack wants to talk with Hannibal. Hannibal wants Jack to wait in the waiting area unless Jack wants to talk about Franklyn. Jack assures Hannibal that his visit is all about Hannibal.

32. INT. HANNIBAL LECTER'S HOUSE - WAITING ROOM - LATER (23:53–23:59)
Hannibal makes Jack wait longer. Finally, Hannibal invites Jack into his office.

33. INT. HANNIBAL LECTER'S HOUSE - OFFICE - CONTINUOUS (24:00–25:50)
Hannibal wants to know what Jack wants. Being cagey, Jack wants to ask Hannibal a few questions first. Jack seems to have no idea Hannibal is a serial killer. He blithely turns his back on Hannibal. He casually inspects Hannibal's office. He asks if they are alone. Hannibal assures him that they are. Hannibal is charming, though guarded. Jack admires Hannibal's drawings. Hannibal notes that a precise pencil lead helps to draw the details. It is easier to make a sharp pencil point with a scalpel.

As Hannibal handles the scalpel, he suggests that Jack is investigating him. Jack reveals that Alana Blum recommended Hannibal. Hannibal puts the scalpel down. Jack wants Hannibal to do a psychological profile.

34. EXT. FBI ACADEMY - DAY - ESTABLISHING (25:51–25:55)
The bright blue sky blazes over the academy.

35. INT. FBI ACADEMY- JACK'S OFFICE - DAY (25:56–28:10)
Jack briefs Hannibal on the Elise Nichols case and the cases of the other missing girls. Will and Hannibal spar. Will realizes Hannibal is psychoanalyzing him. Will leaves to give a lecture on psychoanalyzing.

Hannibal tells Jack that Will has pure empathy. Hannibal believes Will can assume the point of view of those around him. It's an uncomfortable gift. Hannibal thinks he can help Will see the cannibal they are after.

> *Note: This is the first scene between Will and Hannibal. It sets the tone for their relationship. Hannibal will poke Will. He'll probe him, push*

him. He'll manipulate Will. Hannibal will do all of this under Jack Crawford's nose. In fact, he'll do it with Jack's consent.

END OF ACT FOUR

ACT FIVE

36. EXT. HIBBING, MN – FIELD – DAY (28:12–29:25)
Ruthless crows peck carrion. A woman's body has been impaled on deer antlers. Naked, she is on display in this Minnesota field.

Crime Scene Tech Brian Zeller shoos the birds away. Jack tells Will the deer head was stolen about a mile from the crime scene. The papers are calling the killer the Minnesota Shrike. Will says the killer wanted her found. The killer is petulant. He is mocking her or the FBI. Jack wonders where did all of the killer's love go. Will is sure that whoever did this didn't tuck Elise Nichols into her bed. Brian says the killer cut out the victim's lungs. He's pretty sure the killer did this while the victim was alive. Will knows this isn't Elise Nichols' killer.

37. INT. HANNIBAL LECTER'S HOUSE – KITCHEN – DAY (29:26–29:40)
Hannibal lovingly prepares lungs to be cooked.

Figure 4.6: *Hannibal* pilot emotional squeeze.

38. EXT. HIBBING, MN – FIELD – RESUME (29:41–30:06)
Will understands that Elise Nichols' killer wanted to consume his victims. He wanted to keep a piece of them inside of him. The person who killed this new victim thought she was a pig. Jack wants to know if this is a copycat. Getting more incensed, Will says Elise Nichols' killer has a place to do it and no interest in field *kabuki*. Elise Nichols' killer has a house or two or a cabin, something with an antler room.

39. INT. HANNIBAL LECTER'S HOUSE – KITCHEN – DAY (30:06–30:13)
Hannibal sprinkles white wine into a skillet over an open flame. He expertly catches the alcohol on fire. WHOOSH, the flame flows over the meat in the skillet.

40. EXT. HIBBING, MN – FIELD – RESUME (30:14–30:23)
Will realizes the killer has a daughter with the same hair color, eye color, and weight as the other victims.

41. EXT. FACTORY – DAY (30:24–30:25)
The girl who looks like the victims waves to a man who is out of focus.

Figure 4.7: *Hannibal* pilot emotional squeeze.

42. EXT. HIBBING, MN – FIELD – RESUME (30:25–30:58)
Will realizes the daughter is an only child and she's leaving home. The killer can't stand the thought of losing her. She is his golden ticket.

Jack wants to know about the copycat. Will says an intellectual psychopath, especially a sadist, is very difficult to catch. He has no motive. He'll likely never kill like this again. Will suggests that Jack get Hannibal Lecter to write up this killer's profile. In a parting shot, Will says Jack seemed very impressed with Hannibal's opinion. Emotional squeeze

43. INT. HANNIBAL LECTER'S HOUSE – DINING ROOM – DAY (30:59–31:17)
Hannibal enjoys his meal.

44. EXT. DULUTH, MN – MOTEL – NIGHT (31:18–31:22)
A breeze disturbs the branches of a tree near the motel parking lot. Other than that, the motel is quiet.

45. INT. MOTEL ROOM – BATHROOM – NIGHT (31:23–31:36)
Steam rises off the hot shower spray as it pelts Will's body. Slowly, the shower curtain parts. Beyond the curtain is darkness and a misty forest. From the dark forest, a black stag stands and stares directly at us.

46. INT. MOTEL ROOM – DAY (31:37–34:44)
Darkened room. Someone knocks on the door. Will gets out of bed and answers the door to find Hannibal Lecter. Will wants to know where Crawford is. Hannibal says Jack is being deposed in court. The adventure will be Will and Hannibal's today. Will lets Hannibal into his darkened chamber. The sounds of Will taking an aspirin can be heard in the darkness. (32:12)

Hannibal has brought breakfast, which he has prepared himself. Hannibal uncovers a protein scramble for Will—eggs and sausage. Will tries the sausage and says it's delicious. He thanks Hannibal. Hannibal says he has considered apologizing for his ambush, but he fears he would be apologizing again soon and Will will tire of his apologies. Will wants to keep it professional. Hannibal says Will will soon find him interesting.

Not knowing he is speaking to the killer, Will tells Hannibal he doesn't believe the Shrike killed the girl in the field. Hannibal asks what the killer did wrong. Will says everything. Will says the crime scene was practically gift wrapped for him. It was like he needed to see the negative of the picture to see the positive.

Hannibal says that Uncle Jack sees Will as a fragile tea cup, the finest china only used for special guests. Will finds this humorous. Will asks

Hannibal how Hannibal sees him. Hannibal says he sees Will as the mongoose he wants under the house when the snake slithers by.

Note: This is the first scene of Hannibal and Will becoming friends. Bryan Fuller takes a bit longer with this scene, giving it three minutes and change. However, their meal doesn't begin until around 32:12 , so their intimate breakfast takes about two and half minutes. There's a lot to squeeze into a very short time. Bryan pulls this off very well.

47. EXT. CONSTRUCTION SITE OFFICE – DAY (34:45–34:51)
A nondescript sedan pulls into the muddy parking lot in front of a construction office trailer.

48. INT. RENTAL CAR – DAY (34:52–35:34)
Will asks Hannibal why he is smiling. Hannibal says he gets to peek behind the curtain, seeing how the FBI goes about doing its business. Will says they are checking on construction sites that use a certain kind of pipe with a certain kind of coating because they found a metal filing on Elise Nichols' clothes.

49. EXT. CONSTRUCTION SITE OFFICE – CONTINUOUS (35:35–35:38)
Will and Hannibal head toward the construction office trailer.

50. INT. CONSTRUCTION SITE OFFICE – DAY (35:39–36:40)
The SECRETARY talks on the phone, explaining to her friend that Will and Hannibal are going through files. She does this so that Hannibal and Will can overhear her. She asks Will and Hannibal their names. They ignore her. Will finds a suspect: Garrett Jacob Hobbs. Will asks the secretary if Hobbs has a daughter. The secretary says maybe, she doesn't keep company with these people. Hannibal wants to know what is peculiar about Hobbs. Will says Hobbs left a phone number but no address. All the other workers left an address.

51. EXT. CONSTRUCTION SITE OFFICE – DAY (36:41–36:53)
Hannibal, Will, and the secretary load files into the car. Hannibal drops some files. Will picks them up. Hannibal goes back in the office.

52. INT. CONSTRUCTION SITE OFFICE – CONTINUOUS (36:54–37:55)
Hannibal calls Garrett Jacob Hobbs.

INTERCUT WITH:

53. INT. HOBBS HOUSE – KITCHEN – SAME
The daughter answers. It's the girl from factory. She hands the phone to her father, GARRETT JACOB HOBBS. Hannibal warns him.
"They know."

END OF INTERCUT.

END OF ACT FIVE

ACT SIX

OVER BLACK – A light bar swipes the screen indicating a time cut. (37:57–37:58)

54. EXT. HOBBS HOUSE – DAY (37:59–38:09)
Warm, golden light bathes the scene. Will stands, shell-shocked and blood-spattered. A circus of CRIME SCENE PERSONNEL and UNIFORM COPS walk backward.

The light bar sweeps a black frame.

55. INT. RENTAL CAR – DAY (38:10–38:25)
Will sits behind the wheel, blood-spattered. The camera moves around the windshield past the car door frame…

… and Will is CLEAN. We have travelled back in time, before whatever heinous crime happened here. The color is cooler. This is reality.

Will dry swallows an aspirin. He gets out of the car.

56. EXT. HOBBS HOUSE – CONTINUOUS (38:26–39:01)
Through the driver side window, we can see Hannibal in the passenger seat. Methodically, he takes off his seat belt and follows suit.

As Will and Hannibal approach, Garrett Jacob Hobbs shoves his WIFE out of the front door. She is bleeding profusely from a neck wound. Will puts pressure on the wound, but it's a lost cause. Calmly, Hannibal watches from the front yard.

Will watches Mrs. Hobbs die. He unholsters his sidearm and kicks in the front door.

57. INT. HOBBS HOUSE – MAIN FLOOR – CONTINUOUS (39:02–39:08)
Will enters with his gun ready. He calls out, "Garrett Jacob Hobbs, FBI."

58. EXT. HOBBS HOUSE – SAME (39:09–39:11)
Dispassionately, Hannibal looks down on Mrs. Hobbs' body.

Figure 4.8: *Hannibal* pilot hero succeeds.

59. INT. HOBBS HOUSE – MAIN FLOOR – RESUME (39:12–40:21)
Keyed up, Will keeps his gun at the ready. He pushes forward into the darkened house until he finds...

...the KITCHEN. Hobbs has a knife to his daughter's throat. Will aims his gun at Hobbs. Hobbs slashes his daughter's throat. She crumples to the floor. Hobbs rears back with the knife to finish the job, but Will shoots him. Will fires nine rounds into Hobbs' center mass. Hobbs slumps to the floor.

Hobbs' daughter is still alive. The cut is only on one side of her throat. Will puts pressure on the wound, but he is going into shock himself. Will hears Garrett Jacobs Hobbs say something. He turns and Hobbs is smiling. Hobbs hisses, "See?"

Will looks at Hobbs in disbelief. Hannibal saunters into the kitchen just as Hobbs dies. Will desperately tries to stop the daughter's bleeding. Hannibal watches for a moment, observing Will, and makes a decision. Hannibal leans in and takes over. He is a medical doctor. He elevates the daughter's head and calmly applies constant pressure. Shaking, Will looks at Hannibal in awe.

Hannibal saves Hobbs' daughter, ABIGAIL.
Hero succeeds

> *Note: The Will-confronting-Hobbs action sequence takes approximately two minutes. It goes from the time Will gets out of the rental car, 38:26, to the time Hannibal steps in and saves Abigail, 40:21. It seems longer, but as with everything in television, there is an economy to the script, scenes, and show.*

60. EXT. HOBBS HOUSE – LATER (40:22–40:48)
Hannibal walks out with Abigail on a gurney. Blood spattered, Will leans against a car, barely registering what's happening around him. The daughter is loaded into an ambulance. Hannibal gets in with her. The ambulance leaves the scene. Will is left in a state of shock.

61. INT. FBI ACADEMY – CLASSROOM – DAY (40:49–41:16)
Jack finds Alana Blum teaching Will's class. He wants to know where Will is. Alana says she told Jack not to put Will in the field. She told him not to let Will get too close.

62. INT. HOSPITAL – DAY (41:17–41:44)
SLO-MO
Still shell-shocked, Will strides down the hallway. He passes hospital personnel. No one makes eye contact with him.

> *Note: This moment is in subjective camera. First, we're looking at Will walking in slo-mo. Then we see Will's POV in slo-mo. When we're in Will's POV, the camera moves forward and jostles up and down at the same pace of Will's footfalls. This effect puts us in Will's shoes. After the traumatic events of the hero succeeds moment, we need to take a moment with Will. We need to walk with him. We need to see him walking with purpose. We need to believe he will be relatively okay*

for the time being. He'll be haunted by the events and his actions, but he isn't nearly catatonic like he was in the last scene.

63. INT. HOSPITAL – ABIGAIL HOBBS' ROOM – CONTINUOUS (41:45–42:26)
Still in slo-mo, Will enters Abigail Hobbs' room. Abigail lies asleep in her bed. Will finds Hannibal asleep by the bedside, holding Abigail's hand.
END SLO-MO

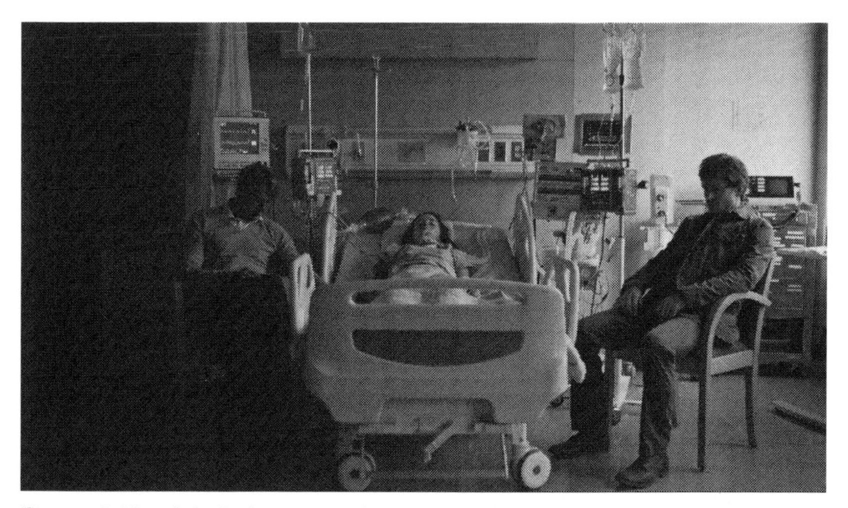

Figure 4.9: *Hannibal* pilot hero succeeds.

Will sits on the other side of Abigail's bed. The three of them rest in the aftermath of their meeting.
Hero's new life

Note: It's really interesting that the slo-mo ends after Will sees Hannibal. This hints at a bit of relief and return to normalcy. It also hints at a need for Will to get out of his own head, if possible. No artistic choice should be made randomly or because it will look cool. Style should always have substance. It should tell part of the story.

END OF PILOT

Bryan Fuller made some brilliant and daring choices in *Hannibal*'s pilot, "Aperitif." For starters, the title character doesn't appear on screen until the midpoint of the show. At the hero succeeds—almost landmark, Will figures out the serial killer they're after is a cannibal. Huzzah! Breakthrough—sorta. In the next beat, Hannibal Lecter simply enjoys a meal. The mere act of watching Hannibal eat gives the audience a thrill and nausea. Will's success is short-lived in the minds of the audience. We know he'll have to face Hannibal Lecter, one of the most infamous (and, fortunately, fictional) cannibals. Our reaction is "Huzzah! Breakthrough! Gulp!"

Bryan also gives us access to Will's complicated mind through fantasy and dream sequences. *Hannibal* is one of the few shows that uses imagery well for the most part. There are moments that are just images. They're not scenes. These images provoke feelings. They convey tone.

Using images, instead of scenes, is fraught with peril. Scenes usually have at least two characters with different wants. Images don't have character wants. Without character wants, the writer loses story drive. Without story drive, the story grinds to a halt. When the story falters, the audience disengages. However, *Hannibal* manages to keep the audience's attention and interest because the images directly connect to the character's emotional logic. *Emotional logic* is the reasoning behind character decisions. Will makes a bad decision because he failed a victim, and he is haunted by his failure. The audience can connect to that emotional logic. This makes the next scene have more meaning.

Hannibal Lecter appears to be delightfully mischievous as opposed to unfeeling. Will has an empathy disorder so he empathizes with killers. Giving serial killers emotion and meaning seems to be the next evolution in the serial killer drama vs. the usual dissociated, unfeeling psychopath. There is more of a spectrum of emotion as opposed to a binary code of emotion. This allows the audience to access the killers. We can get inside their heads like Will gets inside their heads. While they are predators, sharks in our gene pool, serial killers in the world of *Hannibal* have more depth of emotion than the average depicted serial killer. This makes them more fascinating and more terrifying.

Will's journey in the pilot is unique. The point of attack, the first whiff of the problem Will Graham will face, is the idea that we all have thought of killing someone. Not everyone really has thought of killing someone, but clearly Will has, and perhaps frequently. For him, it is normal to think of killing someone. Will has a gift. He can empathize with serial killers. He feels for them and feels like them. He gets lost in them.

At the end of the first act, Will becomes committed to this story when he finds Elise Nichols' body. Elise Nichols haunts him, perhaps like she haunts the man who killed her and put her back in her bed. Will knows the killer feels sorry for this kill. This death was a misstep by the killer. The killer loves his victims, and Elise was different from his other victims. She was sick. The killer never intended to kill a dying girl. Ironic doesn't even begin to cover this issue.

As Elise Nichols haunts Will, he has to solve this case. It's become personal for him. At the emotional squeeze, Will becomes incensed at a copycat crime scene. Unbeknownst to Will, this is a scene orchestrated by Hannibal so Will could see the Minnesota Shrike more clearly. Hannibal understood that Will would see through the copycat nature of his killing. He also predicted Will would be angry on the part of the real killer. Through his anger, Will could understand the real killer better. And Will does. This is when he has his breakthrough. He realizes the killer has a daughter the same age, same hair color, same eye color as the victims. She is the killer's golden ticket. She is the one the killer really wants to possess.

With this new knowledge, Will is able to track down the killer. However, again unbeknownst to Will, Hannibal has warned the real killer, Garrett Jacob Hobbs. When Will and Hannibal get to the Hobbs residence, Garrett Jacob Hobbs has already started his end game. Hobbs slashes his wife's throat and kills her. He is drawing a knife across his daughter's throat when Will interrupts him. Will shoots Hobbs and kills him. Will no longer just empathizes with killers; he has become one. This is the first step into his descent.

His new life involves dealing with his actions. He feels protective of Hobbs' daughter, Abigail. Abigail Hobbs brings Will and Hannibal together. The final image in the pilot is Hannibal asleep on one side of Abigail's bed and Will awake on the other side of her bed. Here are her two guardians of sorts, her new father figures: Hannibal, who has no remorse for setting in motion the climatic events, and Will, who has nothing but remorse.

Spoiler alert! Watch *Orphan Black*'s "Natural Selection," then come back to discover why this show works because of its character-driven structure.

BBC America's *Orphan Black* is a twisty sci-fi drama about 20-something street-wise con-artist Sarah Manning, who watches her *doppelgänger* commit suicide by jumping in front of a subway train. The show balances grounded reality with near-future bio-tech, including cloning. Sarah discovers she is one of many clones. Some of them know they're clones; others are outside the knowledge. Tatiana Maslany delivers a *tour de force* performance as all of the Leda (female) clones. She nimbly slips into many personas and often acts in the same scene with herself.

The technical production aspects required for the multiple clone scenes are impressive. Tatiana must hit her marks precisely and execute her performance exactly the same way. Then she'll go to makeup and costume and come back and perform the reverse side of the scene as a different person. She'll repeat this process until she's acted as all the clones in the scene. She often plays opposite a body double and must memorize her double's movements so she can repeat them when she plays the reverse.[45]

Beyond the production gymnastics, *Orphan Black* is a compelling character drama about living, breathing, thinking individuals. They are humans who may not have the same rights afforded the average person. The clones often are fighting for their very existence against the Dyad Institute, the biotech firm that created them, and the strange Neolution movement that spawned the Dyad Institute. The show has plenty of room for action, thrills, romance, humor, and thought-provoking subject matter. Let's take a look at *Orphan Black*'s pilot.

Orphan Black "Natural Selection" by Graeme Manson; breakdown by Kam Miller

TEASER
1. EXT. SUBWAY CAR – NIGHT (00:00–00:04)
A subway train roars down the track toward the vibrant lights of a major metropolitan area.

2. INT. SUBWAY CAR – MOVING – NIGHT (00:05–00:30)
CLOSE ON the cord of an earbud leading to a sleeping street punk, outsider woman in her later 20s. Meet SARAH MANNING. Her black leather jacket and perma-smoky eye give her a tough but provocative air. She jolts awake, disoriented. She curses, only to find herself near a WOMAN and her YOUNG DAUGHTER. Sarah apologizes. She speaks with a working-class British accent and this seems to be North America. Toronto, Canada, or maybe upstate New York.

3. INT. HUXLEY STATION SUBWAY PLATFORM – MOMENTS LATER (00:31–00:53)
Sarah disembarks and checks her pocket change.

4. INT. HUXLEY STATION SUBWAY PLATFORM – MOMENTS LATER (00:54–03:07)

Sarah talks on a pay phone. She tells whoever she is calling that she is back in town and wants to see Kira. At the other end of the platform, a distressed WOMAN in business attire cries. Sarah gets no love. She pleads to speak with Kira. From her reaction, she was just hung up on. She doesn't have money to call back.

Figure 4.10: *Orphan Black* pilot point of attack.

Sarah notices the crying woman again. Distracted, she weaves her way down the subway platform. The crying woman takes off her shoes and jacket. She neatly places them on the dirty floor next to her expensive pocketbook. As Sarah nears her, the woman turns around.

The woman looks EXACTLY like Sarah.

The woman doesn't respond with shock or surprise. She simply looks into Sarah's face, her own face. Tears stream down the woman's cheeks. The woman turns away and...

...walks directly in front of a SPEEDING TRAIN.

Sarah gasps, cringes, as the train slams into her *doppelgänger*. The train screeches to a halt, blood on its steel wheels. SUBWAY PERSONNEL run toward the train.

Drawn to the macabre scene, Sarah approaches. Subway personnel stop her and others from getting too close. Still, Sarah sees the woman's battered body beneath the train. The whole scene overwhelms her. She turns and sees...

...her *doppelgänger*'s pocketbook just sitting on the floor. No one else seems to notice it. Sarah picks it up.

A SURVEILLANCE CAMERA captures her snatching the purse.

Sarah hurries away from the scene.
Point of attack

> *Note: The entire scene from phone call to purse snatching takes approximately two minutes and 10 seconds. A lot happens in this short time. Two characters are introduced. (I'll discuss character introductions in greater detail in chapters 7 and 9.) A character has a conversation and gets hung up on. Two characters meet their* doppelgänger. *A character commits suicide. And a character commits petty theft. Yet none of it feels rushed.*
>
> *ALSO NOTE: Of course, the name of the subway station, Huxley, refers to Aldous Huxley, author of* Brave New World.
>
> *ALSO, ALSO NOTE: As she approaches the crying woman, Sarah weaves through the columns of the subway platform in a rough approximation of a double helix.*

END OF TEASER

ACT ONE

5. EXT. CITY STREET – NIGHT (03:43–0:3:48)
Still shell-shocked, Sarah carries the dead woman's purse in her arms.

6. INT. OLLY'S TAVERN – BATHROOM – NIGHT (03:48–04:24)
Sarah riffles through the dead woman's purse. She pockets the money. She looks at the woman's ID. It reads: Elizabeth Childs. Sarah finds two cell phones—one black and one pink—and keys. Moments later, Sarah checks herself in the mirror.

> *Note: This is a deceptively difficult scene. Tatiana is a stellar actress. She can pull off talking to herself; not all actors can. Beware: Moments where characters talk to themselves are fraught with peril.*

7. INT. OLLY'S TAVERN – NIGHT (04:28–04:56)
Sarah has a drink. FELIX DAWKINS (early 20s, handsome, gay) meets her. Sarah's face brightens as they hug.

8. INT. OLLY'S TAVERN – MOMENTS LATER (04:57–07:05)
Sarah and Felix have grabbed a table and drinks. Felix wants to know about Sarah's boyfriend, Vic the Dick. Sarah says she hit him first and stole his cocaine. Sarah wants to know if Felix can sell the coke. Sarah wants to get the money and get Kira, her daughter, back.

Felix doesn't think Mrs. S will let Sarah have Kira. He reminds Sarah that it has been almost a year since Sarah left.

Sarah tells Felix about Elizabeth Childs killing herself at the train station. Sarah wonders if she had a twin sister. Felix says anything is possible when you're a foster kid.

Sarah wants to go to Beth's house and maybe rob her place. She also wants Felix to get 20K for the cocaine.

9. EXT. BETH'S APARTMENT – DAY (07:06–07:35)
Nice neighborhood, too nice for Sarah with her fishnets, thigh highs, and shorty shorts to walk unnoticed. She finds Beth's address and uses the keys to get inside.

10. INT. BETH'S APARTMENT – FOYER – CONTINUOUS (07:37–08:03)
Sarah cautiously peeks through the doorway, then quickly comes in. She calls out but there is no answer. She checks out the place. It's modern, sleek, nice.

11. INT. BETH'S APARTMENT – WALK-IN CLOSET – MOMENTS LATER (08:04–08:07)
From the closet, Sarah can be seen entering the master bedroom.

12. INT. BETH'S APARTMENT – BATHROOM – MOMENTS LATER (08:08–08:10)
Sarah digs the master bathroom.

13. INT. BETH'S APARTMENT – BEDROOM – CONTINUOUS (08:11–08:13)
Sarah sits on the edge of the bed. She wants to test it for comfort.

14. INT. BETH'S APARTMENT – WALK-IN CLOSET – MOMENTS LATER (08:14–08:26)
From inspecting the clothes, Sarah susses out that Beth has a boyfriend and they're squares.

15. INT. BETH'S APARTMENT – KITCHEN – MOMENTS LATER (08:27–08:47)
Sarah sees a note from Paul Dierden. He'll be out of town until Saturday. Sarah grabs an imported beer from the fridge. She spies a photo of Beth

and Paul stuck to the stainless steel fridge with a magnet. She takes the photo down and studies it.

16. INT. FELIX'S LOFT – DAY (08:48–10:29)
Felix and a STRAIT-LACED MAN (20s) get dressed. It's nothing romantic, just a friendly fuck. The strait-laced man rubs his finger over his gums. He's testing the cocaine stolen from Sarah's ex-boyfriend, Vic. He says it's shit. He'll give Felix 10K for it. Felix tells the strait-laced man that he can do better than 10K.

There's a pounding at the door. Felix slips the screwdriver out of the "lock" and slides the door open.

VIC SCHMIDT grabs Felix by the throat. He wants to know where Sarah is. Vic rushes the strait-laced man out. Felix motions for the man to call him. Vic demands to know where Sarah is.

Felix says he hasn't seen Sarah in a year. Vic wants to know where the cocaine is. Felix gives him a tiny packet. Vic says he's in trouble with Pouchy, which will bring him pain. Vic will bring pain on Felix until he produces Sarah.

17. INT. BETH'S APARTMENT – LIVING ROOM – DAY (10:30–11:55)
Sarah talks on the phone with Felix. Beth's credit is maxed, but she had a sweet pad and Beth's boyfriend is out of town until the weekend. Sarah pilfers through Beth's bank statements and computer. Sarah is a survivor, and part of her skill set is being a thief.

INTERCUT WITH:

18. INT. FELIX'S LOFT – DAY
Felix tells Sarah that her boyfriend is very much in town. Felix tells her that he can only get 10K for the blow. Sarah says it's not enough to get out of town and set them up with Kira somewhere.

Sarah doesn't know who Beth Childs was, but she had a pretty nice life. Felix wants to know why she killed herself.

Sarah finds a bank statement for Beth Childs that reads: $75,000. The account was opened three weeks ago. Sarah sparks. That's enough to get rid of bloody Vic and get away with Kira. Felix points out that any minute someone is going to ID the body and Sarah will be bounced out of Beth's apartment.

On the news, there's a story about an unidentified woman who jumped in front of a subway train. Sarah has an idea.

> *NOTE: With the exception of the Sarah-and-Felix scene in Olly's Tavern, most of the scenes in act one each take about one-and-a-half minutes. The pacing goes pretty quickly and pulls the audience further into the world of* Orphan Black.

END OF ACT ONE

ACT TWO

19. INT. BETH'S APARTMENT – LIVING ROOM – DAY (11:55–12:05)
ON VIDEO of Beth Childs, she is talking to the person with the camera.

Sarah stands in front of the TV, studying Beth—the way Beth talks, walks, carries herself. Beth seems like a hard ass, but there's a sweetness to her as well. Sarah freezes the frame on Beth's face. She gets close to the TV. She is face to face with Beth. Sarah is becoming Beth.

20. SERIES OF SHOTS over *Bad Girls* by M.I.A. (12:06–13:13)
1) CLOSE ON bank business card. Sarah picks it up.

2) Sarah runs Beth's ATM card magnetic strip against the inside of the refrigerator door. She does this to demagnetize the card.

3) Sarah practices Beth's signature.

4) Sarah goes through Beth's closet looking for the perfect outfit.

5) Sarah watches more home video of Beth. Beth has a flat North American accent.

6) Sarah gets undressed and goes into Beth's bathroom. She finds a bunch of prescription bottles.

7) Sarah lays out some clothes on the bed.

8) Sarah watches video of Beth running.

9) Sarah puts photos of Beth on the bathroom mirror.

10) Sarah watches video of Paul talking to camera, asking Beth if she is ready to push her body. Out of breath, Beth tells the camera: "Damn right." Sarah repeats, "Damn right."

11) Sarah dyes her bleached hair back to her natural color, which is Beth's color.

12) Sarah watches Beth say, "Damn right." Sarah repeats the phrase in Beth's accent.

13) Sarah changes into Beth's clothes.

14) In the bathroom, Beth's pink phone rings. Sarah ignores the call. Then Beth's black cell rings. It's Art. Sarah says in Beth's accent, "Sorry Art. I'm gone for good."

15) Sarah watches Beth say, "Damn right" again. Sarah enunciates the phrase.

16) Sarah holds up a gray dress to herself and looks in the mirror.

17) Sarah leans close to the bathroom mirror (the camera) and says "Damn right" like Beth perfectly.

> *Note: There are 17 shots in this minute-and-10-second montage. All of the shots feel complete. They have a good rhythm to them. And they deliver a ton of information about Sarah and Beth. Plus, they're driven by a character want—Sarah wants to become Beth because Sarah wants to steal Beth's money.*

Figure 4.11: *Orphan Black* pilot hero committed.

21. INT. BANK – DAY (13:13–13:34)
Sarah as Beth strides into the bank wearing black pumps, the gray dress, and subdued makeup. In Beth's accent, Sarah asks for the bank manager, STEVEN RIGGS.
Hero committed

22. INT. OLLY'S TAVERN – DAY (13:35–14:08)
BOBBIE THE BARTENDER wants Felix to either use the phone or hang it up. Felix makes his call. He has called the morgue and says he thinks he knows the woman who killed herself at Huxley Station. It's Sarah Manning.

> *Note: Both Sarah and Felix are preparing to execute their cons. Sarah is going to con the bank. Felix is going to con the city morgue.*

23. INT. BANK – DAY (14:09–14:32)
STEVEN RIGGS (30s, average) greets Sarah as Beth. He talks about his last half-marathon. He asks "Beth" how she did in her last charity race. "Beth" doesn't know.

24. INT. BANK – BANK MANAGER'S OFFICE – DAY (14:33–15:55)
"Beth" wants a large withdrawal from her account—in cash. Steven tells her that he would recommend a cashier's check. "Beth" really wants cash. Steven wants her to know that anything more than $10,000 has to be special ordered. That takes four or five days. "Beth" asks if Steven could expedite that, maybe 24 hours, if she sponsors him in his next charity run. Steven agrees.

Steven tries to run her bank card, but it won't work. He needs to get her another. "Beth" pulls out a safety deposit box key. Steven wants to know if she wants access. "Beth" would love that.

25. INT. BANK – SAFE DEPOSIT VAULT – DAY (15:56–16:32)
Sarah gets Beth's safety deposit box. The pink cell buzzes again. There are texts: "where are you?" "must see you" "have arrived." Sarah ignores the texts. In the box, there is only an envelope. There are birth certificates for Alison Hendrix, Elizabeth Childs, and Katja Obinger. Sarah takes the papers and leaves.

26. EXT. BETH'S BUILDING – DAY (16:33–17:15)
Sarah walks back to Beth's apartment. A parked BLACK CAR flashes its lights at her. However, a nondescript sedan pulls up beside Sarah and blasts its police siren. A MAN (black, 30s, pissed) gets out asking Sarah what the hell she is doing. He tells her to get in the car. He grabs Sarah and calls her Beth. He puts her in the car. He tells her they're late.

The black car leaves.

27. INT. NONDESCRIPT SEDAN – DAY (17:16–18:15)
Freaking out on the inside, Sarah searches for some clue as to what is happening. She sees a name on a police report—DETECTIVE ARTHUR BELL. This is the ART, who has been calling. Art gets into the car and wants to know where she has been. Sarah says she was held up. He gives her grief. Finally, she calls him by name and tells him to drive.

28. INT. MORGUE – CORRIDOR – DAY (18:16–18:27)
Felix sees a body on a stab that has been covered by a sheet. He asks COLIN, the morgue attendant, if that is her. Colin asks if Felix is all right. Felix says he is.

29. INT. MORGUE – CONTINUOUS (18:28–18:54)
Felix is freaking out. Colin assures him that he can do this.

30. EXT. PRECINCT – DAY (18:55–19:34)
The nondescript sedan parks in front. There are COPS everywhere. This is Sarah's nightmare. Art drags her by the arm toward the precinct. He opens the door for her, ushering her inside.

31. INT. PRECINCT – CONTINUOUS (19:35–20:27)
COPS watch her. What the hell is going on? DETECTIVE ANGELA DEANGELIS (30, dark hair, dark soul) tells "Beth" "good luck."
LT. GAVIN HARDCASTLE (50s and as tough as his name) confronts "Beth." He wants to know why she is late. Art says she's here. Hardcastle wants to get going. Sarah still doesn't know what is happening. They lead her to a conference room where a TRIBUNAL awaits.

Sarah halts. Hardcastle tells her to stick to her statement and she'll be fine. "Beth" wants to use the washroom.

32. INT. PRECINCT – WOMEN'S BATHROOM – DAY (20:27–20:48)
Sarah enters. She checks to make sure she is alone. She calls Felix but gets his voice jail. She tells him that she is a cop. *Beth is a cop.* Abort.

> *Note: Sarah and Felix's storylines weave together nicely. The juxtaposition of their scenes amplifies the audience's emotions. Both Sarah and Felix are freaking out during their respective cons. Sarah's con has taken a bizarre turn. She is not only concerned about her culpability, but also concerned about Felix's, which is why she wants him to abort the false report. Felix's con is about to take a different unexpected turn.*
>
> *ALSO NOTE: The Sarah-goes-to-the-cops sequence takes a minute and 53 seconds. She figures out that Beth is a cop who is facing a tribunal. We meet two new characters. Plus, we experience Sarah's anxiety in this situation. All of this happens so quickly it's brilliant.*

33. INT. MORGUE – DAY (20:48–21:21)
Colin pulls back the sheet on Elizabeth Childs' body. Felix freaks at first, but then is oddly fascinated. He feigns disgust. Colin tells Felix that he

can lean on him. Felix accepts, while glancing at the corpse that looks exactly like his foster sister.

34. INT. PRECINCT – BATHROOM – RESUME (21:22–21:44)
Sarah doesn't know what to do. She looks at herself in the mirror, sees the SOAP DISPENSER. She unscrews the plastic container and drinks a bit of the pink liquid soap. She gags. She downs the whole container.

35. INT. MORGUE – RESUME (21:45–22:27)
Colin brings Felix a cup of water. Colin wants to know if the body is Felix's sister. Felix says that it is. Colin wants him to sign a few things. Colin also wants Felix to know if he needs someone to talk to, maybe over a drink, Colin is available. Felix is intrigued.

> *Note: The moods of Sarah and Felix's cons have diverged, yet they're still paralleled. In both, they are drinking something. Felix drinks "morgue water." Sarah drinks liquid soap.*

36. INT. PRECINCT – SQUAD ROOM – DAY (22:28–22:43)
Sarah comes out of the bathroom and is escorted into the conference room by Hardcastle.

37. INT. PRECINCT – CONFERENCE ROOM – CONTINUOUS (22:44–23:15)
"Beth" takes her seat and discovers they are investigating a line-of-duty shooting from this year. Beth shot someone—Margaret Chan—and killed her. The tribunal wants Beth's statement in her own words. They are videotaping this session. They wait for her to spill her guts, but Sarah stalls. Finally, Sarah pukes all over the table.

END OF ACT TWO

ACT THREE

38. INT. PSYCHIATRIST'S OFFICE – WAITING ROOM – DAY (23:16–24:00)
Sarah as Beth waits with Art. Art wants to know where "Beth's" sense of humor has gone. He starts to banter with her. Sarah complies. Art tells her they will figure this out together. He's not such a bad guy.

39. INT. FELIX'S LOFT – DAY (24:01–25:10)
Felix paints a picture of Sarah with Xs over her eyes. Vic pounds on the door. Felix preps himself for the act. When he opens the door, he slaps Vic and stalks to the couch. Felix tells Vic that Sarah is dead. Vic doesn't believe him.

> *Note: As Sarah and Felix's storylines continue to weave together, they continue to connect. In both storylines, they're adjusting to this new normal. Art and Sarah reach an equilibrium. Felix copes with the "loss" of his foster sister through his art. Likely, Art's name isn't a coincidence. Felix relies on his art. Sarah will rely on Beth's Art.*

40. INT. MORGUE – DAY (25:11–25:36)
Once again, Colin pulls back the sheet on Beth's body. Vic breaks down. He holds the corpse and cries. Felix flirts with Colin as Felix consoles Vic—a little, a very little.

41. INT. PSYCHIATRIST'S OFFICE – DAY (25:37–27:05)
Sarah as Beth talks with DR. BOWERS (50s, judgmental, discerning). "Beth" says she is missing herself. She glitched. She's having trouble with detail. She isn't sure she should say anything about the shooting.
Dr. Bowers tells her that she has to talk about that incident so she can move on.

> *Note: Felix breaks the news to Vic and proves to Vic that Sarah is dead by taking him to the morgue. Felix is fully committing to his con and pulling others into his con. Sarah also wades in further to her con by meeting with a psychiatrist as "Beth." Both Felix and Sarah's survivor instincts allow them to embrace the lies they're telling.*

42. EXT. CITYSCAPE – DAY (27:06–27:07)
Time passes as the city hums.

43. EXT. STREET – BETH CHILDS' APARTMENT – DAY (27:08–27:09)
All is calm on Beth's street.

Figure 4.12: *Orphan Black* pilot hero succeeds—almost.

44. INT. BETH'S APARTMENT – DINING ROOM/KITCHEN – DAY (27:10–29:27)
Sarah drinks a beer while looking over documents of Beth's life.
The pink cell phone chimes. There are 12 unanswered messages on the phone. Felix tries to grasp Beth's life. While hopped up on anti-depressants and tranquilizers, Beth shot an innocent Chinese woman. He wants talk about the fact Beth and Sarah are related. This could be Sarah's story, her lost family. "We all dream we're special," he says. "The last thing I am is special," Sarah says.

Felix tells her Vic wants a funeral for Sarah. Sarah says he can't have one. Sad fact is no one would notice if Sarah died, or so she thinks. Felix wants to know about the birth certificates—Alison Hendrix,

Beth Childs, and Katja Obinger—they were all born within the same month as Sarah. She says it's a coincidence. This is just a score.

Sarah will get the money and come back for Felix and Kira. Felix realizes Sarah is going to blow town again. He's furious. He's leaving. Last time Sarah left Kira with Mrs. S overnight, she didn't come back for 10 months. Sarah says she is trying to fix it. Felix tells her to tell it to the angels because she is already dead.
Hero succeeds—almost

> *Note: As the initial phase of their cons are wrapped up, Sarah and Felix share a moment together. Graeme Manson gives Sarah and Felix as well as the audience a chance to catch their breaths. This scene takes two minutes and 20 seconds. It's long enough to break up the churning pace of the previous scenes.*
>
> *Here Felix realizes Sarah is lying to him. Sarah is conning him. She wants to get the money, leave town, and come back for Felix and Kira. Felix sees through Sarah, who has abandoned Kira and Felix for long periods. He knows she hasn't changed. At this point, it's unclear if Sarah is lying to herself or not.*

45. INT. BETH'S APARTMENT - BEDROOM - NIGHT (29:28–29:37)
In a Clash t-shirt and black panties, Sarah comes in from the bathroom drying her hair with a towel. She takes a sweater out of Beth's drawer and tosses it onto a duffle bag.

46. INT. BETH'S APARTMENT - WALK-IN CLOSET - CONTINUOUS (29:38–29:51)
Sarah shops in Beth and Paul's clothes. She hears a creak.

47. INT. BETH'S APARTMENT - FOYER - SAME (29:52–29:53)
The bolt lock turns. The door opens. Someone is coming in.

48. INT. BETH'S APARTMENT - WALK-IN CLOSET - RESUME (29:54–29:59)
Sarah grabs one of Paul's shirts. She paces the closet.

49. INT. BETH'S APARTMENT – FOYER – RESUME (30:00–30:02)
Paul comes in and calls out Beth's name.

50. INT. BETH'S APARTMENT - BEDROOM - RESUME (30:03–30:47)
PAUL (30, leaner, hotter than his photos) comes in. He notes her Clash t-shirt. He wants to know if she is going somewhere. Sarah as Beth says it's just gym stuff. Paul wants to know how the hearing went. Sarah says she couldn't do it. He asks if she skipped it. Sarah heads to the kitchen.

51. INT. BETH'S APARTMENT - KITCHEN - CONTINUOUS (30:48–32:17)
It's almost as if Sarah is running away from Paul and all of his questions. She explains she puked all over the table at the hearing. She moves toward the sink. He follows her. He wants to know what's happened. She's different. He wants to know what she did to her hair. She says she got it cut. He says it looks longer. She says it's just wet. He says something is different. Sarah does the only thing she can think of—she launches herself at him. They kiss, grope, and strip.

Paul wants to go the bedroom. Sarah wants him right here in the kitchen. They rush to strip off their underwear. Paul leans against the table. Sarah pushes him down and straddles him. She takes off her t-shirt. They begin to grind.

> *Note: Graeme gives Paul's introduction a nice chunk of time—two minutes and 15 seconds. We definitely have interest in him. When he creeps into the apartment, we wonder "who is that?" We soon figure out it's the boyfriend. But then, he looks hotter then we expected.*

It's actually written in the script that Paul looks hotter than his pics and video.

We start to have sympathy for him when Paul asks about the tribunal. Wow, he came home early because his girlfriend was going through a difficult time. We get where he is coming from. Plus, we the audience know his girlfriend is dead and the woman who is in his apartment isn't his girlfriend. We start to feel for him. We start to have empathy for him.

Then Paul suspects something is different with "Beth." We start stepping into his shoes. What if we came home and our significant other was acting weird and looked a little different in a way that seems improbable. Then "Beth," fresh from the shower wearing only a t-shirt and panties, launches herself at him. Paul wants her. Okay, we get it. Sarah is hotter than Paul remembers Beth, and he likes it. We have achieved empathy for Paul.

END OF ACT THREE

ACT FOUR

52. INT. BETH'S APARTMENT – BEDROOM – NIGHT (32:20–32:39)
Paul lies asleep in the bed. Sarah slips out from under his arm and out of the bed. Naked, she heads for the closet.

53. INT. FELIX'S LOFT – NIGHT (32:40–34:14)
Pounding on the door disrupts the calm. No doubt Vic wants in. Felix comes out of his bedroom in a very, very short kimono. He slips the screwdriver out of the lock and slides the door open. Inconsolable, Vic wants to come in. He's been in a fight. He's got anger issues. Vic wants to have a memorial for Sarah. Felix, still mad at Sarah, slyly agrees.

Note: Tracking Felix's emotional logic from the previous scene with Felix, we the audience understand he is agreeing to the memorial because Sarah didn't want one. He's doing it to get back at Sarah.

54. INT. BETH'S APARTMENT - LIVING ROOM - DAY (34:15-35:14)
Sarah sneaks out of the bedroom dressed for the gym. She carries her duffle. She steals money out of Paul's wallet. As she is shoving the money down her tights, Paul runs his hands around her. He is way into Sarah AKA new Beth. Sarah tells him she got up for the gym. They walk through the living room to the FOYER.

"Beth" wants to borrow his car. Paul tells her to use her own car. She can't find her keys. He asks her if she looked in "the thing where they always are." Of course, she looked in "the thing where they always are." He opens a small box on the foyer table. Of course, Beth's car keys are in the thing where they always are. Sarah takes the keys and dodges a kiss from Paul.

55. EXT. BETH'S APARTMENT - STREET - CONTINUOUS (35:15-36:18)
Sarah exits Beth's apartment, hits the key fob, and a gorgeous car chirps back. Art's nondescript sedan is parked across the street.

56. INT. NONDESCRIPT SEDAN - SAME (36:19–36:23)
Art watches "Beth" load her duffle bag into the trunk.

57. EXT. BETH'S APARTMENT - STREET - SAME (36:24–36:27)
Sarah gets into Beth's car.

58. INT. NONDESCRIPT SEDAN - SAME (36:28–36:29)
Art puts his car in drive.

59. EXT. BETH'S APARTMENT - STREET - SAME (36:30–36:36)
Sarah drives away. Art follows her.

60. INT. BANK – DAY (36:37–36:44)
Through the bank manager's office window, Sarah can be seen slouching in a chair and talking on her cell phone. It's very un-Beth-like. Good old Steven Riggs, the bank manager, nears the door.

61. INT. BANK – BANK MANAGER'S OFFICE – CONTINUOUS (36:45-37:42)
Sarah, speaking in her blue collar British accent, is leaving a zesty message on Felix's voice jail. Steven overhears part of her message. Sarah quickly gets off the phone. Steven needs her to sign a receipt. As Sarah signs Beth's name, Steven stacks $75,000 in front of her. Almost giddy, "Beth" loads up her briefcase with the cash. She leaves, barely able to contain herself.

62. INT. BANK – CONTINUOUS (37:43–37:46)
Grinning, Sarah exits the bank with a briefcase full of money.

63. EXT. FELIX'S LOFT BUILDING – DAY (37:47–38:13)
Felix's loft is in a bad, albeit artsy, section of town. Sarah drives Beth's car down an alley. Art follows Sarah in his car. A SUMO-WRESTLER-OF-A-GUY dressed in nothing but a towel gets some relief from the heat of the bathhouse next to Felix's loft. Sarah gets out and jogs up the stairs to Felix's. Art gets out of his car with a slim jim and goes to Beth's car.

64. INT. FELIX'S LOFT BUILDING – HALLWAY – DAY (38:14–38:18)
Sarah heads for Felix's door.

65. EXT. FELIX'S LOFT BUILDING – RESUME (38:19–38:23)
Art uses a slim jim to open the trunk on Beth's car.

66. INT. FELIX'S LOFT – SAME (38:24–38:30)
Sarah enters without knocking. Felix isn't there.

67. EXT. FELIX'S LOFT BUILDING – RESUME (38:31–38:33)
Art opens Beth's trunk.

68. INT. FELIX'S LOFT – SAME (38:34–38:35)
Sarah takes off her coat.

69. EXT. FELIX'S LOFT BUILDING – RESUME (38:36–38:45)
Art opens Beth's trunk. He finds the money in her briefcase.

70. INT. FELIX'S LOFT – RESUME (38:46–38:56)
Sarah looks around Felix's loft and finds a flyer for her own memorial service.

Figure 4.13: *Orphan Black* pilot emotional squeeze.

71. EXT. INDUSTRIAL WATERFRONT – DAY (38:57–39:23)
Felix, Vic, and OTHERS have gathered for a memorial service by a river. Vic has Beth's ashes in an urn. He gives an emotional and truthful, in his mind, account of Sarah's personality.

72. EXT. INDUSTRIAL WATERFRONT – VANTAGE POINT – DAY (39:24–39:26)
BINOCULAR VIEW on the Sarah Manning memorial.

73. EXT. INDUSTRIAL WATERFRONT – DAY (39:27–39:33)
Vic continues his eulogy. Felix's cell emits a techno music ringtone. Vic gives him the stink eye.

74. EXT. INDUSTRIAL WATERFRONT – VANTAGE POINT – RESUME (39:34–39:35)
BINOCULAR VIEW on the Sarah Manning memorial gathering as Felix answers his cell.

75. EXT. INDUSTRIAL WATERFRONT – RESUME (39:36–39:37)
Felix answers his cell. He wants to know if it's heaven or hell.

76. EXT. INDUSTRIAL WATERFRONT – VANTAGE POINT – RESUME (39:38–39:40)
BINOCULAR VIEW on the Sarah Manning memorial gathering and Felix talking on his cell.

END BINOCULAR VIEW.

Sarah holds binoculars to her eyes. She didn't want a memorial service for this very reason.

77. EXT. INDUSTRIAL WATERFRONT – RESUME (39:41–39:43)
Felix tells her that she can't do much about it if she's dead.

78. EXT. INDUSTRIAL WATERFRONT – VANTAGE POINT – RESUME (39:44–40:00)
Sarah tells Felix that she is watching.

BINOCULAR VIEW Felix turns to look for Sarah and sees her.

Sarah watches him.

BINOCULAR VIEW Felix walks near Vic.

Sarah thinks this is funny.

BINOCULAR VIEW Felix walks among the mourners, joking around with Sarah. There's a mourner who is still rockabilly after all these years.

79. EXT. INDUSTRIAL WATERFRONT – RESUME (40:01–40:02)
Felix respects the guy's choice to stick with the rockabilly style.

80. EXT. INDUSTRIAL WATERFRONT – VANTAGE POINT – RESUME (40:02–40:06)
Sarah watches, smiling. She notices that Sherry is upset.

81. EXT. INDUSTRIAL WATERFRONT – RESUME (40:07–40:13)
Felix says Sherry thinks Vic pushed Sarah in front of the train.

82. EXT. INDUSTRIAL WATERFRONT – VANTAGE POINT – RESUME (40:14–40:16)
Sarah tells Felix that she got the money. She wants them to be together—Felix, her foster brother, and Kira, her daughter.

83. EXT. INDUSTRIAL WATERFRONT – RESUME (40:17–40:26)
Before Felix can answer, Vic gets mad. Felix has to get off the phone.

84. EXT. INDUSTRIAL WATERFRONT – VANTAGE POINT – RESUME (40:27–40:29)
BINOCULAR VIEW Felix looks toward Sarah. Suddenly, the view glides over and finds a truck coming down the dirt access road. Sarah is immediately upset.

85. EXT. INDUSTRIAL WATERFRONT – RESUME (40:29–40:30)
Felix wants to know what's wrong.

86. EXT. INDUSTRIAL WATERFRONT – VANTAGE POINT – RESUME (40:31–40:32)
Sarah says Mrs. S is coming.

87. EXT. INDUSTRIAL WATERFRONT – RESUME (40:32–40:37)
Shit! Felix rushes toward the truck. Felix stops it.

88. EXT. INDUSTRIAL WATERFRONT – VANTAGE POINT – RESUME (40:38–41:07)
Sarah sees something more alarming.

BINOCULAR VIEW Mrs. S (woman, 40s, tough, no nonsense, Irish) gets out of the truck followed by a little girl...

...KIRA (7 or 8, angelic face, soulful eyes, intelligent beyond her years).

END BINOCULAR VIEW.

Sarah is floored by the idea her daughter thinks she is dead. She is crushed. She wants Kira to know she is alive.
Emotional squeeze

> *Note: As the story progresses to act four, the scenes start cutting back and forth more quickly. It increases the story pacing. For the most part, these quick cuts are done in the edit bay. In the script, the funeral scene is written as one long conversation. This conversation takes place from 38:57–41:07, so it's only about two minutes and 10 seconds. However as you read the intercutting it feels longer.*

As you may notice, reading the intercutting becomes tedious. However, when you watch it, the intercutting keeps the scene lively. Again, the script is written differently, but the effect is this quick intercutting.

Also, you'll note Graeme moves Sarah and Felix through a spectrum of emotions. First, the memorial service is pathetic. Vic is crying over Beth's ashes thinking they're Sarah's ashes. Sarah calls Felix, interrupting the solemnity of the moment. Felix scolds her—he is still mad at her because she planned to leave Felix and Kira again. Sarah and Felix readjust to their usual brother-sister conviviality. They joke about the memorial service and its attendees. Finally, Sarah sees Mrs. S's truck coming and freaks. She's afraid Mrs. S will think she's dead and keep Kira. Then the worst happens: Sarah sees Kira is with Mrs. S. Sarah is crushed. Desperate for her daughter to know she is still alive, she yells for Felix to stop Mrs. S and Kira. She wants them to leave as she watches from a distance.

If Felix and Sarah didn't have the lighter moments, the desperate moment wouldn't have as much impact.

END OF ACT FOUR

ACT FIVE

89. EXT. INDUSTRIAL WATERFRONT – VANTAGE POINT – DAY (40:09–41:13)
Distressed, Sarah heads for Beth's car.

90. INT. BETH'S CAR – CONTINUOUS (41:14–41:27)
Sarah gets into Beth's car to escape the catastrophe of Kira believing Sarah is dead. Suddenly, a women gets into the back seat of the car. She looks EXACTLY like Sarah, except she has short hair dyed magenta. This is KATJA OBINGER (late 20s, German, desperate). Katja carries a pink cell phone. Katja wants to know why Beth hasn't been responding to her.

91. EXT. INDUSTRIAL WATERFRONT – VANTAGE POINT – CONTINUOUS (41:28–42:08)
Sarah gets out of the car. Katja follows. She wants to know why they didn't meet. She brought the samples. Then Katja coughs up blood. Katja wants to see Beth's scientist friend. Sarah gets back into Beth's car and says she can't help her. Katja gets into the back seat.

Figure 4.14: *Orphan Black* pilot hero succeeds.

92. INT. BETH'S CAR – CONTINUOUS (42:09–43:00)
Sarah wants Katja to get out of the car. Katja reveals that Art was following Sarah. Sarah puts it together. Katja was in the black car that flashed its lights. Katja confirms. Sarah wants her out of the car. Katja says, "Just one, I am few, no family, too. Who am I?" It's a riddle, a test. Sarah doesn't know the answer. Katja knows Sarah isn't Beth.

THRAWP – the rush of air, the shattering of glass. A bullet hole appears in the center of Katja's forehead. She jolts backward. Sarah looks at the bullet hole in windshield, then back at the blood covering the dead German and the back seat. Sarah dives below the dashboard as another round pierces the windshield in front of the driver's seat, exactly where Sarah just was. Terrified, Sarah quickly gets her key and puts it into the ignition, starts the car, and puts it in reverse.

93. EXT. INDUSTRIAL WATERFRONT – VANTAGE POINT – RESUME (43:01–43:03)
Beth's car peels backward.

94. INT. BETH'S CAR – MOVING – RESUME (43:03–43:04)
Her face spattered with Katja's blood, Sarah wheels the car around.

95. EXT. INDUSTRIAL WATERFRONT – VANTAGE POINT – RESUME (43:04–43:05)
Sarah maneuvers the car so it's heading in the right direction.

96. INT. BETH'S CAR – MOVING – RESUME (43:06–43:06)
The driver's side window shatters. Sarah ducks again. She's not hit.

97. EXT. INDUSTRIAL WATERFRONT – VANTAGE POINT – RESUME (43:07–43:09)
The tires on Beth's car cut into the turn. The car slings around. This is some expert stunt driving.

98. INT. BETH'S CAR – MOVING – RESUME (43:09–43:10)
Beth drops the car into drive.

99. EXT. INDUSTRIAL WATERFRONT – VANTAGE POINT – RESUME (43:11–43:11)
CLOSE ON a tire as it grabs the dirt, propelling the car.

100. INT. BETH'S CAR – MOVING – RESUME (43:12–43:13)
Gripping the wheel, Sarah floors it.

101. EXT. INDUSTRIAL WATERFRONT – VANTAGE POINT – RESUME (43:13–43:15)
The car speeds away, kicking up dirt.

102. INT. BETH'S CAR – MOVING – RESUME (43:15–43:19)
Sarah crouches behind the wheel, afraid a bullet will find her any second.

103. EXT. INDUSTRIAL WATERFRONT ROAD – SAME (43:15–43:20)
Beth's car roars down the road, putting distance between Sarah and the unknown assassin.
Hero succeeds

Figure 4.15: *Orphan Black* pilot hero's new life.

104. INT. BETH'S CAR – MOVING – RESUME (43:21–43:38)
Freaked out, Sarah tries to hold it together as she gets away. In the back seat, the German's pink cell phone chimes. Sarah is drawn to the chime, but eventually it stops. Then, Beth's pink cell chimes. Reluctantly, Sarah as Beth answers it. "Hello?"
Hero's new life

Note: Action sequences consist of short images. However, the actual script wouldn't be written as it is in the breakdown.

The script description might be written INT./EXT. CAR – MOVING – CONTINUOUS "A tire grips the dirt, spits gravel. The car swerves, fishtails. The car bounces onto the curb. Sarah jerks the wheel back, course correcting."

The script reads more fluidly if the writer captures the vibe and major movements of the action sequence. The writer needs to make the script exciting and fun to read. However, you can get a good sense of the pacing from the cutting in the breakdown format.

ALSO NOTE: From the time Katja gets into Beth's car to the time Sarah gets away—the hero succeeds moment—is only two minutes and five seconds. The hero's new life gets a whole 20 seconds. Orphan Black *churns through story. It squeezes a lot into each scene. Graeme Manson and John Fawcett keep it firmly rooted in character, which is the show's greatest strength.*

END OF PILOT

Creator Graeme Manson, who wrote the pilot, and John Fawcett, who directed the pilot, deftly bring viewers into the complex world of *Orphan Black*. At first, the story seems very small. Sarah Manning, a British con artist, wants to get enough money so she can run away with her daughter and foster brother, Felix.

Coincidently, the perfect opportunity drops in her lap. A woman who looks exactly like her commits suicide and leaves her belongs and life behind. Sarah snatches the woman's purse and her life. It's too tempting for a desperate thief to pass up. However, Sarah doesn't take a moment to consider why this woman, Beth Childs, looks like her, much less why she wanted to commit suicide, despite the fact Beth has a sweet pad and a hot boyfriend.

Yes, the beauty of *Orphan Black* is the character work as well as its care for its audience. Graeme makes sure the audience can participate with the show every step of the way. He introduces Sarah and Beth at the same time. He achieves interest, sympathy, and empathy for both characters—one live, one dead. As Sarah learns about Beth, the audience learns about Beth. The audience knows what Sarah knows. We're with her. And while Sarah is less concerned with the why of her *doppelgänger*, we want to know the mystery behind the connection between the two women. (I'll discuss character introductions and audience participation in greater detail in chapters 7 and 9.)

With an acting dynamo like Tatiana Maslany, Graeme and John have taken great care to make sure *Orphan Black* is character-driven. Character-driven structure effortlessly shapes the pilot story. The **point of attack**, the first whiff of the problem, occurs when Sarah meets a distraught Beth on the subway platform and Beth takes her own life. The event is shocking to both Sarah and the audience. She gasps and we gasp. In this moment, we are bonded to Sarah.

The **hero committed** moment comes at the beginning of the second act. Sarah becomes Beth. She dyes her hair. She studies video of Beth walking, talking, running, laughing. She practices her signature. She chooses the perfect outfit. Gone is the street punk Sarah; the polished, put-together Beth is resurrected so she can clean out her bank account. Sarah is committed to impersonating Beth when she walks into the bank and asks for the bank manager.

However, becoming Beth and *being* Beth are two entirely different things. Beth had a shit-ton of reasons to commit suicide. Her life is complicated—very complicated. And the petty criminal Sarah finds herself in front of a police tribunal about a fatal police shooting. WTF? Beth was a cop. Sarah as Beth is in over her head. Ever the survivor, Sarah thinks quickly and does what she has to do to get through the situation.

The **hero succeeds—almost** moment occurs in the aftermath of Beth's day. In a scene with Felix, who has had his own parallel storyline, Sarah kicks back with a beer. She successfully negotiated a day in the life of Beth, only to find she can't manage her own life. Sarah reveals she'll get the money tomorrow and then skip town. She'll come back for Felix and her daughter, Kira. Felix sees this as yet another one of Sarah's scams. Sarah has made promises in the past and disappointed him. Felix calls her out on her shit and leaves her in Beth's apartment. In other words, Sarah made it through the day as Beth, but she couldn't be real as herself.

A high point in the story is when Sarah as Beth successfully steals $75,000. The elation spreads across Sarah's face. Grinning, Sarah leaves the bank with a briefcase packed full of her future, or so she thinks. It would be easy to think that this moment is the hero succeeds—almost landmark, because Art ends up stealing the money from "Beth" to prevent her from skipping town before the tribunal. However, the true character journey is Sarah becoming Beth, not Sarah escaping with the money. We the audience know from the point of attack that there is more going on here than just Sarah's small problems. We wonder why Beth looks exactly like Sarah. We wonder why Beth really wanted to kill herself. We wonder why a mysterious black car keeps following her and flashing its lights. We wonder what is up with the pink cellphone. Who is on the other end of those calls and texts? Why do they want to get in touch with Beth so badly? So while that moment of triumph in Sarah's smaller goals is quite fun and beautiful, even we know there is more to this story.

The **emotional squeeze** occurs at Sarah's memorial service. Sarah watches from afar as her ex-boyfriend and random friends hold a service over her, well, Beth's ashes. Sarah calls Felix, who is in attendance. At first, Sarah and Felix joke about Sarah's *funeral.* Sarah had said earlier that a memorial service for her would be pointless, because no one would notice if she died. But this isn't true. There are two people who would care and who matter greatly to Sarah. When Sarah sees a familiar truck ramble up the dirt access road to the pitiful clutch of mourners, Sarah's heart drops. It's Mrs. S, her foster mother, and Kira, Sarah's innocent, precious daughter. Sarah stands watching the scene through binoculars. She's across the river, but she might as well be a thousand miles away. She can't stop this dreadful shoe from dropping. Her daughter thinks she's dead.

Often in the emotional squeeze there is a decision between a bad and a worse option. And in a way, Sarah makes a decision here. She decides to tell Felix to stop Mrs. S. She tells him to make Mrs. S take Kira away. Sarah doesn't race over to the mourners and reveal she is alive. She doesn't ask to be put on the phone with Mrs. S so she can prove she is alive. She doesn't ask to talk to Kira. Sarah makes her foster brother attempt to head Mrs. S off at the pass. Sarah shirks her duties as a mother as she has been doing all along. It's heartbreaking.

While Felix is successful at getting Mrs. S to leave with Kira, Sarah is still gut-punched by the incident. With her funeral no longer humorous to her, Sarah gets back into Beth's car to leave. She only has a moment to take a breath before Katja Obinger, Sarah's German *doppelgänger*, pops up in the back seat and we're building to the **hero succeeds** moment.

Sarah wants nothing to do with Katja Obinger. After a tense exchange, Katja figures out Sarah is not Beth. Suddenly, a bullet pierces the windshield and Katja's forehead. Blood spatters in a fine mist. Katja slumps back, dead. Terrified, Sarah dives beneath the dash, turns the ignition, and barrels the car out of the sniper's range.

What we the audience suspected is coming to light. There is way more to this story. Beth was involved in something more disturbing that a police shooting. And there wasn't just one look-alike; there are more. Sarah will need all of her survivor skills to do more than just con people—she'll need them to save herself and her family.

As a stunned Sarah drives away, Katja's pink cell phone rings. While Sarah has been ignoring Beth's pink cell phone, the urge to answer Katja's cell phone is palpable. Should she answer it? Sarah wants to know what's going on. She just saw someone who looked exactly like her get assassinated. That's two dead versions of herself in as many days. Katja's phone stops chiming. After a beat, Beth's pink cell phone rings. Sarah glances at it. If she answers it, it will change her life. She picks it up, hits answer call, and says, "Hello?" This is the start of our **hero's new life**. And we smash to black.

What does Sarah's new life hold for her? We'll have to binge watch the next episodes. And that's exactly what I did. Graeme, John, and Tatiana hook the audience with their character work. While the world of *Orphan Black* is fascinating, we come back because we care about the characters. We care about Sarah and whether she'll get her happily ever after with Kira. We care about Felix and whether he'll have the life he wants with his foster sister and niece. And we grow to care about all of the other characters, including Art, Paul, Mrs. S, and the clone club.

That's what *you* want. You want your audience to become so invested in your characters they will happily, desperately welcome your characters back into their lives episode after episode. Your world may be fascinating, dangerous, and weird, but the draw is the *characters.*

* * *

Spoiler alert! Watch the pilot for Fox's *Empire,* then come back to discover why this show works because of its character-driven structure.

Fox's *Empire* took the 2014-2015 season by storm. Unexpected and overpowering, *Empire*'s success came on the heels of the relative successes of *black-ish, Fresh Off the Boat,* and *Jane the Virgin.* Suddenly, shows with diverse casts were all one color—green.

Empire is soapy drama set in the world of a hip-hop music and entertainment company. Terrence Howard plays Lucious Lyon, the patriarch of Empire Entertainment. After receiving dire health news, Lucious tells his three sons that he'll be grooming one of them to take over the company. This is King Lear with sons. Creators Lee Daniels and Danny

Strong tell the audience as much in the pilot. Lee and Danny have made some smart choices, from casting—Taraji P. Henson as Cookie Lyon is a revelation—to the show's multi-platform marketability. The complete package of *Empire* makes it a potential empire itself.

As with all good shows, the characters draw the audience. They engage viewers. Lee and Danny have infused the characters with fierce drive and tormented backstories. Properly introducing characters—gaining the audience's interest, sympathy, and empathy—invests the audience in these characters' lives. I'll explain character introductions thoroughly in chapter 7 when I discuss your pilot story. For now, let's take a look at *Empire.*

Empire "Pilot" script by Lee Daniels and Danny Strong; breakdown by Kam Miller

1. INT. RECORDING STUDIO – DAY (00:17–00:26)
A FEMALE VOCALIST (20s, beautiful yet funky) sings at the microphone. Her voice is clear, strong, and technically perfect.

2. INT. RECORDING STUDIO – MIXING BOOTH – SAME (00:27–00:44)
LUCIOUS LYON (early 50s, charismatic, magnetic, demanding) watches the singer, no, *judges* the singer. Lucious gets up, adjusts the mix.

3. INT. RECORDING STUDIO – RESUME (00:45–00:47)
The vocalist hits the bridge. Her notes carry above the mix. It's good—great, even.

4. INT. RECORDING STUDIO – MIXING BOOTH – SAME (00:48–00:57)
Lucious cuts the playback. He directs the vocalist to sing like she is going to die tomorrow.

5. INT. RECORDING STUDIO – RESUME (00:58–00:59)
The vocalist nods. She's been giving it her best. *What the hell does this man want?*

6. INT. RECORDING STUDIO – MIXING BOOTH – SAME (00:59–01:11)
Lucious wants the vocalist to show him her soul.

7. INT. DOCTOR'S OFFICE – DAY – FLASHBACK (01:12–01:18)
MOS—Lucious sits on an exam table as two nurses attend him. He clearly isn't getting good news. This is his motivation.

8. INT. RECORDING STUDIO – RESUME (01:18–01:20)
The vocalist puts more heart into this performance.

9. INT. DOCTOR'S OFFICE – DAY – FLASHBACK (01:21–01:24)
MOS—Lucious waits in the exam room. A CAT scan of his brain flashes on screen. This is bad.

10. INT. RECORDING STUDIO – RESUME (01:25–01:27)
The vocalist infuses her performance with verve.

11. INT. RECORDING STUDIO – MIXING BOOTH – SAME (01:28–01:30)
Lucious looks on. His face unreadable.

12. INT. DOCTOR'S OFFICE – DAY – FLASHBACK (01:31–01:34)
Lucious looks to the DOCTOR (40s, 50s), her face unreadable.

13. INT. RECORDING STUDIO – RESUME (01:35–01:38)
The vocalist gets to the bridge. She wails.

14. INT. RECORDING STUDIO – MIXING BOOTH – SAME (01:39–01:57)
Lucious looks distracted as the singer finishes. ANIKA CALHOUN (late 20s, gorgeous) and ROGER the sound engineer (30s) look to Lucious for his opinion. Lucious decides the song isn't there yet. As Lucious strides into the studio, he roughly wakes up BUNKIE CAMPBELL (50s, overweight).

Figure 4.16: *Empire* pilot point of attack.

15. INT. RECORDING STUDIO – CONTINUOUS (01:58–02:23)
Gently, Lucious rubs the singer's shoulders and tells her to remember a year ago when she just found out her brother was shot. What was it like to have to ID his body? The singer relents. Lucious walks back into the mixing booth.
Point of attack

16. INT. RECORDING STUDIO – MIXING BOOTH – CONTINUOUS (02:24–02:28)
Lucious tells Roger to hit it again.

17. INT. RECORDING STUDIO – SAME (02:29–02:35)
This time the singer dredges up a world of pain and puts it all into her vocals.

18. INT. RECORDING STUDIO – MIXING BOOTH – SAME (02:36–02:40)
Anika looks to Lucious, who is still a cipher.

19. INT. RECORDING STUDIO – SAME (02:41–02:48)
The singer pushes through her emotions. The song feels like a catharsis. Her voice climbs like a cry, a plea to God.

20. INT. RECORDING STUDIO – MIXING BOOTH – SAME (02:49–02:49)
Lucious closes his eyes and breathes. This is what he wanted.

21. INT. RECORDING STUDIO – SAME (02:50–02:52)
The singer brings it home.

22. INT. RECORDING STUDIO – MIXING BOOTH – SAME (02:52–02:58)
Satisfied, Lucious touches Anika's arm. They've got it. They smile and hold hands.

> *Note: From the first notes to the final glorious version of the song, the opening sequence takes two minutes and 30 seconds. During this time, we're properly introduced to Lucious Lyon. We also learn the point of attack—Lucious is ill. We understand that this driven man is even more driven after his health news. Lee Daniels and Danny Strong use this technique of intercutting during a scene to give the show momentum as well as connect the flashbacks to the present. We get a sense the past affects the present and will affect the future of* Empire.
>
> *When using this technique, you need to look at the beginning of the intercutting sequence and the last intercut to get an idea of the pacing.*

The shorter the intercuts, the faster the pacing, usually. However, it's easy to fool yourself into thinking all intercutting is increasing pacing. The intercutting has to move the story forward and inform the audience about the characters. If the intercutting fails on either task, the story will founder and become confusing.

23. INT. RECORDING STUDIO – HALLWAY – DAY (02:29–03:06)
The camera pulls back from the recording studio into the hallway to a gold plaque of Lucious' face. A SERVER with wine glasses leads us onto…

24. EXT. YACHT – NEW YORK BAY – CONTINUOUS (03:07–03:25)
…the deck of a sweet yacht where a happening party takes place. The recording studio is on a yacht. Expensively dressed PARTYGOERS enjoy the wine, appetizers, and dancing. HAKEEM LYON (20, hat backward, diamond earrings, gold chains, mesh tank, and $500 jeans) takes a bite of shrimp offered to him by a HOTTIE. He is surrounded by the LADIES. He's the prince of this fairytale.

25. INT. YACHT – LOWER DECK – DAY (03:26–04:13)
While his brother enjoys the party, JAMAL LYON (24, sensitive, shy, talented) works on a composition at the piano. Hakeem joins Jamal. They jam free-style. Hakeem rapping. Jamal chiming in with vocals as he accompanies on the piano. Upbeat, spontaneous, magic. The brothers' chemistry and talent is undeniable.

26. INT. YACHT – UPPER DECK – SAME (04:13–04:20)
ANDRE LYON (27, business suit, business mind) leans on the rail with his wife, RHONDA (26, white, sexy, gym fit, manipulative, Andre's match). Rhonda comments that Dre's brothers are showing off again. He says that's what they do.

27. INT. YACHT – LOWER DECK – DAY (04:21–04:29)
Clearly, Jamal and Hakeem are performers as well as artists.

28. INT. YACHT – UPPER DECK – SAME (04:30–04:41)
Dre comments that his brothers usually show off when his father's around. This is unusual. Dre suggests they go find his father.

29. INT. YACHT – LOWER DECK – DAY (04:42–04:54)
Jamal and Hakeem build to a finish. They're in sync, simpatico.

30. INT. TOWN CAR – DAY (04:55–05:00)
Lucious and Anika arrive at Empire Entertainment. Anika wants to know if Lucious is ready to make his big announcement.

31. EXT. EMPIRE ENTERTAINMENT – DAY (05:01–05:09)
Lucious and Anika get out of the Town Car to a horde of fans. Lucious signs CDs that are thrust in front of him as he and Anika walk toward the building.

32. INT. EMPIRE ENTERTAINMENT – DAY (05:10–05:47)
Lucious and Anika part at the elevator with a kiss. BECKY (23, Lucious' assistant) trails him down the hallway into the atrium. She reels off Lucious' obligations for the day. Lucious mindlessly walks too fast. Becky calls his attention to his rudeness. He warns her that today is not the day. Perceptive, Becky asks about his doctor's appointment. He says it was fine. After this press conference, he wants to cancel all his meetings. He also wants his sons to meet him at his house.

33. INT. EMPIRE ENTERTAINMENT – CONFERENCE ROOM – DAY (05:48–06:15)
There's a basketball hoop in the conference room. Let's just say this place is over the top. Lucious talks to his board of directors. Lucious talks about how the music kept him alive when he was selling drugs to feed himself in Philadelphia.

34. EXT. PHILLY STREET – DAY – FLASHBACK – 40 YEARS AGO (06:16–06:23)
A YOUNG LUCIOUS raps to his fellow corner boys. They're digging it.

35. INT. EMPIRE ENTERTAINMENT – CONFERENCE ROOM – DAY (06:24–06:58)
Lucious talks about how the Internet has destroyed the musician's ability to make money. He wants to change that. He announces that Empire Entertainment has applied to be publicly traded on the New York Stock Exchange.

Figure 4.17: *Empire* pilot hero committed.

36. INT. LUCIOUS' MANSION – DINING ROOM – DAY (06:59–08:20)
Hakeem drinks a beer with his Timberlines resting on the table. Dre comes in. Dre asks how Jamal's friend is. Jamal says he's good, but he wants to know why Dre flaked on dinner last Tuesday because they cooked. Dre says his schedule got busy and he forgot. Lucious comes in and reprimands Hakeem for putting his feet on his $40,000 table.

Lucious tells his three sons that over the next few months he'll be grooming one of them to take over the company. Dre is stunned. He asks if they are all in competition with each other. Jamal asks if they're King Lear now. Lucious says he needs one of them to man up and take over the business, and nothing and no one will tear it down. Hero committed

Note: Lucious telling his sons about the competition among them for Empire Entertainment takes place in the present. It's 1 minute and 20 seconds. It's clear, concise, and it sets up the conflict of the series.

37. INT. PRISON – RELEASE ROOM – DAY (08:21–08:32)
A WOMAN (we don't see her face) signs her release papers and gives her fingerprints. She walks through the interior gate. She is getting out today.

38. EXT. PRISON – FRONT ENTRANCE – DAY (08:32–08:53)
A CORRECTIONAL OFFICER opens the exterior gate for COOKIE LYON (late 40s, sexy, solid, a fierce force of badassery). She walks out a free woman. Cookie is coming home today.

END OF TEASER

ACT ONE

39. INT. GYM – DAY (08:56–10:02)
Two BOXERS spar but one isn't holding anything back.

Lucious and Dre look on. Lucious comments on how much money they're going to make on his fighter. Dre says Lucious sounds like Don King. Lucious tells him not to saying nothing bad about Dr. King. *Huh?* Dre looks at his father, concerned. Bunkie laughs. Lucious asks Bunkie to give them a minute. Bunkie is offended but leaves.

Lucious tells Dre that he knows Dre has put everything into Empire. He's worked at Empire for a long time, even during grad school. But Lucious thinks Empire needs to be run by a celebrity. Dre disagrees. Lucious thinks with the company going public they need to consider it.

Artfully deflecting, Dre asks if Lucious's idea has anything to do with Cookie. Lucious doesn't understand. Dre tells Lucious that Cookie got out.

40. INT. GYM – LATER (10:03–10:38)
Lucious grills Bunkie. How did Bunkie not know Cookie was getting out? Lucious wants to know everything Cookie does. Bunkie asks for $25K for a gambling debt. He swears it's the last time he'll ask. Lucious says no.

41. INT. JAMAL'S LOFT – SOHO – DAY (10:39–11:47)
Jamal thinks Lucious won't give him the company because Jamal is gay. MICHAEL (mid 20s, sweet, handsome, supportive) wants to know what Jamal wants. Jamal won't put out an album. He won't tour. What does he want to do?

The phone rings. Jamal answers. It's Cookie. She wants in. Stunned, Jamal sees his mother through the window.

42. INT. PRISON – WAITING ROOM – DAY – FLASHBACK – ~17 YEARS AGO (11:48–11:59)
A YOUNG JAMAL sits with Lucious, who tells Jamal to go in there and tell his mama that Lucious loves her and don't come back crying. Jamal nods.

43. INT. PRISON – VISITATION ROOM – DAY – FLASHBACK – ~17 YEARS AGO (12:00–12:34)
Young Jamal goes the window that separates him from his mother. He wants to know when she's coming home. Cookie tells Jamal to stop asking her that. Cookie wants to know where his father is. Jamal tells her that his father isn't coming to see her today. Cookie wants to know how Jamal is doing at school. Jamal says he's getting picked on, but he doesn't want to tell his father because his father will tell him to fight.

Cookie tells young Jamal that she knows he is different. Life will be hard for Jamal sometimes, but she's got him. She stands up and gets closer to the window. She puts her mouth to the speaker and tells Jamal that she's got him.

44. INT. JAMAL'S LOFT – SOHO – RESUME (12:35–14:18)
Michael and Jamal rush around the apartment, straightening it while Cookie comes up. Michael wants to know if Jamal told Cookie about them. From Jamal's non-response, Michael gets the impression it's a "no."

The elevator doors open and...

...there's Jamal's mother. Jamal's face breaks into a big smile. He embraces his mother. Cookie holds him tight. This is a family reunion. Cookie smells chicken. Nearly giddy, Jamal drags her into the loft. Michael follows along and gets introduced to Jamal's mother. Both men clearly want Cookie's approval. Cookie wants what's hers.

END OF ACT ONE

ACT TWO

45. EXT. EMPIRE ENTERTAINMENT – DAY – ESTABLISHING (14:20– 14:23)
It's new day at Empire Entertainment, in more ways than one.

46. INT. EMPIRE ENTERTAINMENT – LUCIOUS' OFFICE – DAY (14:24–17:36)
Cookie bursts into Lucious' office against Becky's protests. Lucious isn't there. Alone, Cookie takes in the opulence of the office. It's a stark contrast from what she remembers and what she now sees. Cookie inspects Lucious' awards and photos. She finds a photo of Lucious and Anika.

Lucious comes in to welcome the queen. He is blown away by Cookie's beauty. Cookie wants half of the company. It was her $400,000 that started this company. She spent 17 years behind bars; she wants her half. Lucious says he can't give her half because he doesn't control half, but he can give her a big salary. Cookie wants $5 million a year, plus A&R. Lucious says he can give her maybe $3 million, but he can't give her A&R because he has someone. Cookie puts two and two together and gets Miss Halle Berry AKA Anika.

Anika comes in. Cookie looks her up and down, sizing up her competition. She tells Lucious to work it out.

> *Note: When Lucious sees Cookie for the first time after her prison stint, Lee and Danny give the characters three minutes and 10 seconds to get reacquainted. This is a long scene, but it's a pivotal scene for the series. The Lucious and Cookie relationship started Empire, and it will figure prominently in the future of Empire.*
>
> *Lee and Danny make some smart decisions here. They show us the love and attraction between Lucious and Cookie. They show us why these two characters who will become adversaries were lovers, husband and wife, parents. We get them as a couple. And Lee and Danny show us the promise of divorced parents—that promise children see when*

their parents get along. It's the idea their parents might one day get back together and everything will be okay again. The scene is masterfully done, and it all rests on the characters.

47. INT. HAKEEM'S APARTMENT – LIVING ROOM – DAY (17:37–19:08)
Posh. Very #RichKids. Hakeem gets a haircut. He has a barber's chair in his apartment, which speaks volumes about his entitlement. His GREAT DANES meander through the apartment like horses. Cookie doesn't approve. She tells the BARBER to get out of there. The barber does.

Cookie wants to see Hakeem. She wants to know why he hasn't accepted any of her calls in all these years. Hakeem is dismissive. He goes to sweep up the hair clippings. Cookie says everything she did was for Hakeem and his brothers. She ended up where she did for his brothers and him. Hakeem mouths off. "You want a medal, bitch?" Cookie wants respect. She grabs the broom and beats Hakeem with it.

Note: The production design on Hakeem's apartment is perfection. It reflects Hakeem's personality to a T. There is an huge, outrageous portrait of Hakeem riding a horse and brandishing a sword.

48. INT. LEVITICUS CLUB – NIGHT (19:09–20:55)
Packed and grooving, the Leviticus Club appears to be another one of Lucious' successes. He spies a work in progress, Hakeem, braving his pain as he mounts the stairs. The beating his mother gave him shows on his face—literally. He has abrasions around a bruised eye.

Lucious smiles and says, "I see you met your mother." Hakeem thinks she's a psychotic animal. Lucious tells Hakeem that he is just like his mother. Lucious tries to explain that Cookie isn't a bad person, that he didn't keep the boys away from her because she was bad. They were just in a bad situation and Lucious did the best he could.

Lucious wants Hakeem to get his act together. Hakeem is wasting his talent on bitches and booze. Hakeem says he's working on new material. Lucious knows Hakeem hasn't worked a day in his life. Hakeem is spoiled. But Lucious has written some new material. He wants to take Hakeem into the studio and record these songs and make them hits. Hakeem agrees.

49. EXT. NEW YORK STREET – DAY (20:56–21:07)
Cookie tries to flag down a taxi, but then she sees Bunkie asleep in his SUV. Cookie bangs on the window and wakes Bunkie up. He lets her in the car.

50. INT. SUV – CONTINUOUS (21:08–22:16)
Cookie gives Bunkie a little hell. She knows he's been drinking. She wants to know what's wrong. Bunkie feels like Lucious is keeping him down. Bunkie feels like he raised the boys while Cookie was inside.

Cookie says she has always appreciated him. She is smoothing the way for her next ask. She wants to know if Bunkie is following her at Lucious' request. Bunkie nods. She wants to know what Bunkie is going to tell Lucious. Bunkie says that he didn't see her. She fist bumps him.

Bunkie warns Cookie that something is going on. Something's got Lucious scared and he's been on the warpath. Cookie has his war for him.

51. INT. EMPIRE ENTERTAINMENT – LUCIOUS' OFFICE – DAY (22:17–21:32)
Jamal talks with Becky as he waits to see his father. They share a light moment talking about bathhouses. Lucious comes in and they shut it down. He asks Jamal about one of his previous *friends.* Jamal reminds his father that he is seeing Michael now and that Lucious has met him twice.

Jamal was surprised to get his call. Lucious wants this to be the last time they have this conversation. He believes Jamal's sexuality is a choice. Jamal knows this argument well. Lucious believes he is trying to help his son. Jamal wants Lucius to get to know him. Lucious believes he knows his son better than Jamal knows himself.

52. INT. LYON RESIDENCE – PHILADELPHIA – NIGHT – FLASHBACK – ~17 YEARS AGO (21:33–24:42)
The extended family has gathered. Bunkie and his wife/girlfriend and Vernon and his wife sit in the living room chatting.

Lucious and Cookie sit at the dining room table eating and talking about his new album. Lucious holds baby Hakeem in his lap. Cookie wants Lucious' voice to be higher in the mix. Lucious wants to eat. He hands Hakeem to Cookie so he can eat more.

ANOTHER ROOM – Eight-year-old Jamal steps into pink heels.

Jamal enters the living room wearing the heels and a scarf on his head. The adults disapprove. Lucious sees his son wearing women's clothing and flies off the handle. He rushes into the living room and picks up Jamal. Cookie hands Hakeem off and runs after Lucious, who is out the back door.

53. INT. HOSPITAL – MRI – DAY (24:43–25:55)
Lucious slides into the MRI machine. As he does, the machine fills with light.

> *Note: This Lucious-and-Jamal sequence plays an important role in the series and the pilot. Lucious' opinion about Jamal's sexuality blinds him. Here we see the sequence from Lucious' point of view. He feels he is trying to help his son. He believes homosexuality is a choice. He feels like he knows his son better than his son knows himself, which makes the audience wonder if Lucious has fought homosexual feelings him-*

self. Lucious also sees his life slipping away. He realizes he has limited time to help Jamal.

END OF ACT TWO

ACT THREE

54. INT. ANDRE'S HOUSE – STAIRWAY – DAY (24:57–25:01)
Rhonda pads down the stairs with a glass of water.

55. INT. ANDRE'S HOUSE – BEDROOM – DAY (25:02–26:16)
Andre is in bed reading and moping. Rhonda dances seductively at the end of the bed, but this doesn't cheer him up. She goes to the bedside and hands him the glass of water and some pills. He takes the pills. *What are they for?* As Rhonda gets into bed with him, he slaps her butt. Andre has softened a bit. They resume reading their magazines and newspaper.

Andre is sure Lucious will leave everything to Hakeem and Jamal won't object because he is too passive. Rhonda wonders what would happen if Jamal did object. What if Jamal made a play for the company and Andre's two brothers went to war? Andre might just be the last man standing.

Andre likes this idea. He warms further as Rhonda straddles him and takes off her shirt.

56. INT. COOKIE'S APARTMENT – DAY (26:17– 27:16)
Cookie lies on the floor on her unfurnished apartment. Pounding on the door alerts her. She grabs her gun and goes to the door. It's Andre. She hides the gun and lets him in. They apologize for past hurts and hug. However, Andre has ulterior motives.

57. INT. COOKIE'S APARTMENT – NIGHT (27:17–28:14)
Cookie and Andre sit in front of the fire having a drink. Cookie wants to know why Andre married that white woman. Andre says Rhonda is brilliant. Cookie doesn't approve, but she thanks him for helping her with her apartment.

Andre wants to know if Cookie has ever thought about managing Jamal. Yes, Cookie wants to manage Jamal. She wanted to be head of A&R, but Lucious blocked her. Andre thinks Jamal could be a star, which would position him to be head of the company. Cookie is skeptical. Andre wants the company, but Andre isn't a star so Lucious won't give it to him. Andre connives with his mother to get what they both want.

58. INT. EMPIRE ENTERTAINMENT – CONFERENCE ROOM – DAY (28:15–28:48)
Lucious is holding a board meeting when Cookie comes in and wants to be thanked on this historic occasion. Vernon tries to head her off, but Cookie shuts him down and walks right past him. Lucious asks everyone to excuse them. Andre continues the meeting in his father's absence.

Figure 4.18: *Empire* pilot hero succeeds—almost.

59. INT. EMPIRE ENTERTAINMENT – LUCIOUS' OFFICE – DAY (28:49–30:27)
Lucious meets with Cookie. Vernon is also there. Lucious wants to know what Cookie wants. Cookie wants Jamal. Lucious says she can't have him. Cookie threatens to tell the SEC that she was the first investor in Empire Entertainment with $400,000 in drug money. She knows if the SEC found out about the drug money, Lucious' application for an IPO would be denied. Lucious looks at Vernon, who shrugs. Yep, that's the truth. Lucious wants to know why Cookie is doing this. Cookie wants what is hers. She wants Jamal. Lucious looks to Vernon, who nods. Lucious agrees and says that he never wanted Jamal anyway. Cookie says that she knows.

60. INT. BUSHWICK COFFEE HOUSE – BASEMENT – NIGHT (30:28–30:36)
Jamal plays a soulful song about giving everything, but it still isn't enough.

61. INT. PRISON – VISITATION WAITING ROOM – DAY – FLASHBACK – ~17 YEARS AGO (30:37–30:39)
Young Jamal and a younger Lucious wait together. As Jamal gets up, Lucious grabs his arm. Lucious warns him not to come back crying.

62. INT. BUSHWICK COFFEE HOUSE – BASEMENT – RESUME (30:40–30:41)
Jamal continues to sing, putting his soul into the song.

63. INT. LYON RESIDENCE – PHILADELPHIA – NIGHT – FLASHBACK – ~17 YEARS AGO (30:41–30:46)
Jamal comes down the stairs in the pink heels.

64. INT. BUSHWICK COFFEE HOUSE – BASEMENT – RESUME (30:47–30:48)
As Jamal sings, he fills in his side of the flashback story, his misunderstood motivations.

65. INT. LYON RESIDENCE – PHILADELPHIA – NIGHT – FLASHBACK – ~17 YEARS AGO (30:49–30:56)
Young Jamal clomps into the living room wearing the pink heels and head scarf. Jamal's song reveals he wanted to make people smile, though no one did. Quite the opposite. Lucious rushes from the dining room at the sight.

66. INT. BUSHWICK COFFEE HOUSE – BASEMENT – RESUME (30:57–31:32)
Jamal sings that he just wants to be noticed. He just wants to be good enough. But someone keeps making him jump through hoops. Cookie looks on, impressed with her boy's talent. Becky and Michael watch, grooving in their seats.

It's clear. Jamal has talent.

67. EXT. LYON RESIDENCE – PHILADELPHIA – RESUME – FLASHBACK – ~17 YEARS AGO (31:33–31:36)
Lucious rushes out of the house carrying young Jamal. Young Jamal pleads with his father to stop.

68. INT. BUSHWICK COFFEE HOUSE – BASEMENT – RESUME (31:37–31:38)
Young Jamal's pleas play over Jamal's song.

69. EXT. LYON RESIDENCE – PHILADELPHIA – RESUME – FLASHBACK – ~17 YEARS AGO (31:39–31:39)
Lucious snatches the lid off the garbage can. He puts young Jamal into the garbage can.

70. INT. BUSHWICK COFFEE HOUSE - BASEMENT - RESUME (31:40–31:42)
Jamal builds to his ending. Young Jamal's pleas collide with adult Jamal's voice. Jamal's past pain fuels his current passion, his art.

71. EXT. LYON RESIDENCE - PHILADELPHIA - RESUME - FLASHBACK - ~17 YEARS AGO (31:43–31:44)
Cookie hurries out of the house, coming to her son's rescue.

72. INT. BUSHWICK COFFEE HOUSE - BASEMENT - RESUME (31:45–31:48)
Cookie watches as her son takes center stage and owns it.

73. EXT. LYON RESIDENCE - PHILADELPHIA - RESUME - FLASHBACK - ~17 YEARS AGO (31:49–31:52)
Cookie beats on Lucious with a mother's fury.

74. INT. BUSHWICK COFFEE HOUSE - BASEMENT - RESUME (31:53–31:56)
Jamal sings with a new anger.

75. EXT. LYON RESIDENCE - PHILADELPHIA - RESUME - FLASHBACK - ~17 YEARS AGO (31:57–32:01)
Cookie retrieves her baby from the trash can. She picks him up. Jamal clings to her. Cookie doesn't care that he has a scarf on his head. She doesn't care that he's different. This is her son. She loves him as a mother should.

76. INT. BUSHWICK COFFEE HOUSE - BASEMENT - RESUME (32:02–32:03)
Jamal stands tall.

77. EXT. LYON RESIDENCE - PHILADELPHIA - RESUME - FLASHBACK - ~17 YEARS AGO (32:04–32:07)

Pissed, upset, Cookie holds tight to her son. She kicks out at Lucious, who easily dodges her attack. Cookie marches up the back steps, taking her son back inside where he belongs.

78. INT. BUSHWICK COFFEE HOUSE – BASEMENT – RESUME (32:08–32:09)
Jamal reaches up and sings that he wishes he had longer arms. No matter how much love he has from his mother, he'll always wants his father's love.

79. EXT. LYON RESIDENCE – PHILADELPHIA – RESUME – FLASHBACK – ~17 YEARS AGO (32:10–32:15)
Breathless, Lucious stands in the aftermath of this incident. He walks away.

80. INT. BUSHWICK COFFEE HOUSE – BASEMENT – RESUME (32:16–32:38)
Jamal sings that he will never be big enough to pay his father's dues. Jamal just wants someone to look at him and see he can be someone to love.

Cookie watches, convinced more than ever that Jamal needs her. Becky makes a heart with her hands. Jamal sees Michael with her in the audience.

81. INT. EMPIRE ENTERTAINMENT – LUCIOUS' OFFICE – EARLIER (32:39–32:41)
Lucious watches Cookie leave after her parting shot. She knew Lucious never wanted Jamal. This wounds Lucious more than he can say.
Hero succeeds—almost

> *Note: Here we see the Lucious and Jamal flashback sequence from Jamal's perspective. We hear Jamal sing that he wants his father's*

approval. He wanted to bring a smile to people's faces. It's heartbreaking. The heartbreak makes Jamal's performance beautiful. It's the struggle that makes Jamal's music resonate with the audience.

Lee and Danny use the intercutting technique again to bridge the present with the past. We spend about a minute and 10 seconds intercutting. This is a great way for music to inform the story as well as connect the characters to their music.

We saw how the female vocalist in the teaser could tap into her sorrow and connect with a lyric. We see Jamal knows how to do this on his own, without Lucious directing him (at least consciously).

We also see that Lucious' failure wounds him greatly. Cookie's parting shot that Lucious didn't want Jamal stabs Lucious in the heart. The truth hurts. And it's a truth Jamal has known all of his life. Now he pours the truth into his music. I write more on this moment in the Empire *wrap-up.*

82. INT. BUSHWICK COFFEE HOUSE – BASEMENT – RESUME (32:42–32:59)

Jamal finishes his song to a big round of applause, as big as a coffee house can offer him. Michael and Becky cheer. Cookie smiles, proud. Jamal smiles humbly.

Note: The building of Jamal's song and his talent can overshadow the hero succeeds—almost moment. Lucious' story is the A storyline. He succeeds in getting Cookie off his back, and he tries to make it look like he didn't lose anything. However, the hurt in Lucious' eyes when Cookie tells him that she knows Lucious never wanted Jamal tells us he lost this round. Plus, our knowledge of Jamal's talent lets us know just how much Lucious lost, even if Lucious can't see it himself.

END OF ACT THREE

ACT FOUR

83. INT. BUSHWICK COFFEE HOUSE – BASEMENT – NIGHT (33:02–34:00)

Cookie wants Jamal to know that he got it all—all the talent. He should be showing the world. Jamal feels like he is, just one room at a time. Cookie thinks he should be selling out stadiums and he will.

ANGLE ON – Becky wants to know about Cookie. Michael says Cookie seems genuine. Becky reminds Michael that Cookie just got out of prison.

ANGLE ON – Jamal feels like touring and albums mess with the purity of the art. Cookie tells him he's so pure only a couple hundred white kids in Brooklyn and San Francisco know his work. Jamal says he's not the touring and album guy, but he loves her. She loves him, too. She tells him to go over with his friends. After he leaves, she calls him a stupid sissy under her breath.

84. INT. LEVITICUS CLUB – NIGHT (34:01–34:53)
Hakeem and Jamal have a drink. Hakeem wants to know if Jamal has seen Cookie. Jamal says Cookie wants to manage his career. Hakeem says with Lucious managing his career and Cookie managing Jamal's, they're going to want the brothers to tear each other apart. Jamal promises that will never happen. Hakeem wants to keep drinking. Jamal thinks he should go home because Hakeem is recording tomorrow. Hakeem assures Jamal this is all part of his process.

85. INT. RECORDING STUDIO – MIXING BOOTH – DAY (34:54–36:05)
Lucious watches as Hakeem crashes and burns in the recording studio. It's painful to witness.

86. INT. RECORDING STUDIO – SAME (36:06–35:17)
Hakeem asks to run it back so he can do it again. The engineer marks it as take 37. Hakeem blows up. The music begins and he raps. It's not better.

87. INT. RECORDING STUDIO – MIXING BOOTH – SAME (35:18–35:23)
Andre notes Hakeem is hung over again. Lucious gets angrier by the second.

88. INT. RECORDING STUDIO – SAME (35:24–35:27)
Hakeem stops and asks for the next word.

89. INT. RECORDING STUDIO – MIXING BOOTH – SAME (35:28–35:42)
Lucious tells Hakeem the word is Hakeem is a disappointment and Hakeem is wasting his time. Lucious walks out.

90. INT. RECORDING STUDIO – SAME (35:43–35:44)
Hakeem throws his headphones and says the song is wack. Lucious tells him to shut up.

91. INT. BUSHWICK COFFEE HOUSE – BASEMENT – NIGHT (35:45–35:51)
Hakeem goes to Jamal, who is packing up his gear after performing. Hakeem wants Jamal's help.

92. INT. BUSHWICK COFFEE HOUSE – BASEMENT – LATER (35:51–36:57)
Jamal listens to the song Hakeem recorded. Jamal feels like Hakeem's rap is hot, but Lucious' song is wack. Hakeem says that after Lucious asked him to cut an album, Hakeem has lost his confidence. Jamal asks Hakeem if he wants to be dad. Hakeem doesn't. Jamal turns to his keyboard and starts playing. Hakeem feels it. He starts rapping. He thinks that's hot. Jamal tells Hakeem to lay that down for dad and he'll be fine. Jamal says he'll get the band to hook them up. Hakeem is thrilled.

93. INT. LUCIOUS' MANSION – FOYER – NIGHT (36:58–38:03)
Bunkie knocks on the door. Lucious answers. It's late. They move into the...

...LIVING ROOM.
Bunkie wants Lucious to give him three million dollars. Lucious won't give him three nickels. Bunkie threatens to reveal Lucious killed four drug dealers back in the day. Bunkie pulls a gun out and tells Lucious that he will light a match and burn this bitch to the ground. Bunkie wants what's his.

END OF ACT FOUR

ACT FIVE

Figure 4.19: *Empire* pilot emotional squeeze.

94. INT. RECORDING STUDIO – DAY (38:06–38:32)
Hakeem tears it up. He's energized. He's loving it. This is the song he and Jamal wrote and it's hot. Lucious watches in the mixing booth. Jamal watches, too, and grooves.

95. INT. RECORDING STUDIO – MIXING BOOTH – SAME (38:32–38:33)
Lucious gets up. Andre and Anika are there as well.

96. INT. RECORDING STUDIO – SAME (38:34–38:36)
Hakeem is on top of it. He points to Jamal when he says "prince of America."

97. INT. RECORDING STUDIO – MIXING BOOTH – SAME (38:37–38:39)
Jamal smiles as his brother gives him props. Jamal is genuinely proud of Hakeem.

98. INT. RECORDING STUDIO – SAME (38:40–38:44)
Lucious comes in and tells Hakeem that he is beautiful.

99. INT. RECORDING STUDIO – MIXING BOOTH – SAME (38:45–38:46)
Jamal smiles. He is thrilled his brother nailed it and his father loved it. This is all Jamal wants. He'll be happy to be in the background, assisting, if his father is pleased.

100. INT. RECORDING STUDIO – SAME (38:47–38:51)
Hakeem points to Jamal and tells his father that his brother helped him. Lucious turns an eye on Jamal. "Did he?" There is something in his tone. Is it suspicion? Reproach? Skepticism?

101. INT. RECORDING STUDIO – MIXING BOOTH – SAME (38:52–38:54)
Jamal sees the look and hears the tone. His smile fades. He is not his father's favorite son. He is the son his father threw in the garbage can.

102. INT. RECORDING STUDIO – SAME (38:55–39:02)
Lucious turns his gaze on Hakeem. He is again adoring. He tells Hakeem that Hakeem created this song by himself. Lucious believes it's that monster inside Hakeem, that genius, that made this song. Hakeem eats it up.

103. INT. RECORDING STUDIO – MIXING BOOTH – SAME (39:03–39:08)
Jamal listens as his father denies his contribution, as his father gives his brother undeserved accolades. Jamal leaves.
Emotional squeeze

> *Note: You'll notice the long list of intercuts for the Hakeem recording studio scene. However, the scene itself only lasts about a minute, from 38:06–39:08. Here Lucious sees Hakeem perform better with the help of his less-favored son, Jamal. The pressures of his own prejudices, his perceived societal prejudices, his desire for Hakeem to take over the company, his desire for Empire to succeed after his death, and his undisclosed disease weigh on him. Lucious must choose between these two sons. He must choose whether to acknowledge Jamal's contribution or attribute Hakeem's performance to Hakeem's talent. Lucious chooses Hakeem.*

104. INT. COOKIE'S APARTMENT – DAY (39:09–39:38)
There's a knock on the door. Cookie answers it. It's Jamal. He tells her that she wins. He'll do this for her, but he wants to do this as him. Cookie loves it. Not only is Lucious' son a genius; he's gay, too. Cookie wants to make the gay angle all about Lucious not accepting Jamal and the talent all about Jamal. Jamal wants to come out.

105. INT. PATIENT EXAM ROOM – DAY (39:39–40:06)
The DOCTOR tells Lucious she has bad news. Lucious has ALS. He wants to know how long he has. The doctor tells him three years—maybe more, most likely less.

106. INT. CAR - PHILADELPHIA - DAY - FLASHBACK - ~17 YEARS AGO (40:07–41:04)
Cookie gets into the car. Lucious is in the driver's seat. Cookie has a pocketbook full of money—$10K. She says something felt off about that deal. Lucious tells her she is imagining things. But Cookie knows something felt off. She wants Lucious to promise her if she goes down that he'll keep playing. Lucious tells her nothing is going to happen to her, nothing is going to tear his family apart. Young Andre is sitting in the back seat.

> *Note: Lee and Danny have cleverly connected Lucious receiving bad health news and a death sentence to Cookie coming back from a drug deal that didn't feel right. We can surmise this was the drug deal that landed Cookie in prison, so she got a sentence as well. Pairing these scenes gives them more resonance.*
>
> *While some think of the end of the second act as the all-hope-is-lost moment, it's actually the moment where the main character is pressured emotionally. Often, he must make a choice between two bad options. This is the emotional squeeze.*
>
> *Here, Lucious is told he has ALS—a motor neuron disease that paralyses your body while leaving your mind intact. It's a horrible, incurable disease. One could see this as the deepest, darkest moment. However, the emotional squeeze involves your main character being pressured by external and internal forces. It also involves a difficult decision. Receiving bad news is bad, but it's the* decision *that goes along with it that makes it interesting to a character.*
>
> *When Lucious receives this bad news, he does not have to make a decision in the scene. What's more, we've already seen his resulting decision—he is going to make his sons compete for control of Empire Entertainment. Thus, getting the news about his disease is not Lucious' emotional squeeze. Lucious makes a difficult decision between two of his sons. He chooses Hakeem over Jamal, which may be his undoing.*

107. INT. EMPIRE ENTERTAINMENT – CONFERENCE ROOM – DAY (41:05–41:23)
Lucious sits at the head of the table. He's wearing sunglasses, perhaps to hide his eyes. Cookie sits at the other end of the table. An ATTORNEY tells her that after she signs the contract for the right to manage Jamal, she cannot disclose she was the initial investor with $400,000. Cookie happily signs the document.

108. INT. EMPIRE ENTERTAINMENT – ADJACENT TO CONFERENCE ROOM – SAME (41:24–41:38)
Vernon and Andre stand outside the conference room watching as Cookie signs the contract. Vernon believes Andre is the only one who could truly run this company. Vernon wants Andre to remember him when he is in charge. Andre says he could never forget Uncle Vernon.

109. INT. EMPIRE ENTERTAINMENT – LUCIOUS' OFFICE – DAY (41:39–42:01)
Vernon shows Lucious photos of Bunkie and SHYNE JOHNSON, a crime lord. Vernon says Bunkie owes Johnson $150K. He's dangerous. He's not going to be easy to make go away.

Figure 4.20: *Empire* pilot the hero succeeds.

Figure 4.21: *Empire* pilot the hero succeeds.

110. EXT. BENEATH BRIDGE – BRONX – NIGHT (42:02–43:35)
Bunkie stops to take a piss in the water. Lucious comes up behind him, scares him. Lucious shows Bunkie one of the photos. Bunkie calls Lucious a sell-out. Bunkie wants his money. Lucious tells him that they have been friends since they were 14 years old. He says he never lets anything come between friendship, except a bullet. Lucious shoots Bunkie right between the eyes.

Bunkie's body splashes into the river. Lucious dispassionately turns and walks away.
Hero succeeds

111. INT. YACHT – LUCIOUS' OFFICE – NIGHT (43:36–43:22)
Cookie and Lucious share a moment. It's easy to see the relationship they had. They have an honesty, a realness with each other. Lucious wants Cookie to hear Hakeem's new song. Cookie admits it's gonna be a big fat hit, but she will make Jamal a star. Lucious wants to know why Cookie is doing this. She isn't embarrassed by Jamal. Lucious can't believe it. Cookie says she wants to show him a homosexual can run this company. She leaves Lucious with that thought.

Figure 4.22: *Empire* pilot the hero's new life.

112. INT. YACHT – NEW YORK BAY – DAY (43:23–46:13)
Lucious descends the grand staircase to a packed boat. He toasts Cookie Lyon, welcoming her back. He calls her the heart and soul of Empire Entertainment. He also announces that both of his sons, Hakeem and Jamal, will release albums this year. People clap and cheer. Hakeem, Jamal, Michael, Cookie, and Lucious put on their battle faces.

To the EMPIRE!
Hero's new life

END OF PILOT

While *Empire* is not a perfectly structured TV episode, it accomplishes the vital task of audience participation. It draws the audience into the character's lives and creates interest, sympathy, and empathy for these characters. In the hands of less talented writers, the pilot could have become a mess. However, Lee Daniels and Danny Strong are very talented writers. They've had successful, lauded, and varied writing careers.[46] And they know character. They know character-driven content engages the audience, which is what you want. You want your work to affect the audience. They're very clear on their character wants, and because of this, they maintain story drive throughout the pilot.

The pilot hits all the landmarks of character-driven structure. While there are some timing issues with the landmarks, it's important to remember character-driven structure isn't a formula. It's fluid. It bends. If you create three-dimensional characters and stay on their wants, your episode likely will work. Let's take a look at the character-driven landmark scenes and the structure of *Empire*'s pilot.

The **point of attack**, the first whiff of the problem, happens in the teaser. We're with Lucious Lyon as he listens to a vocalist record her song. At first blush, she's fantastic. However, Lucious is distracted. We flash back to him at the doctor's office. He gets bad news. While we don't know what this news is, we know it's likely a death sentence—Lucious has instructed the vocalist to sing like she is going to die tomorrow. Finally, Lucious goes into the studio and talks with the vocalist. He chooses a particularly painful memory from her past and directs her to tap into her sorrow. The vocalist does. Her voice is transcendent. She surpasses her past attempts. Lucious is pleased. He's created an enduring vocal. He wants to make his mark on this world through music, and perhaps his time is limited. More important than himself is the music, the company, the empire.

Soon after the teaser comes the **hero committed** scene. It comes early in the show, around the seven-minute mark. Here Lucious has gathered his three sons—Andre, Jamal, and Hakeem. He tells them that for the next few months he is going to groom one of them to take over the company. Andre, the eldest, is stunned. He has dedicated his life to the business. He worked in the company as a teen and went to college and grad school for business. He's the most prepared for this opportunity. Jamal, the middle son, jokes that they are King Lear now. A talented artist, Jamal has a mark against him. He is gay and his father doesn't approve of him. Hakeem, the youngest and Lucious' favorite, has little response. Selfish and spoiled, he is more focused on his own interests, whatever they may be at the moment. Lucious tells them nothing and no one will tear down the business. This is Lucious' mission. He wants to keep the business going after his death. He wants it to continue to succeed. He has to make the right choice.

In the next scene, Lucious' ex-wife, Cookie Lyon, gets out of prison early. She has served 17 years of her 30-year sentence, for what exactly we don't know. Here there's a bit of coincidence at play. Cookie gets out at precisely the time Lucious makes his announcement he will be naming a successor. She gets out when the empire is up for grabs. However, we are wowed by Cookie and Taraji P. Henson's performance. We're willing to overlook this coincidence and suspend our disbelief because the character work is so good and the rest of the show feels plausible.

The **hero succeeds—almost** moment doesn't come for another 20 minutes or so. At about the 29-minute mark, Cookie confronts Lucious. At Andre's suggestion, she wants to manage Jamal's career. Lucious refuses. Cookie says she'll reveal to the SEC that she was the first investor in Empire Entertainment with $400,000 of drug money. She believes Lucious' application for an IPO will be rejected if this news comes out. Cookie has just threatened Lucious and the company. Lucious concedes. Cookie can have Jamal. Lucious says he never wanted Jamal anyway. Cookie tells him that she knows.

Cookie's parting shot stabs Lucious in the heart. While Lucious has succeed as a businessman, he has failed as a father. In the next scene, Jamal performs at a coffee house. His lyrics tell his story as we flash back to his childhood. We see Lucious reject young Jamal and put him in a garbage can because young Jamal has put on his mother's shoes and scarf. Cookie rushes to Jamal's rescue, pushing Lucious away from her baby boy.

When Lucious concedes Jamal's management rights—basically, custody—to Cookie, Lucious may have saved his company temporarily. But he may have sunk it in the long run because Jamal is far more talented than Hakeem, Lucious' chosen one. Jamal is smarter, and he has a better work ethic. Lucious has been outmaneuvered by his ex-wife and eldest son. While he said no one and nothing is going to tear down his company, Lucious himself may be the biggest threat to his company.

The **emotional squeeze** occurs when Hakeem comes back into the recording studio and impresses his father with a new song. Previously, Hakeem had disappointed Lucious when Hakeem tried to perform new songs penned by Lucious himself. But now Lucious sees Hakeem can do this. He believes Hakeem has *it*. However, Hakeem admits Jamal helped him. We the audience know Jamal did more than help his brother; Jamal made this song possible for his brother. Lucious glances at Jamal, who is elated that his brother has done so well. All Jamal wants is a pat on the back from his father. He doesn't need the spotlight. He just wants his father's love. However, Lucious has already relinquished Jamal's management to Cookie. Lucious denies Jamal one iota of satisfaction. He turns back to his son and tells Hakeem that his talent did all of this. Hakeem doesn't correct him but rather bathes in his father's adoration. It's in this moment that Lucious sets his fate. Under the pressure of his own ego and prejudice, Lucious chooses his less-talented son over the son who could best helm his company.

The **hero succeeds** moment happens off the family story and focuses on Lucious' criminal past. Lucious defends himself, his company, and his legacy by shooting his longtime friend, Bunkie. A problem gambler, Bunkie blames Lucious for all of his problems. He believes Lucious is trying to keep him down and not giving Bunkie what he deserves. Bunkie has threatened Lucious with a gun as well as with the knowledge that Lucious killed four drug dealers back in the day. Bunkie is blackmailing Lucious for the money so Bunkie can allegedly pay off his gambling debt. But as Lucious notes, Bunkie would bet it instead of erasing his debt.

As Lucious stated earlier, nothing and no one will tear his company apart, and this includes a friend he has had for more than 20 years. Lucious succeeds in defending himself and his company. He has done what he needed to do. We the audience understand Lucious is ruthless.

At the end of the pilot, Lucious is on his yacht surrounded by his family and others. It's an echo of the teaser scene, which also happened on the yacht. Lucious wants to welcome Cookie back. He wants to announce his sons Hakeem and Jamal will both be releasing albums this year. He wants to celebrate his empire, while he can. He raises a glass as do all of his guests. The battle lines have been drawn. This is the **hero's new life**—as he approaches his death.

* * *

Comedy

As I discussed in Chapter 2, comedy focuses on a combination of character traits within your cast. We're going to look at two sitcoms, *Modern Family* and *It's Always Sunny in Philadelphia.* One of these shows uses complementary character traits; the other takes advantage of negative character traits.

Modern Family focuses on complementary characters. These are characters with traits that complement other characters. *It's Always Sunny in Philadelphia* employs negative character traits to create comedy. Let's take a look at these very different but very successful shows.

Spoiler alert! Watch the *Modern Family* pilot, then come back to discover why this show works because of its character-driven structure.

Multiple Emmy-award winning *Modern Family* is a love letter to the families of creators Steven Levitan and Christopher Lloyd. After sharing some of their own families' stories, Steven and Christopher realized their lives could be the basis of a series.[47] This is important to understand as a creator because *Modern Family* is a symphony of *complementary characters.*

All the characters come from a loving place. There are no bad guys. The focus isn't on negative or bad character traits. This isn't *All in the Family.* Jay Pritchett isn't an Archie Bunker-type, even though they are approximately the same ages during their shows. At the beginning of the show, Jay Pritchett isn't comfortable with the gay lifestyle, but he's not un-accepting. He is willing to change. He loves his son. He loves his granddaughter. Over the course of the show, he grows to love his son's future husband and discover they have a lot in common. Finding common ground is the thematic thrust of this show. It's about evolving and changing to get along with your family, as well as realizing that no matter what happens, your family will always love you.

This isn't a dysfunctional family comedy like *Arrested Development.* The characters don't have bizarre, idiosyncratic issues. Rather, *Modern Family* is a *functional* family comedy. The families represent your average American family. In fact, the original title was *My American Family,* though *Modern Family* has a better ring to it. Making *Modern Family* a functional family comedy gave it universal appeal, great ratings, and critical acclaim. The show's success relies not only on the lovely performances by the cast, but also on the creation of the characters by Steven and Christopher. They brilliantly constructed these characters so the audience 1) believes these characters are a family and 2) sets these characters up for comedy while never making them mean-spirited or nasty.

When you're creating characters who are supposed to be related, it's vital to create the emotional logic that formed the characters. In other words, you need to make the audience believe these parents raised these children. *Modern Family* does this like a boss. Claire, an uptight suburban mother and former rebel, and Phil, the goofy dad who wants to be his kids' pal, have three children. Haley is a bit like her mother was when Claire was a teen—pretty, social, not super-smart, and a bit wild. Alex is a bit like her mother is now—a worrier, planner, super-student. Luke is a lot like his dad—goofy, playful, not terribly bright but surprisingly talented. When the audience looks at the Dunphy family, they make sense. Claire and Mitchell are both uptight and strivers. However, Mitchell went to law school and Claire, the rebel, got pregnant and had to quit college. Still, Mitchell, the younger brother, has more insecurities and is more emotionally reserved than Claire. Claire and Mitchell make sense together as siblings. And they make sense as children of Jay. Jay, the gruff father, doesn't always demonstrate his feelings. He's a successful businessman who recently remarried a feisty, younger wife.

I've already mentioned the various complementary character traits among the *Modern Family* characters. The comedy comes from their different approaches to life and their strong wants. The stronger the want, the funnier the scene. What's more, you can pair almost any combination of characters on *Modern Family* and find the comedy because the characters are so well-defined. Cam and Gloria are often paired up, as are Luke and Manny, Mitchell and Jay, Cam and Jay, Claire and Gloria. Let's take a look at the pilot for *Modern Family.*

Modern Family "Pilot" script by Steven Levitan and Christopher Lloyd; breakdown by Kam Miller

ACT ONE

1. EXT. DUNPHY HOUSE – DAY – ESTABLISHING (00:00–00:03)
Camera pushes in on an average American home, maybe like yours.

2. INT. DUNPHY HOUSE – KITCHEN – DAY (00:04–00:48)
Maneuvering around the refrigerator, CLAIRE DUNPHY (late 30s, uptight suburban mother who is constantly trying to keep all the plates spinning) yells up to the kids to come down for breakfast. Checked out,

PHIL DUNPHY (late 30s, goofy father who wants to be his kids' best friend) fiddles with his cell phone. HALEY (16, social, more concerned with fashion than her future) strolls in, fiddling with her cell phone. Haley's wearing a short mini-skirt. Claire tells her she can't wear it. Haley blandly protests. Claire asks Phil to pipe up. Looking up from his phone, Phil tells Haley her skirt is cute. *Thank you!*

Claire rolls her eyes. ALEX (13, smart, sarcastic, over-achiever) enters, dressed appropriately and tells her parents that Luke, their son, has gotten his head stuck in the bannister—again. Phil's on top of it. Where's the baby oil? Claire starts to remind him it's in the bedside table but notices the camera and stops herself.

> *Note: Comedy scenes tend to be quick because sitcoms are only 22 minutes long. The first scene of* Modern Family *introduces four characters and takes only 44 seconds. Whew!*

Figure 4.23: *Modern Family* pilot point of attack.

3. INT. DUNPHY HOUSE – LIVING ROOM – DAY– INTERVIEW (00:49–01:08)

Claire and Phil sit on the couch and talk to the camera. Chyron reads: Phil & Claire, married 16 years.

Claire admits she was wild growing up. Claire just doesn't want their kids making the same bad mistakes she did. If Haley doesn't wake up naked on a beach in Florida, Claire has done her job. Phil chimes in, "Our job." Yes, Claire agrees; she will have done their job.
Point of attack

4. EXT. SOCCER FIELD – DAY (01:09–01:24)
Kids run around on the soccer field as parents cheer—yell, really—from the sidelines. One of the most vocal is GLORIA PRITCHETT (30s, Columbian, gorgeous, protective, hot tempered). Gloria yells for her son, MANNY, (pre-teen, precocious; what he lacks in athleticism he makes up for in romanticism) who is turning around in circles and chasing the ball—always one step behind. JAY PRITCHETT (60s, low-key, not very emotional, successful in business and apparently in love) reads a paper in a folding chair and barely watches the game. He tells his wife, Gloria, that Manny's team is 0 and 6, so she can bring it down a notch.

5. INT. JAY AND GLORIA PRITCHETT'S HOUSE – LIVING ROOM – DAY – INTERVIEW (01:25–01:43)
Jay and Gloria sit on the couch and talk to the camera. Chyron reads: Jay & Gloria, married six months

Gloria admits they are very different. Jay is from the city and she is from a small village. Jay is very successful. Gloria's village is very, very poor but very, very beautiful. She says her village is number one in all of north Columbia for...what's that word? Jay prompts, "Murders." Yes, the murders.

6. EXT. SOCCER FIELD – RESUME (01:44–02:27)
With that extra bit of information, Gloria's "enthusiasm" takes on a different note. She yells at Manny, encouraging him. However, Manny spies a pretty girl, BRENDA FELDMAN, on a bike. His focus is off the

field and the other team scores. One of the OTHER MOTHERS protests to the coach. She tells him to take Manny out. Gloria threatens to take the other mother out. Jay tries to intervene from his low seat. Gloria reminds the other mother that her kid spent the first half of the game with his hand in his pants.

SOCCER DAD (30s, handsome in a Hollywood hipster way) sidles up to Gloria and confesses he has wanted to tell that other mother off for the past six weeks. The dad introduces himself and remarks that Jay must be Gloria's dad. Jay wants to set the guy straight, right after he extricates himself from that damn folding chair.

Note: The substantive Gloria, Jay, and Manny scene is 44 seconds long, just like the first Dunphy scene.

7. EXT. AIRPORT – DAY – ESTABLISHING (02:28–02:29)
A commercial airplane waits at the gate.

8. INT. AIRPLANE – DAY (02:30–02:59)
MITCHELL PRITCHETT (mid-30s, emotionally reserved, lawyer) sits in his seat with LILY (baby girl, Asian). He talks baby talk to her. A FELLOW PASSENGER (woman, 70s, sweet) compliments Mitchell and makes funny noises at Lily. Mitchell says they adopted the baby from Vietnam. Another MAN PASSENGER (60s, nice) says Lily is an angel. He comments that Mitchell and his wife must be thrilled. About that time, CAMERON TUCKER (mid-30s, expressive, dramatic) arrives with the baby bag and snacks. As Cameron squeezes into his seat, the fellow passengers seem to disapprove. Mitchell notices.

9. INT. PRITCHETT–TUCKER HOUSE – DAY – INTERVIEW (03:00–03:16)
Mitchell and Cameron sit on chairs and talk to the camera. Chyron reads: Mitchell & Cameron. Mitchell says they have been together for five years and wanted a baby. They had initially asked one of their

lesbian friends to be a surrogate but—Cameron interrupts and says that they are already mean enough.

10. INT. AIRPLANE – RESUME (03:17–04:03)
Mitchell resents the disapproving looks they got when Cameron arrived. First, they're fawning all over Lily, then they've got to shop SkyMall. Mitchell wants to give the speech. Cameron tries to stop him. They are going to be stuck with these people for the next five hours. Mitchell agrees. He knows Cameron is right. Then a WOMAN comes down the aisle and says to her husband, "Look at that baby with those cream puffs." This sets Mitchell off!

Mitchell stands up to address all those who judge. *Love knows no race, creed, or gender. Shame on you, you small minded, ignorant...* Cameron interrupts Mitchell and shows him that Lily is playing with the cream puffs he bought as snacks. *Oh.* Mitchell sits down. Cameron stands and offers to pay for everyone's headsets.

> *Note: The substantive Mitchell and Cam scene lasts 45 seconds. As you can see, these scenes are quick.*

END OF ACT ONE

Pull out to titles (04:04–04:15)

ACT TWO

11. INT. DUNPHY HOUSE – FOYER – DAY (04:16–05:07)
Phil frees LUKE (10, goofy, dense, immature) from the staircase with baby oil. Haley tries to slip in that she is going to have a boy over today. She would appreciate her family not embarrassing her. Claire wants to know who this guy is. Luke wants to know if Haley is going to kiss him. Phil wants to charge the video camera. Kidding! Or is he? Hero committed

12. INT. DUNPHY HOUSE – KITCHEN – INTERVIEW (05:08–05:24)
Phil sits at the kitchen table and talks to the camera. He confides he's the cool dad. He surfs the web. He texts. He knows all the dance moves to *High School Musical.*

13. INT. DUNPHY HOUSE – LIVING ROOM – DAY – FLASHBACK (05:25–05:32)
Wearing a letter jacket, Phil sings and dances to "We're All in This Together." His children look on stunned and embarrassed.

14. EXT. DUNPHY HOUSE – DAY – ESTABLISHING (05:33–05:34)
Still an average American suburban home.

Figure 4.24: *Modern Family* pilot hero committed.

15. INT. DUNPHY HOUSE – LIVING ROOM – DAY (05:35–06:32)
Alex yells for her parents. She's upset. Luke follows her with an Airsoft gun in hand. Luke just shot her with a plastic pellet. Claire wants to know if Alex is okay. *No, the little bitch shot me!* Phil stifles a laugh. Luke swears it was an accident.

Claire chastises Phil for getting Luke the pellet gun. She wants Phil to reprimand Luke. Phil says, "Buddy, uncool." ***That's it. Oh no.***

Claire wants Phil to shoot Luke with the gun so Luke can understand what it feels like. That was their agreement when Phil got the pellet gun for Luke.

Luke fake cries. Claire calls him out on it. Luke immediately stops. Phil points out that Luke has a birthday party. Claire tells Phil he can shoot Luke afterward at 2PM. They negotiate a time to shoot Luke as they refer to the family calendar.
Hero committed

16. EXT. SOCCER FIELD – DAY (06:33–06:46)
Manny wants to quit soccer because it is a game for children. Gloria believes Manny would have stopped that goal if he hadn't been staring at that girl. Manny corrects Gloria. That was not a girl. She is a woman.

17. INT. JAY'S CAR – MOVING – DAY (06:47–07:41)
Gloria and Manny get into the car. Jay pulls out of the parking space. Jay wants to know why Gloria needed to blow up at that other mother. Jay believes she doesn't have to be so emotional. Gloria likes to live with the drama. Jay tries to get Manny on his side. Manny wants to declare his love for the 16-year-old. Jay is surrounded by emotional people.

Manny wants to go to the mall where the girl works, but first he must go home and get his white silk shirt. Permissive, Gloria agrees to let him do it, if it's what he really wants. Jay warns Manny that if he goes to the mall in his puffy white shirt and declares his love for the 16-year-old, he'll be hanging from the flagpole in his puffy white underwear.

Manny wants Jay to stop the car. Jay does. Manny leaps out. Gloria is upset with Jay for making Manny upset. Jay notes that Manny is not upset. Manny is picking flowers.

18. INT. JAY AND GLORIA PRITCHETT'S HOUSE – LIVING ROOM – DAY – INTERVIEW (07:42–08:04)
Gloria admits that Manny is very passionate like his father. She says her first husband was very handsome and very passionate. All they did was fight and make love, fight and make love, fight and make love. Jay's hearing this for the first time.

19. EXT. TUCKER-PRITCHETT HOUSE – DAY (08:05–08:15)
Mitchell and Cameron arrive home with Lily in a baby carrier.

20. INT. TUCKER-PRITCHETT HOUSE – CONTINUOUS (08:16–08:23)
Mitchell is worried about Lily. Lily was awake the entire flight and she's still awake. Mitchell wonders if Lily has been conditioned to only fall asleep if she feels a woman's shape because she has been at an all-women orphanage. Cameron agrees that it could be possible. Mitchell hands the baby to Cam, who wants to know what the hell this means.

21. INT. TUCKER-PRITCHETT HOUSE – DAY – INTERVIEW (08:24–08:33)
Cameron addresses the camera. He admits he has gained a few pounds while they were expecting the baby. He attributes this to a nesting response where the body retains nutrients.

22. INT. TUCKER-PRITCHETT HOUSE – PANTRY – NIGHT – FLASHBACK (08:34–08:41)
The green tint of a NIGHT VISION lens colors the screen. Cameron chows down on doughnuts in the dark. It's like a nature video of big cats

hunting at night. All the while, Cameron talks over and explains how you just can't fight your body.

23. INT. TUCKER-PRITCHETT HOUSE – RESUME – INTERVIEW (08:42–08:50)
Cameron side eyes Mitchell, who says under his breath, "I'm not saying anything." Cameron tells him that he is saying everything.

24. INT. TUCKER-PRITCHETT HOUSE – RESUME (08:51–10:17)
Cameron leads Mitchell into...

...LILY'S ROOM. Mitchell is stunned. Evidently, Cameron had friends decorate the nursery while they were gone. Andre painted a mural of Mitchell and Cam as angels on clouds wearing toga-like attire. It's hideous. Mitchell wonders if Andre can paint something else. He's upset, but Cameron senses it's about more than the painting.

Mitchell comes clean. He didn't tell his family about the adoption. Cameron knew this. He knew they would be judgmental. He knew it would be a big fight. Mitchell is so relieved Cameron understands. Of course Cam understands. Oh, and Cam invited Mitchell's family over for dinner. *WHAT!*

Cameron heads out to the LIVING ROOM. Mitchell follows with Lily in the carrier.

Mitchell wants to cancel. Cameron tells Mitchell that he is going to tell his family that they adopted a baby—tonight—because Mitchell has avoidance issues.

> *Note: The Mitchell and Cam storyline has fewer scenes than the other storylines, but at a minute and 30 seconds, this is one of the longer scenes. It gives the story and audience a moment to take a breath.*

25. EXT. DUNPHY HOUSE – DAY (10:18–10:21)
DYLAN (shaggy, unkempt, slacker—*awesome, just, awesome*) stands on the threshold. He rings the doorbell.

26. INT. DUNPHY HOUSE – FOYER – SAME (10:22–10:24)
Claire folds laundry. Dylan peers through the windows beside the door. At the sound of the doorbell, Haley yells down for nobody to answer it.

27. INT. DUNPHY HOUSE – HALEY AND ALEX'S BEDROOM – SAME (10:25–10:26)
Haley puts on some lip gloss as she yells that she'll answer the door. She tosses the gloss back into her room and rushes to the stairs.

28. INT. DUNPHY HOUSE – FOYER – RESUME (10:27–11:00)
Haley runs to the top of the stairs as Claire speed walks to the front door. Claire beats Haley to the door. She opens it and introduces herself to Dylan. He's tall. His voice is deep. *How old is this guy?* Haley intercepts Dylan, takes his hand and leads him upstairs. Claire grabs Dylan's sleeve and inquires about his schooling. He's still in high school. He's a senior. Immediately, Claire yells for Phil, who is putting on his sport coat for his house showing.

Claire introduces Phil to Dylan, who is a *senior* in high school. Under her breath, she tells Phil that he needs to scare Dylan.

Phil approaches Dylan, who is on the staircase above him. Phil says, "Let me look at this playa." Phil offers his fist to bump.

29. INT. DUNPHY HOUSE – KITCHEN – DAY – INTERVIEW (11:01–11:20)
Phil looks at the camera menacingly. Phil explains his eyes do all the work. What he says might be friendly, but his eyes say something different.

30. INT. DUNPHY HOUSE – FOYER – RESUME (11:21–11:42)
Phil and Dylan exchange "yo"s. Haley tries to end this moment. But Phil stops her. He climbs the steps and stands above Dylan, trying to get the upper hand. Phil tells Haley and Dylan to keep it real. Dylan has no idea what Phil means. Phil leans on the stair rail and slips on the baby oil. His back goes out.

31. INT. DUNPHY HOUSE – KITCHEN – RESUME – INTERVIEW (11:43–11:50)
Phil continues his litany of eyes vs. mouth communication. The mouth might say, "Where are you from originally?" while the eyes say, "I could defeat you in a physical confrontation."

Figure 4.25: *Modern Family* pilot hero succeeds—almost.

32. INT. DUNPHY HOUSE – FOYER – RESUME (11:51–12:11)
Dylan carries Phil into the... LIVING ROOM. He gently deposits Phil on the couch. Phil comments on Dylan's strength. Phil is lying on his side. Claire, Haley, and Dylan leave him there. Not realizing he is alone, Phil asks to be flipped on his back.
Hero succeeds—almost

END OF ACT TWO

ACT THREE

33. INT. MALL – DAY (12:13–14:08)
Now dressed in his white silk shirt, Manny jogs up the stairs carrying flowers and a sheet of paper. He sees BRENDA FELDMAN (16, bored) standing at the FOTO FUN kiosk. Gloria asks what is on the paper. It's a poem Manny has written for Brenda Feldman. Jay sees catastrophe ahead. Jay offers Manny 50 bucks not to do this. Manny comments that he is 11 years old, what is he going to do with money? Jay wants to know what Manny is going to do with a 16-year-old. Manny is not deterred. He heads to the kiosk.

Gloria notices Jay's terrible mood. Jay attributes it to Manny's impending love declaration. Gloria thinks it's because the soccer dad thought Jay was her father. Gloria wants to buy Jay some younger clothes. Jay is wearing a velour track suit. Jay doesn't want new clothes. He doesn't care what other people think of him. He just doesn't want Manny make a fool of himself. Gloria tells Jay that he is Manny's family now, and he needs to be the wind at his back, not the spit in his face.

Manny returns. Brenda Feldman has a boyfriend. Manny gave her his heart, and Brenda gave him a photo of himself as an Old West sheriff. Manny admits it was stupid of him. Gloria says it was brave. She wants Jay to agree with her. Jay can't. He tells Manny that he'll know better next time.

34. INT. MALL – DIFFERENT LEVEL – MOMENTS LATER (14:09–14:26)
Jay walks determinedly. He's ahead of Gloria and Manny. The SECURITY GUARD stops Jay. The security guard asks that all mall walkers stay to the right. Jay has no idea what he is talking about. Jay looks to his

right and sees a bunch of OLD PEOPLE walking briskly in unison. They all wear velour track suits.

Jay looks to them, then looks at this own track suit. Jay marches into the store with a display for younger, hipper clothes.

> *Note: The Manny-love-proclamation and Jay-mall-walker scenes take a total of two minutes and 13 seconds. When you think about it, the whole production had to set up for these shots, pay a location fee to shoot at the Burbank Town Center, and be on location for probably a day. From that effort, they got 2 minutes and 13 seconds for the show.*
>
> *Here, Steven and Christopher killed two birds with one stone. They wrapped up the Manny wants to proclaim his love storyline and furthered the Jay wants to stay young for Gloria storyline in quick succession. Manny's willingness to make a fool of himself for Brenda Feldman helped inspire Jay to make a fool of himself for Gloria.*

35. INT. DUNPHY HOUSE – KITCHEN – DAY (14:27–15:09)
Claire uses the electric mixer to whip up some icing for a cake. OFF SCREEN, Haley yells at Alex, who is coming into the kitchen. Claire supports Haley and tells Alex she needs to respect her sister's privacy.

After a couple of beats, Claire asks Alex what Haley and Dylan are doing up in the bedroom. Alex says they're doing nothing, just lying on the bed watching a movie. Claire absorbs this information.

Alex asks Claire if Haley ever got pregnant would she pretend like Haley got mono for a few months, then pretend the baby was Claire's. Claire is taken aback.

36. EXT. DUNPHY HOUSE – BACKYARD – DAY (15:10–15:26)
Psyching himself up, Phil marches into the backyard with the Airsoft gun in hand. He faces Luke, who is wearing a parka, safety goggles, two

hats, and six pairs of underwear. Phil tells him to shed the jacket and one of the hats.

37. INT. DUNPHY HOUSE – KITCHEN – RESUME (15:27–15:48)
Alex continues to spin a tale about having a fake baby brother or sister who's really her niece or nephew. Claire calls her on it. She tells Alex that she knows Alex likes to cause trouble for her sister, but it's not going to work. Haley is a good girl, just like Claire used to... Claire quickly leaves the kitchen.

38. EXT. DUNPHY HOUSE – BACKYARD – RESUME (15:49–16:06)
Phil wants to make this a teachable moment. As Phil aims the gun, he assures Luke that he won't enjoy shooting him. Luke asks Phil why he is smiling. This gives Phil pause. He is smiling, or he was.

39. INT. DUNPHY HOUSE – STAIRS – MOMENTS LATER (16:07–16:11)
Carrying folded laundry, Claire climbs the stairs. She thuds her feet on each riser. At the top of the stairs, Claire pauses at the closed bedroom door.

Figure 4.26: *Modern Family* pilot emotional squeeze.

40. EXT. DUNPHY HOUSE – BACKYARD – RESUME (16:12–16:24)
Phil aims the pellet gun at Luke. Luke cringes, waiting to be stung by the projectile. Phil tries to find a place to shoot Luke, but he can't. He can't shoot his son. Luke is scared. Phil thinks Luke has learned his lesson. As Phil is talking, he accidentally fires. A pellet hits Luke in the arm. Luke yelps.

Figure 4.27: *Modern Family* pilot emotional squeeze.

41. INT. DUNPHY HOUSE – UPSTAIRS LANDING – RESUME (16:25–16:55)
Claire gets up enough guts to open the door and bustles into...

...HALEY AND ALEX'S BEDROOM.

Dylan and Haley are, in fact, watching something on her laptop. Haley is upset her mother barged into her room. Claire says they're going to leave the door open because she has seen this show before. She has lived it. Haley is embarrassed by Claire's graphic description. Emotional squeeze

Figure 4.28: *Modern Family* pilot hero succeeds.

42. EXT. DUNPHY HOUSE – BACKYARD – RESUME (16:56–17:12)
Luke's arm is still stinging. Luke accuses Phil of hitting the bone. Phil tries to explain it was an accident. Haley comes out and complains about Claire. Dylan joins her on the deck. Phil accidentally shoots Dylan in the neck with a pellet. Frustrated with the Airsoft gun, Phil drops it on the lawn. It fires again and hits Phil in the shin. Now Phil is in pain, too.
Hero succeeds

> *Note: Steven and Christopher intercut between the Claire-wants-to-interrupt-Haley-and-Dylan and Phil-wants-to-shoot-Luke-with-a-pellet-gun storylines. This connects these two storylines and builds each to the big decisions—does Claire interrupt Haley and Dylan and does Phil shoot Luke?*
>
> *The scenes intercut for about 2 minutes and 45 seconds. This helps ratchet up the pacing. Then the scenes collide when Haley comes to Phil to complain about Claire and Phil inadvertently shoots Dylan with the Airsoft gun. The pacing and story momentum pull the viewer through the story. Plus, the jokes build through the sequence.*

END OF ACT THREE

ACT FOUR

43. INT. TUCKER–PRITCHETT HOUSE – DAY – INTERVIEW (17:16–17:36)
Mitchell and Cameron sit in chairs and talk to the camera. Mitchell complains that Jay still isn't comfortable with Mitchell's gay lifestyle. Mitchell believes Jay always announces himself before he comes into a room so he never has to catch Mitchell and Cameron kissing. Cam comments that he wishes *his* mother had that system. Mitchell taps Cam's arm and says "not now."

44. INT. TUCKER-PRITCHETT HOUSE – DAY (17:37–22:07)
Mitchell and Cam carry food dishes out to the table. Mitchell complains that he can't believe Cam did this to him. Cam tells him to get over it. It's a celebration. The doorbell rings. Mitchell dreads this whole thing. Cam says he is going to get Lily ready and he wants Mitchell to just come out and tell his family.

Worried, Mitchell goes to the door. The Dunphy family comes in. Claire has brought a cake and Phil hands Mitchell wine. Claire tells Mitchell that their dad is following right behind them. The doorbell rings several times in a row. Jay announces that they are coming in. Mitchell tells him that nothing gay is going on.

Jay comes in dressed in colorful, too youthful clothing. Gloria and Manny come in. Phil gives Gloria a nice hug. He compliments Gloria's dress. She says, "Thank you, Phil," but with her thick accent, it sounds like, "Thank you. Feel." Phil runs his hand over Gloria's side. Claire catches his hand and drags him away.

Jay asks about Mitchell and Cam's trip. Mitchell says it was good and he has something to tell them. Jay comments that if Cam comes out here with boobs, Jay is leaving. Claire reprimands Jay. Haley, texting on her phone, comments that she hopes Jay didn't embarrass her. Claire tells everyone not to mind Haley. Haley had her first boy over today and Phil shot him. Mitchell doesn't know what to say to that.

Mitchell tries to get his announcement on track. He explains that a year ago he and Cam had a longing for something more, like a baby. Jay cautions Mitchell that it's a bad idea. Mitchell wants to know what Jay means. Jay means—kids need a mother. He suggests that Mitchell and Cam get a dog. Gloria chimes in to say that she supports Mitchell, even though he is not her son. She looks pointedly at Jay.

Claire tries to defend her dad's stance. Mitchell is a little uptight. Kids bring chaos and Mitchell doesn't handle chaos well. Mitchell is rightly offended. He notes that's not what dad was saying; that's what Claire is saying. He is insulted in a whole different way.

Phil tries to get everyone to chillax. Alex wants to know where Uncle Cameron is. Mitchell thanks Alex for noticing Cam isn't here. Jay puts two and two together and gets the wrong answer. He thinks the big announcement is Mitchell and Cam are splitting up. Jay tells Mitchell a baby wouldn't help keep them together. And Mitchell is better off because Cam was a bit of a drama queen.

Mitchell has had enough. It's time for a speech. His family comes into his house and insults him and his boyfriend, who, by the way, isn't *that* dramatic.

Just then, the theme song to *The Lion King* starts playing and the lights dim. Mitchell has no idea what is going on. Cam enters wearing an orange satin robe and carrying Lily. He stalks into the room to the beat of the song. As the song builds to a crescendo, Cam lifts Lily into the air and a spotlight shines on her as if she were Simba.

Mitchell says, "We adopted a baby." Claire gasps, excited. Everyone but Jay gathers around to meet Lily. Jay interrupts. Everyone waits for the *faux pas* that's about to happen. But Jay tells Cam and Mitchell that he knows he said this was a bad idea, but what does he know. He didn't write the book on fatherhood. He's been trying all his life to get it right and he's still screwing it up. Right, Manny? Manny wrote a song about it in the car. Of course he did.

Jay misquotes Gloria's saying. She repeats it in Spanish and everyone is charmed although they can't speak Spanish. Jay goes to meet Lily.

Figure 4.29: *Modern Family* pilot hero's new life.

> *Note: The Mitchell-and-Cam house scene is the longest scene in the show. It runs four minutes and 30 seconds. The length of this scene gives it weight. It slows down the pacing. It pulls all of the characters together under one roof. The audience can see how the emotional logic from the other storylines affects Mitchell and Cam's big announcement.*

45. INT. JAY AND GLORIA PRITCHETT'S HOUSE – DAY – INTERVIEW (22:08–22:17)
Jay sits on the couch and addresses the camera. He is reading from a piece of paper. "I stand before you with only one agenda, to tell you that my heart is yours, Feldman, comma, Brenda." Jay belly laughs at Manny's love declaration.

END OF ACT FOUR

TAG

46. INT. DUNPHY HOUSE – KITCHEN – DAY – INTERVIEW (22:19–22:21)
Phil addresses the camera. He says that Luke hasn't beaten him in basketball yet.

47. EXT. DUNPHY HOUSE – BACKYARD – DAY (22:22–22:34)
Luke and Phil stand on a trampoline with a basketball goal attached to it. Luke has the ball. Luke shoots. Phil bounces on the trampoline and rejects the ball. In various shots, Phil uses the trampoline to dominate his much shorter son. Phil dunks the ball, but only because he's on a trampoline.

48. INT. DUNPHY HOUSE – KITCHEN – RESUME – INTERVIEW (22:35–22:42)
Phil promises that the day "if," "when," "if/when," Luke beats him, Phil will just tell him "well done."

49. EXT. DUNPHY HOUSE – BACKYARD – RESUME (22:43–22:46)
Phil rejects Luke's shot and the ball soars out of the trampoline enclosure. Phil struts around the tramp as if he is the man.

50. INT. DUNPHY HOUSE - KITCHEN - RESUME - INTERVIEW (22:47–22:50)
Phil says he will want to support Luke and not even go two out of three and see what happens there.

END OF PILOT

* * *

Modern Family's pilot weaves together three storylines—Dunphys, Pritchetts, Tucker-Pritchetts. Each storyline has the character-driven landmarks, although the A storyline—the Dunphys—climaxes an act before the B storyline (Pritchett) and the C storyline (Tucker-Pritchett). Steven Levitan and Christopher Lloyd structured the A storyline this way for a very specific reason: They wanted the pilot to end with a big family scene.

Steven and Christopher were setting up the storytelling infrastructure for the entire series. Many *Modern Family* episodes end with a big family scene that pulls all three families together. The big family scene reminds the characters that regardless of how different they are as individuals, they also love each other. They are *family.*

The *Modern Family* pilot uses a four-act-and-a-tag structure. Let's look at the individual storylines and identify the character-driven landmark scenes for each.

For the A storyline, the **point of attack** occurs in the first scenes. It's crystallized during the Claire and Phil interview. Claire says she wants to prevent their kids from making the same bad mistakes she made. If she can do that, she has done her job. Phil chimes in: "Our job." Claire agrees. If she can prevent their kids from making mistakes, she's done *their* job. That's their *raison d'être.* The Dunphy storyline is about Claire and Phil trying to prevent the kids from making mistakes.

The **hero committed** moment happens when Haley announces that she is having a boy over. This is the first time Haley has invited a boy to the house. Exasperated, Haley considers not having Dylan over because her parents will embarrass her. Claire assures her they won't embarrass her. Claire is committed because she doesn't want Haley fooling around with boys the way she herself did as a teen. Claire already stated this is her mission in life.

Phil and Claire have another parental duty in the pilot. When Luke shoots his sister Alex with the Airsoft gun, it's agreed that Phil must shoot Luke with the pellet gun so Luke will understand what it feels like. Phil gets committed to shooting Luke when they write the appointment on the family calendar.

So for the pilot, Steven and Christopher perform a writing task with a difficulty of 10—they split the A-storyline into two storylines and weave them together. It gives Claire a mission—prevent Haley from fooling around with a boy—and Phil his own mission—shoot Luke with a pellet gun to prevent him from using it to cause others pain. Both missions have the same want: Claire and Phil want to prevent their kids from making mistakes that could lead to serious consequences.

The **hero succeeds—almost** moment happens when Haley's boyfriend, Dylan, arrives and Claire wants Phil to intimidate him. Dylan has no idea what Phil is doing and, perhaps, is a little intimidated. Then Phil slips on the stairs and throws out his back—cut to Dylan carrying Phil like a baby to the couch. Phil's intimidation technique gets completely undermined.

In the third act, there is a very nice building of **emotional squeeze** moments. The episode cuts back and forth between Claire and Phil being tested as parents. Alex wants to wind Claire up. She wants to cause trouble for Haley, and she suggests Haley and Dylan are making out. Claire wants to resist Alex's manipulation. She knows what Alex is doing and wants to trust Haley, but Claire sees herself in Haley. Claire knows Haley and Dylan *could* be fooling around in Haley's room. Claire knows she would have been.

Phil has been charged with shooting Luke. Luke has bundled himself up in layers of clothes to protect himself. Phil has to tell him to shed his parka. Phil wants to make this a teachable moment, but part of him is just a big kid himself. Phil has a grin on his face as he aims at Luke. Luke wants to know why Phil is smiling. Phil understands the nearly irresistible temptation to want to shoot somebody with the Airsoft gun. It's not because he's cruel, but because he knows he's not supposed to.

Claire understands what it's like to be alone with a boy in her bedroom—age appropriately, of course. She understands the temptation to want to make out and maybe more. It's not because she was a bad person, but because she wasn't supposed to do it and, well, hormones...

Both Claire and Phil are under pressure to be the parent and prevent their children from making mistakes, but how far is too far? How much should you trust your children? Claire stands on the threshold of Haley's bedroom. The door is closed. Does Claire open it? Or does Claire trust Haley? Phil stands aiming an Airsoft gun at his son. Granted, the gun fires plastic pellets but still it's gonna hurt. Can Phil pull the trigger?

Claire decides that yes, she can open that door and no, she doesn't trust Haley because she knows herself all too well. She opens the door and totally embarrasses Haley, who wasn't doing anything she wasn't supposed to do with Dylan. Phil decides he can't pull the trigger. Luke is scared and surely has learned his lesson. Whew!

The emotional squeeze moves directly into the **hero succeeds** moment because Phil accidentally triggers the Airsoft gun anyway. Phil shoots Luke. Mission accomplished—though Phil is apologetic. It was an accident.

Haley storms out onto the deck with Dylan in tow. She complains to her father that Claire barged in on Dylan and her. They promised not to embarrass her. Phil tries to smooth things over, but he inadvertently fires the Airsoft gun again. An Airsoft pellet hits Dylan in the neck! If Dylan wasn't intimidated before, he is now. The **hero succeeds** again. Then Phil drops the Airsoft gun and shoots himself. No matter what mistakes Phil and Claire want to prevent their kids from making, they may end up shooting themselves in the foot in their attempts.

The Dunphy A storyline wraps up in act three, but there is still another act to go. Structurally, this looks a little strange. However, we are so hooked into the other characters whose stories will climax in the fourth act, it still feels like we are getting a power-packed episode of *Modern Family*—and we are. Steven and Christopher bring all three families together in the fourth act, which adds energy to the dynamic. It also delivers on the promise of the show: This is a show about three different but related families who love each other. The Pritchett or Jay and Gloria storyline and the Tucker–Pritchett or Mitchell and Cam storyline will come together in act four.

Let's take a look at the Jay and Gloria (Pritchett) storyline next. The **point of attack** for Jay and Gloria happens in act one when Manny sees the girl, Gloria tells off another soccer mom because she insulted Manny, and the soccer dad mistakes Jay for Gloria's father. In act two, Manny commits to expressing his love for Brenda Feldman, the girl he saw at the soccer match. Jay stands firm. He wants Gloria to be less emotional. He also wants to protect Manny from embarrassment and toughen him up. In act three, Manny's **hero succeeds—almost** moment occurs when he goes up to Brenda Feldman at her Foto Fun kiosk and proclaims his love for her. He has accomplished his goal. However, Brenda has a boyfriend. She does give him a photo of himself as an Old West sheriff.

Jay's **hero succeeds—almost** happens when he offers to pay Manny $50 to not approach Brenda but Manny turns him down. Then we enter Jay's **emotional squeeze**. Gloria believes Jay's bad mood is due to the fact the soccer dad thought Jay was Gloria's father. Jay says he doesn't care what other people think of him; he just wants to spare Manny from making a fool of himself. In other words, he cares what people think of Manny, which is kind of sweet.

Gloria wants to buy Jay some clothes with more youthful flair. Jay likes wearing his velour track suit. However, when Manny comes back after being shot down, a security guard mistakes Jay for a mall walker. The combination of the soccer dad and security guard's *faux pas* and Manny's willingness to put his heart out there to be crushed affects Jay. He decides to give in to Gloria's suggestion and get some younger looking clothes. The **hero succeeds** moment happens at Mitchell and Cam's house in act four. Let's take a look at Mitchell and Cam's storyline before we discuss Jay's big moment.

The **point of attack** for Mitchell and Cam's storyline happens in act one when Mitchell wants to shame all of those who judge. Mid-speech, Mitchell learns he has overreacted and made a mistake. Still, that desire to scold people he believes to be judgmental remains throughout their storyline.

The **hero committed** moment occurs when Mitchell learns that Cam invited Mitchell's family over for dinner. Mitchell must tell his family that they have adopted a baby. The **hero succeeds—almost** and the **emotional squeeze** happen in the fourth act in quick succession. Now Mitchell wants to tell his family the news, but his family keeps getting side-tracked with their own lives. He almost succeeds in telling them, but they keep interrupting him.

The **emotional squeeze** comes soon after when Mitchell announces that he and Cam wanted a baby. Jay and Claire warn him against it. Mitchell is insulted. Finally, Jay thinks Mitchell and Cam are breaking up. He says Mitchell is better off because Cam was a drama queen.

Here's where the dam breaks. Mitchell's desire to give the speech rises again and takes us into the hero succeeds moment. Mitchell sets his family straight. They can't come into his house and insult him and his boyfriend, who is not *that* dramatic. Just then, the music from *The Lion King* begins. Cam enters carrying baby Lily. As the music swells, he lifts Lily into a spotlight. Mitchell announces that they have adopted a baby. The **hero succeeds.** Mitchell finally tells his family.

The family gathers around Lily, except for Jay. Jay's **hero succeeds** moment is yet to come. He interrupts his family. They all wait for the other shoe to drop. What ill-informed thing is Jay going to say now? Jay surprises them by saying he doesn't know what's best. He hasn't known his whole life. He's still trying to get it right. Jay says he's happy for Mitchell and Cam. As Jay gets a little misty, Mitchell lets him off the hook. He brings Lily to Jay. Jay says, "She's one of us now." As the entire family gathers around Lily, we glimpse the family's new life. Regardless of the stupid things they do or say, or the things they might not be able to do or say, they love each other. They're a family.

Jay voices over the happy family scene. He says, "We're from different worlds, yet somehow we fit together. Love is what binds us through fair or stormy weather. I stand before you now with only one agenda..." Then we cut to Jay reading off a piece of paper to the camera. He reads, "...to let you know my heart is yours, Feldman, comma, Brenda." It's Manny's love declaration poem. Jay thinks it's pretty funny. It is, and it's sweet, too.

Modern Family includes a tag at the end of their shows. This is usually a gag that may or may not have anything to do with the episode's storylines. In the pilot, the tag involved Phil dominating Luke in trampoline basketball. A big kid himself, Phil uses the trampoline to reject Luke's shots and dunk the ball on the short non-regulation goal. All the while, Phil says in an interview that when Luke finally—well, *if* Luke beats him in trampoline basketball, Phil will be a good sport about it. Hmmm, all evidence to the contrary.

Steven Levitan and Christopher Lloyd found the perfect way to weave together their *Modern Family*'s pilot stories and structure those stories beautifully. They wrote a deceptively simple pilot with a lot of moving parts. They introduced 11 characters, including baby Lily, in 22 minutes. And they made it look effortless.

Remember, character-driven structure is *not* a formula. It isn't rigid. It does help you create emotional satisfying stories. Character-driven structure shows you the landmarks, the scenes that help the character arcs during your episode have shape and meaning.

* * *

Spoiler alert! Watch *It's Always Sunny in Philadelphia's* "The Gang Gets Racist," then come back to see why this show works because of its character-driven structure. Fair warning: This episode deals with some provocative topics, including racism and homophobia.

FX's, now FXX's *It's Always Sunny in Philadelphia* is the raunchy, raucous sitcom about shallow, selfish friends who run a bar in Philadelphia. Actor-writer-producer Rob McElhenney developed the show with Glenn Howerton. Rob, Glenn, and Charlie Day shot a pilot on a borrowed digicam recorder and shopped the show around town. FX bought the show.[48] Suddenly, the three novice writer-producers had to write, produce, and star in their own show. That's called living the dream and sometimes nightmare because suddenly, you have to make a ton of decisions that can make or break your career. In the case of the *It's Always Sunny in Philadelphia* threesome, the gamble paid off big. *Sunny* is the longest-running comedy in cable history and the second-longest-running sitcom in television history. According to *Deadline Hollywood*, the trio signed a deal in 2014 that is said to surpass the $50 million three-year deal they signed with FX in 2011.[49]

The show features five despicable people: Mac and Charlie Kelly along with Dennis Reynolds, Dennis' sister, Sweet Dee Reynolds, and their father, Frank Reynolds. The gang, as they are called, are constantly trying to get one over on the others, whether it's getting out of work or supporting activism to get laid and win a bet. They're always looking out for their own self-interests.

It's Always Sunny in Philadelphia revels in negative character traits. It unapologetically showcases narcissism, selfishness, immaturity, deviousness, and lewd behavior. It mines these negative traits for humor. The deeper they dig, the funnier they get. *Sunny* takes on provocative topics. It pushes boundaries. It has edge. This is why it's been on the air for

10 seasons and counting. Let's take a look at the *It's Always Sunny in Philadelphia* pilot, "The Gang Gets Racist."

It's Always Sunny in Philadelphia "The Gang Gets Racist" script by Charlie Day and Rob McElhenney. Breakdown by Kam Miller.

OVER BLACK LEGEND: 12:45 AM On a Thursday Philadelphia, PA (0:00–0:08)

Figure 4.30: *It's Always Sunny* pilot point of attack.

1. INT. PADDY'S BAR – NIGHT (00:09–01:44)
CHARLIE sweeps up at the end of the evening. MAC pours himself some vodka. DENNIS wants the guys to know they aren't making money and their mortgage is due. SWEET DEE wants to introduce the guys to her new friend from acting class. She also wants them to be cool. They assure her they *are* cool.

An AFRICAN-AMERICAN MAN walks into the bar. Dennis wants him to leave. He tells the stranger the bar's closed. The stranger says he knows. Mac jumps up. He wants to keep the peace and prevent trouble. Sweet Dee wants them to know *this* is her friend, TERRELL.

The guys are very uncomfortable. Mac admits they didn't expect Dee's friend to be black. Immediately, they fall into an awkward silence because they know they look like they're racist.
Point of attack

Title sequence (01:45–02:13)

ACT ONE

2. EXT. PADDY'S BAR – NIGHT – ESTABLISHING (02:14–02:17)
The sign and front door of Paddy's bar are unassuming. They're un-assuming anyone would want to enter, unless your usual dive bar was being fumigated.

3. INT. PADDY'S BAR – NIGHT (02:18–04:10)
Terrell wants to impress the gang with a story about how he packed 400 people into a tiny bar because he is a promoter. He lays the bravado on thick with a story about taking a Hispanic guy out to the back alley and tearing his ass apart.

Figure 4.31: *It's Always Sunny* pilot hero committed.

4. EXT. PHILADELPHIA STREET – DAY (04:11–05:15)
Mac loves Terrell. Dennis wants them to admit there was something off about him. Mac calls Dennis racist. Dennis wants them to listen to him because he is not racist. They grab a table outside a coffee shop. Charlie wants to get the coffees. Dennis wants Charlie to sit down and wait for The Waitress to come outside. Then Charlie can stare at The Waitress.

Charlie wants them to know he is not obsessed with The Waitress. He likes her.

Mac wants the gang to hire Terrell to promote Paddy's. Charlie quotes Terrell using the N-word just as The Waitress approaches. She overhears him and calls him "Hitler." Charlie wants her to know he isn't racist.

Mac wants them to hire Terrell. Dennis wants to get chicks in the bar. Charlie agrees. They decide to hire Terrell.
Hero committed

> *Note: The pacing in* It's Always Sunny in Philadelphia*'s pilot is a little off balance. For example, the teaser lasts about 35 seconds, the Terrell-wants-to-impress-the-gang scene goes a tad long at one minute and 52 seconds, and the hero committed scene—the gang wants to hire Terrell—lasts a minute and 3 seconds.*
>
> *However, because Rob and Charlie, who wrote the pilot, stay on the characters and the character wants, they save themselves. The audience doesn't notice the pacing issues. The audience will forgive you if you stay on the characters and their wants. If you are tracking the emotional and story logic, the audience most likely will stick with you. If your character work is shoddy, the audience will abandon you.*

5. EXT. COLLEGE CAMPUS – DAY (05:16–05:46)
Mac wants to get some friends outside of their own race. Charlie wants to appear not racist. However, he thinks Mac's plan is stupid.

6. INT. STUDENT UNION – DAY (05:47–06:37)
Mac sidles up to two AFRICAN-AMERICAN MEN playing dominoes. He wants to break the ice. He crashes and burns.

An AFRICAN-AMERICAN WOMAN comes up to Charlie and wants to know his name. She wants to know if he wants to play dominoes.

7. INT. STUDENT UNION – LATER (06:38–06:45)
Charlie cleans up at dominoes. He wants to gloat and does. He makes friends.

8. EXT. STUDENT UNION – DAY (06:46–08:37)
Mac wants to know why these people like Charlie more than they like him. Charlie wants Mac to be more sensitive.

Another African-American woman, JANELLE, catches up with them. She wants to give Charlie her number. He wants to throw it away. Mac wants Charlie to call her because it's the perfect opportunity to prove they are not racist. Charlie wants to focus on black men.

Mac wants to know if this is about The Waitress at the coffee shop. He wants to know if Charlie still carries a picture of her in his wallet. Charlie wants him to leave him alone. Mac wants to see Charlie's wallet. Charlie wants to prevent him from getting his wallet. They wrestle. Mac gets the wallet and finds the picture. He wants to tear it up. Charlie wants him to stop. Mac wants Charlie to call Janelle. Charlie agrees to call Janelle so Mac won't tear up the photo of The Waitress.

9. EXT. HIGHWAYS – NIGHT (08:38–08:42)
Philadelphia's Market Street and Schuylkill River look inviting in the night cityscape.

10. INT. PADDY'S BAR – NIGHT (08:43–09:34)
Sweet Dee wants to tell Dennis about her dreams. Dennis wants her to stop because he isn't interested. Terrell comes in. Dee greets him and wants to give him a kiss. Terrell wants to give her a hug. Terrell hugs Dennis and invades his personal space. Terrell wants Dennis to step outside.

11. EXT. PADDY'S BAR – NIGHT (09:35–09:47)
Terrell wants to show Dennis the line of people waiting to get into Paddy's. Dennis is impressed. Terrell wants to check Dennis out. Dennis wants to pretend like he's cool with it.

Figure 4.32: *It's Always Sunny* pilot hero succeeds—almost.

12. INT. PADDY'S BAR – NIGHT (09:48–11:12)
Dennis and Dee are swamped at the bar. Dennis wants to bartend full-time because he's getting tons of tips. Dee wants to know why Dennis is making more money than she is. Mac and Charlie want to comment on how crazy this crowd is. Charlie wants them to notice that it's a lot of dudes.

Dee goes to serve a couple of guys but they want to wait for the "cute one," meaning Dennis. Charlie wants to know if that's Mac's cousin, BRETT, by the jukebox. Mac says it is and wants to say hello.

AT THE JUKEBOX – Brett wants them to know this crowd is something else.

AT THE BAR – Dennis waits on the guys who requested him. One hits on him. Dennis jerks his hand back. Dennis wants him to stop.

The guy compliments Dennis' eyes. Dennis' narcissism gets the better of him. He wants to hear more.

AT THE JUKEBOX – Brett wants to compliment Mac because Mac has come a long way. Mac wants to know what he means. Brett tells him they are running the hottest gay bar in Philadelphia.
Hero succeeds—almost

> *Note: The Paddy's-Bar-is-swamped sequence marries the Dee-and-Dennis-at-the-bar scene with the Charlie-and-Mac-talk-to-Brett scene. All told, the sequence lasts 1 minute and about 20 seconds. It has a good feel for the pacing and intercutting of the two scenes. Plus, it hits the act break hard.*

END OF ACT ONE

ACT TWO

13. EXT. PHILADELPHIA STREET – DAY (11:16–11:20)
It's an average day in Philly.

14. INT. TERRELL'S APARTMENT – DAY (11:21–11:47)
Sweet Dee pounds on Terrell's door. When Terrell opens the door, Dee kisses him on the lips. Terrell wants to extricate himself from the kiss. He wants her to stop. He wants to know what her problem is. Dee wants to know why Terrell didn't tell her he was gay. Terrell is in musical theater. He didn't think it was that big of a secret. Dee has been coming on to him. Terrell thought she was into gay dudes. Dee tells Terrell the guys aren't happy he turned their bar into a gay bar.

Figure 4.33: *It's Always Sunny* pilot emotional squeeze.

15. INT. PADDY'S BAR – DAY (11:48–12:06)
Dennis and Charlie want to celebrate their big gain. They run around with stacks of money. They want to embrace this situation.

16. EXT. COFFEE SHOP – DAY (12:07–13:03)
Mac wants to stop running a gay bar. Mac wants to read the gang a notice about their trendy gay bar. Dennis and Charlie like it. Dee wants to agree with Mac. Dennis and Charlie accuse her of wanting to change things because she didn't make many tips.

Mac wanted to get laid, but clearly that's not going to happen at a gay bar. Charlie is good with the arrangement. Mac believes this is because Charlie has black girls all over him. Mac wants Charlie to know he'll screw it up. Charlie wants Mac to know he has a date with Janelle today.

Dennis agrees with Charlie that it's just about the business.
Dee calls bullshit on him. Dee wants Dennis to know he just likes the attention.

17. INT. PADDY'S BAR – NIGHT – MONTAGE (13:04–13:07)
A parade of guys flirt with Dennis.

18. EXT. COFFEE SHOP – RESUME (13:08–13:58)
Dennis wants Dee to know he just gets along well with those guys.
Dee wants Dennis to know he is leading the gay guys on because he is vain.

Charlie wants to take a vote. He wants everyone who wants Paddy's to remain a gay bar to say "aye." Dennis and Charlie say "aye." Dennis wants to remind the gang that Dee doesn't get a vote because she is a bartender not an owner. Charlie wants all owners who oppose Paddy's remaining a gay bar to say "nay." Mac says "nay," but it's two against one. Paddy's will remain the hottest gay bar in Philadelphia.
Emotional squeeze

> *Note: The emotional squeeze includes two minor moments—Dennis and Charlie rejoicing in money and a parade of guys hitting on Dennis. Both of these moments hook the audience into the emotional logic of the characters. Still, this sequence only lasts two minutes and 10 seconds. It has a nice sense of pacing as well as emotional and story logic.*

19. EXT. PHILADELPHIA STREETS – DAY (13:59–14:01)
We're driving down neighborhood streets. Lots of red brick passes by.

20. EXT. JANELLE'S APARTMENT – DAY (14:02–14:19)
Charlie picks up Janelle. He wants to go get a drink.

21. EXT. COFFEE SHOP – DAY – ESTABLISHING (14:20–14:22)
Not much happening at the coffee shop yet.

22. INT. COFFEE SHOP – DAY (14:22–15:34)
Janelle thought Charlie meant a bar, not a coffee shop. Charlie wants to know what Janelle wants. She says she doesn't drink coffee. Ignoring her, Charlie goes to order.

Charlie wants The Waitress to see his black date. He wants The Waitress to know he's not racist. He wants to go on a date with her. The Waitress wants him to stop asking her. Janelle wants to know what's going on. The Waitress tells her the truth. Charlie wants to know if it would upset her, if it were truth.

23. INT. PADDY'S BAR – NIGHT (15:35–16:27)
Dee holds ice to Charlie's eye. She wants Charlie to see a doctor. He already has. She wants Charlie to keep the ice on his eye. Dee asks if Charlie said the girl's name was Janelle. Yes, it's Janelle Jenkins.

Mac wants Dee and Charlie to see Dennis, who is basically Tom Cruise *Cocktail*-ing it at the bar in a tank top.

Dennis wants attention.

Mac wants to know why the gay guys love Dennis and the black chicks love Charlie. Charlie wants him to know it's not so much that they love them; they don't like Mac. Mac wants to know why. Charlie says because Mac is an asshole. Charlie leaves. Mac wants to know if he is an asshole. Dee wants him to know that it's true. She also wants to talk with him in the back room.

24. INT. PADDY'S BAR – OFFICE – NIGHT (16:28–16:58)
Dee thinks she knows how to solve this whole gay mess. Mac's in. Dee wants Mac to get Dennis drunk on tequila tonight—a lot of it. So drunk he might hurt himself. Mac tells her it'll be no problem. Dee needs to talk with some friends in her acting class.

25. INT. PADDY'S BAR – LATER (16:59–18:00)
Mac pretends to want to know how to do tequila shots. He wants Dennis to show him. Dennis gets so drunk he doesn't realize Mac isn't drinking. Dennis starts passing out in front of Mac.

26. INT. DENNIS' BEDROOM – DAY (18:01–18:58)
The alarm goes off. There are used condoms on the nightstand. Dennis wakes up, hung over. He hits the alarm clock. He realizes someone is in the bed with him. Dennis wants to snuggle. The person turns over and it's a MAN in a BLONDE WIG. Dennis jumps out of bed. Dennis wants to know if they had sex. The guy tells him, "no, it was all hands." Then a SECOND GUY comes into the bedroom and slaps Dennis on the ass. The second guy asks him how that ass is feeling, implying it was *not* all hands.

Note: This unraveling sequence clocks in at about 2 minutes and 30 seconds. Let's track the emotional logic of the characters.

Sweet Dee is upset and jealous that Terrell is gay and not interested in her. She also is upset that Dennis is getting more tips than she is by leading on the gay guys, just as she felt she was led on by Terrell. Terrell thought she was just into gay guys. Dee wants to prevent Dennis from leading on the gay guys and stop working with Terrell.

Mac is upset and jealous because the gay guys like Dennis and the African-American women like Charlie, but no one seems to like him. Dee tells him he is an asshole, which doesn't improve his outlook. Mac wants to stop the gay bar business because it's making him feel insecure and he wants to bring women into the bar so he can get laid.

Charlie seems fine with running a gay bar. He wants to date The Waitress, but he just blew it because he took Janelle to the coffee shop to prove he wasn't racist.

Dennis loves the attention and tips he's getting from the gay guys, though he has no intention of following through on a relationship, much less a hook-up with any of the guys.

Basically, Sweet Dee and Mac have to get Charlie and Dennis to sour on the gay bar angle.

Mac gets Dennis black-out drunk on tequila. When Dennis wakes up, he discovers he has slept with two guys but doesn't remember it. He is horrified. One could see this as homophobic. The show is also dealing with a consent issue. If Dennis was black-out drunk, could he have consented to having sex with anyone? Dennis is traumatized by this incident because he feels violated. Now he doesn't want to run a gay bar.

Most of this happens in two minutes and 30 seconds.

27. EXT. PADDY'S BAR – DAY – ESTABLISHING (18:59–19:01)
Paddy's Bar looks as low rent in the day as it does at night.

Figure 4.34: *It's Always Sunny* pilot hero fails.

28. INT. PADDY'S BAR – DAY (19:02–21:01)
Charlie wants Mac to know he's glad that Mac's embracing the gay-bar angle. Dennis comes in and doesn't want to own a gay bar anymore.

Terrell comes in. He wants to give them some new CDs because the music in the jukebox is stale. Terrell also wants to get rid of the shamrocks because nothing scare blacks or gays more than Irish stuff.

Dennis wants Terrell to know they are letting him go. Terrell wants to know why.

Sweet Dee walks in with Janelle. Charlie wants to know what Janelle is doing there. Dennis wants to know if they know each other. Charlie says the crazy bitch punched him in his eye. Terrell tells Charlie that Janelle is his sister. Mac wants to know if Janelle is Terrell's actual sister. Terrell says Janelle is his real sister.

Mac wants them to know he isn't racist because it sounded like he thought all black people were related. Mac triumphantly says that you people actually are related. This makes him sound racist.
Hero fails

END OF ACT TWO

ACT THREE

Figure 4.35: *It's Always Sunny* pilot hero's new life.

29. INT. PADDY'S BAR – NIGHT (21:04–21:33)
Sweet Dee counts the night's take and it's back to abysmal. They're back to normal.
Hero's new life
Mac wants to know what the guys from her acting class did to Dennis. Dee says she couldn't get ahold of them. It didn't work out. Mac wants to know why Dennis was so freaked out.

30. INT. DENNIS' BEDROOM – DAY – FLASHBACK (12:34–12:35)
The second guy slaps Dennis' ass and asks him how that ass is feeling.

END OF PILOT

* * *

It's Always Sunny in Philadelphia's structure is interesting because it's a *tragedy*, not a comedy. Tragedy doesn't mean the show isn't funny. It doesn't mean someone dies at the end. In this case, it simply means the climax of the show isn't the hero succeeding; it's the hero *failing*. Throughout the "The Gang Gets Racist," different members of the gang want the bar to succeed or fail for their own personal reasons. Eventually, the characters' storylines come together to make the bar a failure again. The show resets to the *status quo*, which is barely making any money at all.

At the **point of attack**, the gang needs the bar to make money because their mortgage is due. The gang commits to making more money when they decide to hire Terrell, who is a promoter. Terrell delivers big. Paddy's Bar is packed and there's a line to get in. The bartenders, Dennis and Dee, are swamped. It's awesome, except Charlie realizes there are a lot of dudes there. Mac sees his cousin, who has never frequented the bar. His cousin congratulates Mac on his personal growth. "You've really come a long way," his cousin says. Mac wants to know what he means. His cousin tells him that he's running the hottest gay bar in Philly. This is the **hero succeeds—almost** moment. The bar is succeeding, but they didn't set out for it to be a gay bar. And while the gang is trying to appear not racist, it is going to have to deal with trying to not look homophobic, too. For the immature, stunted-development foursome, this may prove too difficult.

At the **emotional squeeze**, the gang is rolling in the dough. They get together to talk about their success. Mac wants to stop running a gay bar because he wants to get laid. Dee wants to stop running a gay bar because it feeds Dennis' narcissism. However, Charlie and Dennis want to continue running a gay bar and making money. Charlie finds a loophole that renders Dee's opinion null. Charlie and Dennis outvote Mac. Paddy's will remain successful.

At the **hero fails** moment, Dennis has changed his mind because he woke up naked with two guys and doesn't remember what happened. Mac pretends he's okay with the whole gay bar deal, but he prods

Dennis about his experience, changing his mind. Charlie remains steadfast in his desire to keep making money. Terrell wants to make some changes to Paddy's to make it more gay-friendly. Dennis wants to tell him they need to let him go. Dee brings in Janelle, an African-American woman who went on a date with Charlie. However, Charlie was just using her to prove he wasn't racist to The Waitress at the coffee shop so he could ask The Waitress out. When Janelle found out what was really going on, she gave Charlie a black eye. When Dee brings Janelle into Paddy's, Charlie says, "That crazy bitch punched me in the eye." Terrell takes offense because that's his sister.

Mac wants to know if Janelle is actually Terrell's sister, or if he means she's his metaphorical sister. Terrell means Janelle is his real sister. Mac wants everyone to know he's not racist because he had said black people were related and it turns out they are. This make him seem so racist. Obviously, this isn't going to work out with Terrell. Paddy's has lost its promoter and its gay clientele. Paddy's is back to being a hole-in-the-wall Irish bar.

The hero succeeds becomes the hero fails. You may see this as Mac and Dee succeeding by getting Charlie and Dennis to drop the gay bar angle. However, Mac and Dee have not been the heroes of the storylines. Charlie is the hero of The Waitress storyline. He also has been a big supporter of the bar's success. Dennis is arguable the hero of the gay bar angle. He is the primary attraction and also a big supporter of the bar's recent success. Dennis and Charlie revel in the bar's big earnings. They love rolling in the dough. So Mac and Dee are the antagonists to Charlie and Dennis here.

And failure can be very funny. With the climax ending down, the emotional squeeze will be up—the gang votes to keep the bar a success. Basically, a tragedy is the inverse of a comedy. If you're writing a tragedy, a pilot where the heroes fail in the end, you need to flip the emotional squeeze into a positive. In this case, the characters choose to keep making more money than they have ever made running the bar. This is a good option. They need to make money. However, a positive emotional squeeze signals a helluva downfall to come. The heroes will fail. The major character-driven landmarks you change for a tragedy are the emotional squeeze and the hero succeeds. And sometimes it is funnier for your heroes, especially anti-heroes like the *It's Always Sunny in Philadelphia* gang, to fail.

* * *

This has been a long chapter, but this bears repeating: Breaking down pilots will help you see how professional writers constructed their pilots and launched their shows. When you reverse-engineer outlines for pilot episodes, you get a better grasp on everything you need to accomplish when you begin constructing your pilot. You'll see the character introductions, the details of the world, the delivery of exposition, and the storytelling infrastructure that you wouldn't notice if you simply watched the pilot. Ripping a pilot apart at the seams teaches you the techniques the pros use to convey the essential components of their TV series.

As you can see, character-driven structure works in both drama and comedy. It'll help you create structurally sound and emotionally satisfying stories. Plus, it will keep you focused on your characters and marry your character arc to your story arc.

Understanding character-driven structure as well as tried-and-true writing pro techniques will help make your pilot stand out from the thousands of other pilots on the desks of executives, producers, agents, and managers.

We've just looked at pilot breakdowns, which are like reverse-engineered outlines. In the pilot-writing process, there is a step before the outline, and that's the story grid. We'll look at pilot story grids in the next chapter.

* * *

Assignment

Break down a pilot that is similar in structure to the pilot you want to create. The similarities don't need to be in content. The similarities should be in structure. Do you have an ensemble cast or a single lead? Do you want to write a pilot with a main A storyline and other minor storylines? Or will all of your storylines be of similar weight? Find a show that tells the story the way you want to tell the story.

Your breakdown should follow the basic format for the breakdowns in this chapter. Include scene headings, story beats, character wants, scene ins and outs, act breaks, and character-driven landmarks.

CHAPTER 5

TL;DR chapter 5

TV writers depend on story grids as they break their episodes. They're the first step in the outlining process. Staying on your character wants helps ensure that you have scenes for each scene heading and will maintain story momentum. Story grids save writers time, energy, and heartache. Assignment: Use the breakdown from chapter 4 to create a grid for that pilot.

The Art of the Grid: The Keys to the Kingdom

In this chapter, you'll find story grids for dramas and comedies, including:

- AMC's *The Walking Dead* "Days Gone Bye";
- Starz' *Outlander* "Sassenach";
- Showtime's Episodes "Episode One";
- Amazon's *Transparent* "Pilot"; and
- Fox's *Brooklyn Nine-Nine* "Pilot."

All TV writers rooms have corkboards and whiteboards. TV writers love boards because we're visual people, and we use boards to break story. On those boards, we lay out our episodes in quick beats with scene headings. We'll write the scene heading accompanied by the character wants. We love seeing the story take shape in a physical way before our eyes. We love moving note cards around on the corkboard. Breaking story in this manner is tactile and tangible, and that's why creating the **story grid** is the first step in breaking story.

The grid approach to breaking story also saves us time. We don't have to write the outline to see if the story is working. And we certainly don't have to write the script before making sure the story works. We put our grids up on the wall so other writers can see the whole story in one place. We can get feedback on a story quickly.

With a grid, we see the barebones story. We can tell if we're hitting the landmarks, if our act breaks are strong, if we're hitting the emotional logic and story logic beats, if our main character is proactive, and if the story fits into this season and the TV series as a whole. Creating the skeleton of the story makes it easier for us to change it—or fix it, if necessary—because we haven't committed it to an outline or script.

If you start by writing the outline or script, you can be seduced by your own writing. *I love that turn of phrase! That's exactly what's she's thinking, eating, wearing, etc.* You can fall in love with your own voice. Unfortunately, while you may have a great moment or killer dialogue, you might *not* have a structurally sound story. You might have an inactive protagonist. You may have moments that aren't scenes. I've read pilot scripts that were beautifully written and put to pilot. However, once filmed, the shows didn't work, because they were not based on character wants and didn't have scenes. *If a moment in your script doesn't have a character want, it's not a scene.*

TV story grids represent your entire story in one place. This could be on a whiteboard, corkboard, or single sheet of paper. In writers rooms, we often use notecards on a corkboard. At the top of the corkboard, there are notecards that label each act—teaser, act one, act two, act three, act four and so forth. Below each act title card is a column of individual notecards. Each notecard represents a scene. These notecards are easy to take on and off the corkboard. They're easy to move around on the corkboard, so we can move a scene from the second act to the first act simply by moving a push pin. Plus, it's easy to see if you have too many scenes in one act and not enough scenes in another act.

Until fairly recently, most TV dramas used a teaser-and-four-act structure. As I covered in chapter three, this structure divided the show into equal parts, and it made storytelling flow. Most TV sitcoms used a cold open and a two-act structure because it worked best for that type of storytelling. In the early 2000s, TV act breaks changed. Broadcast networks figured out they could add more commercials throughout their shows, so execs added more commercial act breaks. As a result, the major networks adopted teaser-and-five-acts, teaser-and-six-acts, and several other variations of commercial act break structure. The change left TV writers scrambling to work through the side effects: longer and shorter acts, pacing issues, and other structural script problems. The conversion to more act breaks was great for ad sales, but it wasn't designed for better storytelling.

For shows that do not have commercial act breaks, I suggest using a teaser and four-act structure to break the show. For your pilot, using the teaser-and-four-act structure to break a show with no commercials will help you see whether your landmark scenes are landing in the right places and get a handle on the pacing and flow of the show. If you go straight to outline, all of your scenes will be in one single column. Your show can become amorphous and unwieldy. It also can be difficult to stay on your character wants. Once you've broken your show and know the structure is sound, you can go to your outline and then on to your script. During your final phases, you'll simply remove all of the act breaks to illustrate there are no commercial breaks in your pilot.

If you have a show that needs commercial breaks, you can use the format of the network you think best aligns with your pilot. If you're going to write a kick-ass soapy drama in the vein of Shonda Rhimes, you could start with the teaser-and-six-act structure common to her ABC shows. However, I suggest that you break your pilot using the teaser-and-four-act structure first.

After you break your show that way, you can simply divide two acts—usually acts three and four—into two acts each. You'll wind up with a teaser-and-six-act pilot. Remember, you still need to hit those new act breaks hard with some holy shit! moments that'll keep your audience mesmerized through Doritos and Dodge commercials.

In this chapter, you'll find pilot story grids for current shows. You'll be able to see the skeleton of these stories. You'll see the story beats as well as the character-driven structure landmark scenes and where they fall in the shows. You'll see why these shows *work.*

* * *

Spoiler alert! Watch *The Walking Dead* "Days Gone Bye," then come back to see why this show works because of its character-driven structure.

The Walking Dead has been a ratings juggernaut for the AMC network. It bowed to record ratings (5.35 million viewers with a 2.7 rating in the 18-49 demographic) for the network.[50] In its fifth season, it was still delivering staggering numbers. The 90-minute fifth season finale averaged an 8.2 rating in adults 18-49 and 15.8 million viewers overall.[51]

Frank Darabont (*Shawshank Redemption, The Green Mile*) wrote and directed the pilot episode. He did a masterful job delivering this pilot. Based on the Robert Kirkman graphic novels, *The Walking Dead* had been in development for five years before Frank took it to AMC. Frank had developed the property at NBC. [52] However, after working on the project there, the network decided not to go forward with it. This happens more often than not. Projects may take many years to finally realize.

In an interview with Steve Barton for DreadCentral, Frank said, "I'd gotten turned down enough times, which is no reflection on the material, but no matter what you're trying to sell in Hollywood, you're Willy Loman and it's *Death of a Salesman.* You're out there trying to sell shit that nobody wants. Even if it's good shit." [53]

This is important for you to know as you move forward with your project. Sometimes it's just not the right time for your project, but your time will come. Eventually, Frank pitched the project around town.

He paired up with Gale Anne Hurd at Valhalla. Together, they took it to AMC. AMC decided to hop on board, and the show has been very successful for them.[54]

Frank did some very smart things when he structured the pilot. He kept the character wants clear and simple. He stayed on the characters. For lesser writers and directors, the temptation to focus on the world and gore would be too great, and the characters would get lost. But Frank managed to balance all the elements very well.

Let's go over the pilot in detail and examine its structure.

Please review Figure 5.1 – *The Walking Dead* "Days Gone Bye" grid on the following page. Feel free to refer back to it as you read the next section.

GRID #1 • *The Walking Dead* • "Days Gone Bye" by Frank Darabont (Storyline A – Rick, Storyline B – Shane) / Grid by Kam Miller • *The Hero Succeeds*

Teaser	Act 1	Act 2	Act 3	Act 4
EXT. HIGHWAY – A police cruiser drives down an empty highway, stops. Sheriff RICK GRIMES gets out. He wants gas. **EXT. GAS STATION – Rick walks through abandoned cars with dead bodies inside. He sees a little GIRL. He wants to get her attention, but she is a walker. She wants to eat him. He want to save himself. (Point of attack)**	INT./EXT. POLICE CRUISER – 3 MONTHS AGO – Parked, Rick eats lunch with his partner, SHANE WALSH. Shane wants to talk about women. Rick wants to keep his thoughts to himself. They get a call out. They want to respond. EXT. HIGHWAY 18 – Rick, Shane, and other police officers want to stop fugitives. Fugitives want to get away. The officers and fugitives engage in a shoot out. Rick gets shot, wants to live. Shane calls for help, wants Rick to hold on as we fade to white.	INT. HOSPITAL ROOM – Hazy, Shane wants to Shane to know he's visited. He leaves fresh flowers. **INT. HOSPITAL ROOM – LATER Rick wakes up and looks at the once-fresh flowers, now withered. Rick gets out of bed, falls. He wants help. No one comes. (Hero committed)** INT. HOSPITAL – HALLWAY – Rick wants help. He finds the hospital abandoned. The phones don't work. He sees a mutilated dead body. Horrified, he backs away. Bullet holes and blood mar the wall. A door with a sign that reads: "DON'T OPEN, DEAD INSIDE." It is chained shut. Fingers poke through the door crack. Rick wants out. INT. STAIRWELL – With a lit match, Rick stumbles in the dark. He wants to find an exit. EXT. HOSPITAL – Rick wants help. He finds a mass grave. Rick walks through an abandoned military base. EXT. PARK – Rick sees a bike. He wants the bike. Beside the bike is HALF OF A BODY groaning and reaching for him. WTF? He takes the bike. INT. HOME – Rick wants his family. He yells for Lori and Carl, his wife and son. No one is home. He leaves. **EXT. HOME – Rick wants help/answers. From behind, DUANE wants to subdue Rick, hits him with a shovel. Duane calls for his father, MORGAN, who points a gun at Rick. Morgan wants to know about Rick's wound. (Hero succeeds–almost)**	INT. MORGAN'S HOUSE – Rick wakes up. Duane wants to protect his father. Morgan wants to clean Rick's wound. Morgan wants to know if Rick was bitten. Rick is confused. They want to eat. Rick wants to know what happened. Morgan talks about walkers. A car alarm goes off. They dim the lights. They want to remain hidden. They peek out the windows. Walkers roam. They want to eat. Duane sees JENNY (his mom, a walker) approach the house. EXT. MORGAN'S HOUSE – NEXT DAY – Rick, Morgan, and Duane exit. A walker wants to eat them. Rick wants to protect them. He kills walker with a bat. INT. RICK'S HOUSE – Rick wants a set of keys. He wants to find his family. Morgan tells Rick that if his family is still alive, they're most likely in Atlanta. Morgan and Duane want to go there someday as well. The Centers for Disease Control was working on a cure as well as a large refugee center. INT. POLICE STATION – Rick, Morgan, and Duane raid the gun locker. They want guns and ammo. Rick wants clean clothes, put on his sheriff's uniform. EXT. POLICE STATION – Rick gives Morgan a radio. He wants him to turn it on every day at sunrise and wait for Rick's messages. Rick leaves for Atlanta. He wants to find Lori and Carl. He sees one of his officers as a walker. He wants to euthanize him. Rick shoots him in the head. INT. MORGAN'S HOUSE – Morgan and Duane want to protect themselves. They seal the doors and cover the windows. Morgan wants Duane to read. INT. MORGAN'S HOUSE – BEDROOM –Morgan takes his rifle upstairs and sees his wife outside. He wants to euthanize her. He can't pull the trigger. **EXT. PARK – Rick goes back to the park to find the HALF OF A BODY walker. He wants to euthanize it. He apologizes and shoots it. (Emotional squeeze)**	EXT. CAMP – Shane, along with Lori, Carl, and others, have set up a camp. They receive Rick's message over the radio, unaware it's him. Lori wants to put signs on the highway to warn people away from Atlanta. Shane wants to keep the convoy together. They argue, kiss. They believe Rick is dead. EXT. HIGHWAY – Rick drives until he sees a house. He wants gas. He stops. He finds the tenants dead. He sees a horse, mounts him, and rides. He wants to go to Atlanta and find his family. **EXT. ATLANTA – Rick and horse move through deserted city streets. They attract attention. Walkers rush him, want to eat him. Rick wants to save himself. He abandons the horse. Rick crawls underneath a tank and then inside it. (Hero succeeds)** **INT. TANK – Rick listens to the walkers overtake the tank. They want him. He wants to survive and find his family. A voice comes over the radio, offering help. (Hero's new life)**

The **point of attack** for *The Walking Dead*'s pilot happens in the teaser. Rick Grimes wants gas. It's that simple. He just wants gas. He's at an abandoned gas station and sees a little girl. When he approaches the girl, he wants to help her. She turns and he sees she is dead. The girl wants to bite him. She advances to attack. Rick wants to survive. He shoots her in the head. This is the first, rancid whiff of Rick's problem—the zombie apocalypse. And it just goes to show you that sometimes the point of attack is an actual attack. But it's more than an attack; Rick is forced to shoot a child. He has a moral dilemma—does he shoot the girl and save himself, or does he spare her and let her infect him?

This moral dilemma tells us about the show. It tells us what we're signing on for. It's more than just brain-dead zombie killing. The characters will face moral dilemmas in every episode. They'll face tough decisions. *Drama is decision.* That's why audiences tune in.

If audiences simply wanted to see zombie killings they could play a video game, but this is a television show. The audience falls in love with characters. They care what happens to them. And they care about the decisions the characters make.

The **hero committed** moment happens in act two. Approximately three months before the events in the teaser, Sheriff's Deputy Rick Grimes and several other law enforcement officers wait at an impromptu roadblock. The cops chase criminals in a car. As the car approaches, it hits road spikes and flips, crashing onto the side of the road. A shootout ensues and Rick gets shot. Rick goes into a coma and misses the genesis of the zombie apocalypse. When he wakes up, he is all alone. He has to figure out what's going on. Rick is fully committed. Rick wants to survive. He must adapt quickly.

At the end of act two, Rick wants help. He wants answers. He doesn't understand what is going on. He sees a man walking down the street. He waves at the man. The man veers toward him. It's a walker. We see another person walk up behind Rick. Rick turns to see a young boy. The boy hits Rick in the head with a shovel. The boy's father rushes over. He shoots the walker in the head before coming over to Rick, who lies stunned on the sidewalk. The man wants to know what Rick's bandage is for. He wants to know what type of wound Rick has. Rick passes out. This is our **hero succeeds—almost** moment.

Rick wants help. He wants answers. When he finally succeeds in finding two people who could give him answers, one of them whacks him in the head with a shovel. The other aims a gun at him and wants to know what type of injury he has. Before Rick can get any answers, Rick blacks out.

As you can see from the grid, act three contains the most story. It involves the Morgan and Duane story arc and Rick gets some answers about what has happened in the world. Near the end of the third act, Rick has his **emotional squeeze**, as does Morgan. Frank Darabont does a nice bit of cutting back and forth between Rick and Morgan's storylines to build the tension and emotion. Morgan and Duane have been staying in this small town because Morgan's wife, Jenny, died and now walks here. Rick has decided to leave the small town. Rick wants to find his wife, Lori, and his son, Carl. Rick wants to go to Atlanta where the Centers for Disease Control have set up a quarantine area, which is where Morgan and his family were headed before Jenny got sick.

After Rick and Morgan part ways at the police station, Morgan decides to euthanize his wife. He wants to shoot her in the head. He wants to break the tether to this small town so he and his son can join Rick in Atlanta. Morgan sets up his sniper's roost in an upstairs window of the house he and his son now occupy. He begins shooting walkers. He wants to draw his Jenny into the street so he can get a clear shot. Finally, he sees Jenny. Jenny stops and seems to look up at Morgan. She waits. Morgan has the perfect shot but he can't take it. He can't kill his beloved wife. Will Morgan and Duane remain stuck in this hellish limbo?

Meanwhile, Rick is heading out of town but he has one last mission. He stops at the park where he saw the halved zombie. He looks for it, but it has since moved. Rick walks through the bucolic park. The sunny day and the gorgeous greenery belie the true state of nature. Rick finds the decayed zombie, which is dragging itself through the park leaving a slug trail of innards. Rick kneels next to it. He apologizes to it. He wants it to know he is sorry this happened to it. For all he knows, he might've been friends with this former person. For all he knows, his wife and son may be in the same state of decay somewhere. As the zombie reaches out for him, Rick takes out his gun. He wants to put the zombie out of its misery. He shoots the zombie in the head. This is Rick's emotional squeeze. Unlike Morgan, Rick can pull the trigger. He can now leave his small town and search for his wife and son. He can do what he needs to do.

In act four, we have the **hero succeeds** moment. Rick rides into Atlanta on a horse. At first, it seems deserted. However, Rick and the horse soon attract walkers. They are swarmed. Rick wants to survive. Rick abandons the horse and crawls under a tank. He finds a hatch and crawls inside the tank. Rick has succeeded in making it to Atlanta. This was his goal. However, there is an **emotional twist**. Atlanta seems to be deserted and overrun by zombies. Still, Rick manages to use his wits and escape the zombie throng by giving up his horse and crawling into a tank.

Inside the tank, Rick listens as the zombies mount it and attempt to take it over. Rick wants to survive and find his family. He hears a voice on the radio. It offers help. This is the **hero's new life**. Rick will be on the run from zombies. Hoping to remain uninfected as he searches for his family, he'll also need to rely on the help of others, of strangers. He will need to form alliances and trust people he doesn't know.

Note the positioning of the landmark scenes. It's easy to see on the grid that most of the landmark scenes occur at the end of act breaks. These scenes—point of attack, hero succeeds—almost, emotional squeeze, and hero's new life—are great end-of-act scenes. The point of attack and the hero succeeds—almost are scenes with an element of suspense and maintain the audience through the commercials. Another scene with suspense ends act one. Rick getting shot hits that act break hard and keeps the audience engaged through the commercial break.

The emotional squeeze often isn't a scene that has a lot of suspense. It usually needs to play out and needs a solid resolution. For this pilot's emotional squeeze, Rick doesn't kill the walker for survival; he wants to show it mercy. Rick accepts his post-zombie apocalypse life. He wants to approach it with dignity and mercy. He wants to be able to do what is necessary and make the tough but still moral decisions. He wears his sheriff's deputy uniform, announcing to the world he is there to protect and serve. This scene demonstrates Rick's mindset. The challenge of this scene shows the audience how Rick has changed and launches us into the final act of the pilot. While there isn't a lot of suspense in this scene, the audience is more invested in Rick and his journey. Whether the audience is fully aware of it, they are engaged for Rick's next journey and the series.

Welcome to the world of *The Walking Dead*. It's an edge-of-your-seat thrill ride grounded in family and human drama. It looks at what it means to be human. It tests its characters and pushes them to the point where they might lose their humanity. They face life-and-death moral decisions every day they survive. And we the audience get to wonder what we might do in their situation.

* * *

Spoiler alert! Watch *Outlander* "Sassenach," then come back to see why this show works because of its character-driven structure.

Another ratings queen is Starz' *Outlander*. The series, based on the mega-hit *New York Times* best-selling novels by Diana Gabaldon, set the highest rated multi-platform premiere in Starz' history with approximately 2.3 million viewers. An estimated 51% of those viewers were women.[55]

This show is about WWII British nurse Claire Beauchamp Randall, who gets transported back to 1783 Scotland. She leaves her 20th century husband, Frank Randall, behind and finds a new love, Jamie MacKenzie Fraser, in the past.

The series was developed by Ronald D. Moore (*Battlestar Galactica, Star Trek: The Next Generation*). Ron wrote the pilot, "Sassenach," and John Dahl (*Breaking Bad, Dexter*) directed it.[56] In the pilot, WWII has just ended. Claire and her husband, Frank, have been apart for five years and are on a second honeymoon of sorts in the Scottish Highlands. Frank is a historian. Fascinated with his own genealogy, Frank wanted to visit the area to do some research on his ancestors. Claire sees this as an opportunity for them to get reacquainted. They arrive on *Samhain*, the Gaelic festival that marks the end of the harvest season and the beginning of the darker half of the year. We call it Halloween. It's a time when the ghosts are out.

Outlander runs commercial free on Starz. It's a premium cable network, so you'll see nudity and violence and hear cursing in English *and* Scottish. Because it runs without commercial breaks, I've broken it in a teaser-and-four-act structure. I suggest doing this for all premium cable shows. The teaser-and-four-act structure translates well to the three-act structure as you've seen in the character-driven structure section. As you look at the grid for *Outlander*, you'll see the acts flow nicely and are fairly evenly distributed.

Please review Figure 5.2 – *Outlander* "Sassenach" grid on the following page. Feel free to refer back to it as you read the next section.

GRID #2 • *Outlander* • pilot "Sassenach" by Ronald D. Moore (Storyline A – Claire) / Grid by Kam Miller • *The Hero Succeeds*

Teaser	Act 1	Act 2	Act 3	Act 4
EXT. VILLAGE STREET – CLAIRE RANDALL wants vase in a drugstore window. INT. FIELD HOSPITAL – FLASHBACK Claire, a nurse, wants to save a soldier's leg. A DOCTOR arrives. He wants to take over. Claire steps back. EXT. FIELD HOSPITAL – FLASHBACK Claire hears celebrating. She wants to know why. The war is over. **EXT. VILLAGE STREET – Claire wants the vase and the life it represents. She also wants to walk away. (Point of attack)**	EXT. SCOTITSH HIGHLANDS – ROAD – Claire and FRANK RANDALL want to get reacquainted. EXT. VILLAGE STREET – They want to check into their room. INT. MRS. BAIRD'S BED AND BREAKFAST – MRS. BAIRD wants to welcome them and tell them that it's Samhaim. The ghosts are out. INT. GUEST ROOM – Claire wants to loosen Frank up. Frank wants to do what's proper. INT. MRS. BAIRD'S BED AND BREAKFAST – Mrs. Baird wants them to stop jumping on the bed. INT. GUEST ROOM – Claire wants to have sex. Frank wants to say something. Claire wins. INT. MRS. BAIRD'S BED AND BREAKFAST – Mrs. Baird wants them to have good time. EXT. SCOTTISH HIGHLANDS – ROAD – Frank wants to tell Claire about Cocknammon Rock. Claire wants to humor him. EXT. MIDDLE EAST – FLASHBACK – Young Claire wants to help her uncle on an archeology dig. EXT. CASTLE LEOCH RUINS – Frank wants to explore where his ancestor, Jack Randall, might have been. Claire wants to examine plant life. INT. CASTLE LEOCH RUINS – Frank wants to escape the present. Claire wants to entice him. INT. VICARAGE – Frank wants to research his genealogy. The Rev. Wakefield wants to help him. **INT. VICARAGE – KITCHEN – Claire wants to pass the time. Mrs. Graham wants read Claire's future, discovers two husbands. (Hero committed)** INT. GUEST ROOM – BATHROOM – Claire wants to get the tangles out of her hair. EXT. VILLAGE STREET – Frank wants to know who is watching Claire. Man turns and is gone.	INT. GUEST ROOM – Frank wants to know if there was another man. Claire wants to know what he thinks of her. EXT. CRAIGH NA DUN – Claire and Frank want to see the druid ritual stealthily. The druids want to celebrate the new year. INT. GUEST ROOM – Claire wants to return to Craigh Na Dun. Frank wants to go the vicarage. EXT. CRAIGH NA DUN – Claire wants to know source of a strange sound. She touches the stone and is knocked out. INT. CAR – MOVING – FLASHBACK – In an accident, Claire wants to make sense of it. EXT. CRAIGH NA DUN – Claire wants to get back to her car. EXT. SCOTTISH HIGHLANDS – Claire can't find the car – or road! She wants to know what's happening. **EXT. SCOTTISH HIGHLANDS – WOODS – Claire wants to find her way back. Hears gunshots. Claire wants to avoid getting shot by RED COATS. She finds FRANK dressed as a Red Coat. She wants to know what he is doing. BLACK JACK RANDALL wants to rape her. MURTAGH wants to save her, knocks her out. (Hero succeeds—almost)**	EXT. /INT. COTTAGE – Murtagh wants to take Claire to DOUGAL. Dougal wants to know who she is. Claire wants to escape but wants to stay alive. Claire wants to help JAMIE FRAZER with dislocated shoulder. Rebels want to take her with them. EXT. COTTAGE – Claire wants to protest. Jamie wants to keep Claire warm on his horse. EXT. WOODS/ OPEN TERRAIN – VARIOUS SHOTS – The rebels want to get away from Red Coats. Finally, they ride near Cocknammon Rock. EXT. CAR – MOVING – FLASHBACK Claire remembers Frank talking about British patrol ambushes at Cocknammon Rock. EXT. NEAR COCKNAMMON ROCK – Jamie wants Dougal to know there might be a British patrol waiting to ambush them. Dougal wants to know how Claire knows about the ambush. Jamie wants Claire to hide. The British want to kill the rebels. Claire wants to escape. She runs. **EXT. WOODS – Lost, Claire wants to find her way so she can escape. Finding her, Jamie wants her to come with him. (Emotional squeeze)**	EXT. WOODS/HILLSIDE – Jamie and Claire ride. Jamie wants to join the others. Claire wants Jamie to take care of his shoulder. The others want to celebrate their victory over the Red Coats. Jamie wants Claire to drink from the flask. Claire wants to sooth her hunger pangs. **EXT. HIGHLANDS – Claire wants them to stop. Jamie tumbles off their horse. Claire wants to help Jamie, who has been shot. Claire wants alcohol to disinfect the wound. She wants to dress the wound and have Jamie rest. Dougal wants them to keep riding for 50 miles, another five or six hours. Jamie wants to go so he won't fall into the hands of Black Jack Randall. (Hero succeeds)** **EXT. CASTLE LEOCH – The rebels make it to Castle Leoch, which is not in ruins. Claire wants to get back to her future, but her journey in the past has just begun. (Hero's new life)**

The teaser is the one segment of the *Outlander* pilot that has been demarcated. It comes before the title sequence. The **point of attack** occurs in the teaser, where we meet Claire as she longs for a vase in a drugstore window. We learn a bit about her recent past.

Claire was a nurse in WWII. Determined and compassionate, she has the mettle to do the difficult job of healing soldiers. This will serve her well during the next journey in her life. As she hears the news of the war's end, she celebrates alone. She drinks a toast to her war life, a life where she had a purpose. There is a tinge of regret as the end of this life draws to a close. However, it's her longing for that vase and what it represents that is the first whiff of her problem.

Claire longs for a life where a vase, fragile and beautiful, would be a familiar object, a life where a vase would have a home. It's this life of permanence and safety, a life where the luxury of fresh-cut flowers in a beautiful arrangement has a place. She wants a life where violence isn't a daily occurrence. Still, Claire turns her back on the vase. She doesn't buy it. She doesn't buy into that life. She wants that life, but she also wants more. This is the point of attack for "Sassenach."

The **hero committed** moment happens in two parts. One part happens for the character. One part happens for the audience. The first part of the hero committed moment occurs at the vicarage. Claire has tea with Mrs. Graham. Claire wants to pass the time while Frank talks to the Reverend Wakefield about historical documents. Mrs. Graham wants to read Claire's tea leaves and palm. Mrs. Graham tells Claire she sees a journey in Claire's future and two husbands. Mrs. Graham also sees that Claire's marriage line is forked, as if there are two paths to her married life.

At that point, Claire is committed to living her life. She is the only person who can live it. Remember the point of attack? Claire longed for a life of safety and security, but she also turned her back on that life. She didn't buy the vase. She didn't fantasize about the house where she would put that vase. Instead, she cultivated her interest in botany and healing while her husband explored his ancestry. Claire has chosen her destiny. She may not understand all that it entails, but she has chosen to live an extraordinary life.

The second part of the hero committed moment happens off of Claire. Claire brushes her hair in the hotel bathroom. From the street below, a man in a kilt watches her through the bathroom window. She's in a flowing nightgown and illuminated in soft light. Claire is a vision to this admirer. Frank, Claire's husband, is on the street. He sees the man and realizes he is watching Claire. Frank approaches this stranger and wants to know what he is doing. Without a word, the stranger turns and passes Frank. Then the stranger vanishes as if he were never there. The lights in the village flicker, then go dark. A supernatural event has just occurred. This is *Samhain.* The ghosts are out—for good or for ill.

This supernatural moment signifies to the audience something wondrous will happen. It's a hint of the otherworldly, yet it's grounded in our reality. This is very important for the tone of *Outlander.* When you're working on a supernatural series, you have to understand how much of it will be supernatural. How much magic will be in your world? *Outlander* has very little. *Game of Thrones* has more, but it's also grounded in reality. *Penny Dreadful* is full-on supernatural cranked up to eleven.

For *Outlander,* the hero is committed by her circumstances. Her life, her destiny, and the time of the year draw her into the past. Claire will be swept up. We the audience know a bit more about her circumstances than she does.

Just before the hero succeeds—almost moment, Claire has gone back to Craigh na Dun to find a flower she noticed there during a druid ritual. Once there, Claire hears a strange sound emanating from the largest and most central standing stone. Claire touches the standing stone and she is knocked out.

When Claire wakes, she can't find her car—or the road. She tromps through the woods to find her way back to the village, back to her husband. However, she gets caught up in a battle between the British Red Coats and the Scottish rebels. As she tries to get away, she happens upon a man who looks exactly like her husband, Frank. She soon realizes it isn't Frank; this is Black Jack Randall. Randall tries to rape her, but he is thwarted by the rebels, who think Claire is a druid. The rebels want to save her, but she is making too much noise so one of them knocks her out.

In the **hero succeeds—almost** moment, Claire wakes up in the past. She wants to find her way back to the village, to her husband. She runs from the Red Coats and finds Frank. But Frank isn't Frank. He's a sadistic, cruel captain of his majesty's dragoons, Black Jack Randall. In this moment, she succeeds. She has found her husband. But her success is quickly yanked away from her when she realizes who she's actually found.

You may be wondering why Claire's decisions to go to Craigh na Dun and retrieve the flower aren't part of the hero succeeds—almost moment. They definitely lead into the hero succeeds—almost moment. Remember the point of attack? Claire wants a different life for herself. Getting the flower won't give her a new life. Retrieving the flower isn't on the main thrust of the A storyline. Retrieving the flower is a way to get us on track to go back in time, to Claire's destiny.

Claire's **emotional squeeze** occurs with Jamie. She has been taken by the Scottish rebels. She has helped Jamie with his dislocated shoulder so she has a nurse/patient bond with him. Based on her knowledge from the future, she warned Jamie and the rebels about a possible Red Coat ambush, which turned out to be true. Still, she has tried to escape from this rebel band. She wants to go back to her own time, and the farther away from Craigh na Dun she travels, the less likely it will be that she returns to 1945.

When Jamie finds her lost in the Scottish hills, he wants her to come with him. When Claire asks if he'll slash her with his drawn sword, he smirks. He tells her that no, he won't cut her with his sword; he'll throw her over his shoulder and carry her back. Faced with the decision, does she try to fight Jamie and run, knowing she might get captured by Black Jack Randall, or does she submit because she has a better chance of surviving with the rebels, even if it means losing her chance to get back to the 20th century? Claire decides to go with Jamie.

Often in the emotional squeeze, characters must make a decision between two bad options. For Claire, getting captured by Black Jack Randall or forfeiting her chance to get back to Frank is a difficult decision. She chooses to go the safer, more secure route, though this choice is hardly safe and secure. She chooses to live. The rebels and Claire head out on horseback.

The **hero succeeds** moment happens in act four. Unbeknownst to his fellow rebels, Jamie was injured in the last battle with the Red Coats. Claire is riding on horseback with Jamie when she feels him slump forward. She yells for everyone to stop. Jamie falls off his horse. Claire quickly unfastens Jamie's sling and finds a through-and-through bullet wound. Claire orders the men around for the supplies she needs. She cleans and dresses Jamie's wound. The rebels have 50 more miles to ride, which will take them 5-6 hours. She tells Dougal, their leader, that Jamie needs rest. Dougal refuses and so does Jamie. Jamie doesn't want to get caught by Black Jack Randall, nor does Claire. Claire succeeds in patching Jamie up for the last leg of their long ride.

The **hero's new life** shows us the magnitude of Claire's circumstance. Until this point, her journey into the past could have been a grand scheme, a tremendous prank, perhaps a bad dream. However, when the rebels ride up to an operational Castle Leoch, something Claire saw as a ruin in 1945 just two days ago, she realizes she isn't imagining this whole incident. She is, in fact, in the past. She will have to deal with whatever comes her way. She'll have to live by her wits and find a way to get back to Craigh na Dun if she wants to reclaim her life in the 20th century.

The idea of Claire living two lives is so potent that Ron Moore has Claire imagine her 1945-self at the Castle Leoch as her 1783-self passes by on a horse. The two women seem to see each other. A bewildered look passes between them. This is the struggle for Claire during the series and the thematic thrust of the pilot.

Outlander is a deceptively difficult pilot because our hero, Claire, is primarily reactionary. Like *The Walking Dead*'s Rick Grimes, Claire wakes up in a circumstance that doesn't make sense at first. She, like Rick, must learn the rules of the world before she can be more proactive as a character. Still, both Ron Moore and Frank Darabont have found ways for Claire and Rick to be active. These characters do make choices. They aren't merely swept up by events. They have moments where they take charge, so the audience gets to see a glimmer of their determination and capabilities.

* * *

Comedy

Successful comedies need to be funny, but they also need to have cohesive structure. In fact, some sitcom writers are hired for their story structure sense rather than their jokes and vice versa. All comedy comes from character, so having your sitcom structured on your characters will make it easier to find the funny *and* make the show emotionally engaging and satisfying.

You may be a joke machine—I hope you are. You can learn character-driven story structure. By pairing consistent joke writing with solid character-driven story structure, you'll make yourself an indispensable comedy writer.

We're going to take a look at character-driven story structure within sitcoms. Sitcoms can have a variety of commercial act break structures. Some sitcoms have a cold open or teaser and two acts, three acts, or four acts. Some sitcoms follow a four-act-and-tag structure like ABC's *Modern Family*. Some, like *Episodes*, have no commercial act breaks.

Spoiler alert! Watch *Episodes* "Episode One," then come back to see why this show works because of its character-driven structure.

Showtime's *Episodes* centers on two British comedy writers who bring their award-winning show to Hollywood, only to have the process fuck up their show.

Episodes airs on Showtime without commercial breaks. I've broken down the pilot episode of *Episodes* and put it into a grid. If you put it into a teaser-and-four-act grid, it's beautiful. Plus, it's a show that stays right on its character wants, which makes the jokes clearer and funnier. One of the tricks to funny characters is: Funny characters don't act funny; they take everything seriously. The more seriously the characters take things, the funnier everything gets.

Sean and Beverly Lincoln, the two British writers, take their show, careers, marriage—everything—very seriously, as they should. Normal people would take these things seriously. Sean and Bev are outsiders in Hollywood. They are surrogates for us, the audience. They get to show us how out-of-sync Hollywood is because they think Hollywood is not normal. And it isn't, which can be both exhilarating and challenging, sometimes simultaneously. Hollywood speaks a unique, tonal language, and you can hear it in "Episodes."

Episodes uses non-linear storytelling in its pilot episode. Non-linear storytelling means the story is presented in a non-chronological order. *Episodes* shows us an incident that won't happen until several episodes into the first season. Then it flashes back to Sean and Bev in London. Then it "flashes forward" to the present of the episode. Confused yet? If you've watched the pilot episode, you saw the non-linear time cuts happen seamlessly.

Just so you know, if you want to construct a non-linear story, you do need to know everything that happens linearly. You need to have your timeline well thought out. This helps you get all the details correct when you move back and forth in time. It can seem tricky and clever to viewers. Think *Memento* or *12 Monkeys.* However, if you know what happens chronologically first, you'll be able to construct your non-linear story more easily. Either way, character-driven structure works like a charm.

Please review Figure 5.3 – *Episodes* "Episode One" grid on the following page. Feel free to refer back to it as you read the next section.

GRID #3 • *Episodes* • "Episode One" by David Crane & Jeffery Klarik (Storyline A: Sean & Bev, Storyline B: Matt) / Grid by Kam Miller

Teaser	Act 1	Act 2	Act 3	Act 4
INT. BEDROOM – BEVERLY LINCOLN packs. She wants to go home to London. SEAN LINCOLN wants her to stay in L.A. (Point of attack) INT. FOYER – Sean wants to know what he did to make Bev want to go home. Bev wants to get through the front door. Finally, Bev wants Sean to know she saw him wanking to Morning. EXT. MCMANSION – Bev gets into the car. Sean wants to apologize, but the GROUNDSKEEPER has a leaf blower blaring. Sean wants him to stop. Bev wants to drive away. EXT. ROAD – Upset, Bev drives on the wrong side of the road. INT. MATT LEBLANC'S CAR – MATT LEBLANC wants to call his agent. Car wants to call his mom. INT. BEV'S CAR/EXT. ROAD – Bev hits Matt's car because she's driving on wrong side of the road. FADE to WHITE.	LEGEND: SEVEN WEEKS EARLIER – LONDON INT. RECEPTION – Sean and Bev have just won a BAFTA for *Lyman's Boys*. Bev and Sean want to leave, but they also want to gloat. MERC LAPIDUS wants their show. INT. CAR – Sean wants to go to L.A. Bev wants to stay in London. EXT. SEAN AND BEV'S HOME – They arrive home to a gift basket from Merc. They want to know how Merc knew where they lived. INT. BEDROOM – Sean wants to go to L.A. Bev wants to please Sean and agrees. They have sex. **EXT. STREET – BEVERLY HILLS – Sean drives Bev down L.A. street and it's very L.A. He wants to enjoy it. She wants to disparage it. (Hero committed)**	EXT. GATE – Sean and Bev pull up to the gate at their gated community. They want to get into their new home. The GUARD wants them to leave because he doesn't see their name on the list. Sean wants the resident list. EXT. MCMANSION – Sean and Bev arrive, stunned. INT. MCMANSION – They want to explore the house. INT. MASTER BATH – Sean and Bev find huge bathtub, want to take a bath. They turn on the water, throw off their clothes, and wait for the tub to fill. And wait, and wait. They abandon the bath. EXT. NETWORK OFFICES – ESTABLISHING **INT. NETWORK OFFICES – CAROL RANCE wants Sean and Bev to meet ANDY BUTTON and MYRA LICHT. Carol wants JULIAN BULLARD to audition for Merc. But Sean and Bev have already promised Julian the role. They discover Merc hasn't seen their show. (Hero succeeds—almost)**	EXT./INT. CAR – Bev and Sean are flabbergasted that Julian has to audition. They pull up to their gated community. They want through the gate. The guard still doesn't recognize them. INT. NETWORK GREEN ROOM – JULIAN reads over his part. Sean and Bev want to apologize to him. Gracious, Julian wants to let them off the hook. INT. NETWORK THEATER – Sean and Bev wants to introduce Julian to Merc. Julian auditions and is brilliant. Carol wants Julian to step out. Merc wants to know if Julian sounds too English. **INT. NETWORK GREEN ROOM – Mortified, Sean and Bev want Julian to audition in an American accent. Again gracious, Julian wants to let them off the hook. (Emotional squeeze)**	**INT. NETWORK THEATER – Sean and Bev want Julian for the role. They want Merc to love Julian. Merc wants traditional handsome American star. Julian comes back in, reads with a Texan accent, and falls flat. Julian wants to show himself out. (Hero fails)** INT. MCMANSION – Sean and Bev want to regroup. Bev wants Sean to admit this is a disaster. Sean wants to see the positive side. They get call from Carol. **INTERCUT WITH: INT. CAROL'S OFFICE – Carol wants to pitch them another actor. She pitches them Matt LeBlanc. Sean and Bev are stunned. (Hero's new life)**

Episodes jumps right into the **point of attack**. It's the first scene and the first whiff of the problem. Bev wants to leave LA. Sean wants her to stay. This gives us a running start to the show. It creates story momentum as well as urgency. We don't know who Bev and Sean are. But boy, is Bev pissed at Sean. Sean doesn't know why Bev is pissed. Is it because he went surfing? From Bev's look, it's clearly not because he went surfing. It's good to notice that we're getting a lot of information about Bev and Sean through this fight. They're in California, and from the sound of their accents, they aren't from the Midwest.

As we learn more, we start to side with Bev. She saw Sean, her husband, wanking off to Morning. Please note: Morning is a person. Not only is Morning a person, but Morning also is a person they know! This is more than a celebrity gimme pact, a swing-for-the-fences fantasy fuck. This is a real, legit possible fling, albeit in Sean's mind right now. But still.

See how serious this fight is between Sean and Bev? Their seriousness makes this fight funnier. Sean suggesting Bev is mad about his surfing is funny. Sean's lack of denial at the wanking accusation is funny. Each line builds a joke because these characters are so invested in this fight. These characters aren't acting funny. They aren't wacky. They aren't trying to make us laugh. We laugh because we see ourselves in them. We might see a heightened version of ourselves in them, but it's their relatability that makes them funnier.

This is the **point of attack**, the first whiff of the problem. Bev doesn't want to be in LA. Bev doesn't want to be in Hollywood. Sean wants to make it in Hollywood. Sean is being seduced literally and figuratively by Hollywood. Bev wants to go back to London. Sean wants her to stay. Here are two characters who want different things. They not only want different things—their wants oppose each other. This is the strongest scene you can construct.

The **hero committed** moment happens at the end of act one. After Bev and Sean win BAFTA awards for their show *Lyman's Boys*, Merc Lapidus, president of an unnamed US network, wants them to bring their show to the US. He says he loves *Lyman's Boys* and wants to do it exactly the way they did it in the UK. Sean and Bev wouldn't have to change a word. It's perfect. Sean and Bev thank him but decline. Still, Sean is taken by the idea. He wins Bev over. At the end of act one, Sean and Bev are driving down a glorious Beverly Hills street in a convertible. This is the life. They have committed to bring *Lyman's Boys* to Hollywood. Sean is thrilled. Bev is skeptical but willing.

The **hero succeeds—almost** moment happens at the end of act two. Sean and Bev have come into the network to meet with Carol Rance, their development executive, and the team. They're doing it. They're going to make their show. It's awesome. They've come to work. Once Sean and Bev sit down in Carol's office, they learn in a very Hollywood way that the team loves the show. Loves it! They just need the star of the show, Julian Bullard, to come in for an audition. *Huh?* Sean and Bev don't understand. They've already given Julian the role. It's the same role he played in the UK. He inhabited the role of Lyman, the title character. Julian *is* the show. Merc loved the show. Carol winces. Well...there may be a chance Merc hasn't seen their show. *What?!*

Here is the perfect yank-success-away-from-the-hero moment. Sean and Bev traveled all the way from London to LA to do their award-winning show in Hollywood based on Merc's love of their show—and they discover he lied. Yep. He lied. And now, Sean and Bev have to ask an award-winning actor to audition for a role he's already won awards for, a part they already offered him. Time to regroup and drink.

The **emotional squeeze** happens after Julian graciously auditions for Merc and the development executives. Julian knocks it out of the park. Everyone laughs. It's pitch perfect. Then Julian is asked to give them a moment to talk. Julian leaves the room. Merc ponders, "Does he seem a little too English?" To which, the development executives—who are in fear for their jobs, car leases, alimony, psychiatrists' bills, you name it—heartily agree. Yes, Julian seems too English. Bev suggests that it's because Julian *is* English.

Cut to: Sean and Bev must ask Julian to audition yet again, but this time with an American accent. This is completely mortifying and a perfect emotional squeeze. Sean and Bev are getting squeezed by the president of the network, their development exec, the lead for their series, and most importantly, by themselves and each other. They buckle and ask Julian to audition again with an American accent. And Julian, being very English, graciously accepts. He lets them off the hook. Sean and Bev feel relieved. With the emotional squeeze ending *up*, the structure of the pilot becomes a tragedy. The second audition leads us to the hero *fails.*

Our heroes have succeeded in getting Julian to read again, but this audition tumbles quickly into the **emotional twist.** Julian speaks in an accurate American accent, albeit a Texan accent. However, Sean and Bev's material was written for a British character. It doesn't play for an American character. As an American character, the material's not funny. Julian crashes and burns. Our **heroes fail.** They don't have a lead for the American version of their show. And the idea that they were going to be able to do *Lyman's Boys* exactly the way they did it in the UK evaporates.

Sean and Bev go back to their rented McMansion to lick their wounds. With one phone call, we get the full perspective on our **heroes' new lives.** Carol calls to pitch them another actor—a well-loved TV actor, a big star. Sean and Bev sit up to listen. They see their salvation. Then Carol says, "Matt LeBlanc." No one could be further from the intelligent, erudite Julian Bullard than Matt LeBlanc. Matt LeBlanc is completely the opposite of what Sean and Bev saw for their title character. But this isn't London; this is Hollywood. Sean and Bev respond in stunned silence, and we smash to black.

From looking at the grid, you'll see the writers had the character wants clearly in mind. If you have clear character wants on your grid, your script will have scenes. If the character wants aren't clear, you might not have scenes. This sounds very rudimentary, but knowing that every scene heading has a scene will save you time and sanity. It's so easy to write a moment on a grid or in an outline, only to realize once you start writing it that you don't have a scene. *Again, if a moment in your script doesn't have a character want, it's not a scene.* Even pros make this mistake. When a scene isn't working, the first thing we ask—if we're thinking clearly—is, "What does the main character want?" What *does* my character want? *Crap, I don't know! Grrr!*

Grabbing on to your character wants in the grid will save you a lot of time during the scripting phase because you'll know you have scenes. What's more, your landmark scenes will be focused. You'll maintain story momentum. Your readers and audience will feel like they are in the hands of a master storyteller because you'll be in control of the story through the characters. The *Episodes* pilot excels in these areas. And it's easy to see it on the grid.

* * *

Spoiler alert! Watch Amazon's *Transparent* "Pilot," then come back to see why this show works because of its character-driven structure.

I believe Amazon's *Transparent* is the heir apparent to *Six Feet Under,* which is one of my favorite shows. *Transparent*'s creator Jill Soloway was a writer-producer on *Six Feet Under.* She can tap into the dysfunctional family members who love each other. You may be thinking that *Six Feet Under* was a drama, so *Transparent* is a drama in a 30-minute format. However, Jill has a deep background in comedy.

Jill was the executive producer of *The United States of Tara.* [57] She has written several plays, including *The Miss Vagina Pageant* and *Not Without my Nipples.* [58] Alan Ball read her short story "Courtney Cox's Asshole" and that got her hired on *Six Feet Under.* [59] For several years, Jill, along with Maggie Rowe and Jaclyn Lafer, has produced *Sit 'N' Spin,* which is an open mic/variety show for working comedy writers in LA. It's generally hosted every other Thursday night at the Comedy Central Stage in the Hudson Theater.[60] *Sit 'N' Spin* is a great way to see your favorite comedy writers and comedians perform raw, real, funny work that you can't see anywhere else yet.

Based on Jill's résumé and repertoire, I feel confident calling *Transparent* a comedy. There are very real, heartfelt moments in *Transparent,* because Jill uses her own family experience as the inspiration for the show. Jill shared part of her experience in a *Rolling Stone* article. She said, "It just immediately hit me as this is the show I've been waiting my whole life to write."[61]

That's the way creating a TV show should feel. Your show should come from your heart. It should speak to you, because you're going to have to gestate, birth, and nurture this baby. You'll lose sleep. You might gain weight. You might want to scream. You might want to cry. You might be bursting with pride. And you might experience all of this in a day. You have to be so committed to the project you're willing to endure the roller coaster that is TV show creation. And if you aren't suffering, you aren't doing it right. If you don't believe me, stop what you're doing now and watch *Episodes.*

Seriously, there will be times when others may lose faith in you because a deal falls through, a pilot doesn't go to series, a rep drops you. These things happen all the time; it's just part of the business. Your family and friends outside of Hollywood may not understand that. They may not be able to relate to your experiences. But remember Oscar-nominated writer-director Frank Darabont? It took him five years to get *The Walking Dead* on its feet. Fucking-*Shawshank-Redemption* Darabont! And we're talking about ratings savior *The Walking Dead,* which seems like a no-brainer at this point. Sometimes you think you've got a no-brainer, but you feel like you're walking into rooms with no brains. What's actually happening is that you have a vision, but you haven't convinced others about your vision. Not yet. The TV show creation process is a *process.* It isn't easy, but man, is it awesome when it works.

Back to *Transparent:* This lovely little show streams on Amazon without commercials, so I've broken it down in the teaser-and-four-act structure. Comedies vary, as you'll see in a moment, but the teaser-and-four-act structure makes it very easy to see the character-driven landmark scenes.

Please review Figure 5.4 – *Transparent* "Pilot" grid on the following page. Feel free to refer back to it as you read the next section.

GRID #4 • *Transparent* • "Pilot" by Jill Soloway (Storyline A – Mort/Maura, Storyline B – Sarah, Storyline C – Josh, Storyline D – Ali) / Grid by Kam Miller

Teaser	Act 1	Act 2	Act 3	Act 4
INT. ALI'S APARTMENT – ALI PFEFFERMAN wants to get ready for her day. INT. JOSH'S APARTMENT – BEDROOM – JOSH PFEFFERMAN wants to have sex with his girlfriend, KAYA. Kaya wants to brush her teeth. INT. SARAH'S HOUSE – KITCHEN – SARAH PFEFFERMAN wants to get her kids ready for school. Kids want to play. **EXT. GRIFFITH PARK – Ali wants to tell her friend, SYD, about her new idea and ogle HOT TRAINER. Syd wants to humor Ali. Ali's dad calls. (Point of attack)** **INT. SARAH'S CAR – Sarah wants to get her kids into the car. The kids want to argue with each other. Sarah's dad calls. (Point of attack)** INT. JOSH'S APARTMENT – Josh wants to tweet photos of Kaya's band. Kaya's band wants to relax. Kaya's bandmate wants to re-record her vocals. Josh wants them to hide the pot from his sister Ali. Ali wants to introduce herself.	INT. SCHOOL – Sarah wants to reconnect with ex-lover TAMMY. Tammy wants playdate with kids. INT. JOSH'S APARTMENT – Ali wants to know if Josh has talked to their dad. Josh wants dad to start gifting them money for tax purposes. EXT. PFEFFERMEN FAMILY HOUSE – Sarah, Josh, and Ali want to know why their dad has called them to dinner. Josh wants to speculate Mort has cancer. Sarah wants to speculate Mort's engaged. MORT PFEFFERMAN wants to welcome them. INT. PFEFFERMEN FAMILY HOUSE – Sarah wants to set up for dinner. Josh wants Ali to look at vinyl records. **INT. PFEFFERMEN FAMILY HOUSE – DINING ROOM –MORT wants to talk to his kids. They want to know if he has cancer. He wants to sell the house. Josh wants to flip the house. Ali wants to live in the house. Mort wants to give it to Sarah. (Hero committed)**	**INT. PFEFFERMEN FAMILY HOUSE – OFFICE – Mort wants to give Ali money. Ali wants to know where Mort will live.** **INT. PFEFFERMEN FAMILY HOUSE – Alone, Mort wants to call friend to say he didn't tell his kids. Mort changes into MAURA. Maura wants to get comfortable in a caftan and let her hair down. (Hero succeeds—almost)**	EXT./INT. RITA'S HOUSE –Rita wants Josh to get comfortable. Josh wants Rita. INT. SARAH'S HOUSE – MASTER BATHROOM – Len wants to know if that's all Mort wanted. Sarah wants to have Tammy over for a playdate. INT. SHELLY'S CONDO – Ali wants to know if her mom, SHELLY, will get anything from house. Shelly wants Ali to know her father is selfish. Ali wants to connect with Ed. Ed wants to let Ali know he hears her. INT. JOSH'S HOUSE – Kaya wants to know why Josh kept her waiting last night. Josh wants to deflect. Josh wanted Kaya to sleep in his bed because he can't sleep without her. He wants to talk about his father selling the family home. **INT. LOS ANGELES LGBT CENTER – Maura wants to be herself. The group wants her to be honest. Maura wants the group to know she will tell her children. (Emotional squeeze)** INT. ALI'S APARTMENT – Alone and disgusted with her appearance, Ali wants to change her body. EXT. SCHOOL – Sarah wants Tammy to come look at the house now. Tammy wants to look at the house.	EXT. GRIFFITH PARK – Ali wants trainer to work with her. Trainer wants to discipline her. EXT. PFEFFERMAN FAMILY HOUSE – Sarah wants to know what Tammy thinks about the house. Tammy wants Sarah to know she thinks it's spectacular. INT. JOSH'S HOUSE – Josh wants to tell Kaya he loves her. Kaya wants Josh to shut up. Josh wants Kaya to cover a song. EXT. BACKYARD – Kaya's band covers Jim Croce's "Operator." INTERCUT WITH: EXT. GRIFFITH PARK – Trainer wants Ali to give him 10 more push-ups. Ali wants trainer. INT. PFEFFERMAN FAMILY HOUSE – Tammy wants Sarah. Sarah wants Tammy. They make out. EXT. PFEFFERMAN FAMILY HOUSE – Maura arrives and sees Sarah's car. Maura wants to know why Sarah is there. **INT. PFEFFERMAN FAMILY HOUSE – Tammy and Sarah want each other. They break apart and see Maura. Sarah wants to know why her dad is dressed like a woman. Maura wants to know best way to deal with this situation. (Hero succeeds/Hero's new life)**

In the pilot for *Transparent*, the **point of attack** is a phone call. We don't see Mort/Maura until the end of act one. However, Mort calls his adult children and invites them over for a dinner. He has something he wants to talk with them about. This is the first whiff of the problem, and we see it through the eyes of his adult children: Sarah, Josh, and Ali. At the end of act one, Mort wants to talk with his children over dinner. They think he has cancer. This derails him. He tells them he is getting rid of the house. Josh wants to flip it. Ali wants to live in it. Mort wants to give it to Sarah. Our **hero is committed**. Mort is committed to breaking news to his children. Unfortunately, he committed to breaking the wrong news to them.

The **hero succeeds—almost** happens after Mort's children leave. Mort sheds his clothes as he talks on the phone with a friend. He admits he didn't tell his kids. Mort becomes Maura. She puts on a caftan, lets down her hair, and gets comfortable. Mort has made the first steps in becoming the person he wants to be—Maura. Maura hasn't come out to her children. (The pronouns here are fluid. I refer to Mort as a character and Maura as a different character. I try to keep the pronouns accurate for each character.)

The **emotional squeeze** happens in the third act at the LGBT Center. Maura talks about an incident at Target where she had to show ID for a purchase and the cashier understood her dilemma. Maura's ID didn't match her outward appearance. The cashier didn't make a big deal out of it. Maura felt like that was a victory. However, she comes clean to the group. She promised she would come out to her children last week but she didn't. She is feeling pressure to come out, but she's also feeling pressure from her children, unbeknownst to them, to stay in the closet. Maura also is feeling pressure to be true to herself and her new community.

The **hero succeeds** and the **hero's new life** happen in quick succession. At the end of act four, Maura comes home and sees Sarah's car in the driveway. Maura could choose to leave. She could choose to call Sarah on her cell phone and see why Sarah is at her house. Maura has options. She could avoid seeing Sarah, but she decides to go into her house. Once inside, Maura finds Sarah making out with her college girlfriend, Tammy. Sarah has been in a heterosexual relationship and has two children with her husband, Len. However, Sarah was very serious with Tammy at one time, and Maura knows Tammy.

When Maura walks into her own bedroom and finds her daughter there with her lesbian girlfriend, Maura has successfully come out to Sarah. There isn't a lot of going back from it. It's not exactly how Maura planned it but she succeeded, so yay? The **hero's new life** involves Maura being Maura full-time and finding acceptance from her family and society.

Transparent has the ability to make you laugh one minute and tear up the next. Jill Soloway said she had been waiting her whole life to write this show, and it seems Jeffery Tambor may have been waiting his whole life for this part. He is absolutely wonderful as Maura. He delivers a nuanced, humorous, poignant, award-winning performance.

* * *

Spoiler alert! Watch *Brooklyn Nine-Nine* "Pilot," then come back to see why this show works because of its character-driven structure.

Fox's *Brooklyn Nine-Nine* is a much broader comedy than either *Episodes* or *Transparent.* Beyond the sight gags and in-scene jokes, it employs quick flashbacks that serve as the punchlines for jokes. It centers on Detective Jake Peralta and Captain Ray Holt. Jake is a good detective, despite being immature. Captain Holt plays a serious, dedicated captain, and Holt must bring Jake to heel to make the Nine-Nine the best precinct in Brooklyn. *Brooklyn Nine-Nin*e airs on Fox, so it has commercial breaks. The pilot has a cold-open-and-three-act structure.

Please review Figure 5.5 – *Brooklyn Nine-Nine* "Pilot" grid on the following page. Feel free to refer back to it as you read the next section.

GRID #5 • *Brooklyn Nine-Nine* • "Pilot" by Dan Goor and Michael Schur (Storyline A – Holt, Storyline B – Morgenthau murder, Storyline C – Charles, Storyline D –Pawn shop)

Cold Open	Act 1	Act 2	Act 3
INT. PAWN SHOP – JAKE PERALTA wants us to know the job is eating him. EXT. CITY STREET – Jake wants us to know he's spent all these years trying to be the good guy. INT. PAWN SHOP – Jake's not becoming like them. He is them. Jake wants to play with video cameras. AMY SANTIAGO wants to interview the SHOP OWNER. Jake wants Amy to know he has already solved the crime with a nanny-cam bear. INT. PRECINCT – Jake and Amy want to book the BAD GUYS.	INT. BRIEFING ROOM – TERRY JEFFORDS wants Jake to update them on the Morgenthau murder. Jake wants to joke. Santiago wants to do her job. ROSA DIAZ wants to know about the new captain. Terry says Captain Holt will want to brief them. INT. BULLPEN – Charles wants Gina to give him advice about asking Rosa out. Gina wants him to take Rosa to an old movie. INT. BULLPEN – Jake wants Captain McGinley back. INT. BULLPEN – FLASHBACK – Jake and Gina want to play fire-extinguisher derby. CAPTAIN MCGINLEY wants his detectives to carry on. **INT. BULLPEN – Amy wants a mentor. Jake makes an ass out of himself in front of CAPT. RAYMOND HOLT. Jake wants to smooth over that embarrassing moment. Holt wants Jake to wear a tie. (Point of attack)** INT. HOLT'S OFFICE – Holt wants to know why Terry has been on administrative leave. Terry wants to explain. INT. DEPARTMENT STORE – FLASHBACK – Frightened, Terry wants to shoot first, ID mannequin later. INT. HOLT'S OFFICE – Holt wants to know about the detective squad. Terry wants Holt to know Rosa Diaz is tough, smart, hard to read, and really scary. INT. COPY ROOM – FLASHBACK – Rosa wants Hitchcock to spill about her secret Santa. Hitchcock wants to keep the secret. INT. HOLT'S OFFICE – Terry wants Holt to know Charles Boyle works hard but isn't physically gifted. INT. KITCHEN –FLASHBACK – Charles wants a muffin. Muffin wants to resist. INT. HOLT'S OFFICE – Terry says Amy Santiago wants to prove she is tough. INT. BULLPEN – FLASHBACK – Scully wants to warn Amy about hot sauce. Amy wants to ignore his warning. **INT. HOLT'S OFFICE – Terry says Amy and Jake have bet on who gets the most arrests this year. Holt wants to know about Jake. Terry wants him to know that Jake is his best detective but immature. Holt wants to make this the best precinct in Brooklyn and wants to start with Peralta. (Hero committed)**	INT. APARTMENT – Jake wants to spitball with Amy, Rosa, and Charles. Rosa notes the perp stole a $6,000 ham. Jake wants to joke about Holt's dress code. Holt wants Jake and Amy to knock on doors. EXT. STREET – Charles wants to ask Rosa out. She wants to go to a good movie. INT. HOLT'S OFFICE – Holt wants Gina to tell him about the bet. If Amy wins, Jake will give her his car. If Jake wins, Amy has to go on a date with him. INT. APARTMENT BUILDING – HALLWAY – Amy wants to do her job. Jake wants to other duty. A SKINNY GUY wants to lie about weed. INT. APARTMENT BUILDING – HALLWAY – Amy wants to know if MLEPNOS knew the victim. Mlepnos wants the photo and shuts the door. INT. APARTMENT BUILDING – HALLWAY – Amy wants to bet Jake $20 the next guy is a hot bachelor. An OLD MAN answers. Jake wants to gloat. INT. BULLPEN – Holt wants Jake and Charles to hit pawn shops. Jake wants to go to places that sell those hams. Charles wants to tell Holt. Jake wants to catch the perp first. INT. BENEFICIO'S – Jake and Charles want to interrogate RATKO. Ratko wants to get away. **INT. HOLT'S OFFICE – Jake wants Holt to know they have a lead but Ratko got away. (Hero succeeds—almost)**	INT. RECORDS ROOM – Jake wants Terry to convince Holt to let him back on the street. Terry wants Jake to respect Holt. INT. TUNNELS – 1981 – The disco strangler wants to strangle girl. Holt wants him to stop. INT. RECORDS ROOM – Terry wants Jake to listen to Holt. INT. BULLPEN – Charles wants Rosa to know he got movie tickets. She wants to call off their date. INT. RECORDS ROOM – Jake wants Holt to know about a lead. Holt wants to commend him. Jake is wearing a tie with Speedos. EXT. BROOKLYN SELF STORAGE – ESTABLISHING **INT. CAR – Jake wants to know why it took Holt so long to get his first command. Holt says he is gay. (Emotional squeeze)** Series of FLASHBACKS – Camera zooms in on a framed article that reads: Openly Gay Captain Appointed. Gina asks if they got the gay vibe? Holt says, "Manscaping." INT. CAR – Jake wants to admit that he's a bad detective because he didn't know Holt was gay. INT. SECOND CAR – Rosa wants to give Charles money for the movie tickets. Charles wants to go out with her. She wants to keep the status quo. **INT. CAR – Holt wants to make the most of his own command. Jake wants to apologize, then he sees Ratko. INT. BROOKLYN SELF STORAGE – VARIOUS Guns drawn, Holt, Amy, and Jake split up. Ratko wants to get away. Jake wants Ratko to surrender. Holt, Amy, Rosa, and Charles have Ratko surrounded. Jake finally gets why he needs to wear a tie. It's a uniform. They're all on the same team. (Hero succeeds/Hero's new life)**

The pilot for *Brooklyn Nine-Nine* by Dan Goor & Michael Schur uses a cold open, which differs from a teaser. The pilot's cold open doesn't affect the show's main storyline, but it does launch the episode's theme.

In the cold open, Jake delivers some dialogue from *Donnie Brasco.* Jake says, "This job is eating me alive. I can't breathe any more. I've spent all these years trying to be the good guy, the man in the white hat. I'm not becoming like them...I am them." This episode is about becoming a team. Jake needs to put his selfish nature aside and join his peers under Captain Holt so they can make the Nine-Nine shine. While Donnie Brasco was talking about becoming one of the bad guys, Jake needs to grow up and become a good guy.

While the point of attack usually happens in the teaser, it happens in the pilot's first act. The **point of attack** occurs when Jake makes an ass out of himself in front of Captain Holt and wants to smooth things over. Holt wants Jake to wear a tie. This is the first whiff of the problem for Jake and Holt. It's going to be a battle of wills.

The **hero committed** moment is on Captain Holt. He will anchor the story. At the end of act one, Captain Holt wants to make the Nine-Nine the best precinct in Brooklyn. To do this, he'll focus on making Jake a team player.

The **hero succeeds—almost** happens when Jake, having ignored Holt's direct order, has discovered the identity of the murder suspect. However, because Jake didn't brief Holt, Jake didn't have the appropriate amount of backup and the murder suspect got away. Holt's team almost succeeded in catching the bad guy.

Jake's attitude causes a major problem. Jake delivers the news that he IDed the bad guy but lost him because he didn't tell Holt what he was doing. Jake gives Holt ice cream as if that's going to make Jake's disobedience okay. Holt is stunned. Holt sees he has a good detective, but with Jake's cavalier attitude, Holt has a liability on his team.

Holt relegates Jake to the records room. To his credit, Jake buckles down and finds a lead on the murder suspect's whereabouts. Plus, Jake is finally wearing a tie. Holt is impressed. However, Jake stands up and reveals he isn't wearing pants; he's wearing Speedos. Holt has the rest of the office come in and appreciate Jake's outfit, which embarrasses Jake. Again, Holt reinforces the idea that the Nine-Nine is a team.

Holt decides to bring Jake along for the stakeout. Jake wants to know why it took so long for Holt to get his own command. Holt tells him that he is gay and the NYPD wasn't ready for an openly gay police detective to become captain. It's through this baring of Holt's soul—Holt's **emotional squeeze**—that Holt inspires Jake to change.

Jake sees how his actions could reflect poorly on Captain Holt and how this reflection could damage Holt's reputation, a reputation Holt worked very hard to build despite prejudices. Holt understands he has to tell his story to get Jake's cooperation.

In a satisfying **hero succeeds** sequence, Holt, Jake, and the rest of the detectives work together to capture the murder suspect. Jake finally understands why Holt wants him to wear a tie. It's part of their uniform. They're a team. They need to appear to be a team. Holt succeeds in pulling together this rag-tag team of misfits. This is our **hero's new life**.

Holt drives the character story. He is the one who catalyzes a change in Jake. Because the character-driven structure depends on Captain Holt, the cold open couldn't have contained the point of attack because Captain Holt hadn't been introduced.

In *Brooklyn Nine-Nine,* Dan and Michael employ complementary character traits: Jake's immaturity to Holt's stoicism. Rosa's opinionated nature to Charles' compliant tendencies. Amy Santiago's by-the-book tough exterior to Jake's devil-may-care goofiness. The casual viewer may think this is just a cast of wacky characters doing wacky things. However, Dan and Michael have carefully crafted characters with specific points of view and traits that deftly play off the other characters. Even with broad humor, the characters have to be grounded in their own truths. The more committed each character is to his or her point of view and want, the funnier the humor will be.

Brooklyn Nine-Nine will go for wacky, broad humor. It's not subtle. Still, the humor is based on the characters and their character traits.

It's been well received, and it was renewed early for its third season in January 2015. Fox clearly has confidence in the show and its unique take on the cop comedy show.

* * *

Assignment

Take your breakdown of the pilot that's similar to the one you want to create and put it into a grid. (To request my **grid templates plus a bonus *Hannibal* pilot grid**, please send an email with "Grids" in the subject line to info@kammiller.com.) If the pilot has commercial act breaks, use that format. If the pilot does *not* have commercial act breaks, use the teaser/cold-open-and-four-act structure.

Include scene headings, character wants, and character-driven landmarks. Get the whole pilot on one page. This will make it easier to see the skeleton of the story. You may need to leave off the time of day or abbreviate the scene headings to make it fit on one page.

Stay on the character wants. You will write the word "want" over and over again. If you stay on the character wants, you'll start to see the essence of the scenes more clearly. Avoid getting caught up in the minutia of the story. You just want to include the essential story beats.

CHAPTER 6

TL;DR chapter 6

Breaking your pilot with the teaser-and-four-act format will help you place the character-driven landmarks and create a satisfying, emotional shape to your story. Assignment: Create your own pilot story grid using character-driven structure.

Creating Your Pilot Story Grid

In this chapter, you'll find:

- definitions of different types of TV shows;
- types of pilots;
- storytelling infrastructure tips;
- gridlock symptoms and cures;
- pilot-y pilots; and
- your own pilot grid assignment.

We've broken down successful pilots. Now you're getting ready to break *your* pilot. Let's take a look at the different types of TV shows and pilots you might be interested in creating.

Serialized shows

Serialized shows are TV series with complex, continuing stories that unfold from episode to episode. Each episode's story builds on the last episode's story. It helps for viewers to have watched the previous episodes to know who the characters are and what is happening.
It is more difficult to jump into the middle of a serialized TV show.

Examples of serialized shows include *Lost, Game of Thrones, Orphan Black, The Walking Dead, Pretty Little Liars, Galavant, Once Upon a Time, Orange Is the New Black, Empire, Nashville, Outlander, Power, Jane the Virgin, Reign, Black Sails, The Royals, Transparent, The Fosters, Switched at Birth, The 100, The Originals,* and *The Last Man on Earth.*

Procedural shows

Procedural shows are TV shows that generally have a self-contained story each week. They have strong story engines. Procedural shows tend to be detective, lawyer, or doctor shows. Often each week's story comes from criminal or patient cases. The cases don't need to affect the characters and the characters' lives in the long run. Procedural shows generally aren't serialized, but they can have ongoing story arcs.

A good example of a purely procedural show is *Law & Order*. Each week the detectives would get a new case, they would arrest a suspect, the district attorneys and ADAs would prosecute the suspect, and the suspect would get a verdict. The show was formulaic, and it syndicated nicely because the audience always knew the story would be resolved by the end of the show. The audience understood their investment in the show. And interestingly, this understanding encouraged audiences to binge watch the show. The *Law & Order* franchises were some of the first shows audiences binge watched.

Procedural shows include *NCIS, NCIS: LA, NCIS: New Orleans, CSI: Cyber, Criminal Minds, Law & Order: SVU, Major Crimes,* and *Scorpion.*

Serialized shows with procedural elements

Serialized shows can have weaker story engines. Often, smart creators will pair a serialized show with procedural elements to strengthen the story engine. Examples of character-driven shows with procedural elements are *The Good Wife, Sleepy Hollow, Homeland, Penny Dreadful, Ray Donovan, Banshee, The Knick, The Affair, Bates Motel, Better Call Saul, Billions,* and *Brooklyn Nine-Nine.*

Procedural shows with serialized elements

Some procedural shows have strong a story engine with some serialized elements. Each week the characters will get a case or cases that will be resolved by the end of the show, but they also have ongoing story arcs. Examples of procedural shows with serialized elements include *Scandal, Grey's Anatomy, The Blacklist, Gotham, Hannibal, The Americans, Arrow, The Flash, Marvel's Agents of S.H.I.E.L.D., Person of Interest, Elementary, Chicago Fire, Chicago P.D., Chicago Med, Castle, Strike Back, The Last Ship, Rizzoli and Isles, Suits, Royal Pains, Graceland, Covert Affairs, Bones, Bosch, How to Get Away with Murder, Blue Bloods,* and *Longmire.*

Stand-alone shows

Stand-alone shows are TV series that have discrete stories within episodes and reset at the end of each episode. In other words, the story doesn't build from episode to episode; each episode's story stands alone. Examples of stand-alone shows are *The Simpsons, Family Guy,* and most of the primetime animated shows. Other examples include *CSI: Cyber, NCIS, NCIS: Los Angeles, NCIS: New Orleans, Criminal Minds,* and *Scorpion.*

Having stand-alone stories can make it easy to put a show into syndication. However, with the binge-watching phenomenon, buyers are looking for more serialized shows because they believe the serialized elements will pull viewers through the series with cliffhangers.

Stand-alone with some serialized elements

Traditional comedies tend to be stand-alone shows. However, they can have some serialized story elements. For example, *Modern Family* is primarily a stand-alone show. Within any season, the majority of the episodes tend to be stand-alones. There can be a few episodes that affect the course of the series. Gloria and Jay having baby Joe and Haley going away to college affected the stories downstream. These life events didn't irrevocably change the series. They didn't change the storytelling infrastructure. They just added a different dimension to the stories that followed. Examples of stand-alone shows with some serialized elements include *Modern Family, The Goldbergs, The Middle, black-ish,* and *Fresh Off the Boat.*

Purpose of the pilot

A pilot must introduce the audience to the characters and world of the show as well as set up the storytelling infrastructure for the next five to seven seasons of television. A pilot also needs to launch the show's concept or premise. That's why pilot writing is the most difficult writing in the town. It's more difficult than writing a feature or an episode of an existing show. And this is not to say feature writing or show writing is easy, mind you.

In fact, franchise feature writing is very similar to television show creation and pilot writing. The *Transformers* features franchise has adopted the TV writers room model and created a feature writers room. Writers for the *Monsters, Star Wars,* and Marvel feature film franchises have done so as well. [62]

As you embark on your pilot writing journey, know that it's difficult. If you're struggling, you are not alone. Professional screenwriters struggle with pilots. TV writers who have been in the industry for 20 years struggle with pilot writing. It's tough looking down the barrel of dozens of hours of storytelling and making all the right choices, or at least making choices that won't back you into a corner. If you're struggling, you're probably doing it right.

What kind of pilot do you need?

Serialized shows and procedural shows need different types of pilots.

Premise pilot

Have a show idea with a complex set-up? Does your show need a bit of exposition or explanation so your audience can understand what's going on? You probably need a premise pilot. A premise pilot shows the beginning of your show's story. It may show how your characters met or started working together. It may show the major event that catapults your characters into a new and challenging pursuit. For example, *Lost*'s pilot thrust the audience into the immediate aftermath of a plane crash. Suddenly, complete strangers had to band together to survive. *Lost* has one of the best premise pilots ever made. It drops the viewer into the middle of this catastrophic event. We understand the stakes from the beginning. We're introduced to the characters through action. We begin rooting for them from the start.

Procedural pilot

A procedural pilot introduces the audience to the characters and world of the show through a big, exciting, buzzy case. A procedural pilot should set up the storytelling infrastructure, or how the show will tell story, for the next five, seven, ten, or more seasons. A successful procedural packs a stellar A-story into the pilot while also introducing the characters, world of the show, and show premise. There are some tried-and-true storytelling tricks to help accomplish all of the necessary elements in a procedural pilot.

One trick is to introduce a main character to an already existing organization. As the "new guy/gal" learns about the organization—precinct, hospital, law firm, etc.—the audience learns about it as well. The new guy or gal is the surrogate audience and knows as much about the organization as the audience does. Examples of shows that used this technique in their pilots include *The Good Wife, CSI: Crime Scene Investigation, Marvel's Agents of S.H.I.E.L.D., Grey's Anatomy*, and *How to Get Away with Murder*.

Another trick is to have an insider character get demoted or promoted in a department or organization. As the insider character adjusts to his or her new position, he or she learns of unknown or secret problems; makes new alliances; establishes new rules or regulations; or creates a new chain of command by promoting, hiring, or firing characters. Examples of shows that used this technique in their pilots include *Strike Back, Homeland, Aquarius, Hannibal, The Fall, Justified, The Bridge,* and *The Killing.*

Another option is to create a big case that pulls the audience into the world of the show. The characters who already exist in this world are challenged beyond their norm. It's this crisis that helps introduce the audience to the characters, world of the show, and show concept. Examples of shows that used this technique include *Longmire, The Last Ship, Dig,* and *24.*

These tricks can be useful in premise pilots as well. Having a character start a new life and/or job, i.e., enter a new world, can launch a show. A&E's *Bates Motel* used this technique when Norma Bates bought a little motel and she and her son moved to White Pine Bay. Their introduction to White Pine Bay was our introduction to it. In Cinemax's *Banshee,* ex-con and master thief Lucas Hood steals the identity of the new sheriff of Banshee, Pennsylvania. As Lucas learns about the town, so do we. In Showtime's *Masters of Sex,* Virginia Johnson gets the job of Bill Masters' assistant. She is our entrée to Maternity Hospital and Masters' daring sex study. In Showtime's *Penny Dreadful,* sharp shooter Ethan Chandler is recruited by Sir Malcolm Murray and Vanessa Ives to join their macabre hunting party for Sir Malcolm's daughter, Mina.

Partners often can divide the duties of introducing the audience to the world of the show, characters, and show concept. In the first season of HBO's *True Detective,* Detective Martin Hart vouches for his newish, pain-in-the-ass partner, Rust Cohle, so they can remain the lead investigators on the freakiest crime their department has ever seen. *True Detective* leans on the huge case and relatively new partner, as well as an entrenched partner who is trying to maintain his standing in the department. This case spans decades. We witness separate interrogations with Rust and Marty by two detectives. They suspect one or both of the partners might have had something to do with the murders. Thus, we have a second set of detectives who help us get to know Rust and Marty as well as this complex case.

In BBC America's *Broadchurch* (originally broadcast on ITV), we get a demotion, new guy storyline, and a big case. Detective Sergeant Ellie Miller must work with Detective Inspector Alec Hardy, a disgraced cop who unwittingly and undeservedly got Ellie's intended promotion. Together, Miller and Hardy investigate a child's murder, a firestorm of a case, in the quiet seaside town of Broadchurch.

In Showtime's *The Affair*, we get several necessary handholds to get into this show. The show is about a Montauk waitress, Allison Bailey, who begins an affair with a New York City novelist/schoolteacher, husband, and father of four, Noah Solloway, who is vacationing on the island for the summer. Allison is a depressed, detached local whose young son drowned. She is our entrenched character with an extended family and a network of nosy island neighbors. Noah plays our new guy and gives the audience a way into the locals' lives. Through *Rashomon*-style non-linear storytelling, Noah and Allison are interviewed by a police detective about a murder that took place on the island. This gives us a big case to draw us further into the lives of Allison and Noah.

Storytelling infrastructure

Your storytelling infrastructure is how you plan to convey your stories for the duration of your series. The storytelling structure in the pilot creates a covenant with the audience. The audience expects you'll use the same storytelling style in the next episode, and the next.

For example, in *The Affair*, Sarah Treem and Hagai Levi set up the *Rashomon*-style storytelling structure in the pilot. Half of the show is told from Noah's point of view, half from Allison's. Each character's POV is unique, even when dealing with the same events. How Noah sees a chance meeting at a restaurant is quite different from the way Allison sees this meeting. They even see the other as wearing different clothes. Their perspectives tell us a lot about them. The audience understands neither character is a completely reliable narrator, but each is reliable to his or her own perspective. It's this promise of understanding Allison and Noah's perspectives that makes *The Affair* unique.

This *Rashomon*-style storytelling is used throughout the series. If Sara and Hagai had only used it in the pilot and used a more linear style of storytelling in the subsequent episodes, they would have been defaulting on a promise they made to the audience.

In your pilot, you want to engage your audience. You want to introduce your audience to the world of your show, characters, tone, story engine, and show concept. Plus, you want to set up your storytelling infrastructure.

Your pilot story grid

Congratulations! Now you're ready to break ground on your own pilot story grid. I suggest using the teaser-and-four-act structure. As you've seen, sitcoms can be broken with the teaser or cold open-and-four-act structure. Dramas are easier to break in a teaser-and-four-act structure. If you decide to break your show using a teaser-and-four-act structure, you can later split an act and create a teaser-and-five-act structure, six-act structure, etc. You also can consolidate acts and create a teaser-and-three-act structure. You can even eventually take out *all* the commercial act breaks if your content warrants.

Just know that your structure is malleable down the line. Breaking your pilot with the teaser-and-four-act format will help you place the character-driven landmarks and create that satisfying, emotional shape to your story. Start with your main character's journey. What are the landmark scenes for your main character?

Point of attack

When does your hero get the first whiff of the problem he will face in the pilot? Who or what signals there is a problem in your hero's life? This could be a dead body, a new partner, a glance from an attractive stranger, a minor malfunction with his computer, a high school buddy who looks great, an acquaintance who just got a new job, a rain check on a date. It could be huge—Sarah Manning seeing her *doppelgänger* jump in front of a speeding train—or small—Claire Beauchamp Randall looking at a vase in a drug store window.

Hero committed

When is your hero committed to your pilot story? What event commits your hero to your pilot story? Your hero needs to fully embrace your story. He needs to commit to the journey of the story. Until this point, your hero could have turned back, gone back to his life before this problem, could've lived without achieving this goal. The hero committed landmark might occur when your hero signs a contract, promises to find his friend's runaway daughter, or agrees to teach his neighbor karate.

The hero committed also can occur when your hero becomes more personally invested in your story. This happens frequently in police procedurals. Detective heroes might become more personally invested and commit to a storyline when the murderer kills someone the detective knows, the criminal comes after the cop's family, the detective finds the body in an unexpected place, or the detective thinks the killer will kill again and no one believes him. Think of ways to get your hero to commit whole-heartedly to your story.

Hero succeeds—almost

What does success look like for your hero? How does your hero succeed, only to have that success snatched away?

The hero succeeds—almost landmark is very important for the audience. They need to see your character have some success. They need to experience the disappointment of fleeting success. Success might involve finding the killer, only to have the killer get away. It might involve getting the girl, only to find out she's got a husband. It might involve landing that record deal, only to find out the label is going under.

Emotional squeeze

What would be the most emotionally difficult decision your character makes in the pilot story? How is your character pressured to make this difficult emotional decision? Who pressures her? Your hero must be tested. Think about the worst decision your character would have to make in your pilot. Be ruthless. During the emotional squeeze, your hero might have to choose between following the law or taking the law into his own hands. Your hero might have to choose to save his wife or his child, but not both.

Hero succeeds

Having made this difficult decision, what is the ultimate challenge your main character faces? What unexpected problem does your main character face as a result of this challenge? Who challenges your main character?

Now that your hero has to live with consequences of his difficult decision, his life may look very different. As a result, he faces his ultimate challenge. This challenge might involve keeping his child alive so that sacrificing his wife has meaning. However, the dangers the father faces are more difficult because his child can't keep up, is terrified, is traumatized, or all the above.

The *emotional twist* might occur when the child figures a way to defeat the enemy. The emotional twist might occur if his late wife appears to the father and helps him navigate safely through a labyrinth.

Hero's new life

Having faced this challenge, what does your main character's new life look like? Now that your hero has survived your story, his life has changed. He has changed. You need to share with the audience what his new life looks like. This might hint at the dilemma your hero has yet to face.

The hero's new life might show your hero and his child have escaped the labyrinth, but they face an empty, long road in front of them. Your hero might have escaped the labyrinth to find he and his child face a horde of zombies. This second ending is called a cliffhanger. It leaves the audience in suspense and makes them want to watch the next episode. Some shows work very well with cliffhangers, like *Game of Thrones* or *24* or *The Affair*. Other shows work better with some resolution and acclimation to the hero's new life, like *Masters of Sex*.

* * *

After you've broken your landmark scenes, place them on your grid. Your point of attack likely will land in your teaser. Your hero committed scene likely will land at your end of act one. Your hero succeeds—almost scene likely will land at the end of your second act. Your emotional squeeze will land between the middle to the end of the third act. Your hero succeeds moment will land in the middle of your fourth act. Your hero's new life will land near the end of act four. Think about it this way—you are six scenes closer to breaking your pilot. It feels good to have scenes set throughout your pilot story. Next you need to create scenes that get your main character to your landmark scenes. These scenes should follow a story logic and an emotional logic.

Story logic

Story logic is the sensible progression of scenes that communicate story to your audience. In other words, the audience should be able to follow your reasoning as your story progresses. Audiences rebel against stories that don't make sense. Do the characters act like humans would act in the circumstances of your story? Does the world work in the way you've presented it? If you're creating a fantasy or supernatural show, does your world follow the rules you've created for the world of your show?

Sometimes it's tempting to cheat and write something that isn't perfectly logical. Maybe you can't think of a better story fix. But hey, we're making all of this up, right?

Not so fast! The audience expects to be transported into the world of your show. The audience can't fully escape if they get bumped by story nonsense. They will only suspend disbelief so far. They expend part of their suspension of disbelief selecting your show in the first place. They know they're watching a television show. They know the characters are played by actors, and they are willing to believe these actors actually are these characters for an hour or more. The audience trusts you'll spend their time and attention wisely. They also expect you won't break the fragile suspension-of-disbelief bubble.

If the audience doesn't believe your story, they will tune out, take you to task on the Internet, or just stop watching. Ever listen to a crowd as they leave a movie theater? If the movie didn't make sense, people pick apart the story logic and identify the plot holes. If *your* story is illogical, your readers and the audience will rip it up.

Emotional logic

The audience tracks your story logic; they also track the characters' emotional logic. They follow your characters' emotions within scenes and from scene to scene. If your main character gets furious because he loses his throne to a usurper, he should still be furious the next time we see him. This might be the very next scene in sequence, or it could be later after spending time with another character's storyline.

In your next main character scene, if your main character is happy and well-adjusted rather than furious, your audience will have emotional whiplash. They will think your character is mentally unstable—literally. Maybe your main character *is* mentally unstable. But if your audience can't follow your character's emotional transitions, they will abandon your character and show.

A pretty good example of tracking the emotional logic of a mentally unstable character is *Homeland*'s Carrie Mathison. Carrie has bipolar disorder. Often she changes emotions within a scene. Most of the time these emotional changes are motivated by a story point. Carrie might be trying to explain an imminent terrorist threat against the American people. Her superiors don't believe her. Carrie becomes frustrated. Suddenly, she's screaming and waving her gun around. The audience can follow her fluctuations, which can be wild. We just need to know what's motivating the change in her emotional temperature. Inviting the audience to participate with Carrie helps the audience buy into her.

As you have story and emotional logic in mind, think about the logical progression from landmark to landmark. Decide on the scenes necessary for the audience to follow the story and characters.

Focus on your main character's storyline first. You may have other storylines, but hold off on breaking them. If those storylines insist and start breaking, by all means, write those scenes down and place them on your grid. However, if this is the first time you've ever broken a pilot, know that you can work on that main character's storyline and come back to your other storylines.

As you put scenes on your grid, only put the story beats. Stay on your character wants. Try not to embellish. Keep it simple. What does your main character want? Who or what opposes his or her want?

With the main character's story and all the other storylines, your whole pilot story should fit on one page. Staying on your character wants and keeping it simple will save you valuable space.

You may ask how many scenes should be in an act. Look back on other shows' grids. Look at your grid from Chapter 6's assignment. Remember, this is a grid of the show you think is similar to the one you want to write. How many scenes does it have? How many scenes are in each act?

Still not sure? Here are some examples. *Bates Motel* usually has three storylines and about 30 scenes. *Scandal* usually has four storylines and 50-56 scenes. If your show is fast-paced, you'll need a lot of short scenes—half-a-page to page-and-a-half scenes. *Scandal* might be a good template to consider. If your show is slower paced, you'll have longer scenes, so *Bates Motel* might be a good template.

Gridlock

Let's say you've broken your story but it's still not working. Part of the story doesn't make perfect sense. The characters behave in an illogical fashion to get to the next landmark. While you can see the story isn't working, you don't know how to make it work. You've put your scenes on the grid, but you can't quite see how to change their order, what scenes you need to cut or add to make your pilot story work.

This is gridlock.

It's not uncommon. And it can be quite frustrating.

How do you fix it?

First, look at all of your landmark scenes and make sure they work. Do they accomplish what you need them to accomplish? Are they hitting at the right places?

If your landmark scenes aren't working, put the grid aside. On a blank sheet of paper, write the landmarks. This is your blank slate. Don't freak out. Just re-break those six landmark scenes.

Focus on the emotional squeeze. What will put the most pressure on your main character? What would be the toughest decision he or she has to make? When you come up with the toughest decision, the elements that would put the most pressure on your main character—this is your new emotional squeeze. It may be very similar to your previous emotional squeeze. It may be identical. It may be completely different.

If it is similar or identical to your previous emotional squeeze, work on the other landmarks so they reflect the emotional logic you need to get to that emotional squeeze. Likely your other landmark scenes are very close to working as well.

If your new emotional squeeze is completely different from your previous emotional squeeze, consider this new storyline. What does success look like for this new storyline? How would your character get the first inkling he or she is heading to this emotional crises? How would your main character get on the path to get to this crisis?

Now go back and look at your point of attack—the first whiff of the problem. Look at the end of act one where your hero commits to this storyline. Consider the hero succeeds—almost scene. You know what success looks like. What could snatch success away from your main character? After your main character's emotional squeeze, what is his or her new goal? How will your hero succeed? What will be the unexpected emotional twist? Finally, what does your hero's new life look like?

Now you should have a list of six landmark scenes. Start with a new grid, put these new scenes into your grid, and re-break your story.

What if your pilot still is not working? Focus on your character wants. If your landmark scenes work, your story will be structurally sound. The characters' wants within scenes and within the whole narrative need to be aligned. Make sure you've written your character wants for each scene. Those character wants will give you story momentum and drive. Remember, all good things come from character.

Still not working? Go back to your character bios. Deepen them. Be specific. Be truthful to your characters. The more specific and truthful you are with your characters, the easier it will be to find the stories within them. You may discover new characters and new possibilities. Be open. You're creating a television series that could live for a hundred hours. You want to be open to as many stories as possible.

Being specific to generate more stories may seem counterintuitive. It may seem like you want to be as vague as possible so your characters can morph into any situation. Some writers leave wiggle room on purpose. However, when the characters are so open or vague they could be anything, they're also nothing.

The more you understand about your characters' motivations, desires, faults, weaknesses, secrets, fears, talents—their physiology, sociology, and psychology—the more opportunities you'll find for them to demonstrate their personalities. You'll understand how they would respond in a certain situations and their actions and reactions will feel honest.

For example, you might have a character who is a doctor, but what kind of doctor you don't know. Your character could be a pediatrician, psychiatrist, immunologist, obstetrician, neurosurgeon, or veterinarian. Each choice gives you different opportunities. What kind of doctor? Where did she study? Where does she work? How long has she been a doctor? Is she world-renowned or a humble practitioner? Does she work for a hospital? Does she work for herself? There are so many questions with answers that lead to more storytelling. So be specific with your characters. Dig as deeply as you can. That is not to say you won't discover things about your characters along the way, but you can only discover things if your character is on her feet to begin with.

Once you excavate your characters, go back to your landmark scenes and see if they still work. Can the landmark scenes be stronger now that your characters are deeper? If so, make changes.

Look at your emotional and story logic. Now that you know your characters better, does your story follow an emotional and story logic that is true to your characters, or do characters serve the plot?

When characters serve the plot, they do things just to make certain plot points move forward. With character-driven story structure, characters should NEVER serve the plot. They should never feel forced to make a decision or take an action because you, the writer, need them to move the plot forward. When the audience can see the writer working, the story isn't working.

Make sure your emotional logic and story logic flow from the characters. When the characters *want* something, they drive the story forward. You don't have to manipulate them to make the story move forward. When your characters are true to themselves and have genuine wants, they drive the story.

After addressing all of these areas, if you still don't think your pilot is working, focus on the end of the pilot. Often if you can see the last scene, moment, or image, it should give you a good idea of where your show is heading. For me, if I can see it, I can write it. I always visualize a moment near the end. I want to have an idea of the destination I'm writing to. Seeing that moment helps me figure out all the scenes I need to get to that point on the horizon. It helps me see my hero near the end of his pilot journey.

Also, picture one of your first scenes or moments. Snapping your beginning and end into focus can help make your pilot feel more manageable. It also can get you psyched to write it. If your landmark scenes work, your character wants are strong, and your characters are specific and true, visualize your beginning and end moments and start writing.

A word on your pilot story

Your pilot story needs to kick off your series with a bang. It needs to be the very best version of your show you can imagine. It needs to deliver on the promise of the show's concept. If you're promising an adrenaline action show, you better have edge-of-your-seat action that would make Jack Bauer weep. If you're promising a big soapy drama, you better have character-driven emotional story twists that French kiss Olivia Pope so thoroughly she thinks she's died and been reborn at the top of the Eiffel Tower. If you're promising raunchy comedy, you better have jokes that make Amy Schumer double over and give Zach Galifianakis sympathetic scrotal retraction.

In other words, you gotta deliver. Plus, your pilot story has to grab viewers by the throat and keep them leaning toward the screen.

Network and studio executives have a word for this type of story. They say—I'm serious here—your pilot needs to be *pilot-y*. Yep, that's your task. Make your pilot pilot-y. And they will tell you if you're falling short by saying, "We think your story needs to be more *pilot-y*." And you'll say, "I can make my story more pilot-y." Know that this means you need to make the best, biggest, funniest, most action-packed, most whatever-you-are-promising pilot. There is more to come on your pilot story in the next chapter.

* * *

Assignment

Create a story grid for your pilot using the grids in *The Hero Succeeds* as guidance. (To request my **grid templates plus a bonus *Hannibal* pilot grid**, please send an email with "Grids" in the subject line to info@kammiller.com.) Use the story grid for the pilot you think is similar to your pilot's structure as a template. Put your character-driven landmarks into your grid first. They most likely will be near the character-driven landmarks of the similar pilot.

Fill in any scenes you need to move logically from your point of attack to your hero's new life. Remember to track your main character's emotional logic as well as story logic. If you need to adjust your character-driven landmark locations, do so. Know that they always will be in the same order—point of attack, hero committed, hero succeeds—almost, emotional squeeze, hero succeeds, and hero's new life.

Stay on your character wants. You will write the word "want" over and over again. If you stay on your character wants, you'll make sure you have scenes, which will save you time and heartache down the line.

Resist getting caught up in the minutia of your story. This may be very difficult. You'll feel the desire to write more. This is the grid. It's the barebones story. Stay on your characters' wants.

CHAPTER 7

TL;DR chapter 7

Your pilot story must set up the world of your show, characters, story engine, tone, and theme of your series. Create audience participation and unforgettable character introductions that hook readers and viewers right from the teaser and never let them go. Assignment: Refine your grid.

Refining Your Pilot

In this chapter, you'll find details about:

- pilot mastery of skills;
- character wants;
- story beats;
- audience participation;
- character introductions;
- the bad pitch out; and
- your grid revision assignment.

Your pilot launches your entire series. It needs to grab the audience's attention and never let it go. It also needs to deliver on the promise of the show. With each idea, the writer makes a promise to the audience. For example, Starz's *Outlander* promised romance, passion, action, and adventure. It promised the supernatural. It promised to take viewers into an unfamiliar world, the past, and strand us there with Claire. The pilot does all of these things.

Remember, your pilot story needs to be pilot-worthy or "pilot-y." It shouldn't be a story we could see as the sixth or seventh episode. It should stand out. For example, let's say you're creating a police procedural. For your pilot story, you've decided to write about a convenience store robbery. A robbery alone likely isn't pilot-worthy. It's not a big enough story to launch your entire series. If the convenience store robbery went wrong and turned into a hostage crisis and one of the hostages is a senator's 16-year-old daughter, then it might be pilot-worthy.

The story also has to set up the tone and infrastructure for the rest of your series. Is your show fast-paced? Is it slower paced with major turns on relationships? Is it dark and gritty? Is it blue skies? The tone of your pilot story should perfectly fit the tone of your show. A convenience store robbery and hostage situation wouldn't be appropriate for the pilot of *Glee* or *Jane the Virgin*. The story needs to set the perfect example of the type of stories your show will tell.

Setting up infrastructure involves the number of storylines, the number of commercial act breaks, the use of a cold open or teaser, and the use of an epilogue or tag. The writer needs to address how the stories will be presented. The writer has a lot of nuts and bolts storytelling questions to answer.

Mastery of skills

Pilots launch your series. They also help you demonstrate a mastery of skills. Those skills include:

- proper script format;
- proper punctuation and grammar;
- character-driven structure;
- scene structure;
- hitting the act breaks hard;
- storyline weave;
- subtext;
- theme;
- character;
- dialogue;
- tone;

- pace;
- orienting the reader;
- audience participation;
- command of the page;
- writer's voice; and
- creating a compelling, character-driven story.

Proper script format

It's imperative that you use proper television format and proper punctuation and grammar. Format plays an important role in production. It communicates clearly with the cast and crew. It determines the episode's budget. Plus, it helps production time out the show.

You probably already know that a page of script is approximately a minute of screen time. The script supervisor can quickly determine if the show is going to be heavy, or worse, light. If your script is heavy, you can cut it down either before production or in the edit bay. However, there is nothing you can do if your show doesn't have enough material to cut together to make an entire episode. You do *not* want to be light on pages.

Writing in proper television script format demonstrates that you get television. You understand the business. You want the industry to know you understand what it needs and can deliver scripts it can use. (I'll expand upon proper TV format in chapters 9 and 10.)

Writing with proper grammar and punctuation demonstrates your intelligence. It's that simple. Most of the folks who work in Hollywood are pretty damn smart. You have to be, too. They're the *crème de la crème*. It's not unusual for an Ivy League physician or lawyer to be on staff with you. It's not unusual for a Fulbright or Rhodes scholar to oversee your script. It's not unusual for award-winning playwrights and novelists to be your peers.

Beyond the writers, the executives are just as accomplished. The people reading your work are smart, and they have a ton of scripts to read. They have little tolerance for half-assed, poorly proofed scripts.

And they are judging you by your work. They do not give you an A for effort. Know that you will be judged, and you won't have any way of knowing *how* you're being judged. No one is going to say they read your script and couldn't make it through all the typos so they're passing. They just pass, and you never get to protest or defend your work. When you turn in a script, you must know it was your BEST work.

Structure and scene structure

I've written about character-driven structure, and we'll hit it again in this chapter. I'll cover scene structure in Chapter 9.

Hitting the act breaks hard

Hitting the act breaks hard refers to building a scene right before the act break that makes the audience want to come back for the rest of the story. It is important to have a big moment, a big question, or a big joke directly preceding the commercial break. This is usually a moment of suspense. You leave the audience with, "What will the character decide to do?" or "How is the character going to get out of this situation?"

You might also think of this as a "holy shit" moment, as in "Holy shit, what is she going to do?" or "Holy shit, I didn't see that coming. How are they going to defeat this person?" If you leave the audience with an element of suspense, they will sit through Charmin and Taco Bell commercials for the answer. You want to retain your audience through the commercials. That's why many shows hit their character-driven landmarks at the commercial act break, as you've seen in the story grids for existing pilots.

The weave

Weaving storylines together in an emotionally satisfying and evocative way is a skill. You know your hero's storyline should include the character-driven landmarks. Your secondary storylines will include some, if not all, of the character-driven landmarks as well. By realizing the character-driven landmarks in your storylines, you'll create a feeling of unity and shape to your script.

When you weave your storylines together, it often helps to cluster the character-driven landmarks for your hero's storyline with your secondary characters' storylines. The juxtaposition of landmark scenes will compound the emotional impact of your landmark scenes. Also, it will give your storylines a satisfying shape and a feeling of inevitability.

In *Orphan Black*, we saw a beautiful weaving together of Sarah and Felix's storylines. In several ways, their scenes were mirrors. They both needed to con someone—Sarah needed to con the bank manager and Felix needed to con the attractive morgue worker.

As Sarah and Felix both moved forward with their cons, the cons became more complicated in different ways. Sarah discovered Beth Childs was a cop. Sarah, the thief and con-artist, needed to con Beth's partner, Art, as well as face a police tribunal about Beth's fatal line-of-duty shooting. Now that's complicated. Felix needed to convince Sarah's ex-boyfriend, Vic, that Sarah was, in fact, dead. Felix had to take Vic to the morgue to see Beth's body and face the flirty morgue worker again. Weaving these storylines together builds tension and makes their landmark scenes more powerful.

Subtext

The subtext of your story is what your story means beneath the surface. There is the coherent superficial story comprised of what your characters say and do. Then there is the underlying meaning of what they say and do.

In *Hannibal*'s "Apéritif," Hannibal talks with a patient, Franklyn, about his anxiety. Hannibal tells Franklyn that his body is acting as if there is a lion in the room when there isn't a lion/predator in the room. The subtext of this scene has to do with Hannibal being the lion in the room. Franklyn is having a very human response, fear, but he doesn't see the predator in the room. Hannibal is manipulating Franklyn. He is trying to convince Franklyn that his anxiety is unfounded when it actually is appropriate.

In *Modern Family*'s pilot, Phil wants to intimidate Dylan. However, Phil throws his back out and Dylan carries Phil like a baby to the couch, which completely undercuts Phil's authority. Dylan is the surrogate father. Phil is the child. This scene demonstrates that Phil will be at the mercy of the guys Haley dates instead of the other way around. Phil can only hope for compassion as his older daughter begins dating.

If your story is only text, only superficial, it will lack resonance.

Theme

A unified theme elevates your script from a clever story to a thought-provoking, enduring story. In *Modern Family*'s pilot, the theme is "all parents want to protect their children." Claire and Phil want to protect their kids from making bad mistakes. Claire wants to protect Haley from herself. Phil wants to protect Luke from being irresponsible with his Airsoft gun. Gloria wants to protect Manny from being judged by the soccer mom. Jay wants to protect Manny from embarrassment after expressing his feelings for a girl. Mitchell wants to protect Lily (and himself) from being judged by society and his family.

Empire's pilot is also about family, but in this case, it's a crueler family dynamic. The themes of *Empire* involve power and love. Lucious Lyon uses power to gain and express love for his sons. He puts the company—the seat of his power—up for competition among his three sons. He doles out his love based on the virtues of his own tortured succession planning. Lucious' favorite is Hakeem. Because Lucious' love is based on power and not emotion or even merit, he is blind to the love his other two sons, Andre and Jamal, have for him. One theme for *Empire* is "love based on power is blind."

Character

Your ability to write character will save you, because the audience falls in love with your characters. Make sure your characters are clear and delineated. Make sure your characters are three-dimensional. Make sure your characters follow emotional logic throughout your story. If you capture your characters, stay on their wants, and follow story logic and emotional logic, your audience will forgive other minor story issues like pacing.

Dialogue

Some people have a wonderful ear for dialogue, while others...not so much. However, your dialogue needs to jump off the page. If you have a great ear, fantastic! You're ahead of the game. If you struggle with dialogue, there are things you can do to improve it. First, make sure your script is structurally sound. Worry about dialogue last. If you know your story is structurally sound, all the dialogue can be tweaked to make it better.

One thing you can do to make your dialogue better is to have a person in mind for the character. Maybe this person is a friend, relative, actor—someone. Listen to this person. Pick up on the cadence of his voice. Learn the go-to vocabulary for this person. Is this person a scientist? Can he say *thermodynamic* and *hydroponic*? Is this person a farmer? Would he say bush-hog or hay bailer? Is this person a teenager? What are teens saying these days? What's consistent with their slanguage?

Next, read your script aloud. Can you say all of the lines of dialogue? If you get hung up on a line of dialogue, change it. If your character is prone to monologues, cut them. In general, your characters should speak like normal people. Most people don't monologue, unless you know an arch villain or two. What's more, monologues can be boring on screen. And they're difficult for actors to deliver.

There are exceptions to these rules. However, these exceptions generally exist because a creator already has cast a role or the creator is very well-known. Aaron Sorkin comes to mind. If you're Aaron Sorkin, hi! Love your work. Thanks for reading. If you aren't Aaron Sorkin, you better trim those monologues.

Next, get friends or, better yet, actors to do a reading of your script. Take notes and have someone else take notes. You'll find all sorts of stumbling blocks, difficult passages, and lines that can be cut.

Again, you want your dialogue to jump off the page. Most readers will read dialogue. Many readers skip description because a lot of description is unnecessary. So make the most of your dialogue.

Tone

Make sure your tone is consistent throughout your script. The words you choose will help convey your tone. "She skips up the hill" conveys a different tone from "she trudges up the hill." Your tone should be conveyed not only by the things that happen, but also in how you describe them.

Pacing

Make sure your pacing conveys the urgency or languorousness of your show. *Mad Men* had a very specific, measured pacing. *Scandal* maintains a nearly breakneck pace. The length of your scenes determines your pacing. Shorter scenes increase your pace. Longer scenes decrease your pace. Generally shows have variable pacing. There may be periods of shorter, faster scenes followed by a longer scene or vice-versa.

If you go back to the breakdowns, you'll see different shows have different pacing. *Empire* tends to have a lot of cutting back and forth between two locations within scenes, which gives the show a sense of urgency. Even with multiple cuts within scenes, the longest scenes run about two minutes. Most run a minute or less.

Hannibal has a more deliberate pace. It tends not to cut a lot between two locations in one scene. This gives the sense of waiting, of suspense. *Hannibal*'s longer scenes still run around two minutes. Two-minute scenes are about the average length for the longest television scenes. On the page, this means scenes tend to be approximately two pages.

Orienting the reader

You must orient the reader and viewer to a new scene and location. You must have description beneath scene headings. You must tells us who is in the scene. You must describe the location in size and vibe. You need to orient the reader and viewer geographically. When the reader and viewer don't have a clear idea of the geography, you've lost them. They won't stick with your story because they can't see it. It's essential that you take care of the reader and viewer by orienting them to the location.

Audience participation

You want your audience to participate in your story. Often writers withhold information from their readers and audience because they have a big reveal planned for the final act. Unfortunately, a lot of readers won't make it to the final act if they can't participate with your story. If they don't know what's going on and can't speculate what is going to happen, they lose interest. You want your readers and audience to be invested in your story. I'll discuss audience participation in depth later in this chapter.

Command of the page

Television writing is different from feature writing. In features, director is king. In television, writer is king. We want writers to take command of the page. We want writers to show us something. Often in feature writing classes, writers are taught not to use camera angles, not to direct on the page, not to show us exactly what you see. However, in television, we're much more open.

If you see something very specifically, show us. We don't always have a lot of time to storyboard a script, so we want as much information as possible. "Pull back to reveal a gigantic pyramid-shaped spaceship." Okay, we see it. "Zoom in on circuit board as a tiny wire sparks and blows out." Okay, we can shoot that.

We want you, the writer, to take command of the page. We want your vision. You're the creator. This is your world. This is your show. Show us your show.

Writer's voice

We want your voice. We want to hear you in your script. The words you choose tell us about you. They tell us who you are as a writer. There are some consistent choices that will make your voice stronger.

Eliminate passive voice whenever possible. We write moving pictures. We want active characters. Use crunchy, chewy action verbs. We love action verbs.

Eliminate long, clunky sentences. Long sentences tend to be confusing. They also tend to be run-on sentences. If you have a long sentence, find a place to break it up. Remember, a period is a perfectly respectable punctuation mark. We will read that next sentence if you use a period. You don't have to fool us with multiple comma splices to keep us going.

Eliminate stream-of-consciousness writing. Many writers write as they think; they believe this is their "voice." But stream-of-consciousness writing tends to be cumbersome and confusing. Your first draft might have some stream-of-consciousness writing. If so, then rewrite it so you can be as clear, active, and concise as possible.

Be careful with exclamation points. In our texting and microblogging society, we tend to overuse the exclamation point! See? It's easy to think you'll add excitement with an exclamation point. The excitement should already be in the sentence without one. If it isn't, adding one won't make your story more exciting.

A compelling, character-driven, unforgettable story

Hollywood is looking for writers who can tell compelling, character-driven, unforgettable stories. Remember, character-driven stories can be action-oriented. If the story comes from character, it'll have a better chance of resonating with the reader and audience. If you've used the character-driven story structure and hit all your landmarks, you're more likely to have created a compelling story. If you've created unique characters, ones who have clear story goals and obstacles, you're more likely to have created an unforgettable story.

Take *Game of Thrones,* for example. Within *Game of Thrones* you'll find an array of unforgettable characters—Tyrion Lannister, Daenerys Targaryen, Arya Stark, Jon Snow, Petyr "Littlefinger" Baelish, Melisandre—the list goes on. These characters have very specific goals. The audience can participate with Arya as she recites her list of people she wants to kill. The audience can get on board with Daenerys as she wants the Iron Throne. The audience can get behind Tyrion as he wants love, then revenge. These are unforgettable, character-driven stories.

Character wants

When you're breaking your story, the most important question you can ask is, "What does my character want?" Your main character's want drives your story. In *Raiders of the Lost Ark,* Indiana Jones wants the ark. In *Game of Thrones,* powerful families want to rule the seven kingdoms. In *Masters of Sex,* Dr. William Masters and Virginia Johnson want to pioneer the science of human sexuality as they navigate their own complicated sex lives. In the CW's *The Flash,* Barry Allen wants to prove his father's innocence and get him out of prison. Character wants give you story drive.

Every scene should have character wants. *If a moment in your script doesn't have a character want, it's not a scene.* Let's look at the bare minimum requirements for a scene. A scene has at least two characters with different wants. These wants can be very simple. Character A wants to get coffee. Character B wants to talk about their relationship. These aren't mutually exclusive wants. While Character A gets coffee, Character B can talk about their relationship. The more focused Character A is on getting coffee and the more focused Character B is talking about their relationship, the stronger your scene will be.

Scenes with characters who have diametrically opposed wants are the strongest scenes you can create. Imagine writing these scenes:

Character A wants to break up. Character B wants to stay together.

Character A wants to execute the prisoner. Character B wants to save the prisoner.

Character A wants to jettison the fuel. Character B wants to keep the fuel for the return flight home.

All of these scenes have characters with opposing wants. The characters have different points of view. Opposing wants and different points of view make these scenes easier to write and push the story forward. Building scene after scene with strong character wants pulls your audience through your script and your show.

As you're breaking your story, focus on your character wants. In every scene, crystallize your characters' wants. If you stay on your character wants, you'll maintain story drive and you'll make sure you have scenes.

Story beats

The story beats are simply the major movements of the scene. For example, here are the beats to a scene about Character A wants to break up and Character B wants to stay together: Character A wants to move her stuff out of the apartment. Character B wants her to wait another month because their lease will be up. Character A decides to stay another month.

The beats are very basic. You can immediately see if you have a scene. You will use your barebones beats for your grid. Use simple language—Character A wants X and Character B wants Y.

Limit your story grid to one page. If it's all on one page, it's easier to see how your story is truly laying out. Is it working? Do you have scenes for every moment? Do you have story drive?

Audience participation

Some writers think of their stories washing over the audience. They tend to think it's a passive experience for the audience. However, the audience wants to *participate* with your story. They want to be immersed in the world of your show. They want to deliberate as your characters make decisions. And you want the audience to participate with your story. If your audience is participating with your story, they are engaged and you're affecting them.

As you're writing, you should always think, "Where is the audience sitting with the story?" In his great script-analysis class, esteemed USC writing professor Ted Braun (*Darfur Now*) notes there are three positions of audience participation with your story:

1) The audience knows the *same* information as the characters;
2) The audience knows *more* information than the characters; or
3) The audience knows *less* information than the characters.

Audience = Character

When the audience knows the *same* information as the characters, we're learning as the characters learn about a situation. For example, at the beginning of *Orphan Black*'s pilot, we're with Sarah Manning. As she is intrigued by the woman at the other end of subway platform, we're intrigued by her as well. Sarah approaches the woman who has taken off her jacket and shoes. The woman has folded her jacket and placed it next to her shoes and her pocketbook on the grungy subway floor. Sarah and the audience want to know what the woman is doing. When the woman turns around, Sarah sees that the woman looks exactly like Sarah. It's a big "WTF?" moment. Then the woman turns and walks off the platform in front of the oncoming subway train. In an "OH MY GOD!" moment, Sarah's *doppelgänger* commits suicide right in front of us.

We the audience know as much about the situation as Sarah. For the most part, throughout the pilot of *Orphan Black*, we only know as much as Sarah knows about her situation. As she investigates *doppelgänger* Beth Childs' life, we learn about Sarah and Beth.

Audience > Character

When the audience knows *more* information than the characters, the audience sits in a superior position. This dynamic often gets used in suspense, thriller, or horror shows. The audience knows someone or something is stalking a character who is completely oblivious. We want to yell at the screen, "Turn around!" or "Run!" or "Don't go into the basement!" Our knowledge keeps us engaged with the story. It makes us hope and fear for the characters. We'll sit on the edge of our seats when we know more than the characters.

Often shows only employ this audience participation style in certain sequences. It would be difficult to maintain this level of suspense for the duration of the story. However, a show can create a superior position for the audience if the audience knows more than some of the characters.

An example of the audience knowing more than some of the characters would be *Hannibal* or *Dexter*. In both shows, the audience knows that Hannibal and Dexter are serial killers. For the first seasons of both shows, most of the other characters didn't know the truth about Hannibal and Dexter. The audience got the voyeuristic pleasure of watching a serial killer interact with other characters. The audience is in on the secret when people share a meal with Hannibal. The audience understands Hannibal or Dexter could turn lethal at any moment. A character being rude or a character committing a crime could flip the switch in Hannibal or Dexter.

When the audience knows more than the characters (or some of the characters), they become invested in the story. This is a great way to get the audience to participate with your story.

Audience < Character

When the audience knows *less* than the characters, we're in the dark. Generally, this is the weakest position for the audience. The audience has little invested in the story, so participation can be difficult. We've all watched shows that withheld too much and didn't allow us to participate. Bafflement and confusion and I-don't-know-what's-going-on! can result from the characters knowing more than the audience.

Some writers like to keep the audience in the dark. They like to "save" information. Unfortunately, when the writer saves information for a later reveal, the audience may have checked out by the time the writer wants to reveal the deep dark secret.

However, there are a couple of shows that have characters who always know more than the audience—and we love them for it. The BBC's *Sherlock* is one of these shows. No one knows more than Sherlock Holmes. (Well, maybe Mycroft knows a bit more at times.) Sherlock can figure out a person from a 15-second observation. He's 17 moves ahead of us, and we marvel at his deductive ability. It's his superpower.

The show *Sherlock* works because the audience is with John Watson. Watson is the surrogate audience. He marvels at Sherlock's ability. He wonders how Sherlock does what he does. He is brought into Sherlock's strange, hyper-intellectual world. And as Watson learns about Sherlock, we learn about Sherlock. With Watson, the audience knows what the character knows. With Sherlock, the character knows more than the audience.

Character intros

Each major character deserves a proper introduction. An introduction will hook your audience into your character. An introduction on screen and on paper requires three distinct elements: interest, sympathy, and empathy.

We tend to have interest in a character when he is flawed and/or he does something out of the ordinary. Sympathy doesn't mean feeling sorry for a character. It means we understand where a character is coming from. We might not agree with the character, but we understand his point of view. Empathy means we know what that character feels. We feel what the character feels.

In the *Orphan Black* pilot teaser, we nearly immediately have interest in Sarah Manning, the main character. First off, Sarah is dressed in black ragged short shorts, fishnet hose, thigh-high stockings and black leather boots. She's street-tough, rough. She boldly displays her sex appeal, daring strangers not to notice her. However, when we meet Sarah, she is asleep on a subway car. She looks exhausted and needy. We the audience unconsciously ask ourselves, "What's her story?" We have interest and the first tickle of sympathy.

Jolted awake, Sarah curses, not realizing a mother and her child sit within earshot. Sarah apologizes. At this moment, Graeme Manson is steering the audience toward sympathy and empathy. While many of us have may not have experienced life on the streets, we might have fallen asleep on a train or plane and been jolted awake. We've experienced waking in an unfamiliar place and being momentarily disoriented. Many of us have uttered an inappropriate word in front of tender ears. We can understand where Sarah is coming from in this moment of surprise and embarrassment.

To fully achieve sympathy, Graeme shows us Sarah talking on a pay phone. Sarah wants to speak to Kira. We don't know who Sarah is talking with or who Kira is; we only know the person on the other end of the line won't let Sarah talk to Kira. The person at the other end of the line hangs up on Sarah, who is frustrated and angry. We've all experienced a frustrating phone call. Maybe you've talked to the cable company, an ex lover, a family member, someone you wanted cooperation from desperately, only to be denied. Most of us have been hung up on at some point. We sympathize with Sarah. We don't know exactly what she wants, but we understand where she's coming from.

Then Sarah sees a woman at the other end of the subway platform. Crying and pacing, the woman clearly is distressed. Sarah and the audience have interest. This is a very smart move on Graeme's part. He is moving the audience into empathy as he introduces another character.

As Sarah approaches her, the woman takes off her jacket, folds it, and places in on the floor next to her shoes and pocketbook. The woman turns to face Sarah. She looks exactly like Sarah. Sarah and the viewer are stunned. However, this woman has *no reaction* to seeing someone who looks exactly like her. This disconnect makes the woman more compelling.

Then Sarah Manning watches her *doppelgänger* step off a subway platform and get smashed by a speeding train. Sarah gasps and puts her hands to her mouth. We the audience gasp at the same time. At that moment, Graeme has achieved interest, sympathy, and empathy with Sarah Manning, his main character. From that point, we are with Sarah for this crazy clone club ride. We also have extreme curiosity about the woman who jumped. While we might not understand why she committed suicide, we know she must've felt hopeless, lost, overwhelmed. We have some sympathy for her. In the next few scenes as Sarah learns more about her *doppelgänger*, Beth Childs, we gain empathy for her.

As we've discussed, *Orphan Black* begins with the audience knowing the same amount of information as the characters. It's a bit easier to gain interest, sympathy, and empathy when the audience is on par with the characters or when the audience knows more than the characters. But what if you're writing a pilot where a character knows more than the audience? You can still have a great character introduction and create interest, sympathy, and empathy. Let's look at the BBC's *Sherlock*.

When we first meet Sherlock Holmes in the BBC's *Sherlock*, he is looking into an unzipped body bag. Okay, that's a little kooky. Then he hits a corpse with a riding crop as hard as he can. He definitely has our interest. *What is he doing? Who does that?*

Then Molly, the shy morgue assistant, asks if Sherlock would like coffee. She is trying to ask him out on a date. However, Sherlock is oblivious. He asks for his coffee with two sugars, effectively ordering Molly to get him coffee.

We gain sympathy for Sherlock. Remember, sympathy doesn't mean feeling sorry for someone. It means the audience starts to get where Sherlock is coming from. Most of us have misinterpreted another person's agenda. We've not picked up on someone else's signals. We've been socially inept. While Sherlock has a super-intellect, he has trouble relating to other people. He lacks social graces. We've all felt awkward at one time or another. We might feel a twinge of self-consciousness on behalf of Sherlock. He doesn't have any clue that he just missed Molly's invitation and hurt her feelings.

Steven Moffat, the writer of *Sherlock*'s pilot, has achieved quite a feat. He generates interest, sympathy, and the beginning empathy for Sherlock as well as interest, sympathy, and empathy for Molly. We become fully invested in Sherlock when he meets Dr. John Watson.

A mutual friend introduces Dr. Watson to Sherlock. Sherlock deduces that Watson needs a flatmate. Watson accuses the friend of telling Sherlock about him, but the friend assures him that he hasn't said a word about him to Sherlock.

Sherlock suggests that Watson come look at a flat Sherlock has had his eye on. Watson can't believe Sherlock would want to move in with him without knowing anything about him. Sherlock breaks down Watson's life story. He knows Dr. Watson was in Afghanistan. He was a military doctor. Watson has a sibling, someone Watson doesn't get along with, but they do still care about each other. Watson stands stunned. From his expression, we see it's all true.

We watch Sherlock use his superpower on Watson, the surrogate audience. In other words, we watch him dissect us. And we are amazed. He impresses Watson and us.

When we have empathy, we understand what it's like to be in someone else's shoes. We understand what they are feeling. While we completely empathize with Watson, we also want to *be* Sherlock. Our empathy with Sherlock lies partly in our desire to be Sherlock.

If you're creating a character who knows more than the audience and other characters, you need to make her so compelling that we want to *be* that character. Like Sherlock Holmes or Tony Stark in *Iron Man,* we want to have that super intellect, even just for a short time.

The bad pitch out

In the room, writers have an apologetic phrase that is supposed to help save face while we get an imprecise idea across: "This is the bad pitch out." We know we need *something* to happen at a certain point, but we don't know what that is right now so we pitch out something like it, but not as good.

I bring this up because even professional writers know we have less-than-stellar ideas. We know the first thing that jumps to our minds probably isn't the greatest. We know that clichéd trope we just flashed on isn't the fix. We know that almost-heroic save or almost-clever comeback could be better. AND we know we can make it better.

Carole Kirschner explains this phenomenon as the 4, 5, 6 rule. She says that most of time, the first idea you come up with is a 1, 2, or 3 on a scale of 10. If you think on it some more, you can get it to the 4, 5, 6 range. What you want to do is come up with an idea that's a 7, 8, 9. If you're lucky, you'll think of a 10 out of 10 idea.

Remember to challenge yourself. Don't blindly and blithely accept the first idea that comes to your mind. Is it a 4, 5, 6 idea? Is it a 7, 8, 9? As you become more discerning about the quality of your ideas, you'll start seeing the spectrum of good and not-so-good ideas. You'll also know when you have just nailed that Triple McTwist 1260-degree turn of an idea.

The flip side can also happen. Your inner critic 'roid rages all your ideas until nothing seems worthy. If this happens, go with the ideas you have. Get words on paper. You can't rewrite, revise, rethink unless you have words on paper. Give yourself permission to put words on paper and evaluate your ideas after you've got them on the page.

* * *

Assignment

Take your initial pilot story grid and focus on the elements from this chapter. First, make sure your pilot story is pilot-worthy. It needs to be edgy and noisy to launch your show.

Once you're sure you have a pilot-worthy story, make sure you have a proper introduction for your main character. Decide how your audience is going to participate with your pilot. Will the audience know more knowledge than the characters, less than the characters, or the same as the characters? Remember, if the audience knows *less* than the characters, that's the weakest position for audience participation.

If you have commercial act breaks, make sure you have a big scene with an element of suspense or a difficult dilemma before each one. You want your audience to come back after the commercial break. Plus, you want to demonstrate that you have the writing skills to pull the audience through the commercial break.

Stay on your character wants. You will write the word "want" over and over again. If you stay on your character wants, you'll make sure you have scenes, which will save you time and heartache down the line. Resist getting caught up in the minutia of your story. This is the bare-bones version.

Think about how you want to tell stories every week. How many storylines will you weave together? How are you going to weave them together? Make sure your secondary storylines have landmark scenes. Place them on your grid. You'll likely want to group your various storyline landmark scenes.

Make sure your story jibes with the tone you want for your series. If you want a lighter tone but have darker events in your pilot, it can confuse your readers and viewers.

Now check your main storyline to make sure it still works and the landmarks still land where they need to land. All good? Fantastic! You're ready to move on to your outline.

CHAPTER 8

TL;DR chapter 8

Stellar outlines convince studio and network executives to let you make your show. Crushing it on your outline is just one step in the campaign to sell your pilot and series. Assignment: Write your pilot outline.

Your Outline: Don't Skip the Outline!

In this chapter, you'll find details about wordboarding and the assignment to write your pilot outline.

Excellent, you're moving from your story grid to your outline. You're super-excited! Right? I'm going to let you in on a little secret. Many writers don't like to write outlines. I get it. The allure of hearing your characters banter can seduce you into going directly to script.

However, and this is a big however—as professional TV writers, we usually have to write outlines to get paid. The outline is part of our contract. If we don't write it, we could leave money on the table. We hate leaving money on the table. And what's worse, the outline often dictates whether we get to write the script. Executives gain confidence in the writer and the story through the outline.

One of the banes of a Hollywood writer's existence is an executive saying, "There isn't any, I don't know, *umph*. We need to jazz it up." And the writer knows the *umph* is in the script. This is an outline! By definition, the outline should have less *umph*.

I've written scripts for producers who didn't require an outline, and it was glorious. Some producers do understand that the *umph* isn't in the outline; it's in the script. They also understand we can rewrite the script, so they let us have at it and pay us for it. Awesome!

But the studios and networks are different animals. And the majority of the time we must write outlines to get to the next step, which is writing the script. So, professional TV writers need to know how to write killer outlines. I suggest embracing the outline.

Every time you put words on a screen or on paper, you have an opportunity to wow someone, to gain a fan, to entertain someone. Isn't that why writers do what we do? We want to thrill readers and viewers with our stories. Adopt this mentality for your outline. This is a chance for you to sell yourself. This is a chance to keep or make the studio and network executives, producers, agents, assistants, etc. as fans. This is a chance for them to know they hired the right person because you write with joy.

Think about how much stuff executives, producers, assistants, and agents have to read. TONS. They have virtual stacks of scripts, treatments, outlines, and novels in their iPads bogging their weekends down. They never get through their TO READ list. And think about all the crap they have to read, just joyless crap. Have you ever tried to wade through 20 bad scripts in a row? It's wordboarding. You feel like you're drowning in words.

Now imagine there's a stellar piece of work mixed in with all the crap. You're so grateful, so excited to read joy on the pages. It reminds you of why you got into the business to begin with. This one document is an oasis. Instead of drowning in words, you're replenished with words. You're rejuvenated.

Be the oasis. Always write with joy, regardless of what you're writing. Send the gift of your writing out to your partners. Make their day, their weekend, their week!

To be the oasis, your work should be fun to read. Yep, that outline you're writing should be fun to read. It shouldn't just be a skeleton of your story. The skeleton of your story is the grid. The outline should be written in your voice. You should use crunchy action verbs. You should paint a picture with your words. The reader should get a vibe of your show through your words. There's no place for passive voice in the sands around your oasis. Only rich, vivid visuals; active, living, breathing characters; and sturdy, juicy concepts survive in the desert of the reader.

How to write an outline

First, start with a title and your name. Center these elements at the top of the first page. I suggest not only titling your series, but also titling your pilot. Even if you only have working titles, these titles will make your project more real to you and your readers.

Number your pages and your scenes. Numbering makes it easy for everyone involved with the project to talk about specific story points.

Also, use a serif font like Times New Roman or Courier. I know. I hear you. Sans serif fonts are in vogue right now. They're clean. They're modern. They're all the rage. And they're flipping difficult to read. There's a reason Amazon gives you the option to use its Kindle Bookery font for all of your digital books. Bookery is serifed and relatively easy to read. Google offers the serif Literata font for your e-books.

What's the difference between serif and sans serif fonts? The serifs. One sort has serifs, one doesn't. Serifs are the downstrokes or tails at the end of letters. Serifs tend to lead the eye to the next letter, much in the same way cursive writing leads the eye through a word. This subtle easing the eye through a word makes the experience of reading more enjoyable and easy. And you definitely want your readers to have an easy read with your work. Choosing an easy-to-read font instead of a font that represents your individual style will help you gain more readers and, one hopes, more fans of your writing.

In your outline, you'll write your scene headings exactly how you would write them in your script. This is important. The outline is the first production document. We can see how many days in and out we have for this shoot. If we have too many days out—production days not on our soundstages and standing sets—we may need to make changes.

Shooting days out costs more than using our own sets. In a pilot, we'll be looking at the sets we need to build and the sets that will become our standing sets. Standing sets figure greatly into series production costs.

Novice writers often don't realize they need to think about building sets, so they write with abandon. However, if you demonstrate that you understand the need for standing sets, you'll demonstrate a bit of understanding about the overall production budget. Also, if your pilot takes place in locations that aren't going to be locations for your series, you'll be in big trouble financially. Generally, the pilot for a show costs more than any other episode of the show. We're establishing everything. However, if your pilot launches your story but doesn't establish locations, you'll have to essentially shoot another pilot in your second episode to build your sets. I don't recommend this.

Think about the world of your show and where your characters will spend a lot of time. Make sure you include those locations in your outline and pilot.

Scene headings also are important because they tell production how many days and nights we're shooting. Nights cost more than days and are harder on the cast and crew. Trust me, I've done shoots that go all night. While an awesome experience, it's also a loopy experience. A punch-drunk state tends to set in about an hour before dawn. Man, it can be difficult to get anything done. If possible, you want to balance your days and nights.

As you can see, the outline is an incredibly valuable document, and it can signal a need to make changes before you spend time writing the script.

Scene headings should be separated from the scene description by a line. Often it helps to underline your scene headings. Underlining them sets them apart and attracts the reader's eye. You'll also include act breaks, which should be set apart from the scene headings and scene description. You can center these or keep them left-justified.

Beneath the numbered scene headings, describe the location—quickly. You just need to give the reader the vibe of a location. A bar might be described like this: A dark, dismal dive full of bikers, barflies, and black sheep. Use your voice. Have fun with your descriptions.

Make sure you give a thumbnail description of your characters. Your readers, including your reps, your producers, and your execs, honestly may not remember your show's details. They have tons of projects. Make it easy for them to get into your story by giving them all the handholds they need. Give them quick, punchy descriptions of characters. A character might be described like this: Helga (late 20s, a dirty blonde white girl with MMA fighter physique).

You'll still need to write what happens in the scene. Refrain from writing dialogue. If you include dialogue, it better be awe-inspiring, character-defining, pivotal dialogue. Remember, you can always write "they discuss the heist with its unbreakable barriers, DARPA-tech security measures, and fragile-yet-explosive booty." Cool. "They discuss their failed marriage and subsequent affairs in stiletto jabs to the heart and psyche until finally, Diego grabs Layla and kisses her passionately." Great. We don't have to read the back-and-forth yet. We just need the vibe of their conversation and the result of the conversation.

Include the characters' wants. The result or decision of the scene should lead to the next scene with these characters.

Scenes with action likely will benefit from strong action verbs and bits of the action included. If a character slams into a door or busts through a wall, the outline may benefit from having this visual. The reader will get a better idea of the level of action and the particulars of the action. Is the action a car chase, a bar brawl, a space battle? What is the scope of the action? You'll want to include that in your scene description.

If your scene description has more than one paragraph, please break it up into multiple paragraphs. For some reason, writers tend to corral their scene description into one big block under their outline scene headings. Reading a big block of text is more difficult than two or three smaller paragraphs. The paragraphs function as all paragraphs do—they consist of sentences that pertain to a specific thought or action.

Your paragraphs should all be left-justified and separated by a line from the previous paragraph.

How to write an outline

Do you want your script to have more acts? After you've outlined your script, you'll be able to see big, suspenseful scenes where you can break up an act. Usually you'll find this scene in the third or fourth act.

Breaking up a later act will help you keep your reader and your audience. Having longer acts at the beginning of your script and episode hooks the reader and audience into your story. They're less likely to change the channel or put your script down if the front half of your script feels full and rich.

If you have too many commercial breaks, your script will feel clunky. You've watched TV. You know how it feels when a show comes back for a couple of minutes then goes back to commercial break. It feels weird and takes you out of the story. Try to limit the number of short acts so you can keep your readers and audience.

Let's say you want fewer acts. Likely there will be an end of an act that isn't particularly suspenseful or doesn't have a great capper of a joke. That's a point where it is great to marry two acts.

If you want to take out all of your act breaks, you might want to wait until you have a rough draft of your script. It's easier to deal with your script and rewrites if you can find your landmark scenes easily and the script is divided into smaller segments like acts.

Another consideration is content. Premium cable, Amazon, and Netflix currently have a non-commercial break structure for their series. However, you need to have content that is appropriate for these buyers. If you've written a show that could go to broadcast or basic cable but you don't have commercial act breaks, you will look like you don't understand the television business. Also, some readers and buyers are looking for writers who can hit those act breaks hard. This is a marketable skill. You want to make sure you're demonstrating your knowledge and skills in each writing sample you have in your portfolio.

Assignment

From your pilot story grid, write your outline. Make sure you use complete and proper scene headings. Single space your outline and number your scenes and pages.

Remember to capitalize characters when they first appear on the page. Also, give a thumbnail character description that includes age and ethnicity.

Write your outline in your voice. Give us the vibe of your show with the words you choose. Use action verbs. Have fun with it. Great outlines will help sell you to showrunners, executives, and producers.

Flesh out all of your scenes. Put some *umph* into your outline. Make sure your landmark scenes still work. Make us feel for your characters and show.

CHAPTER 9

TL;DR chapter 9

After nailing your story grid and outline, you're ready to release the hounds and write that crucial rough draft. Now you'll focus on the nitty-gritty of scene structure. Scene structure will give your scenes an emotionally satisfying shape and completeness. Assignment: Write your script as fast as you can.

Your Script: Write It As Fast As You Can!

In this chapter, you'll find details about:

- Character introductions;
- Scene structure (one, two, more-than-two characters);
- Scene resolution;
- Micromanaging your actors (don't do it);
- Format including scene headings;
- Act breaks; and
- Your rough draft script assignment.

Yes, we're finally here. You've broken your show—your characters, the world of your show, the story engine, tone, and season arcs. You've written your treatment. You've broken your pilot story and completed your grid with your character wants. You've written your outline and fleshed out your scenes. You are READY to start your pilot script.

A lot of writers started out as "pantsers." They would get an idea and jump into writing the script and hope everything would turn out okay. They would begin writing before exploring their characters, the world of their show, the story engine, tone, or story arcs. They had no other way to approach writing, so they started with just the idea.

Then they tried this professional process. It feels foreign, even constrictive at first. However, by the time they get to this point—the time to write—they feel confident. They know their TV series. They know their characters. They know where their show is going. Surprisingly, what used to be the hardest part of the process suddenly becomes more manageable, more logical, even easy and fast. They feel in control of the narrative. This doesn't mean their characters don't surprise them. This doesn't mean they have all the answers. It does mean when they make changes, when their characters do something unexpected, these writers know what they're sacrificing—and what they're gaining—by making changes.

In the writers room we often say, "What does this change buy us?" If the change buys us something worthy, we go along with it. If it costs us more than it buys us, we think of another direction. Having a good handle on your show allows you to make smart decisions and write with confidence.

Let's say you're still not feeling confident. Let's say you're reading this on your own without a writers room or a class. Take a breath and remember this is your rough draft. It doesn't have to be perfect. It's not going to be perfect. Professional TV writers don't write perfect rough drafts. In fact, we don't even call our "first drafts" first drafts. There are several steps before our first draft. There's the rough draft and writer's draft. Plus, there are *versions* of the rough and the writer's draft. Some writers write a reader's draft. Then after the first draft, we keep rewriting and rewriting. So let yourself off the hook.

New York Times best-selling novelist Anne Lamott offers some excellent writing advice about rough or first drafts in her book *Bird by Bird:* "For me and most other writers I know, writing is not rapturous. In fact, the only way I can get anything written at all is to write really, really shitty first drafts."[63] Embrace your rough draft as imperfect. Again, you're simply putting words on the page. You have time to go back and make those words pretty on subsequent drafts. You'll be able to add all the connective tissue on later drafts.

Move forward

At this point, the most important task is to put words on the page. Use your outline. You don't have to write in sequence. Write the scenes you're most excited to write secure in the knowledge you already know the story. You know how to get from point A to point Z.

Whatever you do, get words on the page and don't rewrite—not yet. Work to get your complete pilot story in script form. You need to see the story from start to finish before you know what needs to be changed.

As you're writing, keep your character wants in mind. Every scene will have at least two characters with different wants. If you feel your story flagging, check your character wants. If you stay on your character wants, you'll maintain story drive.

Spoiler alert! Watch the teasers for *The Good Wife* and *How to Get Away with Murder* pilots, then come back to learn how these shows crush it on character introductions.

Character introductions

As you write your pilot, consider your character introductions. First, your characters need a quick description. This description should include age and ethnicity as well as important personality and physical traits. You'll want to type your characters' names in all caps when we first meet them. Then you can simply include your quick description in parentheses. You also can write your character description as an extra sentence in your description. After you've described your characters, you want to introduce them emotionally.

Your characters shouldn't just walk on camera and perform the functions you need them to perform for your scenes and story. You need to introduce all of your main characters emotionally. And remember, to properly introduce a character, you need to generate interest, sympathy, and empathy for that character—*in that order.* You can't just skip a step. If you try to skip directly to empathy, it's like skipping the foreplay and going directly for the orgasm. Maybe it could work for some people in your audience, but for most people, it won't. You need to give them interest, sympathy, then empathy.

Interest simply means your audience needs to be curious about your character. Maybe your character is wearing something unusual. Maybe your character did something unusual. Maybe your character is being ignored by everyone in a press conference except the camera. Why is she at the press conference? What is her role in the press conference? Who is she? Maybe she's Alicia Florrick, the wife of the disgraced state attorney general who has been caught in a sex scandal. Maybe she's a cub reporter on her first job at the White House. All you need from your audience is interest.

Next you'll earn sympathy. Sympathy doesn't mean we feel sorry for a character. Sympathy in character introductions means we know where a character is coming from. We understand a character's point of view. We might not agree with it. We might not have experienced it, but we understand it. We might not know what it's like to be married to a politician, but we can understand Alicia's point of view. We might not have ever been a reporter or needed to ask a question at a high-profile press conference, but we probably have experienced a first day on the job or at school. We probably understand the cub reporter's point of view.

Now that your audience feels like they understand your character's point of view, you need empathy. Empathy means we know what it feels like to be that person. We're in that character's shoes. When Alicia hears her husband deny using government funds to buy hookers but admit to using *his own* money to pay for sexual services, we can put ourselves in Alicia's shoes.

Most of us probably know what it's like to be in a relationship. Within that relationship, we hope we have trust. We can imagine what it's like for that trust to be violated. Most of us have been cheated on, or know someone who was cheated on by a boyfriend or a girlfriend. Most of us have thought about what we would do. We might say, "If my significant other cheated on me, I would..."

What's more, we probably know what it's like to enter an agreement with a significant other or loved one. This could be a very simple level of trust. A significant other promised to come to our birthday party but didn't. A significant other promised to meet us at 7PM and left us hanging. Now magnify that trust to sharing a bank account. A significant other promised to love and cherish us, forsaking all others. Plus, we promised to share all worldly goods, including our money. Then he uses OUR money to pay for sex. *Oh, hell no!*

At this point, the audience is feeling for Alicia Florrick, the good wife. When Alicia's husband asks if she is okay, she slaps his lying, cheating face. As an audience member, we can get behind that action. We are cheering. *You go, girl!*

While we might not have been cheated on in this very public way, we probably know what it's like to have been deceived and humiliated, even in a small way. It could be a moment from our childhood. We might remember when a sibling told a lie to our parent and we were punished for it. We might remember a misunderstanding between friends. We might recall our first heartbreak. Our understanding of the character's emotion doesn't have to come from an identical experience, which is why you the writer need to establish interest and sympathy first. By laying the emotional groundwork, the audience can get on board with your characters.

Character introductions are powerful tools in a TV series. You want the audience to fall in love with your characters. You want the audience to invite your characters into their homes over and over again. You want your audience to miss your characters when your season or series ends. (I miss you LaDonna, Antoine, Big Chief, Davis McAlary, and the rest of the residents of *Treme*!)

What about anti-heroes?

Anti-heroes are basically bad guy protagonists. These are heroes who lack the usual positive traits of heroes—courage, integrity, morality—or who also have heaping doses of other, less-appealing traits. Think Tony Soprano, Walter White, Vic Mackey, John Luther, Dexter Morgan, Tyrion Lannister, Jimmy McNulty, and Jack Bauer. We most often think of anti-heroes being men, but there are plenty of women anti-heroes in TV, including Annalise Keating, Olivia Pope, Cersei Lannister, Arya Stark, Carrie Mathison, Jackie Peyton, Piper Chapman, Galina "Red" Reznikov, Alex Vause, Nancy Botwin, Elizabeth Jennings, Grace Hanadarko—the list goes on. One of the great aspects of television is its focus on character, all kinds of characters. The fragmentation of television opens up new avenues for TV show creation and new characters. There's room for almost any character you want to create.

Let's look at an introduction of an anti-hero. Here is the polar opposite of Alicia Florrick: *How to Get Away with Murder*'s Annalise Keating. Annalise is another defense attorney, but other than that, she's nothing like the good wife.

Peter Norwalk, the creator of *How to Get Away with Murder,* employs an interesting trick when introducing Annalise Keating. He introduces her through the points of view of her students. The show begins with four 20-somethings arguing whether they should retrieve a body. The audience doesn't know who they are. We don't know the identity of the dead body. All we know is the four conspirators are desperate, and they are trying to get away with murder because they tell us so. We have interest in them. How did they get in this situation? Who are they? Who did they murder? *Did* they murder someone? What is going on? There is lots of interest happening here. Finally, one of the co-conspirators, Wes Gibbins, takes charge and tells the others they are going to flip a coin to determine whether they go back for the body. We see the coin ascend and reach its apex.

Cut to—three months ago. It's a bright sunny day in Southern California, though it's supposed to be Philadelphia. (That's totally the

University of Southern California's campus. Shonda Rhimes, one of the show's EPs, is an alum.) And we see the *leader* of the murder conspirators, Wes Gibbins, on his way to class. However, here Wes seems completely naive, innocent. As he enters the auditorium-style lecture hall, he overhears a girl say she threw up four times this morning because she was afraid the professor would call on her. Someone else says the professor is a ball-buster, but he interned this summer with Chief Justice Roberts, so he feels prepared. Another student compares Professor Keating—this is the first mention of her name—to defense attorney Alan Dershowitz, who has defended several high-profile clients, including O.J. Simpson. The student says that Dershowitz is the better academic, but Keating is the better defense attorney. That's high praise.

Professor Keating's reputation precedes her. The audience has interest in Keating before they even meet her. We know she's tough, demanding, smart, intimidating.

Wes is unfazed by the dread that Keating evokes. He is ready for the class to start, or so he thinks. When he sits in the front row and tries to talk to another student who will eventually be a co-conspirator, she tells him she is engaged and the seats are assigned. There's a chart at the front of the class. Clearly, Professor Keating has prepared for this class. She has chosen to seat her students in particular seats. Why? Hmmm...

It's important to note that while we're being introduced to Keating, we're also being introduced to Wes Gibbins. He is the surrogate audience. He is us. We have interest in him. In the first scene, Wes stepped forward at a desperate moment and took charge. We know what his future will bring. We wonder how he got to that point.

Then we have sympathy for Wes. It's his first day of class, maybe his first day in law school. He's hopeful, excited, giddy even. We can understand his point of view. As his future co-conspirator shoots down his attempt at friendship, we start to have empathy for him. She tells him she is engaged and the seats are assigned. The seating chart is at the front of the classroom. In other words, move and leave me alone.

While we might not have gone to law school, we all have probably experienced a first day of class. We've probably tried to make friends in a new situation, which can be difficult and make you feel vulnerable. We have probably been in a situation where we have felt unprepared for what lies ahead. We're in Wes' shoes at this moment.

Another future co-conspirator tells Wes that he doesn't want to be a sitting duck when the shooter gets in the room. Wes is perplexed. His fellow student tells Wes that he has no idea what he just walked into. As Wes makes his way to his seat, Professor Keating enters off screen.

We don't see Professor Keating's face as she greets her class with these ominous words: "I don't know what terrible things you've done in your life up to this point, but clearly your karma is out of balance to get assigned to my class. I'm Professor Annalise Keating and this is Criminal Law 100, or as I prefer to call it…" Annalise writes on the blackboard, creating a wonderful dramatic pause. Then she turns to face the camera and the class. She says the new words on the board: "…how to get away with murder."[64]

As I've mentioned, we have all kinds of interest in this bad-ass professor. Then we have sympathy for her—we understand her point of view—when Annalise admits she knows her students will have a hard time in her class. She's offering her sympathy, in a manner of speaking. Plus, she's slightly self-deprecating. "…clearly your karma is out of balance to get assigned to my class." In other words, I know taking my class will be a bitch. Annalise owns her reputation. She embraces it. Many of us wouldn't choose that tactic, but we can respect her for doing so, She demonstrates that she is a strong person. This is when sympathy starts to turn to empathy.

We all have a desire to see ourselves as the hero of our own stories. We tend to identify with characteristics that make us heroes in our own stories. Annalise being a strong person is something we can identify with. We start slipping our toes into her Manolos.

When Annalise discards the dull academic title for her class, Criminal Law 100, and boldly writes a more enticing title on the board, we start strapping on her heels. When she turns around and faces the camera, when we finally see her face, and she delivers the line, "How to get away with murder," we empathize with her. She has something we want. She has knowledge we want to have. In that moment, we want to be Annalise—bold, commanding, enticing, seductive, intelligent, demanding, confident, self-possessed. She's a hero, or technically, an anti-hero.

Think back to the beginning of *The Good Wife*. Annalise is everything Alicia is not. The difference is really quite stunning. And while we may not always agree with Annalise or Alicia, once we've bonded with them, we're hooked into their shows. This is what you want to do with your characters. This is one way your hero or anti-hero succeeds.

Scene structure

Remember, you carefully structured your pilot. You laid out the character-driven landmark scenes that helped you create a structurally sound and emotionally satisfying story. Those character-driven landmarks helped you create your main character arc. On the story level, you've seen how valuable structure is. The same is true on the *scene* level.

A scene should be shaped or structured like a mini-story. It will have a beginning, middle, and end. A scene structure is driven by character wants. Again, a scene usually has at least two characters with different wants. If those wants are diametrically opposed, that's the strongest scene you can write.

If you've never structured a scene, this may feel forced and constrictive. You may just want to write how you feel. When you write how you feel, you can never be sure your story or scenes work. You have no measurement other than your feelings. You run the distinct risk of writing scenes that don't work.

And here's the real kicker. If you don't take the time to structure your scenes, your competition will. And your competition's script will be stronger, sharper, and leaner for it.

Let's look at a scene from the pilot of *Hannibal.* Check out the FBI men's bathroom scene that starts around 16:06. Will Graham has his face in a basin of water. Blood seeps into the basin. Will emerges from the basin, his face dripping with water. He wipes his face. The image illuminates his state of mind. His mind is flooded by the blood of the victim, Elise Nichols. It's confusing, obscuring, uncomfortable. That moment is designed to put us in Will's shoes. Our hero's want is to understand Elise Nichols' murderer.

Then, Jack Crawford comes into the men's room. Jack is the obstacle. He wants to know what Will knows now. The problem is, Will is confused by the killer. Jack uses several tactics to break through to Will. First, he uses surprise and accusation. Jack wants to know what Will is doing in the men's room. The implication is, why are you wasting time in here. Will is quite intelligent. He doesn't fall for this ploy. He deflects it with humor. "I like the smell of urine cake." A worthy opponent, Jack doesn't fall for Will's humor. He dismisses it. Then Jack yells at another agent who is coming into the bathroom and undoing his fly. "Use the ladies' room!"

Jack's display of anger and frustration penetrates Will's defenses. Then Jack uses another tactic. He puts Will on the spot and asks if Will respects his judgment. What's Will going to say? *No, I don't respect you, Jack.* Not likely. Will has no other choice but to say he respects Jack's judgment. Getting Will on his side helps Jack further break through to Will.

Jack then wants Will to know that Will is the FBI's best hope. Jack believes in Will and Will's gift. The implication: Start using your damned gift already.

Almost apologetically, Will tells Jack that he is on the case, but he is confused. We have movement. Our hero's want is to make sense of this confusing killer. Acknowledging Will has a problem gets him closer to a solution. Will admits he doesn't know this psychopath. He's never even read about him. Will doesn't even know if the killer *is* a psychopath.

Again, we have movement. Will understands the killer might not be a textbook psychopath. That's new information.

However, Jack isn't satisfied. He pushes further. He wants to know what Will knows. Jack knows Will knows something specific about this killer, because Will said putting Elise Nichols into her bed was an apology.

Bryan Fuller and Hugh Dancy do a fantastic job of tracking Will's emotions. In this scene, Will is using his gift. He is empathizing with the killer. He is getting into the killer's mind, and Will is becoming the killer. Elise Nichols was an apology. Will himself is almost, if not quite, apologetic. He experiences the emotions of the killer, which is how he knows the killer has emotions. Will admits the killer felt bad. He believes the killer felt like he could show Elise Nichols that he loved her.

Jack continues to push back. He questions the killer's love. Will believes the killer loves one of the victims and by extension, all of them. Jack escalates his questioning. He reminds Will they didn't find semen or saliva on the victim. Elise Nichols died a virgin!

Here Will *decides* to become the killer. He decides to react the way the killer would if Jack were pushing him. Will defends the killer. He tells Jack that's not the way the killer loves them. Will is appalled, disgusted even. Will says the killer kills his victims quickly and mercifully.

Finally, Jack is satisfied. He believes he has squeezed the information out of Will. "A sensitive psychopath," Jack says.

As the scene resolves, Will's demeanor has changed. He says with anticipation that the killer will take another girl soon. The killer knows he is going to get caught—one way or the other.

I adapted a scene-structure approach I learned from Lance Gentile (*ER, Third Watch*), the Emmy-winning physician and USC professor. A scene can be broken down into its basic components: the hero's want, obstacle, escalations, decision, and resolution. A scene will have all of these components. An escalation *escalates*; it increases friction, tension, flirtation—whatever's appropriate for the scene—and pushes the story forward. An escalation can cause a character's emotions to change from the beginning of the scene to the end of the scene. The decision is like the climax of the scene. The resolution includes the result of the decision, and that all leads us into the next scene with these characters.

Here's a breakdown of the Will and Jack men's room scene. This scene takes approximately a minute and 57 seconds. It has 14 escalations. We know the hero's want and the obstacle before the scene starts. The first escalation begins the scene.

Hero's want: Will wants to make sense of this confusing killer. He wants to understand him.

Obstacle: Jack wants to know what Will knows—now.

Escalation: Jack wants to know what Will is doing in the bathroom.

Escalation: Will wants to deflect with humor.

Escalation: Jack bats the humor away and yells at another agent. He wants Will to know that he is pissed and frustrated.

Escalation: Jack wants to know if Will respects his judgment.

Escalation: Will wants Jack to know that he does respect him.

Escalation: Jack wants Will to know that they stand a better chance of catching the killer with Will's gift.

Escalation: Will wants Jack to know that he is working on it, but he is confused.

Escalation: Will wants Jack to know that he doesn't know this type of psychopath. He doesn't even know if the killer *is* a psychopath.

Escalation: Jack wants to know what Will isn't telling him. He knows Will knows something.

Escalation: Will wants to appease Jack. He believes the killer wanted to honor the victim.

Escalation: Jack wants to know what kind of crazy this killer is.

Escalation: Will wants to give Jack what Jack wants. He believes the killer wanted to show the victim he loved her.

Escalation: Jack pushes back. He wants to know what Will means.

Escalation: Will wants Jack to stop pushing him. He believes the killer wants to love one of the victims, and by extension, he loves all of them.

Escalation: Jack wants Will to know they didn't find semen or saliva on the victim.
Decision: Will reacts. He defends the killer. It's as if he *is* the killer. He is appalled. That isn't how the killer loves them. The killer kills them quickly and mercifully.
Resolution: Jack believes Will. He believes they're after a sensitive psychopath. Will knows the killer will take another girl soon because the killer knows he's going to get caught.

* * *

The men's room scene has a satisfying shape to it. It works with the story logic and emotional logic of these two characters. It delivers important information about the case, but it also gives us insight into the characters. Note how the characters' emotions changed from the beginning of the scene to the end. From here, we can follow Jack and Will's emotional logic and story logic.

In the next scene with Jack, Jack wants Dr. Alana Blum to do a psychological profile of Will Graham. Jack has just seen Will struggling. He has seen Will adopt the killer's emotions. He's concerned about Will, but he also has seen Will have a breakthrough about the case. Jack needs Will on the case, despite the psychological risk to Will's psyche. This is why he has approached Alana Blum.

In the next scene with Will, he is in the crime lab with Dr. Beverly Katz, Jimmy Price, and Brian Zeller. Will avoids looking at Elise Nichols' body for as long as he can. He wants to remain himself. He wants to remain in control of his own emotions. When Will does look at it, he is mesmerized. He enters the mind of the killer. He sees Elise Nichols as the killer saw her. Will's gaze is drawn into the blackness of the body bag. He fantasizes about Elise Nichols being mounted on deer antlers and slowly coming back to life. The Jack-and-Alana-Blum scene and Will-in-the-crime-lab scene are perfect evolutions from the emotional logic and story logic of the men's restroom scene.

Again, in both scenes, we have beginnings, middles, and ends. Each scene can be broken down into a hero's want, obstacle, escalations, decision, and resolution.

Scenes with multiple characters

The Will-and-Jack scene is a great example of a scene with two characters who have different wants. However, you might have a scene with multiple characters with multiple wants. How do you pull that off? Good question. You'll still have a hero for your scene. Your hero may change from scene to scene. For example, Will was the hero of the Will-and-Jack men's restroom scene. But Jack was the hero of the Jack-and-Alana scene. Your hero will have a want for the scene. Some of the other characters likely will oppose the hero's want.

Spoiler alert! Let's look at a scene with multiple characters with multiple wants. Check out the exterior woods scene at the beginning of the *How to Get Away with Murder* pilot. It starts at about 31 seconds into the teaser.

In this scene, two characters want to go back for the body and two characters want to leave the body. We have opposing wants. Wes Gibbins finally decides to flip a coin to determine whether they're going back for the body. Wes is our hero. His want: Retrieve the body and bury it so they can get away with murder.

What is opposing Wes? What is his obstacle? Two of the four co-conspirators want to leave the body. They are afraid they will get caught red-handed with a corpse. This is a reasonable point of view. Michaela believes retrieving the body is stupid. She thinks they'll never get it across campus without being seen because this is the busiest night of the year. Tonight Middleton University is holding a raging pep rally for their Warrior football team. Connor believes even if they could get the body out of the house without being seen, the ground is frozen; they wouldn't be able to dig a grave.

Laurel believes Wes is right. They have to get rid of the body. She points out that they have all night to dig—frozen ground or not. They argue. Wes tells them to shut up because they have to make a decision. It's two against two. Wes decides to flip a coin. They have to make a decision fast and commit to it. If anyone has a better idea, they need to speak up now. None of the others speak up. Wes tosses the coin.

In this scene, Wes' want is to retrieve the body and bury it so they can get away with murder. Conner and Michaela oppose Wes and, by extension, Laurel, because Laurel agrees with Wes. Connor and Michaela are the obstacle to Wes's want. Each time Connor and Michaela speak up, they escalate the situation. And each time Laurel argues with them, she escalates the situation. Finally, Wes makes a decision.

The spine of a scene's structure is the hero's want. The obstacle opposes or interferes with the hero's want. You need to know these elements at the beginning of a scene. Each time the opposition collides with the hero's want, it escalates the situation. Each escalation makes it harder and harder for the hero to achieve his want until finally the hero makes a decision. You can have as few as three escalations in a scene before the hero makes a decision, but it's better to have more. More escalations give the scene time to build and breathe. In this *How to Get Away with Murder* scene, for instance, there are 11 escalations. With each escalation, we get more exposition about the murder and the co-conspirators through conflict. Once the hero makes a decision, that decision leads to the resolution. The resolution should lead the hero into the next scene. This scene takes a minute and 40 seconds of screen time. Here's a breakdown of that first scene in *How to Get Away with Murder.*

Hero's want: Wes wants to retrieve the body and bury it so they can get away with murder.

Obstacle: Connor and Michaela want to leave the body where it is.

Escalation: Wes meets Connor, Michaela, and Laurel in the woods. He has the murder weapon.
Escalation: Michaela wants Wes to take back the murder weapon.
Escalation: Laurel wants to clean it up and hide it in plain sight, right after they bury the body.
Escalation: Michaela wants to leave the body where it is.
Escalation: Connor agrees with retrieving the murder weapon, but he disagrees about retrieving the body.
Escalation: Laurel believes the body will get them caught. She wants to bury it.
Escalation: Michaela wants an option that doesn't require them to carry a body across campus on the busiest night of the year.
Escalation: Connor notes that even if they could get the body out of the house unseen, the ground is frozen.
Escalation: Laurel says they have all night to dig.
Escalation: Connor challenges Laurel. What is she talking about?
Escalation: Laurel admits that this is murder; none of them know what they are talking about.
Decision: Wes tells them to shut up. It's two against two. Wes wants to flip a coin to decide whether they go back for the body or leave it. The others protest. Wes asks them for a better solution. No one has a suggestion.
Resolution: Wes flips a coin.

Each co-conspirator has a good point. As they make their cases, they reveal the stakes. The audience understands the task's difficulty. Peter Norwalk, the creator, is conveying exposition through conflict, which is one of the best, most compelling ways to do so.

Spoiler alert! Watch the first Piper scenes in *Orange Is The New Black*'s "The Chickening," then come back to learn about scenes with one character.

Scenes with one character

A scene usually has at least two characters with two different wants. A scene can have more characters in a scene with different wants. And a scene could have one character with a strong want. Now wait, how does that work? Character wants drive scene structure and story. If there isn't a strong character want, it's not a scene. A moment without a character want is simply a moment, an image.

One show that uses moments and images pretty well is *Hannibal. Hannibal* shows moments and images through Will Graham's perspective. These moments and images are not scenes, but they do give the audience access to Will's frame of mind. They help propel the story forward by letting the audience know what Will is thinking and feeling.

Will's emotions are always evolving. The images and moments don't repeat emotions. In other words, the moments focusing on Will's evolving emotions push the story forward because the audience understands Will is changing. They can follow Will's emotional logic and hook into the story through the emotional moments and images. If you're going to use moments or images, make sure those moments aren't repetitive and do illustrate evolving emotions.

Be careful with moments and images within your script. Moments and images don't have character wants. Without character wants, you lose story momentum. Your story can grind to a halt.

So what's this about scenes with one character? You can have a scene with different wants and only one character. The character needs to have a strong want. The opposing want often comes from the world or the environment. For example, the *Orange Is the New Black* episode "The Chickening" starts with Piper being awakened by the PA system on a

Sunday morning. The voice on the PA says, "In a world filled with hate, we must still dare to hope. In a world filled with despair, we must still dare to dream." This sets the tone and theme of the episode. This is the challenge of the environment. Then the voice on the PA rattles through a list of worship services, none of which appeal to Piper. Piper grabs a granola bar, peanut butter, and her *Gone Girl* book. She gets coffee from the cafeteria. Piper goes outside to the yard, sits under a tree, and tries to enjoy her granola bar, coffee, and book. Unfortunately, she is interrupted by a chicken.

At first glance, these seem like a string of moments. However, Piper has a distinct want. Piper wants to enjoy her Sunday morning ritual. On the outside, maybe Piper used to have a cup of coffee and read *The New York Times* on Sunday mornings. Maybe she used to go down to the coffee shop and read a book. Piper wants to enjoy her Sunday morning ritual as best she can. Her opposition is prison. Prison intrudes on her life, her rituals, her Sunday morning. Even outside, where she might be able to pretend she isn't in prison, she has to put up with a random chicken. Her life as she knew it is gone.

Piper does have a scene with Correctional Officer O'Neill in the middle of this sequence. Piper has gotten her coffee and is leaving the cafeteria. O'Neill scolds her about missing breakfast, the most important meal of the day. Piper thanks him. O'Neill makes a snide comment because she doesn't listen to him. Piper tries to smooth it over. O'Neill tells Piper he is doing the four-hour body. Piper says she doesn't know what that means. O'Neill implies that soon she'll be able to see the difference in his body and then she'll know what it means. Piper decides to wish him good luck and leaves.

In this little scene, O'Neill is trying to establish a ritual, the four-hour body, whatever that means. He also is trying to impart a ritual—eating breakfast. So this scene is on point with Piper's want. Piper wants to enjoy her own Sunday ritual. The opposition is the prison, represented by O'Neill. Prison wants to control Piper's life, including her Sunday morning.

If you have a scene with one person, make sure it's really a scene. Make sure it has at least two different wants. If it doesn't have wants, it may be a moment or an image. If it's a moment or an image, make sure it's illustrating something new about a character, a new emotion, and it's not simply repeating something the audience already knows.

The escalations in a scene can be lines of dialogue or actions. In *Orange Is the New Black*'s "The Chickening," most of the escalations are actions. It's wise to have actions as escalations because it forces you the writer to show, not tell the audience what is going on. It also immerses the viewer in the show. If all of your escalations are oral, your audience doesn't have to watch your show. Your TV show turns into a radio show. The audience can just listen to it.

Find ways to move the story forward through actions. Find actions to give the audience access to your character's emotions and state of being.

Resolution of scenes

When a scene ends, the audience and reader should know where the hero of the scene stands emotionally. We used to use a technique at the end of scenes where we would indicate a character and an emotion. It would read something like this—"OFF Piper, perplexed..." The reader and director knew we wanted the scene to end with Piper's face reflecting that emotion. We don't use this technique as much as we used to, because we don't have every scene end on a face. We might end a scene on a master shot.

Still, you want the reader and audience to know the resolution or resulting emotion of the scene. The scene shouldn't just end with dialogue, as if all the skeletal, pertinent information was delivered and the audience and director can figure out for themselves what to do with the end of that scene. You the writer need to decide how to end the scene. And you the writer need to decide what emotions your characters are feeling. Resolving your scenes will not only help the actors, directors, and audience, but also make your script feel complete.

Micromanaging your actors

While you want your scenes to feel complete and help your director and actors know the emotional temperature of a scene, you don't want to dictate every little movement the actor makes. Some writers take the show-don't-tell maxim to heart, and they try to think of an action that demonstrates every emotion. Unfortunately, this makes actors puppets. And actors aren't puppets.

Writers often micromanage the actors because they forget actors are real people. Yep, Laurence Fishburne, Uzo Aduba, Viola Davis, Vera Farmiga, and Peter Dinklage are all real, actual people. More than that, they are real, actual people who are smart actors. Respect your actors. When you write a character scratches her nose, says a line, sniffles, rubs her inner arm, and bites her lip—you're micromanaging the actor.

Directing the actors on the page helps no one, including you. The more extraneous, fidgety movements you give your characters, the harder your script is to read. Readers will start to skip over all of your description when the description isn't important. **You're actually training readers to skip your description.**

Some writers can write an entire page of description and readers will love it because everything those writers write is important. Readers will read the words on the page if they are vital to the story. However, if they're not vital, readers start skimming.

Some writers say they feel like they need to break up dialogue so the reader won't get bored. Breaking up dialogue has exactly the opposite effect. The reader gets really bored reading about a character stirring a cup of coffee or shuffling her feet if it isn't essential to the scene.

There's a scene in *Breaking Bad* where stirring a cup of coffee is absolutely essential to the story. However, if you've been abusing your reader with stray character directions, the reader won't know when something is essential. Again, the reader likely will skip over your description and only read the dialogue. Micromanaging your actors—don't do it.

Format

You *must* write in proper television format. I'm not going to go into a lot of detail about format, but here are some basics.

```
                         TITLE
                   Title is centered.

                     ACT ONE (Acts have a 4 inch left
                     margin.)

EXT. SOUNDSTAGE - DAY [SCENE HEADINGS HAVE 1.5 INCH LEFT
MARGIN AND 1 INCH RIGHT MARGIN]

Description or action lines have 1.5 inch left margin and a
1 inch right margin.

                  CHARACTER NAMES HAVE A 3.5 INCH LEFT
                  MARGIN AND ~1.75 RIGHT MARGIN
              (Parentheticals have 3
               inch left margin and a 4
               inch right margin)
           Dialogue has a 2.5 inch left margin
           and a 3 inch right margin.

                                          TRANSITIONS ARE
                                          RIGHT-JUSTIFIED
                                          WITH A 4.5 INCH
                                              LEFT MARGIN
```

Figure 9.1: Basic TV drama format and margin sample.

Final Draft has templates available for more than 50 TV series. These templates will automatically give you the right style for margins, act breaks, transitions, dialogue, character names—all the elements you need in your pilot script. If you want to use the template for *Mad Men* or *South Park*, you simply create a new file from "New from Stationery" and choose the show you'd like to emulate. Don't see any template you like within the software? You can download the TV templates from Final Draft.

I also suggest finding pilot scripts online that are similar to the type of show you want to write. You can find digital scripts for many of your favorite TV shows with Internet searches. Once you have a copy of a show you like, you can jack the style of that TV script. However, you'll likely find production scripts on the Internet. You want to make sure you're copying the style of a *non-production* script. How do you know the difference? Pilot scripts do NOT have scene numbers.

It's good to note that single camera sitcom and multi-camera sitcom scripts are formatted differently. Single cams are single spaced. Multi-cams are double-spaced, including the dialogue.

You will see a lot of variations from script to script, which can get tricky. One of the major areas that tends to confuse people is scene headings. For all original pilot scripts—drama and comedies—you need to consider act breaks and have proper scene headings.

Writing accurate scene headings makes you look like a pro. They communicate very specific information to production and demonstrate that you understand television production. One of the things production does first is track the days in and out—how many interior scenes and how many exterior scenes you have in your script. They also look at how many day scenes vs. night scenes are in your script. They look at how many scenes are on standing sets and how many scenes are location shoots. As I mentioned earlier, exterior and location scenes are more expensive than interior scenes on your standing sets. However, there is a caveat. You want to make sure you have both interiors and exteriors, because too many interiors can make your show feel claustrophobic.

Day and night scenes on your standing sets are equivalent, but exterior night scenes are much more expensive and harder on the crew. Unless you have a show about vampires, you'll want to make sure you have day shoots as well as night shoots. Use day or night for the time indication. Avoid using dawn, midnight, dusk, noon, evening, or other specific times of day. If you write dawn, production will plan to shoot specifically at dawn on that day. They will time it out to the minute. Again, unless you're writing a show about vampires and the precise time of day plays an important part in your story, only use day and night.

A proper scene heading will begin with either INT. or EXT. This communicates quickly to production how many days in and out we'll need to shoot.

The next element is the location. You need to go from the largest location to smaller location. For example:

INT. WHITE HOUSE – OVAL OFFICE – NIGHT

This is a proper scene heading. Notice there are spaces between the em dashes in TV script scene headings. The elements need to be separated. The scene heading starts with interior so we know we're shooting inside, probably on our sets. The next location is the largest location—WHITE HOUSE. This communicates with production where the scene takes place. Production can count how many scenes take place in the WHITE HOUSE very quickly. The third element is the smaller, more specific location—OVAL OFFICE. This tells production the exact set they need to prep for that scene. Finally, the scene heading indicates the scene takes place at NIGHT. Production will know which mattes to put behind the windows as well as the intensity of the lighting on set for this scene.

You may see all kinds of variations on this format, but this is the standard format. Using the standard, accepted format will demonstrate you understand how to communicate clearly with production through your scene headings. It's a skill that will demonstrate you're an industry professional. I'll cover more pro formatting tips in chapter 10.

Act breaks

Some writers only want to write for HBO. They're willing to forego all the other buyers in the town and only write for one, maybe two buyers. Some buyers, like HBO and Showtime, currently don't have commercial breaks. So when the HBO-centric writers are writing their pilots, they sometimes choose not to have commercial act breaks. They think it makes a statement of intent about the potential buyer. However, some writers who make this stylistic choice then go on to write content that's not appropriate for premium cable. HBO and Showtime want noisy, edgy content with sex and violence. If you're writing content that could fit on the CW, it's not going to be right for HBO.

If your show's content could be on broadcast network or non-premium cable, you need act breaks. Writing with act breaks will demonstrate that you understand television. It will demonstrate a skill. Being able to write stellar commercial act break scenes that make the audience want to stick with your show through commercials is a marketable skill. Leaving out act breaks can make you look like you don't understand television and that you don't understand the market for your show.

Length

For a drama pilot, your script can be anywhere from 55 to 65 pages. Single-camera sitcom pilot scripts usually run around 30-35 pages. Multi-camera sitcom scripts usually run around 50-56 pages because they're double-spaced.

* * *

Assignment

Off to script! By this time, you're probably itching to start. You see your pilot clearly. You know where you're going with the story.

Using your outline, begin your script. Write as fast as you can. Get words on paper. If you haven't found the perfect word, use the word that springs to mind and keep going.

In most university settings, you're getting notes along the way. Take the notes and keep pushing forward. Resist second guessing. Trust that you've done all the prep work. Now you need to see the living, fire-breathing script.

If you're writing on your own, write with the door closed, as Stephen King suggests in his wonderful book *On Writing*. Writing with the door closed means you keep your work to yourself while you're writing this draft. This technique helps keep those critics—internal and external—at bay. It gives you permission to use that not-so-perfect word or turn of phrase. You know no one is going to see your naked, bawling, vernix-coated rough draft.

CHAPTER 10

TL;DR chapter 10

Rewriting is not merely tweaking words or sentences. Proper rewriting will help you sharpen and deepen your script by jettisoning moments that aren't scenes, scenes that aren't working, dialogue that is leaden, and boggy description that micromanages actors. Assignment: Rewrite your rough draft.

Your Second Draft: Writing Is Rewriting

In this chapter, you'll find details about:

- warm reads;
- beginnings of scenes;
- cold reads;
- the polish;
- the art of the easy read;
- character descriptions; and
- your second-draft rewrite assignment.

Congratulations—you've finished a draft of your pilot script! What an accomplishment. Now you're ready for the rewrite. Here are the things you'll want to consider for the next draft.

Save this draft

Save this draft of your script and do a "save as" version to start the next draft. Title the file accordingly. You'll want to make sure you save your script often and that you save anything you cut out of your script. I have a catch-all document, cleverly titled "cut-outs," where I paste anything

I cut out of my script. I always want to make sure I have that exact wording in case I ever need to go back to something I've written.

I write fast, so sometimes I save a new draft every day. Make sure you have a robust backup system that makes sense and works for you. It can be devastating to lose a draft of your script and try to recreate what you wrote from memory. If you ever lose a draft, start recreating it as soon as possible. It will be easier to recall your logic and changes sooner rather than later.

Rewriting

Rewriting can be a confusing, difficult, and sometimes painful process, but it's absolutely necessary. Professional TV writers don't write perfect first or rough drafts. We rewrite, rewrite, rewrite. And I'm not talking about little tweaks here or there. I'm not talking about changing a word or two. We rip the script apart, write entirely new sections, rearrange sequences—we do heavy lifting. Often we rewrite until the script is shot. Then we hit the edit bay and have at it again. If you don't like to rewrite, this isn't the job for you.

What constitutes a rewrite? How do you know what to rewrite? How do you know when to stop rewriting?

First, read your script aloud to yourself. If you stumble over dialogue or description, change it. This is one of the easiest steps to rewriting. Hearing your words aloud forces you to justify each word. If you can't justify each word, you need to rewrite.

I print a copy of my script for each oral read-through and make notes on the page. This helps me resist making changes digitally as I go and rewriting the script during the read-through. It also helps me catch more typos.

After your first oral read-through and revision, consider having others read your script. It's always good to have other writers read your work. The notes writers give you will be different from notes other people, even people in the business, will give you. Writers and trusted readers may be the best first-round readers for your new work.

This will be your warm read. The warm read includes people who know about your project. They might have read your treatment or outline. You likely will have talked to them about your TV series idea and pilot script, so they'll have an idea of what you're trying to accomplish.

Once your warm readers have read your work, listen to them. You don't need to defend your work. Just listen and take notes. You'll think you'll remember everything, but you won't. You'll forget that gem of a note because you're emotionally invested in your work. Write everything down so you can process it later.

After you've gotten notes from several readers, see if there are similarities in the notes. If there are similarities, you can be pretty sure you have a problem in that area. Then look over the notes and see if there is anything you agree with already. One of your readers might have identified an area you already knew was weak, or an area that you struggled with on the first pass. Make sure you address that note.

Also, look for notes that just get under your skin. Notes you think are horrible, awful, stupid notes. Probably, there is something to these notes, and that's why they're bugging you so much. The note itself might not be precise, but your mind is rebelling against the note for some reason. Often those notes point you in a direction that needs to be addressed. Start thinking of ways to address the note. You'll be surprised how often there is a simple fix for these types of issues—and how often you do need to fix them.

Storyline problem

Let's say you're having a particular problem with a storyline. Your entire b-storyline isn't working. Strip the storyline out of your script and work on it in its own document. Make the storyline work on its own, without the other scenes and storylines cluttering your mind.

Seeing the storyline on its own will help you see what needs to change. It also will help you identify any story logic or emotional logic issues. Plus, you'll be able to see where the major landmark scenes of that storyline land. *What landmark scenes?*

Major storylines need the character-driven landmarks just like your main character's storyline. For a major storyline, you'll have at least six scenes—point of attack, hero committed, hero succeeds—almost, emotional squeeze, hero succeeds, and hero's new life.

For a minor storyline, you'll likely have fewer landmark scenes—hero committed, hero succeeds—almost, emotional squeeze, and hero succeeds. You want all of your storylines to have a nice shape. Often the storyline landmark scenes land around the main character's landmark scenes. The juxtaposition of landmark scenes makes them pack more of an emotional punch.

Once you've made a storyline sing on its own, you can put those scenes back into your pilot script. You'll likely find your pilot is leaner, stronger, and better as a result.

Story logic issues

Story logic issues equal plot holes. They can also mean your characters are making illogical decisions, decisions normal people wouldn't make. Your characters are making these bizarre decisions because it serves your plot. Whenever something serves your plot, it will feel forced.

If you have story logic issues, you need to track back to at least a scene before the logic problem, maybe a couple of scenes before it. Often we get focused on the scene that has the logic issue and think if we can just fix that logic issue, we'll fix everything. That's like saying if we put a Band-Aid here, it'll fix this broken leg. But the problem often runs deeper. It starts before that troubling scene.

Remember your scene structure. A scene always has a decision. The decision leads us into a resolution, which takes us into the next scene. The *previous* decision may be faulty. Go back in your script and see if there is anything you can change in the run up to that problem scene that makes better sense. The bad decision in the problem scene often is due to a bad prior decision. If you change the set up, you can change the current decision and make a better one.

Emotional logic issues

Let's say you have an emotional logic issue. Emotional logic involves the psychology of your characters and how their emotions affect the story. Characters make decisions because of emotions. The audience tracks your characters' emotions. In fact, your audience watches your show to experience emotions vicariously through your characters. If your characters' emotions are inconsistent, you'll lose your audience. Also, if you imagined your characters one way and they feel false, your audience will sense the falseness.

If your character's emotions are inconsistent, go back a couple of scenes and track his emotions. Perhaps there is something you need to highlight to make sure your audience understands *why* your character's emotions change. Perhaps your character needs to make a different decision to feel differently. Perhaps the character needs more knowledge to feel differently. Maybe he needs to know his girlfriend is cheating on him. Maybe he needs to know his boss is thinking of firing him. If you want to generate a feeling of paranoia, for example, your character (and your audience) needs to understand why he *should* be paranoid.

If you have a reluctant hero, for the love of all that is green and good, make your protagonist proactive. Make your protagonist want the case, patient, guy, job, cocaine, whatever. Giving your protagonist a want, a positive want, will save your sanity.

"Doesn't want" is not a want. An actor can't play "doesn't want." If my main character doesn't want ice cream, what does that look like? He doesn't order ice cream and we move on. If my main character *really* wants ice cream, I can do a lot with that scene. I can put him on a diet, then plop him in front of a Ben and Jerry's. He could be broke so he has to panhandle for spare change. He might have to ask his new partner to buy him a double scoop of Rocky Road. He might have to sneak into the basement so his wife doesn't catch him eating a Klondike bar. He could take his kids to the ice cream truck, buy them King Cones, and selflessly lick the drips off the sides so their little fingers don't get sticky. There's so much to do with a character *wanting* ice cream. When a character *doesn't* want something, it makes your job much more difficult.

* * *

After you address the problems your first round of readers noted, read your script aloud again. The oral read-through will help you catch spelling, punctuation, and grammatical errors, as well as clunky passages. If you have long sentences, shorten them. A period is a perfectly respectable punctuation mark.

Some writers believe that screenwriting is writing-lite. They believe Hollywood doesn't care about conventional, institutional things like typos, punctuation, and grammar. They think, *We're the artists. We're the rebels. We play all day. Criminy, we just make television and movies! This isn't literature or something important like a doctoral dissertation.*

While it is true we play all day and we are rebels—we *do* feel very strongly about spelling, punctuation, and grammar. My friends have had Twitter rants about serial commas. In case you're wondering, the rant was in favor of the clarity serial commas deliver.

I've known showrunners who don't like to allow the abbreviation "O.K." and don't particularly like "okay" either. There can be all sorts of particular in-house rules, like no gerunds, no exclamation points, the use of double dashes to signify an em dash, and so forth. You may have no way of knowing those in-house quirks, but you absolutely can get all the elementary rules of writing—spelling, grammar, punctuation—correct. Violating any of the elementary rules of writing can get your spec script scuttled. If you think for one minute a great story twist or character will compensate for sloppy writing, please think again.

Let's say you are up for a job in Hollywood. There are literally thousands of writers who want that ONE job and probably hundreds who are qualified for that ONE job. Your script has to be stellar on all counts.

Passive voice

Passive voice also will get your script dropped in the recycling bin. We write moving pictures. We write about active protagonists. We want to read crunchy, descriptive action verbs as opposed to stagnant "to be" verbs whenever possible and appropriate. "Paul is slammed against the refrigerator and kissed by Sarah" feels very limp compared to "Sarah slams Paul against the refrigerator and Frenches the breath out of him."

Sometimes passive voice is the right choice, but if you can find another way to describe your action—and that's what you're doing, describing action—choose action verbs. Even at the beginning of scenes, you can use action verbs. You might have a scene that begins: "Claire is sorting through her herbs." That's serviceable. However, you also can start it: "Claire sorts through her herbs." You don't need the "is sorting" to denote we're joining her while she is doing something. Claire will sort herbs at the beginning of the scene. This subtle tweak to your writing will launch your scenes faster. Plus, it will make your voice stronger.

Your voice

Your voice should infuse the script. It should communicate the tone and vibe of your show. The words you choose and the way you put those words together say a lot about who you are. Your voice also should tell the world you love writing. Limp, labored writing suggests a journeyman writer who would rather *have written* than write. Executives, agents, managers, and producers search for writers who love to write, because we have to write and rewrite and rewrite and rewrite. There are writers who hate the process of writing. Those folks are no fun to work with. Boooo!

Again, your voice should come through on everything you write. You should have a blast writing everything—arena documents, outlines, treatments, and scripts. If you don't, do something else. Being a writer is hard work. It requires many thankless hours behind a keyboard. If that doesn't thrill you, and I mean *thrill* you, do something else that does.

As far as I know, we only get one life, and it shouldn't be filled with drudgery.

Beginnings of scenes

Whenever you have a scene heading, you need description. A scene usually doesn't start with just dialogue. The reader needs to know what the room looks like and who is in the room, even if they aren't speaking. If a character suddenly "shows up" in the middle of a scene, it jars the reader and takes the reader out of the scene. The reader may go back to see if he missed something. *Was this character always here? Did I miss this character entering the scene? What else did I miss? What's going on in this scene?*

Even if your scene is continuous or resumed, you need description after the scene heading. If your characters walk into a room, the reader doesn't know if there are other people in the room, if the room is empty, or what the room looks like. If you are going back to a scene in progress, the reader doesn't know if anything has changed since we left this location. Did someone else enter the location? Did someone leave? You need to orient your reader to the location after a scene heading.

Scene-by-scene

I had the great privilege of taking "Directing Actors" at USC with Oscar-nominated Hollywood legend Nina Foch (*An American in Paris, Spartacus, The Ten Commandments*). She would say, "Each scene is a pearl, and we want to make a string of pearls."

Go through your script and make sure every scene is a pearl. Each scene should have at least two different character wants. Each scene should have a hero's want, obstacle, escalations, decision, and resolution. Your scenes should be no longer than about two pages.

If you're having trouble with a scene, copy and paste it in a new document and focus on it. Along with the length, you'll be able to tell if it has a beginning, middle, and end. Do the characters' emotions track throughout the scene? Does the story logic work? If it's a landmark scene, does it fulfill the promise of the landmark scene? Does it move the character forward in her story?

I take my scripts apart scene by scene and study each scene. I want to make sure each scene works and achieves the story potential. The reader and viewer want to feel like this story comes from a master storyteller. You want to make sure your scenes work rather than *feel* like they work. What's more, when you get notes, you'll know exactly what you're losing by changing a scene. You'll be able to see the story potential if you make changes. You'll be able to guide the notes and execute them more easily.

Theme

I covered theme in the treatment and story idea sections. Now you'll go back and see if your theme remained consistent. Let's say you started with one theme, but as you wrote, your theme fell by the wayside. That's fine. You're cool. Seriously.

As you look at your script now, do you see any new themes begging to be explored? You may find a line of dialogue that hits on something that runs through your script. Awesome. You may find that several characters grapple with a specific problem and handle it differently. Fantastic.

If the original theme remained the same from the idea phase to the rewriting phase, great. If it didn't, mine your current script for theme and see if there are ways to highlight the new theme throughout the script. You'll likely find in both cases—a consistent theme or a new theme—that you'll be able to elevate the theme by tweaking dialogue or actions. A lot of times, small changes can make your theme pop and resonate. The reader and viewer will think you're amazing because you deliver thematically unified scripts. And you *are* amazing because you've gone back and highlighted your theme.

Launching a series

You're doing more than writing a script; you're writing a *pilot.* You're launching a series. By the time a reader gets through with your pilot, he should know where the series is heading. He should be able to predict what the next episode will entail. He should have a good idea what to expect if he tunes in next week, and the next, and the next. If the reader doesn't know what to expect, you've missed the mark.

You need to figure out how to convey your series in the pilot. You may need to go back to your treatment to remember what your series is about. Sometimes as we're writing, the characters and story take off. It's a great feeling. What a rush. However, in a pilot, you have to be cognizant that you're setting up 60 to 100 hours of television. This is why pilot writing can be harder than feature writing. You're thinking 100 hours in advance.

Now is the time to go back and see what you need to change so your reader and audience know your series from your pilot. You may be able salt valuable pieces of information throughout the pilot that will adequately prep your audience for your series. You may need to add a storyline or a runner that deals with the continuing world story. A runner usually has three scenes—a beginning, middle, and end—spread out during the episode. Or you may need to rethink your series. Maybe your original idea was interesting, but you've latched on to a more compelling series while writing your pilot.

If this is the case, you may need to go back through your pilot to strengthen your new perspective on your series and make sure you're consistent throughout your pilot. How do you know if you've successfully projected your series in your pilot? Welcome to the cold read.

Cold read

You've revised and revised. You've reworked, retooled, and restructured your script as necessary. You've addressed the issues from your warm readers. Now it's time for the cold reads. Cold reads are when you ask someone who knows nothing about your script to read your script. You haven't pitched a logline. You haven't explained your whole writing process. You haven't talked about any of the characters or story points. The reader knows nothing.

I'm stressing that the reader needs to know nothing because many writers talk a *lot* about their writing—with everyone they know. This makes it difficult to find cold readers. From the beginning of your process, I suggest that you save a couple of your smartest, toughest friends for your cold reads and don't tell them anything about your work in progress.

At this point, you are very close to your work. It's difficult to be objective. A cold read is as close to objective as possible. This can be very beneficial, especially if your world or concept is complicated. Cold readers, those who know nothing about your story, can tell you if something's confusing. They will tell you if you have story or emotional logic issues. They will tell you if it was easy/fast read or a hard read. They will tell you where they were most engaged in your story. They will tell you if something needs to be highlighted. Many times some key bit is already in the script, but it is lost in the description or buried in the dialogue. The cold reader's feedback can help you fine-tune your work.

I suggest that you ask your cold readers where they think your story is going. If they can articulate your series based on only reading your pilot, huzzah! You rule! If they struggle or completely misunderstand your series, ugh! You'll need to go back and figure out where you got off track. However, you have a valuable resource—your cold readers. Ask them why they think your series is going in a particular direction. Ask them what were the most outstanding elements that helped them *understand* your world. They'll be able to point you to exactly the areas you need to address.

Polish

Once you've addressed the issues from your cold read, it's time for the polish. Again, read your script aloud. It's the best way to catch typos and other errors. Read it aloud slowly and record it. After you record it, listen to the recording and follow along with your script, because you may have filled in orally something that isn't on the page.

Do a pass on your scene headings. Make sure your scene headings are formatted consistently and spelled correctly. Do a pass on your act breaks. Make sure you have formatted your act breaks correctly and you have included your transitions. Do a pass on your characters. Make sure when they are introduced their names appear in all caps and you have a thumbnail description.

Create your title page if you haven't created one already. Save your script as a PDF. Make sure this version includes your title page. Read this version aloud. Also, look at the formatting of the PDF. Don't leave end-of-act tidbits at the top of a page. Rescue all your widows and orphans. Widows and orphans are typesetter's terms for short lines at the top or bottom of a paragraph. They look like they are dangling from the body of the text.

Make your changes and save as a new PDF. Print a copy from your PDF and read it again. You'll want to make sure your printed version matches your PDF version because some people print scripts to read. You'll want those folks who print scripts and invest the time to read them to have the best reading experience possible. If someone prints out your script, they want it to be good. Make the print version as awesome as the PDF version.

Be radioactive

Not only should your script be stellar in form and format, your original pilot script also should have unforgettable characters and story. Your script should be so hot it burns the reader's hands. Readers should flip those pages so fast sparks fly. They should leap to tell their bosses—*I just found the best fucking script of the year!* Your script should emit rays. It should glow. Your pilot needs to be so hot it's radioactive.

Being radioactive can mean several things. The characters are so well-drawn, so consistent that the reader becomes immersed in your characters' lives. The world of your show is unique and enthralling. You have done such a great job of creating a world and populating it with interesting characters that the reader wants to live there. The action, thrills, chills, or humor your characters experience captivate the reader. Your voice buoys the script, evoking the show's tone and vibe.

You'll want to make sure your teaser is phenomenal. Your teaser should get the reader into your world elegantly and introduce your main character. It needs to grab your reader by the lapels and never let him go. If your teaser doesn't rock, you'll lose your reader before your story has a chance to get on its feet. Make sure you work on your teaser. Make sure it sells the promise of your show and your hero. Along with these considerations, your pilot needs to be a joy to read. It should be a fast, easy read that conveys the joy you had while writing it.

The art of the easy read

You want readers to fly through your script. You want them to forget they're reading. You want them turning those pages so fast they can't wait to figure out what happens next. You want your readers to get into FLOW. Flow means the reader is immersed in the story and forgets she's reading.

Many of the suggestions I've already made help make a read easy. For example, eliminating passive voice whenever possible, orienting the reader at the beginning and end of scenes, eliminating typos, using proper punctuation and grammar, using proper format, and providing thumbnail descriptions of your characters help the reader enjoy the read. Some of an easy or fast read has to do with the characters and story. Most of it has to do with presentation of the text. Creating an easy read is an art in and of itself.

How the eye travels over the text also determines whether the read will be an easy read or a hard read. When the eye meets the page, it is drawn to certain elements. The white space on the page helps direct the eye. The more white space you have, generally the faster the read.

TITLE
Title is centered.

ACT ONE (Acts have a 4 inch left margin.)

EXT. SOUNDSTAGE - DAY [SCENE HEADINGS HAVE 1.5 INCH LEFT MARGIN AND 1 INCH RIGHT MARGIN]

Description or action lines have 1.5 inch left margin and a 1 inch right margin.

CHARACTER NAMES HAVE A 3.5 INCH LEFT MARGIN AND ~1.75 RIGHT MARGIN
(Parentheticals have 3 inch left margin and a 4 inch right margin)
Dialogue has a 2.5 inch left margin and a 3 inch right margin.

TRANSITIONS ARE RIGHT-JUSTIFIED WITH A 4.5 INCH LEFT MARGIN

Figure 10.1: Basic TV drama format and margin sample.

For drama scripts, scene headings and description start at the 1.5 inch left margin and go all the way across to the right margin. With dialogue, character names start approximately at a 3.5 inch left margin. Character dialogue appears underneath the character name. The dialogue starts at approximately a 2.5 inch left margin. The parenthetical starts at approximately 3 inch left margin and has a 4 inch right margin. The transitions are right justified. The act beginnings and breaks start at approximately the 4 inch left margin.

When the eye scans the page, it's drawn to the dialogue automatically because the dialogue has more white space around it. It's like a funnel. However, the eye will start reading from the 1.5 inch left margin if there is description. It will read the description, then travel to the character name, which is further centered than the dialogue. Then it reads the dialogue. If there is a parenthetical, the eye will catch it on the way to the dialogue. All is good. Your words are being read.

However, the eye needs encouragement to travel from the dialogue back out to the description at the 1.5 inch margin. The eye would rather stay in the center of the page. If the eye has to repeatedly shoot out to the description margin from the dialogue margin, it will fatigue. This fatigue makes the read hard. The reader likely will subconsciously skip the description and just read the dialogue.

There is a caveat. If the eye has to shoot out to the description margin from the dialogue margin for a block of description three lines or more, the eye has time to get used to the new margin and likely will read that section. But if the eye has to read a line of dialogue, then three lines of description, then a line of dialogue—the eye will fatigue and the reader may put down your script.

Limit the number of times the reader's eye must change margins. Make sure you keep as much description together as possible and dialogue together as possible. Grouping your description with other lines of description as well as grouping dialogue with other lines of dialogue helps your readers' eyes flow over your material.

The same holds true for comedy scripts. The margins are a bit different, so be sure you have the proper single-camera comedy or multi-camera comedy margins for your script. Think about the white space and where the eye will be drawn on the page.

Easy read character description

Try not to bury a new character and her description in the middle of scene description. Set the character apart in some way. Start a new paragraph. Make sure your new character stands out from your description.

Important stuff

Avoid putting important stuff like new characters or pivotal story points at the bottom of a page. Readers tend to skip or forget the bottom of pages. They read and remember more from the top of pages. So while you want to save your widows and orphans and prevent end-of-act tidbits from the dangling onto the next page—you also want to make sure your important information is at or near the top of your pages.

Puppy vs. small dog

You've finished your polish. You've revised your pilot so it's a fast read. Is it ready? Do you feel it's ready? Do you find yourself tinkering with small things like changing out words that mean basically the same thing? This is the puppy-or-small-dog phase. And if you're debating over the nitty-gritty, you're probably done.

Save that sucker. Create a new PDF. Print out that PDF. Do your oral read-through. Make any tweaks. Save it. Create a final PDF. Check your PDF to make sure it's the saved version as your final draft. Then register your pilot script with the WGA.

* * *

Assignment

Congratulations, you're a creator! You've finished your pilot. You've captured your characters, world of your show, show concept, story engine, and tone in script form. Readers will be able to read your script and visualize your series. They also should be able to project where you want to go with your series.

Here are the steps you'll need to work through for your rewrite.

1) Save a draft of your script. Save your script throughout the rewrite process.

2) Make sure your script is within the ballpark of proper length. If it's too long, make cuts. If it's too short, YIKES! Consider adding another storyline. Find a way to flesh out your pilot story so it's the proper length without sacrificing good scene structure, scene length, character-driven structure, and all the other aesthetics I've covered.

3) Read your script aloud. I suggest printing your script for this process.

4) Ask receptive friends to do a warm read for you.

5) Address the notes. Do the heavy lifting. Push yourself.

6) If you're having a storyline problem, strip out all the scenes in the storyline and copy them into a new document. Address any story or emotional logic issues. Make sure each scene has proper structure—hero's want, obstacle, escalations, decision, resolution. Make sure the resolution leads into the next scene in the storyline. Make sure each scene is the proper length. Once you're satisfied with each scene and know the storyline works, re-insert the scenes into your script.

7) After you've addressed all your notes, check for typos as well as spelling, punctuation, and grammar issues.

8) Try to eliminate passive voice. Use crunchy, descriptive active verbs whenever you can.

9) Infuse your script with your voice. Choose words you love and that convey the vibe of your show.

10) Make sure you have stellar description at the beginning of your scenes. Make sure you resolve each scene so your readers know your characters' emotions and motivations.

11) Make sure each scene is a lustrous pearl.

12) Search for your theme. Did it remain consistent from the beginning, or has a new theme surfaced? Find ways to elevate your theme throughout your script.

13) Make sure your pilot launches your series. Your readers should know where your show is going.

14) Invite cold readers to read your script. Listen to their notes. Ask them if they know where your series is going. Do their ideas match your expectations? If not, ask them why they think your show is headed in a specific direction. Consider making changes to address this issue, if needed.
15) Make sure your script is the proper length. Make changes as needed.
16) Read your revised script aloud. I suggest printing out your script for this process. Make changes. Save your widows and orphans.
17) Make sure your script is an easy read.
18) Create your title page. It should include the title of your series, title of the pilot, your name, your email address, and cell number.
19) Create a PDF. Read through your PDF to make sure everything is on the page where it should be. If you make changes, save again and create a new PDF.
20) Once you have your polished final pilot script in PDF format, register your script with the WGA. Do not put any WGA registration numbers or copyright information on the title page. Doing so makes you look amateurish or paranoid. People expect you to be professional and to have registered your work with the WGA. They also expect you to treat them like professionals.

CHAPTER 11

TL;DR chapter 11

After you have polished your gleaming, radioactive script, you should go back to your treatment and update it. You may have made character, world, tone, or other changes that should be reflected in the treatment. That way, you'll be able to pitch your series at a moment's notice. Assignment: Update your treatment.

Revising Your TV Series Treatment

In this chapter, you'll find all the details for your treatment rewrite and your treatment rewrite assignment.

You've written your pilot, lived with your characters, walked around in the world of your show, refined your story engine, crystallized your series concept, homed in on your tone, and projected your series' future. Your show likely has evolved from the beginning of this process. Now is the perfect time to go back to your treatment and update it while your evolved show is fresh in your mind. You may have new characters. You may have fewer characters. You may have a better grasp on your series concept now that your characters are on their feet and your world has been solidified in your mind.

Revise your treatment now because you'll need to pitch your show. Yep, I know you just wrote that pilot, but you'll still need to pitch your show. In chapter 1, I mentioned that we don't pitch the pilot story; we want to know about the *show*. A pilot script can get people interested in your show, but you still need to tell them about the whole series.

Your revised treatment will be the most valuable document of your project. It's YOUR reference tool. It's not a selling document. Don't hand over your treatment with your script. It won't sell your show. But it'll help you prepare to talk with people about your series. It's YOU the executives and producers want to know. YOU are the most important part of the equation because *making* a show is a marriage. Executives and producers want to ask you questions. They want to interact with you. A pitch meeting will tell them about your show and give them an indication of how easy it will be to work with you.

If you have a great idea but are a pain in the butt, they won't work with you. A great idea doesn't sell a show; it's a combination of the idea and the creator. And it's more the creator than the idea. Working on a TV show requires long, grueling hours. You spend more time with the show than you do with your family. Think about that. You spend more time with the cast, crew, studio, and network than with people you love. And all these people spend more time with you than their loved ones. They want to get to know you.

Part of the pitch meeting is pitching your series, but part is proving you're a professional and a person people want to work with. Be a good person and be prepared. Rewrite your treatment now so you'll be able to wow Hollywood when you have a chance to pitch your series.

Assignment

Now that you've written your pilot script, revise your treatment. Include any changes you've made or revelations you've had during the writing of your pilot. Trust me, you'll be glad you took this extra step now, while all your additions and changes are fresh in your mind. You never know when an executive, showrunner, or producer might read your pilot and have questions. If you have all of your show info up to date in your treatment, it'll be easy to review it and look like a pro in your meetings.

CHAPTER 12

TL;DR chapter 12

Congratulations! Hollywood wants to hear your voice.

You Succeed: Your New Life

Thank you for reading *The Hero Succeeds.* It's been my pleasure to share concrete tool and skills that have helped me in my career. I hope they will help you succeed as you create your TV series and write your pilot.

Now you have a logical method to break your TV series and pilot. You know all the elements you need to create your show. Plus, you have the secret decoder—character-driven structure—to create emotionally satisfying TV scripts.

The Hero Succeeds offers a professional approach to the pilot-writing process. If you've been writing along with this book, you've finished your pilot script and TV series treatment. You rule! Congratulations! I'm psyched for you, and I can't wait to see the shows you develop.

Hollywood wants to hear your voice. We want to know what you're passionate about. The resources page at kammiller.com has links to more than 20 television writing contests and programs. Put yourself out there. Be undeniable. You have fans. Some of them just might not know it yet. Cheers!

APPENDIX

I recently had the pleasure of working with some promising young writers—Henry Boyd, Eli Brenna, Mac Davies, Aryeh Harris-Shapiro, Sarah Kenny, and Aleeza Klarman—on their first original pilots. I was impressed by their writing *and* their generous personalities. They have graciously agreed to share some of their early treatments and outlines with you.

In this appendix, you'll be taken to the kingdom of Altea; the corrupt city of Crittenden; the rural community of Jerusalem, Tennessee; the competitive world of collegiate diving; the heightened world of musical theater; and a place you're probably familiar with already—Hollywood, albeit the B-movie industry of schlock and ugh. You'll find drama and comedy, dark and light.

Treatments and outlines are living, breathing documents. As we worked on their pilots, some elements changed and evolved, so the treatments and outlines might not perfectly match their finished pilot scripts. That's the way it's supposed to work. I believe you'll find the thought these writers put into developing their TV shows inspiring and helpful.

It was a blast to work with each of these writers on their projects. I thank them for sharing their early work with you. For more information about these writers and their completed pilots, please send your request to info@highandlowmedia.com.

* * *

Drama

Jerusalem, TN **by Aryeh Harris-Shapiro:** *Jerusalem, TN* is a drama about Luke McCullough, a farmhand whose developing messianic powers embroil the residents of his small town in a conflict between the Southern Baptist Convention and an emergent cult.

Aryeh Harris-Shapiro
Aryeh's characters, themes, and subtext are just lovely. He's a deep thinker and a focused writer. He pushes his scripts to work on many levels. With *Jerusalem, TN,* he wanted to tackle religion and faith as separate concepts. He also wanted to create a hopeful message in a dire, desperate setting.

You'll see Aryeh's in-depth character work in his treatment. He carries it through his outline, giving his three main characters—Luke, Kacey, and Ann—their own distinct character-driven story structure. During the pilot writing phase, Aryeh primarily worked on cutting down his 85-page first draft. Talk about killing your darlings! There was so much good writing left on the floor. He completed a terrific character-driven pilot that opens like a bloom as you progress through the story.

* * *

Girl Out of Water **by Aleeza Klarman:** *Girl Out of Water* is a family drama about an ambitious collegiate athlete, Sierra Patterson, who suffers a mental breakdown after a life-altering injury.

Aleeza Klarman
Aleeza has a gift with characters and dialogue. She finds the voices of her characters with ease, and they never feel forced. She wanted to tell a truthful, poignant, long-arc serialized story of acute mental illness and its effects on a family. She carefully balanced tragedy with hope and created gut-wrenching scenes.

You'll see subtle changes from Aleeza's treatment to her outline, including her main character's chosen sport. Changing Sierra's sport from soccer to diving required Aleeza to go back to the research phase because she knew little about collegiate diving. She interviewed the assistant athletic director and women divers at her university. As you'll see in her outline, the change creates a wonderfully suspenseful character-driven structure.

During her pilot writing process, Aleeza mainly worked on her character introductions and elevating her pivotal scenes visually on the page. She completed an impressive family drama. All of her storylines weave together nicely, creating a cascade of emotion.

* * *

Minotaur* by Eli Brenna*: *Minotaur,* an action drama, tells the story of Leon, who adopts the alter ego of the Minotaur to take on the scum and villainous conspiracies of Crittenden. Leon will not survive.

Eli Brenna

Eli went big and created a high-concept, character-driven project. He focused on tone, world building, and terrific visuals. He wanted to tell a dark, gritty tale of crime gone awry in a fictitious economically devastated city. His main character is a psychologically damaged vigilante who dresses up like a minotaur. As I said, Eli went big.

You'll see from Eli's treatment that he quickly drops into story mode. He wants to tell you the story of the Minotaur. He's keenly aware of his audience, which is smart. You'll also notice in his outline that he weaves together his two leads' separate investigations nicely. He also injects his action scenes with verve.

During the pilot process, Eli deepened his character work. He added character beats for his main character to help the reader better understand his motivations and emotions. Eli also added procedural beats to give his dual—police and vigilante—investigations more turns. He delivered an intense, tight pilot full of terrific action set pieces.

***The Guardian* by Mac Davies:** *The Guardian* is a fantasy drama set in a fragile world recovering from a long conflict, a world where a young girl with supernatural powers must rise up to save humanity.

Mac Davies

Mac has been thinking of *The Guardian* for a long time. In this fantasy drama, he created a consistent, cohesive world where magic and technology work together. Then he populated his world with accessible, emotionally relatable characters. You'll see in Mac's treatment that he skillfully focuses on world-building. He quickly describes the different kingdoms and the friction among them.

During the pilot writing phase, Mac's action pieces were visceral and visual. They leapt off the page. His story changed significantly from the outline in the final acts, which is why his outline isn't included here. He focused a lot of his efforts on his final acts, where he had two storylines he needed to weave together. These storylines needed to build on their own as well as off each other to create suspense. Mac's completed pilot offers a fresh, captivating sword-and-sorcery fantasy drama.

Comedy

***Exit Stage Left* by Sarah Kenney:** *Exit Stage Left* is a single-camera musical comedy about Georgia Moss, an aspiring theater director whose parents give her an ultimatum: Major in a STEM field or pay for college herself.

Sarah Kenney

Sarah had worked on this idea earlier, but she hadn't quite broken it yet. Her characters were already solidified in her mind. She needed to find an ongoing character conflict for the series as well as a focus on its current social relevancy.

Sarah drew inspiration from her own life. The economic decisions facing recent college graduates are reflected in her family. Sarah was a theater major; her brother pursued a STEM field. Her brother has had more employment opportunities. Still, Sarah felt pursuing the arts would hold much more satisfaction for her. She wanted explore this dilemma through her series.

You'll get a flavor of Sarah's humor in her treatment. She describes her characters with zest. You'll also see how she tackled the challenge of a show set in college as she arcs out three seasons. In her outline, you'll see the scale of her show. Sarah has created a much bigger canvas than the usual sitcom.

During the pilot writing process, Sarah worked on creating the emotionally satisfying character-driven structure. She trimmed her opening daydream sequence to get into her episode faster. She also needed to maintain story momentum during her main character's pot-smoking foray. Sarah created a wonderful musical daydream that gave the reader access to her main character's internal struggle and propelled the story forward. She wrote a charming, laugh-out-loud pilot.

* * *

***B-List* by Henry Boyd**: *B-list* is a workplace sitcom about a talented director, Roger Larson, who labors as the assistant of a prolific B-movie producer as he watches his own arthouse film dreams vanish.

Henry Boyd

Henry wanted to examine the allure and reality of Hollywood. He juxtaposed the outrageousness of B-movies with a young director's ideals of cinema. He populated his world with unique characters, and he did a great job of projecting possible episodes so the reader could see the humor immediately.

You'll get a flavor for Henry's humor in his treatment. He does a good job creating three-dimensional characters with distinct foibles. He has a great handle on his tone and gives appropriate, helpful examples. He answered the big questions very well. He knocked it out of the park with his proposed episode loglines. They made me laugh, and I totally got Henry's show.

Henry made quite a few changes from his outline to his pilot, which is why the outline isn't included here. His secondary characters popped. They were singular, quirky, and hilarious. Henry focused on creating the character-driven structure for his main character, who wound up playing the straight man in the jokes. Henry worked on deepening his main character to give the reader access to his motivations and emotional logic.

* * *

Treatments

Jerusalem, TN
Treatment
by Aryeh Harris-Shapiro

Type of show
A serialized, character-based, supernatural family drama.

Logline
Luke McCullough, a Tennessee farmhand, develops messianic powers, embroiling the residents of his small town in a growing conflict between the Southern Baptist Convention and an emergent cult.

World of the show
Jerusalem, Tennessee. The small town is pretty much the entire world of the show, although we do get small glimpses of the world beyond. Nashville, the headquarters of the Southern Baptist Convention, makes a few appearances. Major locations in the town include Luke's home, the pastor's home, the church the town is built around, the struggling factory farm that employs most of the town's residents, the high school, and the local bar. The town is built right along the Mississippi river, which plays a major role in the town's landscape as well as the pastimes of its residents. Aside from the messianic element at the center of the

show, the world of the show is grounded in realism. Miracles and magic occasionally puncture this realism, but they occur rarely and are always treated with a sense of real-life consequence.

Characters

Luke McCullough: A big man with perpetual bags under his eyes, Luke is a farmhand on the rocks. He's coping with a recently deceased wife, a stepdaughter he barely knows, a job that's as good as gone, and a monster of a drinking problem just waiting for him to let his guard down. He's a near-broken man, filled with a consuming need to be loved and a gnawing fear that he doesn't deserve it. He had it once. He lost it. The yawning emptiness at his core threatens to tear him apart.

Luke has a stepdaughter. He doesn't know her very well. He knows she's in pain, just as much as he is. But he doesn't understand her. He doesn't know how to help. It's just another thing he can't handle, he tells himself. His self-pity blinds him to the very real sins of inaction he's committing.

Luke has a lot of skills. He's mechanically inclined, good with his hands. He's a skilled hunter and fisherman. He's a hard worker, good at keeping his head down and being useful in all the mundane ways that help him distract himself from what he sees as his fundamental existential impotence. Luke knows with all his heart the kind of life he wants to live. But he can't bring himself to try and make it a reality again. He did once and was punished for it. So he'll look for love in other places. There are plenty of people who might love him now that he can heal the sick. Now that he can walk on water and feed the hungry. Now that he can raise the dead.

* * *

Pastor Ann Michaels: Ann became the town's pastor when her husband passed a year or two back. This isn't a traditional arrangement in the Baptist church, which discourages female pastors, but the arrangement that Jerusalem needed. Her husband hadn't groomed a successor, and none of the men in town had the knowledge or the luxury to choose to just up and leave their jobs to lead the church. So the choice was between having the SBC send a stranger and ordaining Ann. There was a lot of heated debate. And in the end, the town settled on Ann, who they knew, who they trusted.

Ann is in her late 60s, willowy and wind-beaten, white hair pulled back in a perpetual ponytail—still a rancher's daughter in frame and demeanor despite the intervening years. She has grown children living lives in Memphis and Nashville. More than anything, she'd like them to move back home. She knows that it's not likely. But she was raised in Jerusalem. Her husband was raised in Jerusalem. Her kids were raised in Jerusalem. It's a good place. A good place that makes good people. She's convinced of the rightness of her town and its importance in the terrifyingly amorphous landscape of the 21st century United States.

The way the town is splitting apart under the economic pressures facing the factory farm terrifies her. It terrifies Ann to see the good people of Jerusalem suffer and find their way to the bottle, the needle, or simply the vices that live in their own hearts. She believes that they can be better, that they can be saved. People are getting used to the idea of her as the town's spiritual leader. She knows these folks inside and out. She can help them. She knows it.

Then Luke's blessings awaken. The SBC descends. And Ann can feel her authority slipping through her fingers. She can feel her charges moving farther and farther out of reach.

* * *

Kacey Reardon: Luke's stepdaughter. Sandy-haired and short with a sturdy frame. Looks like a smaller version of her mother. She's in her last year of high school. She's absolutely devastated by her mother's death, and then her own near-death before Luke managed, beyond all odds, to heal her.

To meet her, you'd think Kacey was older, in college at least. She's responsible in a matter-of-fact way. When she was younger her father left the picture and she had to take care of her mother, an addict. Her mother wasn't well for a very long time.

Kacey's mother got better. Then her mother met Luke. And then her mother was gone. After her mother died, Kacey found herself taking care of Luke. She choked down her own grief so she could make sure Luke got home safe from the bar every night and he went to work the next morning.

More than anything, Kacey wants out. Her greatest fear is to live in Jerusalem for the rest of her life. But escape seems almost impossible. Luke is terrible with money and her mother wasn't much better. Kacey was trying to secure a scholarship to the University of Tennessee, but her mother's death and her own accident sidelined that. And Kacey's not one to walk away from responsibility. It's one of the things she holds onto in order to separate herself from the people around her. Luke, somehow, has become her responsibility.

Her relationship with Pastor Ann is one of the few places she allows herself to really be vulnerable. Ann was a surrogate grandmother to her growing up, and her support and acceptance mean a lot to Kacey.

Kacey is the human center of the show. Luke and Pastor Ann are tangled up in things larger than themselves, things they represent, things they fight to get away from, things they lose themselves in. Institutions. The church. The cult. Their faith itself. Kacey is only herself, nothing more, nothing less, and the show can never lose sight of the emotional impact the story has on her.

* * *

Nick Blair: One of Luke's coworkers at the farm. Early 20s. African-American. Razor-thin, eyes on fire. A high school dropout, the youngest of many employed at the farm. Furiously religious, completely embittered toward the mundane. He grew up surrounded by the worst of Jerusalem: the tweakers, the junkies, the drunks.

Nick's known Luke for a long time. Never thought very much of him. The fact that Luke is, by all rights, the second coming, confuses the living hell out of him. On one hand, Luke represents everything Nick hates about Jerusalem. Drunk, pathetic, aimless. On the other, Nick can't deny what's in front of his face.

Nick's terrified that the thing he's invested all his hope in, the transcendent glory of the hereafter, is no different from the world he's running from. He has two options: disbelieve the miracles he sees, which he'd never do, or remake Luke into something he can tolerate—whether Luke wants him to or not.

* * *

Caroline Allman: Staff writer for the *Baptist Press*, the official SBC publication. African-American, early 40s, maintains an unfussy, professional appearance out of place in Jerusalem. The go-to writer to investigate reported divine phenomena to see if they're newsworthy.

Fundamentally skeptical despite her employer, Caroline's religion is something she more or less takes for granted as a part of her life. Her faith in the truly divine is something she's had beaten out of her by endless charlatans and frauds. She struggles to represent the interests of her organization while dealing with her reawakened sense of awe. She also struggles with her stance toward Pastor Ann. She attempts to reconcile her Convention-mandated stance that Ann should not be ministering to this town with her own respect for Ann as a leader and a woman. As the town begins to slip out of Ann's control, Caroline is forced to choose between the interests of the SBC, Jerusalem itself and the interests of a woman she's come to see as something close to a friend.

* * *

Sheriff's Deputy Keith Rayburn: Early 20s, white. Handsome and clean-scrubbed in a way that sticks out like sore thumb in Jerusalem. Born-again and fundamentally kind-hearted, Rayburn seems like the perfect small-town cop. Fair, firm, and friendly—that's the motto he lives by. At least until he has to manage the crisis brought on by Luke's newfound divinity. His judgment impaired by his faith, Rayburn struggles to find a way to see clearly as the situation rockets toward the point of no return.

Season plan

Season one: This season is very, very small scale, focusing on the intimate ramifications of Luke's newfound powers as well as the local politics and structures of Jerusalem. The impending closure of the factory farm provides the major thrust for the season, as it places many aspects of the town in crisis, economically and psychologically.

There are two serialized plots developing in the background. The first is Caroline Allman's observation of Jerusalem and Pastor Ann, which comes on the heels of Kacey's near-death and miraculous recovery. The second is Nick Blair's ongoing efforts to convince Luke of his calling and convince the community of Luke's divine nature. The latter rears its head in the back half of the season, when Nick begins to push Pastor Ann to ordain Luke as co-head of their church.

This push causes major friction between Ann, Kacey, and Luke. Ann gives in to public demand. Nick and Luke's success tears open a schism between the three main characters as the two begin to push the town to break away from the SBC completely. This turn, reported back the SBC by Caroline, leads to a delegation from its Nashville headquarters traveling to Jerusalem.

This impending intrusion leads Ann and Kacey to attempt to repair their relationship with Luke, but it's too late—they arrive to find that Luke's following has rapidly coalesced into a cult. Their access to him is cut off. Things have begun to spin into deadly motion.

Luke's powers in season one are fairly limited. He can heal the injured, the sick, and the disabled, as well as walk on water. He does not gain new powers, only sees his extant powers increase. At first, his powers demand moments of emotional crisis to function, and they are unpredictable and unreliable. However, as the season progresses, he exercises more and more control, to the point that he can use them at will by the end of the season.

Season two: Season two expands the scope and raises the stakes of the first season by kicking the developing storylines of season one into high gear. The SBC arrives in Jerusalem and immediately begins to attempt to co-opt Luke and transform him into a national story. Luke's cult expands and becomes increasingly clannish, adopting stranger and stranger internal policies and doctrine. The town becomes a sea of shifting alliances.

The SBC and the cult form tentative ties in order spread news of Luke's gift, ties that fall apart in the face of their dogmatic differences. Pastor Ann finds her religious and social authority threatened by the presence of the SBC delegation and must find a way to stand her ground without alienating the very group that might be able to fight the tidal growth of the cult.

Kacey joins the cult in an attempt to reach Luke and find some way to bring everything to a peaceful conclusion. Nick and Luke struggle for control over the cult and its direction, a conflict that ends in Nick's favor, with Luke reduced to a figurehead, a potent icon with no control over his own destiny. At season's close, Luke discovers that without his knowledge, the cult has begun to arm itself.

Luke's power expands greatly this season, becoming much showier as he's called on to perform more and more as a public figure. He feeds the entire cult despite their limited means of food production, he rebukes a tornado heading straight toward Jerusalem, and, most noticeably, he begins to emanate a messianic radiance. In the final moments of the season, Luke, alienated from the cult, from his "family," thinking of the story of Lazarus, attempts to raise his wife from the dead. He succeeds in the darkest possible way, in a way he regrets deeply the moment it happens.

Season three: Season three skips forward in time, opening with the beginning of the ATF siege of the cult's compound, which is built into the husk of the closed factory farm. The siege takes up the duration of the third season. The siege lasts for weeks.

The ATF is paralyzed by the national attention that the SBC and, later, the mainstream media have directed at Jerusalem. Their desire to avoid a second Waco leads to a stalemate.

This season focuses very heavily on the practical details of the siege and their implications, examining the ramifications of faith turned hard-line dogma in a relentlessly pragmatic world. Ann finds herself in the position of mediator, attempting to negotiate a peaceful surrender by the cultists, one that they're unwilling to give. Kacey and Luke attempt to find a way to escape the cult without being taken into custody.

The three main characters join forces to defuse the conflict. They are unsuccessful. Various maneuvers by the ATF (attempting to insert a mole into the cult, attempting to flip an extant cult member, attempting to gas the compound and flush the cult out) and incendiary public statements by cult leadership drive the siege toward its violent conclusion, a firefight that leaves many on both sides dead or wounded and Luke in federal custody.

Luke's powers play less of a role here than they did in earlier seasons—though the cult prods him to go on the offensive against the ATF, his powers are simply not of that nature. He is reduced in the season's final moments to simply healing those he can, saving their lives so that they can continue to slaughter those on the other side.

Themes

This show has two central themes, one intellectual and one emotional, both linked. The first is the function of faith and its place in society, the way religion can save a person and destroy a community—or vice versa. The second is the brutality and the elusiveness of hope, the way that the chance miracles and moments of transcendence that allow us to survive the punishments of day-to-day life do not save us from ourselves.

Story engine

The story in this show comes from collisions between institutions and individuals. The individuals are outlined above. The institutions include the church, the Southern Baptist Convention, the factory farm, the emergent cult, and the town itself.

The primary story model is Luke or Pastor Ann either feeling threatened by one of the institutional forces or seeing a way to get what they need through one of the institutions and acting appropriately.

Another story model would be a conflict between two of the institutions (the town and the SBC, the SBC and the cult) that places one or more of the main characters right at the center, in a place to solve it, exacerbate it, or be destroyed by it. The internal politics of the institutions also generate story insofar as they affect the main characters.

Tone

The tone of this show is fundamentally empathetic, a compassionate humanist look at broken people doing broken things in an attempt to make themselves better. At its highest and lowest, the show contains moments of great beauty and moments of gut-wrenching despair. The dominant mode of the show is a deep-focus excavation of the tiny tragedies and victories that make up the passage of life. The goal is not melodrama—nothing is played to excess. The show just recognizes that life, even at its most sedate, is a high-stakes emotional game.

I think we're all feeling the squeeze a little harder than we used to. There used to be this idea of a safety net, especially during the Clinton boom years. But between 9/11, Afghanistan and Iraq, the recession, the housing crisis, and the endless news of mass shootings, the bottom has fallen out. This show touches on economic concerns, but it's truly relevant because it gets at that feeling that everything is falling apart underneath our feet, and our impossible but inevitable task of holding it all together.

Empathy is the fundamental tenet of this show. Someone—I can't remember who—said that we consume art to learn empathy. Cynical, brutal, uncompromising art is important, crucial, but a show that reaches out to everyone, that holds faith in humanity even when doing so seems impossible—I think that has value.

How is the show unique? How does your show push the envelope?

It's rare for a show in the modern era to focus explicitly and heavily on religious faith, and even more so when that show itself is not made by and for those of faith. We see condemnations of religious hypocrisy and programs echoing religious dogma fairly often. Still, given the United States' ongoing difficulties reconciling religious and secular interests, a show that provides an empathetic, even-handed perspective on faith deserves a place on the airwaves.

What are your influences?

The first two films by writer-director Jeff Nichols, *Shotgun Stories* and *Take Shelter*, operate in the same rural milieu, and the quiet depth with which Nichols draws his challenged, challenging characters is a huge inspiration.

The music of the Mountain Goats is a major tonal influence. Lead singer/songwriter John Darnielle imbues his songs with radical empathy toward their protagonists, finding the emotional truth of the silliest subjects (two minor characters from the movie *Scarface*, for instance) and locating the essential mix of hope and despair that sustains people in deep personal crisis.

Why me?

I have a certain perspective on faith that I would call uncommon—a critical, secular viewpoint that nevertheless takes into account the positive effects of faith, the need it fulfills, and its value to us as individuals and us as a society. I stand at a distance from faith, but I am not alienated by it or embittered toward it. This show requires a delicate touch. It has to convince the secular audience of the centrality of faith in these characters' emotional lives without seeming as if it's proselytizing. It also has to take a critical position on faith when that position is deserved without the religious portion of the audience feeling as if they are under attack. I believe I'm uniquely suited to strike that balance.

Girl Out of Water
Treatment
by Aleeza Klarman

Type of show
Serialized, character-driven family/medical drama.

Logline
An ambitious college student, Sierra Patterson, suffers a breakdown after losing her athletic scholarship, and she and her family must reconcile the repercussions for their lives.

World of the show
The show mainly centers on Sierra's school and family home, as well as the offices of her physical therapist and psychologist.

Themes
The show will explore loss, finding one's self, and what makes us human.

Story engine
The stories will come from sports and sporting events, the mental-health system, business ventures, and family.

Tone
Girl Out of Water addresses an issue that is underrepresented on television. Mental illness affects approximately 58 million adults in the U.S. alone—and that figure does not include children, teenagers, or those indirectly affected, like family and friends. I want to focus on an accurate, non-melodramatic story with a mentally ill teen protagonist, and the way she and her family relate to her illness. Many movies have focused on mental illness, but the most famous ones, like *One Flew Over the Cuckoo's Nest,* have a decidedly negative view of the treatment process. There is also still a great deal of stigma associated with mental

illness, and a television show centered on a family struggling with this issue could be revelatory.

Character bios

Sierra Patterson

Physiology: You can tell 18-year-old Sierra is an athlete even without the team sweatshirt she always wears like a badge of honor. She is thin but solidly built, with muscles poking up even where she occasionally wishes they wouldn't. Sierra stands firm, straight and proud—she likes her body, and she is only just beginning to discover its power over boys. She hasn't quite mastered the use of makeup or high heels, but a little help from her college teammates is going a long way toward scrubbing off those vestiges of childhood innocence.

Sociology: Sierra is from a lower-middle-class family trying to pretend they're slightly wealthier than they really are. She is used to working, whether at low-paying summer jobs or as part of school work-study programs. Sierra was never going to win any academic awards, though not for lack of effort. She got Bs when she studied and Cs when she didn't. It only took her family a couple of years of schooling to realize that Sierra was going to have to capitalize on her athletic talents if she wanted a shot at a good college education. The full athletic scholarship to college was her first real break, and to Sierra and her family, it felt as though God had sent it down on a chariot.

Psychology: Sierra is a little hardened. She'll win or die trying, and she doesn't understand people who just give up. She's spirited, determined, and impatient to start a career as a professional soccer star, no matter how many times people tell her that female soccer players rarely have successful careers. Sierra laughs in their faces, goes home, and watches clips of Abby Wambach on YouTube, because Abby is her touchstone.

In middle school and high school, Sierra rarely had time for dates, so college is the first time she's been able to explore sexuality, and she is enjoying the hell out of it. Small town America has no place in a giant public college, and there are no watchful eyes here to lecture her about cows giving the milk away for free. Despite that, she's not wanton—she loves to flirt and make out, but she's hesitant to go all the way.

Sierra's focus is first and foremost on the prize—the game, the scholarship, and her career. She feels the pressure of expectation every single day, but it's a coating on her skin that she's gotten so used to, she barely notices it anymore. She has a singular gift of performing right when she is needed most.

After her accident, Sierra's determination is tested. She struggles with depression over the potential loss of her athletic scholarship, and, more importantly, her career. She has only ever wanted to be a soccer player, and now she doesn't know what her future will hold. She begins to believe she has no future at all, and her work with her physical therapist and her psychologist sometimes feels like a futile effort. Signature trait: Sierra is a winner in a losing game. She is a fighter.

* * *

Felicity Patterson

Physiology: Felicity is Sierra's 12-year-old sister, and that's basically how everyone sees her. Like Sierra, Felicity is athletically gifted; she loves gymnastics and she is excellent at it. She dreams of being in the Olympics, but the public school she goes to doesn't have the best teams, and she can't afford the best private coaching. Felicity is petite; she's on the pretty side of plain, but she is not a beauty.

Sociology: Felicity is in the 7th grade. She gets excellent grades, even with the extensive time commitment her sports require. She does not share her mother's religious beliefs.

Psychology: Felicity is the hand-me-down sister. Nearly everything she owns came from Sierra or her mother. She gets along well with her mother, but she is often ignored by her father, who focuses only on

Sierra's soccer career. Felicity worships Sierra, but she rarely gets much more than the time of day in return. They were close when they were both little, but when Sierra became a middle-school soccer star, Felicity was left in the shadows.

Felicity doesn't date yet, although she often has crushes on the boys in her class. She sometimes feels invisible, and though she is outwardly resigned to being "Sierra's little sister," internally she hates it. Sierra's accident gives her a chance to move out of the shadows. Signature trait: Felicity is hardworking and insightful, and her empathy provides some of the show's most touching moments.

* * *

Maria Patterson

Physiology: Maria Patterson is a once-attractive Latina woman who has been prematurely aged by stress and fatigue—not to mention the illness that stole her breasts. She has been in remission for years, but the scars of her surgeries are painful reminders of what she has been through.

Sociology: Sierra and Felicity's mother couldn't be more overworked if she had to walk uphill both ways to work every day. She is a very tiny cog in a very large, Walmart-esque machine. She hates having to serve customers whom she knows from outside of work, but the town is too small for it to be avoided. Cranky and out of sorts, Maria comes home with sore feet and wounded pride. But she does it because she loves her family, and someone needs to bring home a paycheck. She relies on prayers just to get through the day.

Psychology: Maria is resigned to her role in life, but she resents having to work as hard as she does. She often fights with her husband, Steven, because she doesn't feel like he pulls his weight. Maria loves Felicity a great deal, and they have a real bond—two women who feel overlooked by the world, both working as hard as they can. However, Maria is sometimes jealous of Sierra, who is everything that she misses being.

Maria desperately wants to feel attractive again. She wants to put her feet up and hire someone else to do the cleaning. Instead, she often feels like a cross between a 1950s housewife and a slave to a corporation. Signature trait: Maria is one of the most discontented people on the show. Her anger often causes problems and controversy.

* * *

Steven Patterson

Physiology: Steven Patterson is a good-looking, weathered Caucasian man in his late 40s. He is long and lean, with more than a hint of gray in his hair and smile lines around his mouth. He is a former athlete, and he has the look of a team coach.

Sociology: Steven came from a comfortably middle-class family, and he still has trouble keeping to the budget his wife sets. He is completely non-religious. He believes that the only things you get in life are things you earn for yourself.

Psychology: Steven Patterson was a college athlete in his day, and the only language he speaks is sports. He loves his wife and both of his daughters, but he is laser-focused on Sierra, who is picking up the sports mantle. Sierra possesses the rare gift for athletics that he used to have, and he is proud that he is the one who got her involved in soccer as a child.

When he's not attending Sierra's team practices or games, or running drills with her in the small backyard, Steven attempts to get his sports apparel business off the ground. He truly believes it will be the next great thing. However, the red ink in his books is a huge line of contention between him and his wife, which makes Sierra's career even more important to him.

After Sierra's accident, Steven loses his compass. He is forced to face the fact that she might not be able to bail him out of financial debt with her hypothetical soccer-star salary. He can't let go of the dream of having a famous athlete for a daughter, which throws his relationship with Sierra into jeopardy. Signature trait: Steven is lovable, but his immaturity and obvious lack of business sense can be infuriating. His relationship with Sierra is one of the most complex on the show.

* * *

Christian Buteau
Physiology: Christian is a tall, handsome, muscular black man in his early 30s. His face seems stern, but his hands and heart are gentle as he helps his physical therapy patients recover.

Sociology: Christian and his wife struggle to support their growing family on relatively small salaries, but he loves his job as a physical therapist and wouldn't change it for the world. He is a former soldier, and his sergeant-like manner is something Sierra, who is used to coaches, learns to respect.

Psychology: Christian has a no-nonsense attitude that patients either love or hate, and he has a take-me-or-leave me attitude toward them. He has seen injury after injury, and he wants to help each person to the absolute best of his ability. It drives him crazy when people don't take their recovery seriously, but the patients who do want to get better hold a special spot in his heart.

Christian only regrets the patients he can't help and the friends he couldn't save during the war in Iraq. He is sometimes overly protective of his children, because he has seen the terror in the world. He grows to see Sierra as one of his daughters.

* * *

Isabella Howard
Physiology: Isabella Howard is the girl you wish you were. She is Caucasian, gorgeous, and popular. She is the captain of Sierra's soccer team and Sierra's best friend before the accident.

Sociology: Isabella can afford to pay for college. Her parents are upper-middle-class. She does well in school and is always leading some besotted boy around like a puppy.

Psychology: Isabella wants to be the best. She sometimes resents Sierra's talent, and the accident makes her feel guilty for those feelings. She starts avoiding Sierra, and their friendship begins to dissolve.

* * *

Annie Brooks
Physiology: Annie is a young, attractive Caucasian woman who is barely out of grad school. She's still wet behind the ears, and it shows.

Sociology: Annie works in the free clinic where Sierra gets some of her treatment. Annie is from an upper-middle-class family; they don't approve of where she works or what she does. She has a fiancé, and she wants to have a family of her own, but it's starting to seem as though she might not be with the right person after all.

Psychology: Annie is new to the free clinic. She is desperate to prove herself and save the world one patient at a time. Armed only with tissue-paper thin idealism, the pain and chronic nature of mental illness is a shock to her. However, she is good-hearted and smart, even if her naiveté is sometimes grating to Sierra.

* * *

Season one

Sierra is just beginning to acclimate to college life when she injures her knee. She returns to school to find that everything has changed. She works with Christian, a physical therapist, but she has many ups-and-downs in her recovery. When she finds out that she's losing her athletic scholarship, she sinks deeper and deeper into depression until she attempts suicide.

Felicity has to adjust to the new family dynamics. She feels new pressure to excel at sports so she can take Sierra's place as the family star. She recognizes that something is wrong with Sierra's mental health, though the rest of the family is too distracted to notice.

Steven's family relationships are struggling, so he throws himself into his sports apparel business, which experiences several obstacles. He can't get a loan from the bank, there are problems with the manufacturer, and a competitive brand nearly puts him out of business before he even begins. However, he invents a product that goes viral and puts him back on the map.

Season two

Sierra enters a treatment program for depression, where she makes new friends, some of whom her family do not approve of. She moves back home and becomes closer to Felicity. She finds other goals, though her father still pressures her to find a way back into athletics. Her depression and therapy with Annie have several ups and downs.

Meanwhile, Steven's profitable business is threatened when he is sued by another sports apparel company for patent infringement. Maria, who has quit her job to help with Steven's business, must again look for work. She is dismayed to find that her old job is no longer available.

Felicity is offered a scholarship to a private high school, but she must deal with the stigma of being one of the poorest kids in school. As she grows better and better at sports, it becomes clear that new opportunities may be opening for her—possibly even a shot at the Olympics.

Season three

Sierra attempts to get back into college, but she is hampered by her grades and the stigma around her depression and publicly known suicide attempt from season one. The discrimination prompts her to seek a *pro bono* lawyer, and she files suit against her former college.

Felicity is on the verge of admission to the Olympics. Steven is finally taking an interest in her, but the pressure is overwhelming. As she continues to compete, Felicity finds that her potential teammates are not as friendly as she had hoped.

Steven's business is shut down for good, and he is essentially bankrupt from the patent lawsuit. He throws all his energy into Felicity's Olympic bid, while contending with the welfare system. Things go from bad to worse for Maria when she discovers that her cancer is back. She tries to hide it from her family, because she knows that they do not have the money for healthcare bills. She does not want to derail her daughters. Her greatest wish is to see Felicity win a medal at the Olympics.

* * *

Minotaur

Treatment

by Eli Brenna

The minotaur waits in the center of the labyrinth. Many enter, hoping for reprieve. None survive. The Minotaur waits in the city. He seeks those criminals who would make his city a worse place. None survive. *Minotaur* tells the story of Leon, who adopts the alter ego of the Minotaur to take on the scum and villainous conspiracies of Crittenden. Leon will not survive.

Minotaur is a serialized, prestige superhero crime drama with procedural elements. There is no magic. The characters and action will be grounded and gritty. The bulk of the show takes place in Crittenden, and it will have a mostly realistic feel. Crittenden combines the down-and-out, luckless den of despair and poverty of Detroit, with its sprawl and foreclosures, with the cityscape, violence, and culture of Philadelphia. Guns take precedence over swords or magic. The show asks, what is acceptable for the greater good? What does evil look like? And how are we all corrupted? The message of the show involves the belief that humanity is easily manipulated.

The Minotaur meets his match in Sabine, a policewoman who picks up one of his murders and sets out on a mission with an end she could not imagine. At the same time, Leon's guardian, Franklin, sees Leon's potential and interferes in Leon's debatably noble activities. Over the course of the series, Leon is the minotaur to the maze that is his city. He is an animal off the chain. Sabine's determined to catch the Minotaur and bring him to justice. At the end of the series, when Sabine catches the Minotaur and he is executed for the whole town to see, the populace cheers.

Main characters

Leon: White, male, late 30s. He is about 5'9" and appears to be of average weight, but more than the average amount of that is muscle mass. He has built himself up to protect himself from a world that has hurt him for too long. He has dark hair and wild eyes. Leon stands with his head slightly down, shielding his eyes. The Minotaur, on the other hand, looks straight ahead. Leon is better looking than average, but he would never be considered for a modeling contract. He has scarring across his back from when his parents beat him with a hot frying pan. His parents were cruel.

Leon had an older sister, who one day called child services to come and save them. Their mother found her on the phone and beat her with it. She was unconscious when the police arrived. She has never woken up. Since then, Leon has lived with Franklin, his guardian.

Leon has no sex life to speak of. He has definitely had it, but probably with a prostitute when he was 19. He wants to live in a safer city. This is the only city he has known, and he does not want to leave. He has a strange optimism in his own abilities, but he is pessimistic about the nature of humanity and has seen the inefficiency of the city's law enforcement at work. He is not easygoing, but is soft-spoken. He is militant and determined. He is introverted, and reads quite a bit.

Today, Leon is a troubled man. He has been corrupted by the world around him. The trauma he experienced has pushed him toward instability in his adult life. He finished high school and found an interest in literature. However, after failing to find a calling, he worked manual labor odd jobs for years. Leon does not believe in any god—god has never fulfilled the justice he promised. The Minotaur does. The Minotaur judges the city's worst residents.

Leon is of above average intelligence, but he is by no means a genius. He is easily manipulated, which ties in to the abuse he received as a child. Leon is broken. The Minotaur is not. The Minotaur is strong. As the Minotaur, Leon fears nothing. As the Minotaur, he wants it all. He wants justice. He wants his city to be a safer place, even if his methods are cruel. He is frustrated by the cruel, even if he may be cruel himself.

Leon has no deep personal relationships besides Franklin, who of course has been betraying him. He moves through the world as a hulking specter, a monstrous masked man. Leon lumbers around avoiding contact. The Minotaur seeks it out. He believes that humanity does not deserve reprieve. He believes in death, and his own judgment. It is final.

Sabine: Black, female, early 30s. She is just above average height, average weight, with dark hair and bright eyes. She stands like someone a foot taller than she actually is. She is subtly beautiful. She looks like a cop. She is tidy and organized, hair pulled tightly back. Her parents moved to Crittenden back when the city wasn't as miserable, and the schools weren't half-bad. Sabine had a good education, but in an economic downturn, the schools lost a lot of funding and her favorite teacher during her senior year of high school. Now she is middle-class, earning a cop's salary. She loves the work but hates the job—the bureaucracy and lack of promotion. She is a little religious. She believes in God, believes in mercy, but also believes in the law. She holds herself and others to a high moral standard, yet she is able to get what she wants from others.

Sabine is one of the best detectives on the force, but she has constantly been held back due to her race and gender. Her superiors are not directly racist, but part of the institutional system of disenfranchisement that limits her without being noticed. She has a keen eye for detail and is a great people person. The form of manipulation she embodies is not malevolent, but rather she is able to manipulate humanity through her empathy. She's no pushover, though. She is confident and strives to make a name for herself. She fears mediocrity. She also fears death. Her will to survive is strong, and her fear of death may be the one thing holding her back from her full potential.

Sabine desires to rise in the ranks and has a strong urge for justice, much like the Minotaur. She is driven by the pain of others—where others fall, she rises. When others need defending, she will defend. She is frustrated by the way her race and gender count against her, and by the way her inferiors rise above her.

Sabine is unmarried. She has a boyfriend, but it is only semi-serious. Her world view is overall positive, which is why she is so driven when the darker parts of humanity reveal themselves. She moves through the world in kindness and slowness. She is self-corrupting by the end of the series.

Franklin: White, male, late 60s. He is of average height and of above-average weight. He is light of skin, hair, and eyes. He stands like a war veteran. He definitely used to be very handsome. He has liver spots and is greying.

Franklin is Leon's guardian. Franklin took care of Leon after Leon was removed from his parents. Franklin used to work as the British ambassador to a couple of different countries. He was very well educated and came to America after he retired. America worked well as a center for his conspiracy group. Separately from his involvement with Leon, Franklin is part of a larger conspiracy of questionable morals.

Franklin's own parents were upper-class, and they raised Franklin to believe that the world was his for the taking. Franklin feels entitled. When he discovers that Leon has become a superhero, he decides to use Leon for his own purposes. He begins pulling the strings. He holds the Minotaur's leash.

Franklin is extremely intelligent, and he is extremely compassionate toward Leon. He believes he is using Leon toward the greater good, and Franklin can easily forgive himself. Franklin is self-corrupting, but also corrupts Leon. Franklin has good standing in society and does some small work in his community. He is easygoing and cordial, but he is hiding more than he's showing. He fears a world beyond his control. He demands control and will not be convinced that his world view isn't the only true one. He also desires to control others. In his conspiracy web, he is ambitious and wants to become the number one guy. He is frustrated when others, including Leon, do not do what he wants them to do. He has no deep personal romantic relationships, but he cares very much about Leon. He moves through the world silently, but like the moon, he controls the tides wherever he goes.

Story engine

The story engine comes from Leon's superhero antics and personal life; Sabine's cases, bureaucracy, and tracking down Leon; a large web of secrets and conspiracies, which Franklin and eventually Leon are privy to; and the rise and fall of villains and allies. The tone embraces city life. It is mysterious, thrilling, and dark without trying to be *The Dark Knight.* It is moody and violent. The audience should feel despair for these characters, and for the state of humanity. Every week, we get to see Leon as the Minotaur; every week, we get to see Sabine deal with criminals on the lawful side of things, and edge closer and closer to catching the Minotaur.

Seasons

I envision each season having 13 episodes. Over the course of the first season, Leon will investigate the murder of a supervillain and prepare for the inevitable rise of whichever powerful being must have killed him. Sabine will investigate the murder of some minor criminals, only for the cases to go cold. Near the end of the season, she will discover more murders with a similar M.O., and by the end of the first season Sabine will realize she is hunting the Minotaur. Also over the first season, Franklin will introduce the audience to the larger conspiracy.

In the second season, Sabine will be promoted due to her discovery of the Minotaur's web of murders. She will be in charge of a taskforce dedicated to finding him. Leon will have to evade a city and law enforcement more aware of his actions, while also trying to do his "job." During this season, Franklin will push the limits of his control over Leon. He will push Leon harder and further than he has before, and he will come very close to being caught.

In season three, Franklin will be faced with a choice between Leon's life and the life of another operative who Leon is hunting. Franklin chooses to save Leon, but at the end of the third season, Leon will discover that Franklin has been pulling his strings the whole time. Also during this season, Sabine's superiors begin to lose faith in her abilities to find the Minotaur. They bring in outside agents to assist, one of whom becomes a supervillain.

Markets

This show would probably fit best on FX. They already go for moody, violent, prestige programming like *American Horror Story, The Americans, Sons of Anarchy, Justified,* and *Fargo.* However, they do not have a superhero show. It would fit in well with their lineup. They do air old episodes of *Buffy the Vampire Slayer,* which, while not a superhero show, has a superhero-like protagonist and story structure. HBO also may be a good home, as they also do not have a superhero show and are committed to sex, violence, and prestige programming. Showtime, A&E,

or even NBC might be a good fit as well (NBC did air *Hannibal,* after all). Amazon could sign on to compete with Netflix and their Marvel deal.

Relevance

This show is relevant right now. It will reveal the darkness of humanity that people attempt to push aside. It will appeal to teenagers and adults, as the superhero genre often does, but will take that appeal and use it for the greater good—the exploration of humanity in a realistic (if action-heavy) way. The leap of faith to the superhero element will lead to places superhero shows rarely go. I cannot promise it will improve the quality of the audience's lives as far as happiness goes, but it will fulfill them and appeal to the obsession with darkness in all of us. I also believe it fills a need in society for dark shows that appeal to that obsession. It can be a way to live vicariously evil through these characters, as well as explore the ways they themselves may corrupt or be corrupted by others. In addition, today's society has embraced the court of public opinion, from Zimmerman to Cosby. We judge others and make up our minds before they have even gone to trial (and sometimes they never go to trial). This vigilante spirit is embodied by Leon, who believes his own judgment to be infallible. If he believes someone is guilty, no one can convince him otherwise. He takes justice into his own hands. Of course, eventually the court of public opinion will come around and judge him just the same way.

How is this show unique?

This show differs from other shows in its unique combination of the superhero genre with true darkness. Other superhero ventures attempt darkness, but the hero rarely dies, and often dark superhero ventures verge on the camp. *Minotaur* will kill its hero at the end of the show, and the unique betrayal Leon will experience from Franklin is a twist on the classic Bruce Wayne/Alfred dynamic. This show will push the envelope with the fact that Leon will commit murder, unlike Batman. He is an antihero in a way that most superheroes just are not. The format will also focus on both Leon and Sabine every episode, setting them up as dual protagonists (who must eventually duel) with Franklin as the strong behind-the-scenes supporting character who can connect us to the larger world of the show and its vast conspiracies.

Research

I would very much like to use research on Greek and classical mythology. This will particularly influence my conceptions of the supervillains and of the show's story structure. The name of the city of Crittenden, for example, is influenced by "Crete," where the minotaur was held in Greek mythology, and it also sounds like "cretin's den."

Influences

Other art that has influenced me include the television shows *Orphan Black, Hannibal, Breaking Bad, Lost,* and *The Wire.* The format, conspiracies, and progression of *Orphan Black* are spot-on, and it is a brilliantly structured show. The procedural elements and darkness of *Hannibal* are an inspiration, and *Breaking Bad*'s format and character structures serve as an interesting starting point, as well as its realistic depiction of darkness, corruption, and violence. *Lost*'s endless sense of mystery made it the first show I ever loved, and *The Wire*'s singular view of a city is extraordinarily influential. I am also influenced by Greek and classical art and literature (as may be clear by the show's title). Obviously Batman is an influence as well, in the way I plan to twist its traditional characters and structure.

Why are you the only person who can create this TV series?

I am the only one who can write this series because I specifically want to explore the way each character embodies a different prism of corruption and manipulation. I believe humanity is inherently neutral, but it is easiest to be evil. Humans find it easiest to be selfish, and even if they do not intend to do so, often end up corrupting themselves and those around them. I also believe that superhero stories do not need to be cheap, or simply fun action for young audiences. In addition, others could easily see Leon's murder policy as just. I do not support capital punishment, and I will be able to keep in mind Leon's sins throughout the series, where others might forgive him. In the end, justice will come for the Minotaur as well.

* * *

The Guardian
Treatment
by Mac Davies

Type of show
Serialized fantasy, sword-and-sorcery epic drama.

Logline
In a fragile world recovering from a long and terrible conflict, a young girl with supernatural powers known as 'the guardian' must rise up to preserve balance and prevent the collapse of humanity.

World of the show
The world of the show is the entire world also known as Altea. Altea is a complete world much like that of Middle-earth and other epic fantasy type worlds. It consists of different landmasses, continents, nations, oceans, seas, forests, mountains, etc.

There are dragons lurking deep in the north, hidden from the world. Spirits can cross between both human and nether realms. And in this world, after the horrible war, little do the people of Altea know that such a tremendous conflict fractured the divide of spirit world and human world. The new guardian will not only have to face enemies common to the human dimension, but also those of fallen spirits, demonic entities, etc.

The nations

Vir

In the cold, icy, and unforgiving north resides the fallen empire of Vir. Vir has been reduced to a figurehead monarchy run by the joint control of Vaia and its allies from the war. Vir was once a proud empire of strong men and women built by their bond of endurance. The people of Vir (Virions) suffer through endless winters. They survive on hunting and trade, and the use of fire magic crystals that provide the heat for industry. But Vir is most known for its warriors. Fierce, strong, and unified like family through their struggles. Their greatest warriors were trained very young and are often referred to as the most feared men of an age.

One man believed that Vir should spread its values with other people. He was Lord Sargon, a respected warrior and commander of his time. Perhaps the best there was. Sargon believed the world did not respect Vir, and looked down on its people. Soon he created the first army of Vir known as the Dragon Legion. Naming them after the dragons that once roamed the cold north, the dragons being the oldest tradition of their people. He used his army of elite soldiers and fire magic to expand. Threatening the balance of the entire world. Cities fell, and many perished in bloody battles. Until the nation of Vaia allied itself with other nations and fought back with the help of 'the guardian' who was a woman known as Maya.

Maya proved to be a greater warrior than even Sargon. She led the forces of the allied nations to victory in the bloodiest war the world had ever seen. Though the exhaustion of war and the wounds she suffered against Sargon ultimately killed her. She could not live on for the restoration after the war. The time when Altea needed her most.

Without Maya, the nations of the world divided the empire of Vir back to their original nations. They punished the Virions with heavy taxes, and crippled their economy. The army was reduced, and the proud people of Vir began to wither. Many now rely on petty theft to survive. The code of honor that existed within the once proud people seems to have disappeared.

Kaia

At the center of Altea is the nation of Kaia. It has become the bastion of power within Altea at the conclusion of the 'War of the Dragon.'

Within Altea, there is a wealth of opportunities. At the start of this series, Altea is fragile as a world. All the nations are recovering from the brutal conflict. Kaia appears to be doing the best of all. The aftermath of the war and the study of Vir's use of magic crystals for war technology pushed Kaia to the forefront of technological prowess. Use of magic crystals within machines has created superior forms of irrigation and sewage systems. The use of magic technology is even creating new forms of travel. Kaia is near the point of having motorized vehicles.

However, the war has still sapped a lot of military strength. Most nations are in the same situation as Kaia. How does the world run now with a completely crippled Vir? It's been more than a decade after the war, and Vir is worse off than ever. With new technology and empty seats of power, the world is in serious trouble. For Kaia, mobster like gangs take advantage of country farmers and monopolize the incomes of shop owners within the industrious, democratic, bustling capital city called Mayahn (named after Maya).

Cytan

A country formed as a group of islands on the Calm Sea. The Cytani people are peaceful. They are a nation of farmers and fishermen. And Cytan is known for its use of different types of fabrics for creating all sorts of different clothing.

The land is lush and has beautiful grasslands, oceanic views, and mountains. It's a spiritual place of harmony and tranquility. Cytan is neutral. They never enter any war. The people are extremely spiritual. A gate that leads to the spirit world exists at the highest peak of one of their mountains. Though anti-war, Cytan actually has warriors who might be more than a match than the warriors of Vir. To reach ultimate happiness, Cytani believe a person must acquire strength of spirit, a tranquil mind, and a compassionate heart. Only with peace can a person achieve happiness.

Feyvern

Feyvern is a kingdom and ally of Kaia. Completely surrounded by forest and other woodland. Its people consider magic to be sacred, and there exist deep wells of magical energy and crystals harboring that energy within their forests.

The people of Feyvern are typically exclusive to other societies, but ultimately saw they needed to stop the march of Vir. As a society, the Fey (people of Feyvern) are seekers of knowledge. Old relics and tomes of information are of high value. Many Fey become priests or priestesses of magic and worship at shrines where they honor 'The First Ones.' The First Ones are the original people of all of Altea. Magical beings that made the world as it is today.

While still allies with Vaia, Feyvern has returned to its isolationism. They are in the middle of a struggle with the fractured rift of the spirit world. New evils have entered the woodland realm.

Magic

Magic within Altea is strong. It is the evidence of the existence of The First Ones. Although there is an abundance of magic within the world, there are very few who are actually capable of wielding it without the help of war technology.

Those who can are sorcerers and sorceresses. For them, the ability is mostly weak. They can be brought into wars as healers, able to perform medical practices that non-magic medics cannot.

But in groups, magic users could alter the fields of battle. Together, chanting ancient magical spells, they can change the weather to support their cause. Some could possess other people on the battlefield and assassinate an enemy commander. Abilities of sorcerers and sorceresses vary depending on their proficiency and area of study.

There is one person who has far greater power than anyone in Altea. That is the guardian. The guardian is reborn after each death. Always brought back to preserve and create balance within the world. Sometimes when the guardian dies, he/she is suddenly reincarnated into someone who has already been living for several years. Or they are reborn as a new child. It is entirely up to fate where the guardian is brought back. But it is the guardian's choices that decide the fate of Altea.

The guardian has a natural skill for fighting. He/she instinctively has skills of the guardians who came before them. But it takes time to remember/re-learn all of it.

With magic, the guardian has great destructive force. They can cause the ground to quake beneath their enemies, turn arrows into dust before they hit, create shockwaves with their hands, and even make it rain fire. But such use of magic has great cost to their well-being. It can cause exhaustion, even death.

To find the new guardian, each nation has a specific tower dedicated to the location and protection of the guardian. The rebirth is marked by great beams of light emanating from the sky, hitting the seeker crystals of each tower. From there, the seekers can find which nation the guardian is in. Then they must bring the crystal and search. To discover the guardian, it is in the eyes. Their eyes will glow blue when the crystal is close to them.

Characters

Terra

Physiology: Lithe, athletic, and strong. Youthful. A sense of curiosity and wonder for what the world has to hold in her eyes, and a determination to find out.

Sociology: The daughter of Sargon, Terra was a princess until war broke out. When Sargon was killed, Myron, Sargon's brother, took Terra away from the empire. She was no longer raised in an upper-class environment. Title of princess and potential empress no longer having any meaning to her. She was young when the war happened, and during the assault on Sargon's fortress, Myron managed to get her out. The order of seekers thought it best that Terra did not know her history. The trauma of the event affected her, and Myron had no choice but to follow the order's wishes otherwise the seekers planned to kill Terra out of fear and bigotry toward Virions. So Myron helped the seekers use their magic and alter Terra's mind.

Terra has no memory of being from Vir, or her sister, Kaelyn. She was raised on an island with the protection of the seekers and the tutelage of Myron. Terra believes she was some orphan girl wandering the streets of Mayahn and brought in by Myron to learn the ways of the guardian. He has educated her on history, language, combat, and some of her magic. As the guardian, people should love her. But with a long absence in between Maya's death, the guardian isn't as favored as she once was. Terra doesn't have much experience with the outside world and she needs to find out despite Myron's wishes to keep her protected for a while longer.

Psychology: Terra wants to be the best guardian to have ever lived. She's strong willed, stubborn, and incredibly determined. She is extroverted by nature and always speaks her opinion whether or not people like it. In training, if things don't go her way, her temper gets the best of her. She wants to know more about herself and find out what the world is like. But Myron and the seekers keep her hidden. It irritates her. She knows as the guardian she needs to be exposed to the outside world. A skilled swordsman, Terra is talented in all fields of fighting and a naturally gifted magic user. She is naïve and doesn't know how difficult the road as the guardian really is.

Myron

Physiology: An older man, a little over 50 years old. His hair is graying and his face shows signs of age. A man who has been through a lot. There is a scar on his face where Sargon hit him with a blade when Myron chose not to join his cause.

Sociology: Myron is a well respected seeker within his magic order. As a seeker he is responsible for finding the next guardian reincarnated into the world. It's a difficult job but he is the most skilled. Also his duty includes training and mentoring the guardian. He has been alive to witness Maya and see her grow, and now he must help Terra do the same.

Myron's brother was Sargon. Emotion tempted Myron to follow the call of his brother and help him with his cause. However, selfless responsibility and duty placed him against his brother.

Myron's well educated, of Virion blood, and has a deep feeling of regret about how the previous war turned out. While respected amongst the seekers, there is mistrust due to his Virion blood. He believes while the war has been won, the winning side seems to be growing corrupt and falling into chaos.

Psychology: Myron is a caring man who looks after Terra like she is his own daughter. Part of this is due to his relation to Sargon. Terra is his niece. With his wife long dead, he is a bit withdrawn sometimes.

With his experiences, Myron has a lot of wisdom. He learned from great teachers, but in the end forged his own path.

Can be a little manipulative with Terra, but he believes it is for the best and for her protection. He is her guiding hand. Myron sticks to his traditional methods of teaching, although he himself has a lot to learn from Terra.

Laike

Physiology: Laike is in his 20s. He is often unshaven, though he looks boyish and has innocent eyes.

Sociology: Laike is the brother of Dain. They're both native Kaians who were forced to grow up in harsh situations as orphans. Their parents died in the war, and so it was up to Dain and Laike to survive on their own. Education was limited for Laike. He enjoyed wandering and getting into trouble. Home life was inconsistent. He lived in different orphanages, and sometimes in different alleyways. Oftentimes it was Dain looking after Laike because Laike was the younger brother.

Psychology: Endearing and fun loving, Laike gambles and tries to help out Dain with money for their not-so-great home. His habits put him in more trouble than they help with anything.

Laike really just doesn't want to disappoint Dain, but getting involved in criminal activity is the only way he knows how to help. It's hard for him to get it through his brain that there are alternatives.

Generally Laike is positive and optimistic about life. He doesn't like always being treated like a kid by Dain, and he's frustrated he isn't like Dain. Laike is a trickster and skilled at manipulating others.

Dain

Physiology: Dain has a young face with the look of an older man. His beard and lines of stress on his face belie he's only 21.

Sociology: Dain helps get by along with his brother, Laike, by serving as a member of the law enforcement. He's one of the youngest members of the squad. His peers treat him as though he still needs to earn his spot. Dain wants to be one of the chief investigators of crimes throughout the city. The loss of his parents has been difficult especially because Dain has had to focus on the little education he could get while also keeping Laike out of trouble. Often a loner within the community, Laike gets along well with people, whereas Dain can be a bit cold and off putting.

Psychology: Focused on his work, Dain doesn't find the time for women or much of anything fun. It doesn't seem like he's had a good laugh in a long time. Dain is frustrated that he can't keep Laike in line all the time, and his advancement in law enforcement is taking too long. Dain wants to bring down the gangs because he hates people who take advantage of others. Dain can be negative and cold. He doesn't trust others easily. He is a good fighter and a skilled observer.

Kaelyn

Physiology: Beautiful, fit, and strong, Kaelyn has a regal presence about her and a seductive flair.

Sociology: The eldest daughter of Sargon, Kaelyn has been through a rough life. She has had to depend on her wits and her beauty to survive. After enduring years of slavery, Kaelyn finally became a self-made woman._Kaelyn's considered low-class, but she has a comfortable and steady income. Kaelyn is the owner of a bordello, a courtesan. She is well known amongst political leaders and gang leaders. Well educated and sharp, Kaelyn's prejudices are against everyone excluding Vir. She hates how she and her people have been treated in the aftermath of the war. Kaelyn has many connections within the city, and it makes her very influential and powerful.

Psychology: Despite being a prostitute, Kaelyn is actually a talented warrior. Sargon trained her, after all. She has natural talents as a fire magic user. Her morals lie within the gray. She will use whatever methods she deems fit for survival.

Kaelyn's outlook on life is full of anger and the desire for vengeance. She speaks with a soft and alluring voice, but her motives are dark. To others, Kaelyn's the most beautiful woman in the city. To herself, she's the rightful heir as empress to Vir. Her current position is a means to an end, and is only waiting for the right chance to return to Vir and seize power.

Jin

Physiology: A foreigner's appearance (Asian), Jin wears Cytan martial artist garb. He is in his mid-30s.

Sociology: Raised in Cytan and follows the ways of the Cytani spirit warriors. Unlike others, he is one of the very few Cytani to actually leave their mainland and explore the world.

Psychology: Thoughtful and philosophical, Jin left Cytan because he believes his people have been isolated for far too long. Jin is a man who has visions and believes he is a seer. He sees glimpses of a possible future. His goal is to alter and prevent the dark ends he foresees. Jin has no ambitions but a simple life and peace.

Lyanne

Physiology: Pale white, unusually so, and almost ethereal in her appearance, Lyanne has an unnatural grace about her.

Sociology: From the woodland realm, and thus, Lyanne believes she has a higher knowledge than most people.

Psychology: A bit of a know it all, Lyanne has a lot of knowledge about magic that can help the guardian. Also on a mission to find out why the severed wall between the human and spirit world is having adverse effects on her homeland.

Nirua

Physiology: Ex-military, Nirua is grizzled and scarred in his mid-30s.

Sociology: Nirua was born within the divide of the two gangs. He, like many others, has fallen victim to their wars._Gangs and political leaders—Nirua hates them both. He's the leader of a growing movement within the city to overthrow the gangs and the entire political system of the area.

Psychology: He's militant and enthusiastic. His strong belief in his cause is contagious to other people. He is a strong public speaker. Nirua is a great fighter, and he believes he has found a way to defeat both gangs. It turns out his plan gets him possessed by a demonic spirit who is far more manipulative and powerful. It turns his cause from a minor threat to lethal.

Bael
Physiology: Tall, well dressed, and fit, Bael always has a look of superiority in his eyes. Bael is in his late 30s.

Sociology: Bael is the most powerful gang leader in the city of Mayahn. Bael was born in the upper class, and the gang was handed down to him by his father. He is well educated and has a sense of nobility. His brothers work for him. His parents are dead but he has a reverence for his father. His only enemy in the city is Revis and the law enforcement. Revis is his rival within the streets.

Psychology: Bael likes the way things are. The upper-class and his gang sit in power where they belong. Hierarchy is a natural order where the higher class should always sit on top. He believes in noble birthrights. He enjoys life and the luxurious elements his position grants him. He fears Revis' capability of rising and overthrowing him. The sole power of the gang scene is his goal. He is reserved and calm.

Revis
Physiology: Revis is the same age as Bael, which is the late 30s. He's bulky and his face has seen better days.

Sociology: Revis was lower-class from the day he was born. Revis is a self-made man who had to earn everything he got. With parents who were hardly able to keep him alive, Revis had to lie, cheat, steal, and kill to survive. He received no education but had enough street smarts to build a gang of his own that is now the second largest within the city. The gang's numbers grow every day, especially considering lower-class people prefer one of their own over Bael. Revis hates noble, upper-class people. Their sense of superiority and entitlement, taking advantage of the poor drove him to violence.

Psychology: Revis enjoys much "baser" entertainment than Bael. He goes to bordellos, watches men fight to death in arenas, etc. Revis has a quick temper, but he shows real signs of affection for the lower-class people. Although he gives out some of his money to help, he still takes advantage of what they have to fight Bael.

How is your show relevant now?

My show is relevant now because fantasy is becoming more popular every day, especially with the recent success of *Game of Thrones*. It's relevant because within its setting, it mixes both fantasy and the advance of technology. A new world rising as the old world goes to the wayside.

It's relevant because it will take serious looks at different modern issues such as concepts of modern USA imperialism. Paralleling the actions of the nation of Kaia intervening with countries around it that don't want them to intervene.

How is your show different from other TV shows?

Not many fantasy shows within a fantasy setting add technological twists to them. And depending on the storylines being followed, it is flexible. It may have moments that seem like horror, others a traditional drama, or even investigative mystery. The styles will interweave wherever the journey of Terra takes the audience.

How does your show push the envelope?

My show pushes the envelope because it will take stances that might not be the popular opinion. It may show the other side of a 'terrorist' cause to reveal that those on the other end are also human beings. It will push the audience to really think about what it means to be truly compassionate and empathize with all people. The show will not be afraid to kill off characters and throw incredible plot twists.

What did you discover through real-world research about your idea? How did you incorporate it into your show?

I looked at customs of Vikings, ancient Spartans, Greeks, and the Samurai to base certain values for different nations and their societies. The nation of Kaia is meant to be like that of Athens as the center of a progressive society. While fantasy, there is an essence of industrial revolution taking place as well. I also looked at World War I for details of warfare that depict a lot of the horror for how I envision the war Maya fought in. The Virions are based on strict warrior codes from Spartans and Samurai. Vir's landscape is meant to be cold and icy like that of the Vikings in the Scandinavian countries.

What other art has influenced your TV series idea?

I'm heavily influenced by *Game of Thrones* for its sword-and-sorcery style of television. The epic fantasy storytelling is something I'm a huge fan of. But the magic in my television show is more inspired by the likes of *Avatar: The Last Airbender* and *The Legend of Korra.* Those shows have been a part of a long stretch of my life and the world within it inspired many of my ideas. *Buffy the Vampire Slayer* is also a huge inspiration.

* * *

Exit Stage Left
Treatment
by Sarah Kenney

Type of show
Serialized, character-driven single-camera sitcom with some workplace-type situations.

Logline
Exit Stage Left is a single-camera comedy about Georgia Moss, an aspiring theater director whose parents give her an ultimatum: Major in a STEM field or pay for college herself.

World of the show
Glenshee College, a tiny liberal arts institution near Ohio's Amish country. More specifically, Bixby Theater, home to the college's theater and dance programs. Students largely identify with one of the three major cliques: techies, costumes, or actors. The techies live their lives in the scene shop, the control booth, or anywhere but center stage. They like to imagine themselves beyond the drama that is the actor's turf, but they are in fact prone to histrionics and flights of fancy. They make the best of the terrible shows the professor/directors choose to produce. They are the people who are never in the actual spotlight, so they are always striving for attention and respect.

Themes
The show will explore themes of self-discovery, competition and ambition, and the bond that can develop amongst a group of underdogs.

Story engine
Each new show brings a fresh round of building/directing/prop-finding challenges. Week to week, Georgia has to balance her life at the

theater with classes for her biology major, a social life, and other campus activities.

Tone

The show will be very high-energy with irreverent humor.

Character bios

Georgia Moss

Physiology: Twenty-year-old Georgia has brown hair, green eyes, and is a little above average in height but isn't headed for the WNBA anytime soon. She isn't overweight, but her freshman 15 has probably followed her into junior year. Because of this, and also because she goes to college in the middle of nowhere and doesn't particularly care about dressing up, she wears a lot of stretchy pants with longer tops. She wears tortoise shell glasses that might as well have come from Vogue Optical's "Look at Me, I'm Sarcastic" collection.

Sociology: The Moss family lives in a very middle-middle-class county in the middle of Maryland. Georgia's parents both work. Her father is a manager for a popular East Coast grocery store chain and her mother is head of speech therapy for the public schools. Georgia is an only child.

Georgia's self-deprecating humor can sometimes get a little awkward, but it's mostly endearing. She is one of the few people who gets along well with fellow techie Victor Reis. They have the common goal of wanting to actually make a living in theater production despite being repeatedly told to focus on something safer. They don't have a romantic relationship. Because she's the only girl Victor doesn't either ignore or attempt to seduce, some of their coworkers expect something's bound to happen between them. Georgia knows too much about Victor's party-guy past to want to go there.

Georgia's relationship to the rest of her college is facilitated through her roommate and only non-theater friend, Stephanie Pin, whom everyone calls "Spin." Their dorm room is Georgia's break from the theater's insanity. Spin is pre-med, but she somehow finds the time to know where all the best parties are. She forces Georgia to enjoy the college experience. She is also the only person who can get Georgia to put on pants that don't have a stretchy waistband.

Psychology: Georgia wants her parents to take her seriously. Being their only child has long forced Georgia to balance her own dreams with those of her parents. She's always been a good student, but being away at college has made her realize she needs to live her own life. This may or may not be the one her parents dreamed their daughter would have. Georgia might not be bad at math and science, but she doesn't love it the way she loves theater.

Though she is mostly good-natured, Georgia has a pretty fierce temper. It takes a lot to anger her, but she has a breaking point. And when it's hit, she explodes. Her father has a similar temper, but her parents have always told her to control herself. She tries to keep her issues inside, which turns her into a bit of a pressure cooker.

Victor Reis
Physiology: Victor is 20 and tall, dark and good-looking in a non-traditional way. He's Jewish, but he only observes when he can use it as an excuse to get out of class. He's self-assured and unapproachable until he gets to know you...but he probably won't want to. Unless you're a hot girl he hasn't met yet or a professional tech director.

Sociology: His family is *nouveau riche*. His father, Jed, runs his own construction company in Long Island, New York, which is why Victor is so good at scenic design and set building. His dad isn't happy that his son is using his skills in hopes of a career in theater. Jed doesn't understand why Vic doesn't take business classes so he can just step in to the construction empire. Vic has a sister, Abbie, who is ten years his senior. While in Israel on her birthright, she decided to stay and work on an organic farm. Despite their age difference, they had been very close, and she had protected him from some of their parent's intensity. When she left for and then stayed in Israel, eight-year-old Vic felt abandoned.

Free from his overbearing father for the first time in college, Vic joined a frat as a freshman and had a couple of wild years. He quit at the end of his sophomore year when, as a scene shop assistant, he came to work hungover and had a near-mishap involving the table saw. The scene shop supervisor, Zlatka, who recognizes his talent and treats him like a son (she's pretty mean to everyone else), urged him to get his act together.

Psychology: Victor loves the impermanence of theatrical sets. For every new show he gets to start over, and at the end he gets to tear it all down. He's gifted at recycling the walls or platforms from old shows to look brand new for the current production. Although his finished sets are works of art, he is never attached to them. He is always ready to start on something new. Much as he is with his sets, he tires of people quickly. Aside from Zlatka and Georgia, he doesn't like to build lasting relationships. His sister's abandonment has left him somewhat polarized about women.

Stephanie "Spin" Pin
Physiology: Petite, Korean, cute and free-spirited. She has her nose pierced with a small stud and a few colorful streaks in her black hair. She is completely comfortable with herself and dresses like an off-duty supermodel at Burning Man: perfectly imperfect.

Sociology: Adopted as a baby by a couple of Portland, Oregon, hippies, Spin has "old parents" who raised her to believe she could be anything she wanted to be. Unlike her roommate, Georgia, Spin actually *does* want to be a doctor. She also wants to learn to play a new [insert bizarre instrument like a didgeridoo here] every week, and she and her friends in the philosophy department like to tag buildings around campus with huge chalk murals. Georgia is constantly amazed by Spin's ability to do so much on campus and still easily make straight As.

Spin has an easy confidence and go-with-the-flow attitude that should backfire on her in a major as intense as pre-med, but somehow it never does. She's just one of those people. Her easy-going nature and genuine happiness drives some people (like Vic) insane, but most people find her spirit infectious. This sometimes annoys Georgia, but for the most part she's just happy to have a port in the storm. Spin is a really good listener, but sometimes her suggested solutions are a little too reliant on "opening your mind with some of this top-notch medical-grade marijuana I'm working on!" She dates an unpredictable array of guys...and girls.

Psychology: Spin sees the good in everyone, whether they like it or not. She sees possibilities where Georgia sees obstacles. While she's comfortable with who she is, she doesn't like being pigeonholed. Some of her relationship choices seem to be motivated more by an urge to continue to defy categorization than actual romantic interest.

Zlatka Novobilski

Physiology: Scene shop supervisor Zlatka is Polish and in her late 40s. She is about 5'6" and compactly built. She dyes her long hair pitch black and wears it severely pulled back. She wears stovepipe jeans from the 90s that probably haven't been washed since they were first bought, huge steel-toed boots and a permanent "don't fuck with me" expression. The freshman and actors are terrified of her.

Sociology: In her youth, Zlatka was Poland's great hope for an Olympic medal in figure skating at the 1984 Sarajevo games, but she failed to live up to those dreams when she fell in love with a Bosnian athlete. He went missing during the Bosnian War, and she immigrated to the U.S. in the mid-90s, assuming her lover dead. She now believes romantic relationships are a waste of time and regularly dispenses this helpful advice to her female students. She does not, however, have a problem with a woman taking advantage of a man if it helps her advance herself. She is a big proponent of "being sneaky about it." Despite having lived in the United States for well over a decade, Zlatka still speaks with thickly accented English, peppered with Polish expletives. Zlatka definitely comes off as harsh, but she has a soft spot for Vic because he responds to her angry tirades with affectionate insults.

Psychology: Zlatka is extremely mercurial; eccentric and funny one day and filled with rage the next...these are what Vic refers to as her "Old Country" days. Zlatka's experiences have hardened her, but the young girl in the sparkling skating costume is still within her. She comes out to visit every now and then.

Iris Williams

Physiology: Iris, 21, is a statuesque, classically pretty African-American woman. She dresses simply and stylishly. She moves like a dancer. Her grace and impeccable manners give her an air of approachability, but people tend to be in awe of her. She knows it, too.

Sociology: Iris comes by her dancer's carriage honestly; her mother had been a dancer in New York in the 1980s. Iris' father moved the family to Ann Arbor, Michigan, when Iris was a baby. He owns a popular farm-to-table restaurant.

Iris had been making her own costumes since she saw a video of her mother in an off-Broadway production of *A Chorus Line*. Iris' mother regularly takes her on "show trips" back to New York to see ballets and the latest Broadway productions. Iris' parents have always encouraged her talent. She is extremely detail oriented, and her work is always flawless. Iris chose to attend Glenshee over the larger, bigger-named schools she was accepted to because she was told if she came she would also be hired as the head costume designer for the theater department.

Iris was Georgia's randomly assigned roommate freshman year and they deeply hated living together. Their relationship has not improved with their theater work, but they can't avoid each other. Iris and Victor have a secret hook-up going on that Georgia doesn't know about.

Psychology: Iris firmly believes that the secret to getting what she wants is to just be naturally good at it, and it will come to her. Consequently, when she finds something she is not so good at, it terrifies her and she avoids it at all costs. Iris easily manipulates people with her charm. She is always able to get her freshman assistants to cater to her every whim.

Harold Harman

Physiology: Harold is a nervous man in his mid-30s. He keeps his limbs drawn in when he's sitting. He parts his hair harshly to the left and wears only black.

Sociology: A visiting professor, Harold's in an awkward place socially at the school. He thinks he's too young to hang out with the other professors, but he's probably a little too old to be hanging out with the students. Though that hardly stops him from trying.

His last regional theater play in Salt Lake City, Utah, having been a bust, Harold came to Glenshee as a temporary replacement to on-sabbatical department head Maude Mahon-Walsh. He was supposed to serve as an advisor to Georgia while she directs the first musical of the school year, but he wants to stay on when the department head returns.

He decides the only way to do this is to impress the department with his original work, *Witness! The Musical,* based on the 1985 Harrison Ford movie. He will serve as writer, director, and choreographer. Harold sometimes mentions a wife in Utah, but the circumstances surrounding that are mysterious.

Psychology: Harold is the poster child for delusions of grandeur. He never thought he would deign to teach, and so in his mind, he is putting on Broadway caliber shows. He's completely oblivious to the fact that he's stepping all over the students he's supposed to be teaching, which is directly at odds with his desperation to be liked. He sees this as his best chance at theatrical glory.

Season arcs

Season 1: As the first season begins, Georgia is back at Glenshee for her junior year. Her parents tell her that they won't continue to help her pay for college if her only focus is theater. She agrees to double major in biology as a compromise. When she gets to the theater for the first production meeting, she learns that the Sondheim musical she thought she was going to get to direct has been bumped in favor of Harold's vanity project. She decides she's had enough. She'll just go the "stable" science route, like her parents want. This lasts a matter of hours before realizing biology doesn't excite her, and that even the worst musical on the planet is still theater. She determines to make the best of it.

Over the course of the season, Georgia must mediate a bitter and fast-escalating feud between Iris and Zlatka over the storage space underneath the stage. The students endure a night of forced post-rehearsal "bonding" with Harold that includes smoking a great deal of weed in his oddly Spartan apartment. Victor and Iris' secret attraction is revealed. Georgia enlists Spin to help her throw a killer cast party after the show finally closes. Although *Witness! The Musical* turned out to be exactly as stupid as she had worried it would be, Georgia embraces it. It can't get any worse.

Season 2: The students return from Thanksgiving break and are ready to get started on the winter straight play. As a result of the poor attendance and high production costs of *Witness!*, the department is in financial trouble. Georgia suggests they scrap the high-concept version of *King Lear* that Harold had planned. Rather than his vision of a "post-industrial, digital kabuki-mythos" Shakespeare, she thinks it might be better if they do a classic Neil Simon comedy. It would be something students and people in the community might actually have heard of, and it would be way less expensive. Plus, everybody loves a comedy!

Harold considers comedy to be an art form that is beneath him (despite having inadvertently directed one at the start of the year) and decides they could save money *and* get an audience by doing a play with a small set and high shock value: Sarah Kane's *Blasted.* The play is filled with horrifying content, and the college won't let the department produce it unless they "clean up" about 90% of the action. Every week they have to make new adjustments to the script to censor the nausea-inducing portions. Sarah Kane's estate finds out about the rampant censorship and puts an injunction on the school to stop them from doing the play. Harold is beside himself, convinced he'll be fired. Georgia steps up and decides that because they already have a hotel room set, they'll do Neil Simon's *Plaza Suite.* When the show sells out, Harold takes the credit.

Season 3: The season begins after winter break. When Theater Department Head Maude Mahon-Walsh returns from her sabbatical spent in the Appalachian mountains, Georgia is relieved to talk to her about Harold's terrible play selections. They aren't appropriate for the actors or the student body, and they don't offer much in the way of diversity. Maude initially seems like the voice of reason and the ally Georgia needed last semester, agreeing with her on all counts and noting that Harold will have to be "not replaced, but placed elsewhere" within the department. Georgia needs Maude to agree to be her advisor for her senior project. Being Maude's assistant director for this play could make or break Georgia's senior year. Maude tells Georgia she thinks Georgia will appreciate her "truly innovative concept" for the spring musical: A retelling of Gershwin's *Porgy and Bess.* Maude's "edgy" idea involves switching the casting of the traditional black and white roles and "updating" it by making Sportin' Life a meth dealer.

Georgia is completely at a loss for how to fix this. She can't figure out how to turn this blatantly racist, wildly offensive bastardization of an important classic into art. She decides to wash her hands of this one and applies for a young professionals workshop in New York with Vic and Iris. While there, an off-off-Broadway producer is impressed with Georgia's work and offers her a directing position. Georgia must decide between taking a chance and staying in New York or honoring her parent's wishes that she finish college.

How is your show relevant now?
We are living in a world where the economy is so bad that majoring in something other than STEM fields essentially means you don't want to have money, ever. Yet students graduate from college year after year with degrees in the arts because they believe in themselves and they can't imagine working in any other field. Their confidence may be delusional, but it's a confidence anybody would want to have. Even in a dire job market, there's something about youth and college that makes you think it will all work out.

How is your show different from other TV shows?
While there have been shows in the past focusing on the world of theater such as *Smash, Glee,* and *Slings and Arrows,* this one tells the stories of the people behind (and above) the stage who make the spectacle possible. Each season will cover the construction, rehearsal, and coming together of one show.

How does your show push the envelope?
Each season tracks one theatrical production. There are several productions per academic year. This means that the same students would be in college for between six and eight TV seasons. It provides a real sense of the week-to-week progression of rehearsal and construction.

Theater kids are notoriously crazy on most college campuses. Everyone I've ever met and spoken to about their college experience acknowledged that this group can get especially wild. Theater kids are prone to choosing the most creative solution to a problem, rather than the simplest or most efficient.

What did you discover through real-world research about your idea? How did you incorporate it into your show?
While seeking a career in entertainment has always been a risky endeavor, studies show that future prospects may be even worse for such graduates today. I'm curious about why young people still take that risk, when they could theoretically set themselves up for a better life by choosing to pursue a degree in a STEM field that might secure them a better lifestyle and also help the economy. In the past decade, STEM jobs have grown three times as fast as other fields. When you're 18-20 years old and you're making choices that affect the rest of your life, but you don't even know what you want for the rest of your life, how does that inform your behavior?

What other art has influenced your TV series idea?
- Stephen Sondheim's "Merrily We Roll Along"
- "I Was Meant for the Stage," The Decemberists
- "Choose your own adventure" type stories
- the ability of lighting to instantly change mood, tone, and perception
- TV shows: *Slings and Arrows, Spaced, 30 Rock, Glee, Mozart in the Jungle, Breaking Pointe, Smash*

Why are you the only person who can create this TV series?
After "not being a great fit" as an actor in any of the already poorly chosen plays at my undergrad, I spent all four years working backstage on the productions in almost every capacity possible. I felt really ambivalent about where I wanted to be. For everyone I was working with, theater was a little microcosm within the school where we could try to figure out who we were in our own way. We also sometimes drove each other nuts, but it was a great community. I also have a younger brother who was a biology major, and he makes more money

three years out of college than I do after almost eight. I've definitely gotten a real-world education on the value of a degree in theater.

* * *

B-List
Treatment
by Henry Boyd

Type of show
B-List is a single camera half-hour sitcom with 13 episodes per season. The show is procedural in that every episode will revolve around one of the films being made, but there is also room for character-driven stories within that setting.

Logline
Roger Larson tries his best to crawl out of the world of cheap budgets, low quality, and lower expectations after winding up trapped as the assistant of Ken Johnson, a prolific and aging producer in the B-movie world.

World of the show
Modern day Los Angeles and the surrounding area. Most of the sets will be local and as cheap as possible, but there is the opportunity to travel to different locations depending on the fictional film's budget.

Characters
Roger Larson (20s) has dreamed of being a filmmaker his entire life. He went to film school, made some impressive short films and even won best short film at USC. But somehow he ended up without a job and was forced to sign on as Ken Johnson's personal assistant. All Roger wants to do is make great films and become a famous director. But the more he works for Ken, the less likely it seems that will happen. Roger is slowly being pushed into obscurity, and he's afraid that he'll never make it.

Roger is too arrogant to see the value in what he's learning from Ken and his films, even if they aren't as good as Hollywood's A-list movies. He's blinded by the fact that he thinks he's above all of this as well as everyone else, and he refuses to believe the job is helping him at all. Every time he believes he knows better than others, it almost always turns out that he's wrong.

Roger considers himself an artist and a connoisseur of film (constantly referencing art films or foreign movies). His main flaw is that he's all artist. He has no sense of the business side of things when it comes to selling movies or to selling himself.

Physiology: Roger is a young, somewhat attractive guy who doesn't know it. He dresses straight out of a Wes Anderson movie, which seems to match his lanky but average-sized physique.

Sociology: Roger comes from an upper-middle-class home with regular parents and no siblings. He's worked plenty but never really had to endure any hardships or want for anything, which he always resented his parents for because it makes for a terrible biography of a famous filmmaker.

After spending most of his childhood making films, he graduated from USC looking to get started on his career, only to end up working as Ken's assistant. Roger has a keen eye for everything that technically makes something great. He has no idea what he's doing as far as putting actual heart into a film, and a lot of his work comes off as either robotic or just copying someone else's style. He has a strong prejudice against anyone who doesn't have a good pedigree of films they've watched or would consider their favorites. Most of his current friend circle in LA has been restricted to people who are exactly like him in almost every way. He hasn't noticed how he alienates himself like this yet.

Psychology: Roger is all about becoming the best filmmaker ever, and his entire psychology resolves around that. He is usually excited and fun, but he can become angry and frustrated when things don't go as planned (which is often the case in film). However his anger comes off as ridiculous, so no one takes it seriously.

Roger sees himself as a budding young filmmaker beginning the first few steps of his climb up to greatness, and different/unique compared to everyone else working in film. While Roger is fairly smart, he is no stranger to making dumb mistakes that often set him back. He thinks anything obscure or foreign is more likely to be cool and cultured, so in his off time he spends his money looking for hard-to-find films on any possible format (film reel, DVD, VHS, etc...) or studying the works/writings of the greats.

Ken Johnson (white, 70s) was on the top of the B-movie world during the second half of the 20th century. After serving in Korea (as a chauffeur for MacArthur) he returned home and started working as a driver for the studios, which led to him financing part of the sleeper hit, *Attack of the Brain Monsters.* After that he became a producer, helping finance low-budget films that always made a profit, quality or not.

Plenty of famous directors and actors passed through his films over his career before moving into the big leagues (and even a few he just says worked for him). As the years progressed he made less and less money (which he blames on a lot of directors, including the ones he trained: Hitchcock, Polanski, Kubrick, Clint Eastwood, Ron Howard etc...) Ken has experienced a slight resurgence in the past few years now that terrible movies have become something of a novelty. So Ken has been pulling out all the stops to make the next big terrible movie. He's the most mediocre of Stan Lees.

Ken is obsessed with the bottom line, all business and little film. He doesn't even watch movies, and he only cares about getting out the cheapest films for the largest amount of return. Because of his vast experience in film he'll stumble into genius sometimes with the work he does, but only by accident. He'll do anything to get his films made on schedule and under budget, cut any corners, and resort to any means necessary, shady or otherwise. Ken's biggest fear is becoming a failure in business and losing his money. He also has a very loose sense of etiquette in work, constantly throwing away screen credits to solve his problems or being very insulting/politically incorrect in the way he speaks to others.

Physiology: Ken is a small, bulky bully of a man. He will wear outfits from the 50s and smoke the same cigars that Patton did.

Sociology: Ken was born and bred in the working class, and he assumed he would be there his entire life until he stumbled his way into the film industry. He has almost no formal education, but has enough war stories to fill a library. (Every story is a war story for Ken).

Ken is prejudiced against practically everyone, including white people who he also can't stand, and he has the mindset of a politically insensitive cartoon that would make you squirm if it came on while you were in an ethnically diverse room. If it makes it any better, he really just doesn't like anyone at all equally. But despite all of that, he still knows everyone. He has a never-ending list of people who either owe him favors or he can talk into helping him for one reason or another. You couldn't call them friends but at least it's something.

Psychology: Ken's psychology and mindset is the sum of everything that is wrong with the film industry today (from Roger's point of view). He is also shaped by business, focused on costs and revenues while being attached to an outdated model of business. He refuses to change his methods, which have always worked for him. However, Ken is also the kind of person you would call sharp. His street smarts are impressive enough to help him continue to profit from his work even as the industry has changed over the past few decades.

Sarah (20s) is Ken's script girl. Her official title is script supervisor, but Ken calls her the script girl because he has always had one. Sarah is trying to become a screenwriter, and she hopes that she can eventually get Ken to film one of her scripts. She supervises everything involved with the script and concept, sometimes even writing out scenes quickly if they're needed. Sarah is desperate to succeed but also has a very blunt and realist personality that sometimes puts her at odds with some of the cast and crew.

Physiology: Sarah is a young woman with a slight Midwestern accent that she tries to hide for work. She has a presence that inspires confidence and says that she knows exactly what she is doing. This presence turns to standoffish when she has to deal with issues that come up between the cast and crew.

Sociology: Sarah comes from a middle-class family in Michigan. She graduated from college with a degree in historical literature, but fell in love with screenwriting after reading the script for *50/50.* After working a series of assistant and script reader jobs that went nowhere, she ended up as Ken's script girl. It was the only job that actually let her do some writing, even if it is for bad horror flicks and low budget scifis. She also has a network of contacts from different agencies and production companies that Ken needs her to use often in order to get ahead of the competition.

Psychology: Sarah is similar to Roger in that she wants to become the best screenwriter she can, but she has a much more realistic expectation about what to do and a real plan for how to get there. She gets frustrated from time to time by Ken's outdated method of doing things, but thinks that what she's learning about actually making movies outweighs his horribleness for now.

Sarah is usually very blunt and sassy at times, which puts her at odds with a lot of the cast and crew when dealing with problems. She also has a fear of failure that sometimes creeps up on her. Outside of work she really just loves to read, and she has an enormous personal library that barely fits into her apartment.

Jane (30s) is definitely not actually named Jane. She is the go-to camerawoman/cinematographer for Ken on his films. An easygoing woman with a vaguely foreign accent that sounds like she was in *Highlander*, no one knows what country Jane is actually from. Jane's only experience with camera work is from working at a photography studio that did family and school portraits. Her biggest problem as a camerawoman is that she has no urge to try anything daring with her work. Jane prefers to keep it simple with her shots and not stray from the norm.

Physiology: Jane is an average sized woman with average features that don't match her voice or accent. She will intimidate anyone who tries to disagree with her about the camera work, but other than that she is usually very removed from everyone else.

Sociology: No one knows anything at all about Jane's background, and she never talks about herself with anyone or gives her opinion. She simply appeared one day and made Ken give her a job as his camerawoman.

Psychology: Jane is aggressive when necessary for what she wants, but outside of that she is easygoing and quite polite. She has no ambitions to move up or be the best. She likes what she does now just fine. Although we have no knowledge of her background, she displays a very high IQ and will occasionally let slip an insanely specific fact about a subject such as chemistry or a far-off location.

Don (late 40s) is Ken's editor who never goes outside. He moved into film after working for a decade at a news station. He is overly fond of narration, which he will provide himself whether anyone asks him to or not. He thinks he has a great voice. While he is great editor once he gets started, he is technologically inept outside of editing software and often needs help from others.

Physiology: Don is a younger version of Tom Brokaw, with a slightly annoying pitch in the way he speaks.

Sociology: Don came from a family of highly successful news anchors. All of his relatives work at a news station in some capacity. Don found himself immediately ostracized by everyone except for his supportive wife and three kids when he left to work in film. A lot of his news-anchor family still won't talk to him.

Psychology: Don is a real friendly guy; Ned Flanders' sweetness combined with the nicest and most supportive father you could imagine. No one can not like Don. Don's real goal is to become a voice actor, and he was hoping he could use his connections as an editor to make that happen. But Ken won't let him do any narrations because of his weird voice, and most people tend to run off when he plays his demo reel. Don doesn't particularly enjoy the films he works on, but it makes him happy enough to be able to support his family for now while working toward his dream.

Liam (30s) is Ken's prop guy. When not working on insane concepts or monsters or props, Ken also makes him be the male stunt double on set even though he doesn't look like anyone he doubles for. Not only that, but Liam is timid, nervous, small and weak. Everything you wouldn't want in a stunt double.

Physiology: A small stature describes pretty much everything about Liam. He is constantly shrinking away from everyone and everything around him.

Sociology: Liam grew up an outsider and has managed to stay that way while trying to work in props for films, despite his encyclopedic knowledge of films regarding their set and creature designs. *The Thing* inspired every career choice he has ever made. His works were considered too controversial and strange for even the workshops whose jobs are to think that stuff up. Ken was the only one who would take him on (for cheap, of course). Liam might have a place within the science fiction/fantasy realm, but who knows if we'll ever meet anyone who works in that side of the industry. Usually he is just hunkered down in the dark props room working on a new creature or prop.

Psychology: Liam just wants to do the prop design that he loves all the time without being bothered or having to deal with anything. He hates getting involved with movie decisions and anything outside of his work, which is probably why Ken loves to make him the male stunt double for all of the movies they make.

Penelope (30s) is Ken's stunt coordinator. She is also the female stunt double. She doesn't look like anyone she doubles for because she is much taller and bigger than anyone else. But Ken hires her and Liam every time they need any stunt work. She is also very aggressive when it comes to doing the biggest stunts possible, at the risk of everyone else.

Physiology: Penelope is tall, strong, energetic, and not afraid of anything. Everyone is intimidated by her except Ken.

Sociology: Penelope grew up in an extremely wealthy family from New England, and she spent most of her life disappointing them by doing the exact opposite of what was expected of her. She grew up taking any MMA and martial classes she could find, weightlifting, and competing in fight clubs, legal or otherwise. On the side she would ride and service illegally modified cars. She spent some time as a prizefighter in the UFC. She decided to head out to LA after seeing the *Mission Impossible* movie where Tom Cruise rappels on the side of the Burj Khalifa. She doesn't have too many friends due to her intimidating nature, but she is trying to be friendlier in order to make connections with other stunt coordinators. She sees Ken as a mentor/father figure and is somewhat protective of him.

Psychology: Penelope is all about bigger, better, louder, and more dangerous. She lives for the day when she'll have a large enough budget to do the most insane stunts ever dreamed up. Although she is constantly frustrated by her lack of a strong budget and Ken's inclination to scale down her ideas to cut costs, Penelope appreciates the opportunity and does enjoy the challenge of making everything work with so many limited resources. When she isn't working, she's dreaming up and designing more stunts, even if there's no movie for them to be used in.

Film cast and crew: While the main characters will usually be in every episode, the rest of the cast will rotate every episode for the actors, production crew, and extras. However, there will be some recurring characters—extras, who Ken keeps hiring, sometimes even putting into more than one role on the same film. There will also usually need to be a different director every episode, unless Ken decides to direct. Each new director will have distinct personality/film traits that can clash with the main characters. There is also the possibility to have famous actors and directors cameo in those roles as well.

Theme

The show will explore the idea of success/quality, what that means, and how you obtain it.

Story engine

Each week the show will feature a film project. Stories will come from filmmaking—really low quality films, film industry jobs, every job involved with making a film, financing a film, props/costuming/ production design, critics' reviews, networking in the entertainment industry, location scouting, fighting over film credits, screen tests, selling to distributors—anything that can go wrong or right with making a movie. Also stories can come from the interactions between cast and crew members as well as their relationships with other people outside of the film world.

Tone

I want the tone to be similar to *Brooklyn Nine-Nine and Parks & Recreation,* but with a little bit more sharpness that tends toward a darker/more adult humor area similar to *Extras.*

The show will definitely have plenty of lighter sight gags, parodies, situational stuff, exaggeration, and slapstick/screwball stuff because there's so much of that to work with. Everything concerning the characters and their lives will be pretty light. However, I want to also have some darker comedy because there will be plenty of poorly made horror/slasher movies as well as the characters' politically incorrect behavior.

While I don't believe the show should have an HBO tone in terms of the content, I do think the show should be able to acknowledge and talk about the nudity/profanity/gore that would be in some of these films. Ideally I could see this show on a channel like FXX, Comedy Central, or Adult Swim.

Sample episodes

1) After Ken buys a combination of terrible foreign movies from all over the world in a cheap package deal, Roger has to help Don edit everything into an actual movie and get Jane to film scenes that can be put in between the footage.
2) Ken needs a wealthy sardine importer to finance his next film, so he convinces Roger to be his honeypot.

3) Ken finds that Don has put narration over all of the audio for *It Came from Beneath the Beneath,* so Roger and Sarah have to recreate the audio for the entire film themselves.
4) After Penelope's car stunt for *Dirty Riders* destroys the only camera, Ken has to hide his pride and go ask an old friend for a loaner.
5) After finding out that a competitor's company is also releasing a movie about killer Mole People, Ken drives everyone to the breaking point to finish in order to get their version sold and released first.
6) Ken hires Sarah to write her first entire script, a scifi about a weatherman who saves the world from an alien weather machine.
He enlists Don to help, who grudgingly contacts his weatherman cousin to assist them.
7) After coming up with an insanely specific lists of locations he needs to shoot *The Killer Killers,* Ken offers a reward to the first group that can get it for him.
8) After a critic offers a bad and extremely personal review for *College Girl Horror Dorm,* Ken decides to get back at a critic for the first time.
9) After the lead actor drops out of *Baby Killer,* Roger and Sarah have to find a replacement.
10) After the final cut of *Attack of the Green Flamingoes* comes back especially terrible, Ken needs to convince a distributor to buy it so he can maintain his winning streak.
11) With nothing to do and nothing currently shooting, Ken offers a series of challenges to the crew, and the winner gets an executive producer credit on the next film.
12) After sticking up for Liam because he was being bullied by the delivery boy from the nasty Chinese food store, Roger finds that he inadvertently lost Ken his source for cheap set food and has to find a new replacement.
13) Roger has a nightmare that Alfred Hitchcock is disappointed in him, and he has to make his horror/suspense masterpiece out of Ken's next film.
14) Attack of the Giant Clam.

How is your show relevant now?

Recently there has been a large increase in interest in B movies, most notably with the release of movies such as *Sharknado, Iron Sky,* and also big-budget films with terrible critical reviews such as *The Happening* and *The Wicker Man.* The Transformers movies have been panned by critics while still grossing an enormous amount. There has also been the entrance of exploitation films into mainstream film, the best example of this being Quentin Tarantino's films. With the developments in digital distribution, a really bad movie has a much greater chance of being seen and bought solely based on its low quality creating a huge entertainment value.

In addition, the show explores the idea of how you succeed in your goals and the right way to go about doing that. All of the characters come from a variety of backgrounds and are trying different ways to reach their own version of success, which is something everyone goes through. In Roger, we see the example of what might be considered the proper way to become a successful filmmaker, whereas in Ken we see the self-made idea of how to get into film.

How is your show different from other TV shows?

This show is a celebration of poor quality and exploitation. There has always been a cult following for low quality or what you could call bad movies that are almost their own genre of comedy throughout film history. Sometimes they are made with a goal to look poorly made or ridiculous in concept, but other times what starts off as a promising film turns into something terrible. But most shows or movies that explore this area of film just laugh at them, not with them. *B-List* would take an inside look at how B movies are made, and the fact that there is a lot going on behind every movie.

How does your show push the envelope?

While this show is going to be a celebration of bad movies, it will also be a critique of what's wrong with Hollywood film right now and in the past. *B-List* will use parody and satire to point out the problems of current films in regards to diversity, gender, sexual orientation, the process of creating a film, special effects, and the makeup of the current studio system.

What did you discover through real-world research about your idea? How did you incorporate it into your show?

The majority of my research so far has been looking at the history of Roger Corman, the most famous producer/director in the B-movie world. A lot of what I learned was the ingenious things that were done in order to cut costs, find quality talent, and almost always turn a profit.

Roger Corman used exploitation through provocative titles and posters to draw in viewers, reused sets and small budgets to keep costs low, and hired talented young actors by offering them experience and lead roles they wouldn't be able to obtain through the normal studio casting. I'm going to integrate the idea of keeping costs down, using whatever means necessary, as well as the exploration of ideas used in creating a B movie throughout the show. The most important part of these movies is getting people to watch them no matter what, which will be reflected in the production process.

What other art has influenced your TV series idea?

While I haven't done much research in other mediums outside of film, I think any art people see and have a horrible fascination with will definitely influence the show. The main other influences are exploitation in nature such as the *Sin City* graphic novels by Frank Miller, or the trend of exploitation traits that permeates some of the most popular modern video games.

Why are you the only person who can create this TV series?

I will watch anything, and I grew up watching bad movies with my friends: *The League of Extraordinary Gentlemen, Killer Klowns from Outer Space, Troll 2,* the *Jack Frost* horror movies, and countless others. And sometimes they accomplish things that you wouldn't ever be able to achieve with a big budget film.

We also spent most of high school making bad movies and roping other friends into helping out. Any time we had the opportunity for a project that gave us free choice we made a movie, whether it was from European history, US history, satire class, Spanish class, or even health class. We always had no budget, terrible equipment, and god-awful acting supplied by ourselves, but we always managed to make something redeeming that was either funny or at least fun to watch. And we always had an amazing time making those films that we managed to carry over into the final product.

I know that I can put that kind of atmosphere into *B*-List and the characters. I've also noticed that I'm usually able to find something redeeming and enjoyable in even the worst movies that makes seeing them worth it. I know these movies and what makes them great.

* * *

Outlines

Jerusalem, TN
Pilot Outline
"Not Beyond Repair"
by Aryeh Harris-Shapiro

TEASER

1. EXT. MISSISSIPPI RIVER – DAY

The sun rises over the Mississippi river. LUKE MCCULLOUGH (white, early 30s) sits on the riverbank. He tips a bottle back and drains the whiskey pooled at the bottom. He's a big man, shaggy, bags perpetually under his eyes. He chucks the bottle into the river.

2. INT. CHURCH – DAY

A small church, packed for Sunday service. PASTOR ANN MICHAELS (white, 60s) stands at the head of the congregation. She's a rancher's daughter and looks it, willowy and tanned, a shock of white hair hanging down her back. She delivers her sermon with spirit and urgency. The topic is charity.

Ann calls attention to George Mason, a thick-set man with his leg in a cast. She tells George's story, the story of a man injured on the job, unable to provide for his family. She calls the community to action, exhorts them to save their brother from the iniquities of poverty. She brings the service to a big finish, passion radiating from the pulpit.

The response is muted. NICK BLAIR (black, early 20s), the fire-eyed church deacon, brings a collection basket around to the whole congregation. His gaze draws some loose change but not much else. KACEY REARDON (white, late teens) avoids his gaze when he passes by. She pulls her small frame tight, shrinking in her seat.

3. INT. CHURCH OFFICES – DAY

After the service, Nick and Ann total their donations in Ann's modest office. Not enough to pay Mason's bills. Ann feels defeated. She vents to Nick about how difficult it's been getting people to accept her as pastor. Nick shrugs off her complaints—no real sympathy on his end.

Nick brings up an old idea that Ann tries to shoot down the moment it leaves his mouth. He persists: They need to call the Southern Baptist Convention.

4. EXT. LUKE'S HOUSE – DAY

Kacey walks up to a small, run-down house surrounded by uncut grass, connected to civilization only by a dirt road. A police cruiser sits in the driveway. Luke sits on the steps, half passed-out. DEPUTY KEITH RAYBURN (white, 20s) sits next to him. When Rayburn sees Kacey, he goes to her and informs her that he found Luke passed out by the side of the road. She apologizes. Rayburn tells her that he likes Luke but that this can't keep happening.

Kacey tries to get Luke inside, a massive physical struggle. Luke apologizes to her over and over, tells her he's not her responsibility. She tries to comfort him. She calls him "dad." Luke tells her that she doesn't have to call him that. Kacey can't bring herself to respond.

5. INT. LUKE'S HOUSE – LUKE'S BEDROOM – DAY

Kacey gets him in bed.

6. INT. LUKE'S HOUSE – KACEY'S BEDROOM – DAY

Kacey goes to her room and breaks down sobbing.

END OF TEASER

ACT ONE

7. INT. LUKE'S HOUSE – LUKE'S BEDROOM – DAY

Dawn. Kacey tries to get Luke out of bed. It takes a lot of effort to wake him, let alone get him upright. She gets him showered, fed, and out the door to work.

8. EXT. LUKE'S HOUSE – DAY

After a couple of minutes, Kacey checks outside. Luke's sitting in his truck, head in his hands. Kacey shoves him over to the passenger side and drives him to work.

9. INT. FACTORY FARM – DAY

Luke shovels feed into the huge metal chutes that line the cattle pens in the factory farm. The place is dingy: filth, metal, and stink. Nick does the same to the next pen over. Nick quietly brings up the fact that he didn't see Luke in church the day before. Luke keeps his head down.

Nick gets less casual. More pointed. Accusatory. Luke reams him out, venting his grief and hate in a screed against god and the church. Luke's wife enters the conversation, and Nick oversteps his bounds. The other factory workers have to pull the men apart to end the fistfight that follows.

10. INT. FACTORY FARM – MANAGER'S OFFICE – DAY

MARTIN WORTH (40s), the factory manager, shoots straight with Luke—he's on the rocks. Luke can't show up to work hung over. He can't keep fighting with people. The manager is under pressure to make cuts at the farm, and it's getting very difficult to keep Luke on.

Luke nods, says "yeah" a bunch. Wants to be miles away. Finally, his boss tells him to get back to work.

11. INT. HIGH SCHOOL – DAY

Kacey walks through her high school, glances and stares following her.

CARTER and BETH walk up to her. They're scruffy kids with bad skin, scary-thin frames hidden by big, bulky sweatshirts. They try to strike up conversation with her, but Kacey is distant. One-word answers. Trying not to get drawn in.

Carter and Beth ask if Kacey knows where to score any crank. She doesn't. The addicts' questions turn nasty, and she rushes away before she gets drawn in.

12. INT. HIGH SCHOOL – DAY

Kacey meets with the school guidance counselor. The counselor expresses sympathy for Kacey's grief, but he tells her that she's missed almost every in-state college application deadline. Kacey presses him, urgent. She needs to get out of this town. The guidance counselor tells her that there is a school that might take her—one with rolling admissions.

Kacey asks about financial aid. Less luck there. Every deadline has passed. There's nothing.

13. INT. LUKE'S HOUSE – NIGHT

Kacey attempts to talk to Luke about college. She brings up their financial situation and asks if her mother left her any money. Luke is drunk. He doesn't want to deal with it. He just wants to watch TV.

Kacey calls Ann. She needs to talk to Ann. Can she come over?

14. INT. ANN'S HOUSE – KITCHEN – NIGHT

Ann lets Kacey in and offers her some chicken. Kacey wolfs it down—she hasn't been eating much recently.

The two catch up in front of the evening news, dancing around the real topic. Finally Kacey asks the question—can Ann help her pay for school?

Ann breaks it to her gently—she can't. She'd been supporting Kacey's mother for years, and when she passed Ann started supporting Luke. She was happy to do it—is still happy to do it—but she doesn't have the money.

Kacey starts to ask the question—what if Ann stopped supporting Luke?—but she's interrupted by the news. A town an hour away had a mad cow scare. Ann cuts Kacey off and turns the volume up. The broadcaster mentions that mad cow scares can destroy the economy of any small town reliant on farming.

Ann picks up the phone and calls the SBC.

END OF ACT ONE

ACT TWO

15. INT. FACTORY FARM – DAY

Luke and Nick shovel dung out of the chute that runs behind the cattle as they grind their way through their shift.

One of the cows starts butting against the pen. Nick grabs a stun gun, but Luke holds him off. He tries to soothe the animal instead, stroking it and whispering. The cow gets more and more violent. Nick grabs Luke and barely manages to drag him out of the way of a vicious kick.

Luke and Nick manage to hold the pen door shut as the cow slams its head over and over into the steel. Its skull breaks open. Its brain leaks out. Blood flows.

And then the cow dies.

16. EXT. CHURCH – DAY

CAROLINE ALLMAN (black, 30s), a staff writer for the *Baptist Press*, steps through the front doors of the church, her professional sharpness contrasting with the church's homey interior. Ann rushes out to greet her, laying on the folksy charm.

Caroline rebuffs her, not cruelly, but it's time to get down to business.

17. INT. FACTORY FARM – OFFICES – DAY

Ann and Caroline meet with Martin Worth. Ann presses him to tell Caroline that the town is in trouble. Martin gets into the hard numbers of a mad cow scare and outbreak, scaring Ann even more in the process. He tells both women that management was already considering closing the farm, and that it's a certainty now that they have an actual case of mad cow.

18. INT. MILLENIUM SAVINGS BANK – DAY

Kacey meets with SUZANNE MACINTYRE (50s), one of the loan officers at the local bank. Suzanne knows Kacey because one of her daughters is in Kacey's class. Kacey presses her to tell her what a student loan might look like. Suzanne tells her that with Luke's abysmal credit, any loan would have astronomical interest attached.

Suzanne asks Kacey whether she's going into a profitable field, and Kacey tells her she doesn't know, she just wants out. Suzanne strongly warns her against it. Kacey begins to break down, unable to see a way she can leave the town. Suzanne apologizes but says she needs to take another meeting.

19. INT. FACTORY FARM – DAY

Ann and Caroline run into Luke and Nick on their way out of the farm. They're disposing of the dead cow. Blood streams across the floor into steel drains.

Ann tries to pull Luke aside to talk about Kacey. Luke brushes her off—he needs to focus on this job, right here and now.

20. INT. LUKE'S TRUCK - NIGHT

Luke pulls his truck into the driveway, exhausted. He sits for a moment, then pulls a bottle out of his glove compartment and takes a long, deep swallow. Then another. Then another.

21. INT. LUKE'S HOUSE - NIGHT

Luke stumbles into the house and finds it empty. The lock in his liquor cabinet is broken. A small bottle of cheap whiskey sits, empty, in the sink. Several other bottles are missing. Luke checks Kacey's room—empty. He pulls his coat back on and rushes outside.

22. EXT. CEMETERY – NIGHT

Luke drives his truck slowly through the town cemetery. He finds Kacey, hammered, sitting by her mother's grave. She's a wreck, screaming and sobbing her way through a conversation with Luke. She's almost incoherent but things come across. Rage. Despair. Blame. Endless blame, directed mostly at Luke.

Luke piles her into his truck and drives her out of the cemetery after taking a swig for the road.

One swig too many.

The truck slams into a tree. Luke's head smashes into the steering wheel. He blacks out for a moment, but pulls himself around. He staggers out of the truck. There's something lying in front of the truck. Something wheezing and bleeding. And there's a giant hole in the windshield.

Kacey.

She's incredibly hurt, broken and bloody, a huge gash pumping away in her neck. Luke pulls out his cell and calls 9-1-1, describing Kacey's injuries to the paramedics. They tell him to put pressure on the neck wound and wait for them.

Blood pours out between his fingers no matter how tight he grips. Kacey isn't going to make it. Luke closes his eyes. He prays.

The wound closes. Red and blue lights slowly illuminate the road.

END OF ACT TWO

ACT THREE

23. INT. HOSPITAL – NIGHT
Luke sits in a heap next to Kacey's comatose form. She's hooked up to an endless series of machines, her broken body held together by very little. Luke barely has a scratch on him, but emotionally he looks close to death.

Deputy Rayburn enters gently, all sympathy and light touch. He asks simple, straightforward questions. When? Where? How? Luke answers each one honestly. Rayburn tries to ascertain whether Luke is a suicide risk. It could go either way.

Rayburn comforts Luke. Tells him to stay at the hospital, not to go to work. Rayburn says he'll go fill in Luke's bosses. Luke should be with Kacey.

Rayburn steps out of the room, finds the attending nurse. Rayburn asks how Kacey's prognosis looks. The nurse says they're trying to get the swelling in the brain down. Kacey's also lost a lot of blood. She says it could be better, but they expected it to be worse—Luke reported a gaping throat wound that just wasn't there.

Rayburn asks the nurse to keep an eye on Luke. Make sure he doesn't hurt himself. The nurse asks whether she should prevent Luke from leaving if he tries. Rayburn says he hasn't figured out whether to press endangerment charges yet, that it'll depend on whether Kacey comes out of her coma. The nurse says she'll keep Rayburn posted.

24. INT. FACTORY FARM – DAY

Rayburn arrives at the factory farm in his cruiser. Asks the nearest employee where to find the manager.

Nick, helpful as ever, tells him that the manager's indisposed, talking to management all day about the mad cow thing. Nick offers to take a message. Rayburn considers.

25. INT. MASON HOUSE – DAY

Caroline and Ann sit with George Mason. Ann implores Mason to tell Caroline his story. Caroline pays close attention—this has the makings of a great story.

Mason tells his story, mechanically. Like the words were put in his mouth. Like he doesn't really believe what he's saying.

Ann asks if he's alright. Mason lays into her. He's not some victim. He's not some useless cripple. What was she thinking, calling him out like that in her sermon? Insulting him by claiming he can't take care of his family.

Ann protests, but Mason shuts her down. What does she have to show for it? What benefit did that embarrassment give?

Thirty dollars. He throws them out of his house.

26. INT. CHURCH OFFICES – DAY

Caroline and Ann meet in Ann's offices. Caroline returns the SBC's decision. They'll publish a fundraising request in the *Baptist Press*—IF Ann steps down as pastor. The SBC doesn't believe there should be female pastors. They have no problem helping a town in need, but a fundraiser without that stipulation would legitimize Ann as the leader of the community. So she needs to go.

Ann fights back tooth and claw. She appeals to Caroline's pragmatism, her gender, her empathy for the town. Caroline agrees but remains clear: this is the way things are. Neither Ann nor Caroline have the power to change the deal that's on the table. She tries her best to get Ann to see that.

The two go round after round and are about to head into another when—

A knock at the door. Nick. He has news.

27. INT. HOSPITAL – NIGHT

Ann and Nick arrive at the hospital. Ann rushes into Kacey's room. Sits next to her. Shocked. And then it hits her.

Luke isn't here.

Ann's furious. Where the hell is he? Where. The. Hell. Is. He?

Nick has a guess. He says Luke is probably the same place he always is when he's not at work.

28. INT. RIVERSIDE BAR – NIGHT

Luke drinks alone at the bar. Ann storms in, Nick at her heels. Ann unloads on Luke, venting all her spite and frustration at him. Luke doesn't respond, which only infuriates Ann more. She calls him an insult to his wife's memory and storms out.

Nick sits down at the bar. Buys Luke a drink. Tells Luke that he heard from Rayburn about the throat wound. Luke denies it. Nick presses, asking Luke if he prayed the wound away. Luke denies it again. Nick quotes the scripture supporting the existence of faith healing—another denial.

Nick changes tactics. Lays into Luke. Accuses him of not caring about Kacey. That gets another denial, but a passionate, angry one. Nick pushes harder and harder, breaking Luke down, painting a future for Luke where he could have saved Kacey but didn't out of pride. He paints a future for Luke with no life, no love, no nothing. Luke says that he deserves nothing anyway. Nick asks what Kacey deserves.

END OF ACT THREE

ACT FOUR

29. INT. HOSPITAL – NIGHT

Nick and Luke stand by Kacey's bedside. Nick leads Luke through faith healing—laying on hands, prayer—and it doesn't work. Luke clearly isn't investing fully.

Nick asks Luke to tell him about when he met his wife. After some hesitation, Luke tells him. He and his wife met at a bar—of course. He was drunk. She was in withdrawal, hooking to score some cash and get some tweak. He didn't have any money, and she didn't have any takers—word travels fast in a town like Jerusalem, and nobody was looking to sleep with a publicly known whore, especially a junkie. So they just sat at the bar, him nursing the last drink his paycheck could buy, her scanning the room for nonexistent customers. The bar closed. Luke offered her a couch to crash on at his house. She took him up on it. The next day, he got home from work and she was still there. Nowhere else to go. So they talked. He didn't drink. She didn't get high. And they just took it one day at a time from there.

And then she started using again. And it all went to hell.

Nick tells Luke that Kacey is the one good thing from that meeting that still exists. Luke's wife is dead. Luke is drinking again. The one good thing that came out of the marriage was that it probably saved Kacey's life. Just having a house, a stable environment, a sober mother—she's a tough girl, but who knows what could have happened. Kacey was saved. And now she's going. And it'll be like the good part of Luke's life, the only good part, never even happened. If Luke lets her slip away, he might as well have drunk himself to death years ago.

Every word Nick says cuts like a knife, driving Luke deeper and deeper into his despair. On those last words, he starts to cry. Nick stops talking. There's a moment of heavy, deadly silence.

And then Kacey opens her eyes.

30. INT. CHURCH OFFICES – DAY

Caroline enters Ann's office. Ann is there, wearing the same clothes as the night before. Phone by her side.

Caroline states her case: Ann should take the deal. Not because it's the right thing to do—it's not—but because she's clearly overwhelmed. Dealing with personal and social crises simultaneously would be too much for many experienced pastors. Why not let someone else take the wheel while Ann sorts out her own life? And she's cleared it with her superiors that some of the money raised can go to pay for Kacey's hospital bills.

Ann doesn't speak for a long time. Slowly, she begins to tell Caroline why she wanted to be pastor in the first place. She came from money. Her late husband didn't. He knew what it was like at the bottom and wanted to help people climb out. She understood the idea, but struggled to understand the drive, the need to be a caregiver to the weak and sick. Then her husband got very sick—liver cancer. She found herself taking care of him for the first time. It was almost impossible. She almost went into the ground with him.

Ann's husband passed. The burden was taken off Ann's shoulders. She realized what a blessing it was to give that to someone, to relieve their burden. She only had to bear the weight of her husband's death for a few months. There were people in Jerusalem carrying weight their entire lives. She realized that's what she wanted to do—relieve burdens. Ease suffering. Pick up where her husband left off.

Ann thought she knew these people, knew their lives and their struggles intimately. She thought that was why she was uniquely qualified to be pastor. But somehow, this happened. To one of the people she loves most. Right under her nose. She failed.

The phone rings.

31. INT. HOSPITAL - DAY

Ann and Caroline visit with Kacey in the hospital. Rayburn hovers by her bedside. Kacey tells Ann that she's going to be discharged soon—her worst physical injuries have healed over the course of the last 12 hours. Kacey still has breaks and fractures all over her body, cuts and scrapes and other superficial things, but her brain and major organs are all, shockingly, fine.

Ann asks if Kacey remembers what happened. Kacey tries to explain how it felt to wake up, but the experience is so transcendent and alien that she can only partially put it into words. Caroline scrawls down notes.

Ann tells Caroline she's rejecting the offer. She keeps missing the things that matter most—disaster and hope—because she's endlessly, endlessly trying to appease the SBC board. She'd rather be genuinely present for her community, through good and bad, than allow herself to be distracted by old men playing politics. So Caroline can just go back to Nashville and tell them that.

Caroline tells her she can relay the decision, but she's staying in Jerusalem. Kacey's miracle recovery is too good a story to pass up.

Rayburn breaks in. He gently asks Kacey where Luke is. He needs to know. Kacey tells Rayburn that Luke was there when she woke up, but she doesn't know where he is now.

32. EXT. HOSPITAL PARKING LOT – DAY

Rayburn walks to his cruiser and finds Nick, waiting. Rayburn asks Nick if he knows where Luke is. Nick says he does. Rayburn asks Nick to tell him. Nick refuses—Rayburn will just charge Luke.

Rayburn denies this. Says he just wants to talk. Nick, in a low whisper, tells Rayburn about the healing. About Luke's powers. He calls on Rayburn's faith—is Rayburn going to lock up a messenger of god? Is Rayburn going to lock up a holy man? If he is, he'd better lock up Nick right now for obstruction, because Nick isn't going to say a word about where Luke is. He won't betray his faith like that. Nick holds out his wrists. Waiting. Rayburn climbs into his cruiser and drives away.

33. EXT. MISSISSIPPI RIVER – DAY

Luke stands out by the Mississippi River at sunset. He takes off his boots, and then his socks. He steps out onto the river with one foot. And then the other.

He doesn't fall. It's like he's standing on a sheet of glass.

He's walking on water.

END OF PILOT

* * *

Girl Out of Water
"Pilot"
by Aleeza Klarman

TEASER

1. INT. HOTEL POOL – NIGHT

SIERRA (18, lithe, muscular, light-skinned), wearing goggles and a bathing cap, plunges into the water. She swims, embracing the water, at peace in her natural environment. Suddenly, something is thrown into the water beside her, creating ripples. Sierra surfaces.

ISABELLA (19, blonde, slender) is standing at the edge of the pool, next to the small diving board, wearing pajamas. She wants Sierra to come back to the room. If their coach does bed checks, they'll be in trouble. Sierra wants to stay and keep swimming to calm her nerves.

Isabella wins the argument. Sierra gets out of the water.

2. INT. HOTEL ROOM – NIGHT

Sierra comes out of the bathroom in her pajamas, scrubbing her hair dry on a towel. She flops down on the bed. She wants to talk to Isabella, but Isabella is already asleep. Sierra closes her eyes, but they fly open a moment later. She gets out of bed. Isabella grumbles and tosses a pillow at her.

3. INT. HOTEL BATHROOM – NIGHT

Sierra turns on the shower so that the room fills with steam. She lowers the toilet seat lid onto the toilet and climbs up onto it. She closes her eyes, curls her toes over the edge of the seat, and raises her arms in a diving position. The sound of cheering fills her mind.

There's a knock on the bathroom door and the cheering stops. Isabella yells at Sierra to turn off the water; she's trying to sleep. Sierra climbs down off the toilet seat and turns the water off.

4. EXT. PATTERSON HOUSE—DAY

Establishing shot of a small house, in a small yard, situated next to houses that are substantially nicer.

5. INT. PATTERSON HOUSE—DAY

Pictures of the family, including Sierra, litter the front of the refrigerator. No one even glances at them because the morning is in its usual full-swing chaos. MARIA (mid-40s, Latina, perpetually tired-looking) is scraping together breakfast. FELICITY (14, brunette, mixed skin tone) is scarfing down toast and making herself a peanut butter sandwich for practice. STEVEN (mid-40s, Caucasian, blond, athletic) is standing at the mirror trying to fix an uncooperative tie. Steven tells Maria he needs to take the car to get to work. Maria says that they talked about this; she needs the car today. She can't be late. Felicity, sensing a problem, stops making lunch and reminds them that someone is supposed to drive her to gymnastics practice. After a few more moments of arguing, Maria relents and says that she'll take the bus. Steven agrees to drive Felicity, and he hustles her out the door.

6. INT. FAMILY CAR — MOVING — DAY

Steven and Felicity sit in early-morning silence. Felicity fiddles with the radio. Steven wants to coordinate plans with Felicity so that they can get to Sierra's competition on time. He plans to pick her up at the school at noon. He'll give her a note to miss the rest of her classes.

Felicity wants to go to her gymnastics competition. She doesn't understand why she has to go to Sierra's meet—it's nothing she hasn't seen a thousand times. Steven points out that it's a big deal and could lead to the Olympics. Family is supposed to support each other.

Felicity says that if that's the case, maybe he and Sierra should come to her gymnastics. Steven is annoyed. He'll pick up Felicity at noon, because he said so, end of story.

7. INT. HOTEL — DAY

The phone rings. Sierra answers, and a pleasant voice informs her that it's her wake up call. Sierra shakes Isabella awake, and they get to work, shaving their bodies with electric razors (and helping each other shave the parts they can't reach.) They stuff energy bars into their mouths, pick up their gear bags, and run into the hall wearing their warm-up gear. They join a gaggle of other girls similarly dressed. FRANK, Sierra's coach (40s, gray-haired, muscular), does a head count, then tells them the bus is leaving.

8. INT. BUS/EXT. POOL - DAY

Sierra and her teammates arrive at the huge indoor pool, which is already milling with activity. They get off of the bus and assemble in front of the building. Huge signs for the diving event are plastered over the entrance.

9. INT. POOL – DAY
Sierra and her teammates stand in line, waiting to check in. People are cleaning the stands, checking in other competitors, and testing the chemical content of the pool.

An OLYMPIC SPONSOR REPRESENTATIVE comes up to Frank. They shake hands, and he takes her over to Sierra and Isabella, who are gawking.

The sponsor greets them coolly. She mentions that she travelled for several hours to get here today because their coach assured her that she would see the best new diving talent. The sponsor says she hopes she won't be disappointed.

Isabella and Sierra look at each other.

END OF TEASER

ACT ONE

10. INT. GYM – DAY
Felicity finishes stretching and coats her hands with chalk. She takes her place at the end of the gym, performs a vault, and lands smoothly on the mat.

Charlie (50s, kind face, body gone to seed) beckons her over. He tells her he's arranged for a friend who works at a great gymnastics program to be at the gymnastics competition tonight. He wants Felicity to perform her beam routine for him.

Felicity wants to go, but she's supposed to be picked up at noon for Sierra's competition. The coach tells her it's her choice, but opportunities like this don't come around very often. If she's as serious about gymnastics as he thinks she is, she won't miss it.

11. INT. POOL – DAY

The coach calls Sierra out of the pool after a dive. He wants her to adjust her dive—she's still hitting the water at a slight angle. He demonstrates, and she nods. She tells him she wants to correct it, but she admits she's having trouble. She climbs up onto the board to try again.

12. INT. STEVEN'S OFFICE – DAY

Steven collects his papers and hurriedly stuffs them into his briefcase. He shrugs into his jacket and is about to leave when his BUSINESS PARTNER stops him. The partner wants to know where Steven is going. Steven reminds him about the diving meet. The partner wants Steven to stay. The partner has to go to a meeting, and he needs Steven to finish negotiating the lease for their new space. Steven checks his watch. It's almost quarter to noon. He promises to call about the lease from the car. He takes off, leaving the business partner frustrated.

13. INT. WALMART – DAY

Maria, clad in her corporate vest with the smiley-face button, waits outside a closed office door. The door opens and a secretary comes out. Maria wants to know how long until the boss is ready to see her. The secretary says he's still on a call. Maria checks her watch—if she doesn't leave soon, she'll be late for Sierra's meet.

14. INT. POOL – DAY

Sierra and her team, wearing their warm-up jackets, are seated in a panel for a brief press junket. The reporters ask Sierra how she feels with all the pressure on her—they hear she's been having some trouble in practice, which is unusual for her. Sierra notices the Olympic sponsor watching her. She smiles and reassures the reporters that she's very confident. She's been preparing for this for years, and she's sure when her time comes, she'll be ready.

An announcer welcomes the growing audience in the auditorium. The meet is beginning.

END OF ACT ONE

ACT TWO

15. INT. POOL – DAY
Establishing shot of the board where the team rankings are posted. Sierra's team is in second place.

It's Isabella's turn. She pounds fists with Sierra and walks over to the high dive. Sierra has her fingers crossed. Isabella executes flawlessly. Sierra and her team cheer.

16. INT. CAR – DAY
Steven sits in his car and looks at the door to the middle school. He is irritated as hell. He drums his fingers on the wheel and checks his watch. It's 12:15. He calls Felicity's cell phone again. No answer.

Finally Steven curses and zooms out of the driveway.

17. INT. SCHOOL – DAY
Felicity watches Steven's car through the window. When he leaves without her, she smiles grimly. Then she picks up her gym bag and hands her excused-absence note to the woman at the front desk. She leaves the school.

18. EXT. ROAD – DAY

Felicity walks down the road to the bus stop. When the doors open to let people off, she sneaks in the back to avoid paying bus fare. She settles herself into the seat with her gym bag, trying not to be noticed.

19. INT. POOL – DAY

Sierra's teammate makes a big mistake while diving, and she lands with a huge splash. The judges murmur to each other, and give low scores. The team slips down in the rankings.

20. INT. GYM – DAY

Felicity arrives and weaves through the crowded gym, trying to locate her coach. The competition has already begun, and he's busy coaching the rest of the team. When the coach notices Felicity, he tells her to get warmed up. A teammate sprained her ankle, and Felicity is moving up in the program. Felicity asks where the scout is. The coach looks around, and says the scout isn't here yet. Felicity panics; her family will kill her for missing Sierra's meet, and now she has nothing to show for it.

21. INT. WALMART – DAY

Maria's MANAGER (30, crew cut, rumpled suit) calls her into the office. She sits nervously across the desk from him, smoothing her hands on her vest. The manager congratulates her and tells her that her application for assistant manager has been approved. Maria is thrilled. She thanks him profusely, then begins to leave, saying she'll see him bright and early tomorrow morning. The manager stops her and tells her that she's not going anywhere until the inventory is done. Maria points out that she already traded a shift with someone so that she could go to Sierra's meet. The manager says that if she wants to be an assistant manager, she has to make work her top priority. Maria agrees to stay.

22. INT. POOL—DAY

Sierra's phone buzzes. There's a text from her mother, saying she's sorry, but she won't be able to make it. Sierra is disappointed. She scans the auditorium for the rest of her family. She sees Steven coming in through a side door, and smiles. He gives her a thumbs up.

The coach taps Sierra on the shoulder. She's up next.

23. INT. GYM - DAY

Felicity performs her beam routine. She does it perfectly, completely focused, until the last moment. She takes a deep breath, and lands the dismount. Her teammates, and many of the other people watching, cheer. Felicity smiles.

24. INT. POOL - DAY

Sierra is taking deep breaths and loosening her muscles as the coach mutters in her ear. They need this dive to go well if the team is going to win. The announcer says Sierra's name, and she climbs up onto the high dive.

Steven and Sierra's teammates cheer. Sierra smiles, then focuses on taking deep breaths. The world quiets. She sets her feet on the edge of the diving platform. She's ready. Sierra leaves the platform at an angle. As she spins, she hits her head on the edge of the concrete.

END OF ACT TWO

ACT THREE

25. INT. POOL - DAY

As in the first shot of the episode, Sierra is facedown in the water. This time, she's not moving. Again something plunges into the water beside her. It's a lifeguard. The lifeguard grabs Sierra and pulls her out of the pool. She's barely conscious.

Steven is frozen in the stands. When he sees Sierra being pulled out of the water and laid down next to the pool, unmoving, he clambers over the seats to get to her. PARAMEDICS rush to attend to Sierra. Sierra's coach keeps Steven back while they attend to her. There's pandemonium in the room.

26. INT. WALMART – DAY

Maria stands in a silent back room, ticking items off on a clipboard. Her phone buzzes in her pocket. She pulls out her phone. It's Steven.

She doesn't answer.

27. INT. GYM – DAY

Felicity's phone buzzes in her gym bag. She reaches down for it, but a teammate nudges her shoulder. The scout just walked over and is greeting her coach. The coach beckons to Felicity, who goes up to greet him.

The phone goes to voicemail.

The coach introduces NICHOLAI, the scout (40, Russian, slick) to Felicity. The scout saw her beam routine, and he's impressed. He wants to offer her a spot in an amazing gymnastics program at a different school. Felicity is thrilled and immediately says yes. She's so excited that she hugs the scout.

28. EXT. POOL – DAY

Steven hangs up the phone and follows Sierra, now on the stretcher, into the ambulance.

29. INT. AMBULANCE – MOVING – DAY

Steven talks to Sierra, trying to get her to respond. Sierra is barely conscious. The paramedics tell Steven to back off. Steven doesn't even realize he's crying.

30. INT. WALMART—DAY

Maria's phone keeps buzzing as she finishes stocking the register with money. She finally listens to the message. Her eyes widen, and she immediately rushes out of the store—but she leaves the register open by mistake.

31. EXT./INT. HOSPITAL – DAY

Sierra is unloaded from the ambulance and rushed into the … operating room.

32. INT. GYM – DAY

Felicity is congratulated by her teammates. She basks in the attention and glows from the scout's offer. She picks up her phone to call her parents and sees the messages she's missed. She listens to the most recent one. She grabs her bag. The coach sees the look on her face. When she tells him Sierra is hurt, he offers her a ride to the hospital.

33. INT. WAITING ROOM – NIGHT

Steven asks passing nurses and doctors for news about Sierra, but no one has anything new to tell him. He clenches his fingers, frustrated, angry, and scared beyond all reason. His phone rings. He answers it.

Steven's business partner tells him the lease fell through, because Steven never called like he promised. Steven apologizes and tries to tell him about Sierra, but the partner has already hung up.

Maria rushes into the waiting room. She wants to know what happened, and where Felicity is. Steven wants to know where she's been. They argue until Felicity enters. Steven yells at Felicity for not meeting him at the school at noon like she was supposed to. Felicity wants him to stop yelling at her. Maria also wants them to stop yelling.

Steven apologizes.

The DOCTOR comes into the room, looking somber. Maria holds Felicity tightly. Steven stands apart from them. They wait for the doctor's news.

END OF ACT THREE

ACT FOUR

34. INT. WAITING ROOM – NIGHT

The doctor explains Sierra's condition. She hit her head on the platform. They don't know the extent of the damage yet. They can stay with her, if they want to. Maria agrees. Steven says he'll take Felicity home.

35. INT. FAMILY CAR – MOVING – NIGHT

Felicity and Steven drive home in silence. Finally, Steven tells Felicity that she should have been there. Felicity says she knows.

36. INT. FELICITY'S ROOM – NIGHT

Felicity tosses her gym bag in the corner and collapses on her bed. She pulls the brochure of the new gymnastics program the scout gave her out of her pocket. She looks at it for a moment, then tears it up and shoves the pieces under her pillowcase.

37. INT. HOSPITAL ROOM – DAY

Sierra opens her eyes. The world is blurry. She blinks, and Maria comes into focus. Maria is sleeping on a chair, but she wakes as Sierra stirs. Maria asks how she's feeling. Sierra mumbles a question. Maria doesn't understand. Sierra tries again. Did her team lose the meet? Maria doesn't want her to worry about diving right now, but Sierra gazes at her intently. This is non-negotiable. Reluctantly, Maria admits that the team lost. Sierra stares at the ceiling for a moment. Then, to her mother's dismay, she starts laughing uncontrollably.

38. INT. STEVEN'S OFFICE – DAY

Steven shows up, completely exhausted. He greets his business partner and starts to tell him what happened, but he stops when he sees that his partner is packing up. The partner tells him he wants out of their misbegotten business venture. The idea is good, but Steven is snake-bitten. They'll never make it.

Steven wants his partner to stay in the business. It's a good idea, and their luck will turn. Besides, he needs this. He has hospital bills to pay now. The partner apologizes and says the business is now Steven's. The partner picks up his stuff and leaves Steven alone in the half-empty office.

39. INT. HOSPITAL CORRIDOR – DAY

Maria's phone rings. Her friend from work is on the other end.

INTERCUT WITH:

40. INT. WALMART – DAY

The FRIEND watches police officers take a statement from her boss. The friend asks what on earth Maria did. The boss is furious that Maria left the register open. Someone cleaned it out.

END INTERCUT.

41. INT. MIDDLE SCHOOL CLASSROOM – DAY

Two KIDS hunched over, heads together, laughing at something in the corner of the classroom. Felicity nudges her FRIEND and asks what the other kids are laughing at.

Her friend is evasive. Felicity goes over to the kids, and sees them replaying Sierra's accident on YouTube. Felicity snaps. She grabs the phone and hurls it against the wall.

42. INT. HOSPITAL CORRIDOR – DAY

Maria leans against the wall, trying to process the phone call she just received. She can see her whole life going down in flames. Suddenly alarm bells start ringing in Sierra's hospital room.

43. INT. HOSPITAL ROOM – DAY

Maria rushes inside to Sierra, who's trying to remove the IVs and wires covering her, yelling that she has to get out of here; she needs to go home. Maria and the nurses try to subdue her, but Sierra is beyond reason.

44. INT. HOSPITAL ROOM – LATER THE SAME DAY

Sierra is sedated. Steven and Maria want to know what's wrong with her, and why she has been acting so irrationally. The doctor wants to explain that after head injuries, personalities and emotions are unpredictable. No one knows who Sierra is going to be, or how she's going to feel from now on. Only time will tell. Steven and Maria don't want to believe it. Sierra wants them to believe she's asleep, but she's heard everything. She cries silently.

END OF PILOT

* * *

Minotaur
"Pilot"
By Eli Brenna
Outline

TEASER

1. EXT. CITY STREET – NIGHT

A BUSINESSMAN (late 30s) leaves his office building carrying a briefcase. He runs to the corner and tries to hail a cab, but it goes past him. He gets a phone call and answers it, but it is so loud out on the street that he can't hear a thing. He looks around and he is right by an alley, so he goes...

2. EXT. CITY ALLEY – NIGHT

...into the mouth of the alley. He holds the phone up to his right ear, and his left hand up to his left ear. He can hear the phone a little more clearly, but he does not hear a MAN (early 30s) and a WOMAN (early 30s) enter the alley behind him. The businessman paces, talking on the phone, when the man and the woman come up behind him.

The male mugger quickly grabs his phone and the female mugger drags the businessman further into the alley. The businessman looks at the muggers, terrified. The male mugger pockets the phone. They demand the briefcase. The businessman says "no." He shows them the case is handcuffed to him and explains that he does not have a key on him—the key is at his destination.

The muggers take out a knife. They try to undo the handcuffs with the knife, but when it doesn't work, they decide to go about it in another way. The businessman is terrified, and for good reason—the knife goes for his wrist...

3. INT. MUGGERS' APARTMENT – NIGHT

The muggers attempt to open the briefcase, which still has the handcuffs on it, though they are bloodier now than they were. The man looks up—he thinks he heard something. The woman tells him to stop freaking out and to help her with the briefcase. The man goes to the window and opens it. He pokes his head out. He looks up and around. Nothing. He pulls his head back and goes back inside only to see...

...a BEAST, dressed all in black and brown, with horns and a cape and fur, standing with a gun pointed at the woman's head. His face is obscured except for his dark eyes and slightly gaping maw.

The woman is terrified. The male mugger asks the caped man how the hell he got in here, and what the hell he is. The caped man responds by taking out a thin blade. The male mugger approaches, trying to defuse the situation, though he is quite angry. The caped man sticks out his blade and cuts into the mugger's chest. The mugger retreats, clutching his bleeding chest. He looks back up, angrily, at the caped man.

The caped man warns the male mugger that he will shoot the woman. The mugger rushes at him anyway. The caped man shoots the woman in the head. The male mugger jumps at the caped man, who whips his gun around and slams the butt of it into the mugger's skull.

END OF TEASER

ACT ONE

4. EXT. MUGGERS' APARTMENT BUILDING – DAY

The next day, POLICE have arrived and are creating a controlled crime scene. Tape, cars, lab workers. SABINE (30s), a police detective, gets out of her car and walks to the building. She talks to CAPTAIN MILLER

(50s). She asks him what happened, and he says it's a double murder with signs of forced entry.

5. INT. MUGGERS' APARTMENT – DAY

Sabine goes up to the muggers' apartment. She looks around. Woman shot in the head. Man bleeding from chest, head caved in. Blood all over the floor. Sabine inspects the door; the lock has been jimmied open and is now broken. Sabine goes back to the bodies. She talks to CRIME LAB EMPLOYEES. She asks who the hell would do this.

6. INT. LEON'S HOME – LEON'S BEDROOM – DAY

In the corner, on a big chair, a cape, mask, and black and brown outfit sit in a pile. The briefcase is leaning against the chair, unopened.

LEON (30s) lies curled up in bed, asleep. There is a knock on the door. Leon barely stirs.

FRANKLIN (60s) opens the door and enters. He asks where Leon was last night, and Leon asks what Franklin thinks he was doing last night. Franklin brings up that a supervillain he refers to as Agamemnon has been murdered. He asks Leon if Leon killed him. Leon denies it and shows Franklin the briefcase. Franklin remains unconvinced. Leon questions Franklin about Agamemnon. Leon decides to find who killed Agamemnon.

7. INT. CRIME LAB – DAY

Sabine is at the crime lab, and they look into the ballistics of the gun used in the double murder. They are able to use information based on the head injury the man sustained as well as the bullet casings and the bullets themselves. They begin to track down gun registration info for that type of gun.

8. INT. AGAMEMNON'S HOME – DAY

Leon enters Agamemnon's home. It is beautifully furnished with artwork on most walls. Leon snoops around, going to the living room, bedroom, and then the office. But as Leon approaches the office, he hears something. SOMEONE else is in there. Leon peeks in to see someone dressed entirely in black going through Agamemnon's desk. The other person turns and sees Leon. Quickly, this person pulls out a gun and shoots at Leon, missing just barely. Leon ducks. The person grabs something from the desk and runs through another door. Leon follows, chasing this person all over the first floor, until this person opens and leaps out a window.

9. EXT. AGAMEMNON'S HOME – DAY

Leon runs outside just in time to see the mystery person get in a car. Leon has time to memorize the license plate before the person speeds away.

10. INT. SABINE'S CAR – MOVING – DAY

Sabine is on the phone with the crime lab tech; he has given her an address. It is the address of someone who owns a gun matching the murder weapon. The gun owner had been reported missing by her daughter this morning.

11. EXT. OLD LADY'S HOME – DAY

Sabine surveys the scene. She looks in a window but can't make anything out. She goes to the door, which is unlocked.

12. INT. OLD LADY'S HOME – DAY

Sabine enters. The home is dark. The blinds are closed and no lights are on. The home is dusty and dirty. Sabine pulls out her gun and looks around the first floor and doesn't see anything. She goes upstairs. In the bedroom, she finds a dead OLD LADY (80s) rotting in her bed.

END OF ACT ONE

ACT TWO

13. INT. OLD LADY'S HOME – DAY

Crime lab has arrived. Sabine believes that the muggers' murderer could be the same as the old lady's. Captain Miller says that's certainly not impossible, but he does not want to run on that assumption yet. Politically, it makes it seem like there's a serial killer in the city, and he also does not want Sabine to take on both cases.

Anyway, the old lady and the muggers are entirely different from one another—what could be the MO of their killer? Sabine wants the old lady case, but the captain says, "No." The captain gives the old lady case to another detective, MAXWELL (early 40s). Sabine leaves to go back to the station.

14. INT. OLD LADY'S HOME – DAY – LATER

Maxwell is at the crime scene with the crime lab. Maxwell is focused very heavily on the cause of the old lady's death. He sees the throat has been slit and asks the crime lab to find out what kind of blade or tool might have been used. The crime lab shows Maxwell that some sort of animal fur has been discovered around the house, but there is no sign of a pet. Maxwell says it was probably an old pet that ran away.

15. INT. LEON'S HOME – DAY

Leon is on his computer. He looks up the license plate of the mysterious person who was in Agamemnon's home. The car comes up as belonging to Agamemnon, but registered to a different address. Franklin comes by.

Franklin and Leon discuss Leon's plan. Franklin is concerned that Leon does not have one, and Leon wants to just keep following the trail as it is laid out. Franklin tells him it isn't a trail, it's a maze.

16. INT. POLICE STATION – DAY

Back at the police station, Sabine looks at photos from the crime scene. She also has photos of the old lady. She looks at the injuries each victim sustained. Captain Miller approaches Sabine and berates her for handling Maxwell's assignment badly. Sabine apologizes politely but briefly and goes back to studying the photos.

Miller wants Sabine to know that Maxwell is a good detective with a career to watch. Sabine retorts that Miller must think her career isn't one to watch. Miller starts to fire back, then Sabine studies the photo closely and looks at shots of the whole crime scenes. Suddenly, Sabine realizes she has discovered some sort of lead. She stands up, apologizes to Miller, and says she has to run to the crime lab.

17. EXT. CITY STREET – DAY

Leon looks up at a building and checks an address he has written down on a scrap of paper. He enters.

18. INT. APARTMENT BUILDING – DAY

Leon is outside the apartment of the mysterious person from Agamemnon's home. He breaks in the door, and right as he does...

19. INT. APARTMENT – DAY

...Leon is attacked. It is a WOMAN (late 20s). Leon fights back, but the woman has the upper hand; she knows her apartment. She moves behind a corner. Leon moves carefully to find her, but she sneaks behind him and knocks him down. Leon falls but drags her down with him. He pulls out his gun and she knocks it away. He knocks her in the face with his elbow, and she grabs his arm. The woman is able to escape his grasp. She pulls a gun and Leon headbutts her. She drops the gun. They wrestle until exhaustion and stop fighting.

The woman asks why Leon is there, and he tells her he wants to know why she was at Agamemnon's house. She says her name is Claire, and Leon isn't the only one interested in Agamemnon and his death. Leon says he is investigating Agamemnon's death. Claire does not want to give Leon any information on how she knows about Agamemnon, but she does show Leon that all she took was a business ledger. She says Leon can scan it with her scanner, but she is keeping the original.

END OF ACT TWO

ACT THREE

20. INT. POLICE STATION – DAY

Sabine goes to Maxwell and tells him that she wants them to work together to solve both of their cases. Maxwell says he wants to work on his own. Sabine points out similarities between the murders of both the muggers and the old lady. Both were injured with very similar blade wounds. Maxwell tells Sabine he doesn't care—the captain clearly doesn't like her, and he wants to distance himself from her. He has a whole career to think about, not just one case. Sabine then shows Maxwell one more thing—at each crime scene, the crime lab found traces of bull fur.

21. INT. LEON'S HOME – DAY

Leon is resting. Franklin wants to know what happened to Leon, because Leon is hurt. Leon tells Franklin to stay uninvolved. Franklin helps treat Leon's injuries.

22. EXT. CITY STREET – DAY

Leon walks up to the Argive Technologies building, home of Agamemnon's company. Leon is dressed as a delivery man.

23. INT. ARGIVE TECHNOLOGIES BUILDING – DAY

Leon walks inside. He shows that he has a package for the second floor. He is let in.

24. INT. ARGIVE TECHNOLOGIES BUILDING – SECOND FLOOR – DAY

Leon goes to the second floor and opens the package, which only contains a roll of tape. He crumples up the box, which he throws into a janitor cart trash can. He finds the fire escape door and tapes shut the door latch. He leaves the building.

25. INT. POLICE STATION – CAPTAIN'S OFFICE – DAY

Sabine goes to Captain Miller. She wants the captain to assign her and Maxwell as partners, so they can solve both cases. The captain says no; as he already told Sabine the old lady case wouldn't be assigned to her. She tells the captain about the lead she has. Maxwell insists that they not be made partners. The Captain asks Maxwell if he has made any progress on the case. Maxwell admits he has not.

The captain tells Maxwell to start showing results. He tells them they can work together to solve both cases, but he warns them he will be watching carefully.

26. EXT. CITY STREET – NIGHT

Leon goes to the Argive Technologies building. He peeks inside and sees SECURITY GUARDS all over the first floor lobby.

27. EXT. CITY ALLEY – NIGHT

Leon walks around to an alley next to the building. He sees if the building has a fire escape. It does, but the stairs are retracted. Leon becomes the Minotaur. He climbs up the fire escape of the building on the other side of the alley. He walks many floors up. He finds a door and uses a blade to unlock it. He goes inside, turns around, and runs. He runs toward the fire escape, leaps forward, and lands...

28. EXT. ARGIVE TECHNOLOGIES BUILDING – CONTINUOUS

...on the fire escape of the Argive Technologies building. Leon walks up to the second floor, where he finds the door he taped open earlier.

29. INT. ARGIVE TECHNOLOGIES BUILDING – CONTINUOUS

Leon goes inside. The building is half-lit. The only people here are security guards. Leon evades them and finds the main stairwell, as using an elevator would be too noticeable.

30. INT. ARGIVE TECHNOLOGIES BUILDING – STAIRWELL – CONTINUOUS

In the stairwell, Leon finds a SECURITY GUARD (40s). Leon hears the guard coming and waits around a corner of the stairwell to knock the guard out when he reaches him. Leon walks all the way up to the top of the building.

31. INT. ARGIVE TECHNOLOGIES BUILDING – TOP FLOOR – CONTINUOUS

Leon exits the stairwell to find a SECURITY GUARD (40s). The guard pulls out his gun. Leon charges the short distance at him and grabs the gun away. The guard calls for backup. Leon headbutts the guard right in the mouth. Leon whips around behind the guard and covers his mouth before choking him out. Leon finds Agamemnon's office.

32. INT. ARGIVE TECH BUILDING – AGAMEMNON'S OFFICE – CONTINUOUS

Leon breaks in. An ALARM sounds. Leon frantically searches through drawers, cabinets, and desks, trying to find anything suspicious. The top of Agamemnon's desk shifts slightly. Confused, Leon wipes everything off the top of the desk. He moves it around. The desk has a false top.

Leon removes it. Underneath, there is a small area with a lid with a keyhole in it. Leon takes out his blade and picks the lock.

Inside, Leon sees a few scattered DVDs and Polaroids. The Polaroids depict women tied up and bleeding. Leon takes them.

33. INT. ARGIVE TECHNOLOGIES BUILDING – STAIRWELL – CONTINUOUS

Leon rushes out of the office as security guards stream toward him. He fights his way back to the stairwell.

34. INT. ARGIVE TECHNOLOGIES BUILDING – TOP FLOOR – CONTINUOUS

Leon charges down the stairs. Security guards come at him and Leon shoots them or fights them back. Leon escapes.

35. INT. LEON'S HOME – LIVING ROOM – NIGHT

Leon goes to the TV. He inserts one of the DVDs. It depicts a SCRUFFY, TALL MAN (40s) beating a woman tied to a chair. The man then takes off his belt. Leon keeps watching. Moments later on the recording, the man takes his belt and wraps it around the woman's throat.

END OF ACT THREE

ACT FOUR

36. INT. LEON'S HOME – LIVING ROOM – DAY

Leon watches the DVDs. Franklin comes in and sees what Leon is watching. Franklin wants to know where Leon got the DVDs. Leon shows Franklin that he is using a face-matching technology that he hacked into in order to discover who the scruffy, tall man in the video is. Leon wants to find him.

Franklin turns off the video. He urges Leon not to watch this, as it is damaging. Leon tells Franklin he needs to check it thoroughly. Franklin tells Leon he should have turned them over to the police. Leon tells Franklin that the police wouldn't have known what to do with this.

Franklin wants Leon to stop while he's ahead—as in, alive. Agamemnon was no joke. Leon is getting into dangerous territory. Franklin tells Leon he won't be able to help if Leon gets caught. He says he won't help Leon get himself killed. He mentions Leon's sister, Tehya, and tells Leon he doesn't have to avenge her. Leon turns the video back on. He wants to kill the man.

37. INT. MARCUS' HOME – LIVING ROOM – DAY

The scruffy, tall man, MARCUS, is in his living room. He is gathering his documents and belongings, including a pile of DVDs. Marcus is trying to get out of here, fast. There is a knock on the door. Marcus stops what he's doing and pulls out a gun. Marcus looks through the peephole. No one is there. Marcus goes back to packing more frantically. The Minotaur comes up behind Marcus. He knocks Marcus out.

38. INT. OLD LADY'S HOME – DAY

Sabine and Maxwell investigate the crime scene. They want to find more evidence than just similar knife wounds. They look over the whole crime scene before Sabine asks how the killer could have gotten in. Sabine realizes the door was unlocked when she got there the first time. She goes to the door and sees that the lock has been broken by being picked—same as in the muggers' apartment. They realize that the killer uses the same blade for picking locks and for killing. The start of an MO.

39. INT. MARCUS' HOME – BASEMENT – NIGHT

Marcus wakes up in his basement. He is tied to a chair. He tries to escape. Leon, as the Minotaur, stands in front of him. The Minotaur demands that Marcus tell him about Agamemnon. Marcus says he won't.

The Minotaur takes off his belt. He beats Marcus with it. He tells Marcus he saw the DVDs. He tells Marcus that Marcus can do nothing to save himself now, except maybe talk. The Minotaur punches Marcus in the gut and in the face. Still, Marcus won't talk.

The Minotaur takes out a knife and sticks it down Marcus' pants. Marcus finally gives in. He screams out and tells Leon to find Claire.

40. EXT. CITY STREET – DAY

Sabine and Maxwell get out of a police car. The captain is already there. He asks them if they found anything, and they say they did. He congratulates them and tells them they'll continue to be partners—and they have a new case. They walk into a house.

41. INT. MARCUS' HOME – BASEMENT – DAY

The Captain shows Sabine and Maxwell the dead, bloody body of Marcus, still tied to a chair. Sabine looks down. She crouches. She picks something up. She stands and stares at something in her hand—bull fur.

42. INT. HOSPITAL – A ROOM – NIGHT

Leon enters a hospital room. He cautiously approaches the bed. In it lies TEHYA (40s), hooked up to machines. She is unconscious, in a coma. Leon sits down on the bed with her. He strokes her face.

43. INT. LEON'S HOME – LIVING ROOM – NIGHT

Franklin is home. He goes to the living room. He sees the DVDs stacked up on the table. Next to them are the stapled-together scanned pages from the business ledger. Franklin looks through them. On the last page, he sees a transaction recorded for an enormous sum of money. The name on the account is Daedalus. Franklin tears out the page.

END OF PILOT

Exit Stage Left
"Pilot"
Outline
by Sarah Kenney

TEASER

1. EXT. GLENSHEE QUAD – DAY

GEORGIA MOSS, 20, in her uniform of glasses, leggings, and oversized shirt, walks across the Glenshee College quad. Her phone buzzes from a text. She sees it's from her friend Victor. He claims to have "received solid intel" on the production announcement meeting happening that afternoon.

Georgia shrieks loudly enough to disturb three FRISBEE GOLFERS, two guys and a girl, playing nearby. Georgia tries to call Victor several times, then texts him, but he texts back that he'll meet her later at the theater. She shouts, "No! You can't do this to me!" and takes off in the other direction for the dorms, further disturbing the Frisbee golfers.

2. EXT. GLENSHEE DORMS – DAY

Georgia sprints up the stairs to the boys' dorm and throws open the door.

3. INT. GLENSHEE DORMS – HALLWAY – CONTINUOUS

Georgia needs to find out what Victor knows and nothing is going to get in her way. Except maybe the BRO with a towel wrapped around his waist exiting the bathroom. As Georgia smacks into him, his towel falls. She doesn't have time for awkwardness at this particular moment. As she resumes racing to Victor's room, she yells to the bro that he should really invest in a belted robe if he's going to run into people like that.

Georgia reaches Victor's door and pounds on it excitedly. VICTOR REIS, 20, tall and darkly good-looking (although currently disheveled) groans and opens the door. Georgia wants the details on the rumor. He indicates that he "has company," but Georgia will not be deterred: "You can't just drop a hint about what could be the most important show announcement of my college theater career and then leave me hanging."

Victor really wants Georgia to leave. He says he can meet her at the theater in a half hour. Victor tries to shut the door. Georgia, not leaving, sticks her foot in the door before it closes. She has her obligatory "graduation strategy meeting" with her parents now, but she needs to hear what Victor knows before she can deal with that nightmare.

Victor's unseen one-night stand (because they're ALL one-night stands) starts to pull him back to bed. Georgia tries to peek in to see who it is this time, and Victor definitely wants to keep that a secret. His attention pulled in opposite directions, he shouts "SONDHEIM!" through the crack. Georgia starts in disbelief and takes her foot out to jump up and down, but her "WHAT?!" goes unanswered as the door slams shut. It doesn't matter. Georgia is overjoyed.

4. EXT. GLENSHEE QUAD – DAY

Georgia exits the dorm and practically skips down the quad sidewalks. She reaches the middle and pauses—if she doesn't do something with this excitement, she's going to burst. Georgia sees the Frisbee golfers still at it, and she has an idea.

5. EXT. GLENSHEE QUAD – DAY– DAYDREAM

Her demeanor shifts from excitable to calm and authoritative. Georgia calls "Places!" to the Frisbee golfers, who instantly drop their game and, fixing their clothes and hair, rush over to an arrangement of rocks on the quad. When they are set, Georgia calls "Action" and the Frisbee golfers begin performing "Opening Doors" from Stephen Sondheim's *Merrily We Roll Along.*

As the song progresses, Georgia directs some passersby on the quad to take parts as needed. She directs others to bring in more set pieces. As the number progresses toward the archway in the building at the end of the quad, each location in the song gets more detailed. They move from the rocks to a section with a piano and folding chairs designating an apartment. After that, a segment of lawn with easy chairs, a desk, and a standalone door designating a producer's office. By the end of the number the archway has been turned into a nightclub with a stage and lights. As her "cast" wraps it up behind her, Georgia heads off to meet her parents, invigorated.

END DAYDREAM.

6. INT. TINY CAMPUS CAFE – DAY

The mood is decidedly different in the cafe. Georgia's parents, CARTER MOSS, 50ish, wearing an odd combination of button down and baseball cap, and CHERYL MOSS, 50ish, the sort of woman who has gone gracefully gray and would look weird with makeup, sit across from her.

It's Georgia's junior year and Carter wants Georgia to think seriously about her future. Georgia tells them she is serious about theater. She's been begging professor and faculty director Harold Harman for the past two years to do Sondheim instead of another one of his original compositions, and she just heard he's finally agreed. She's going to get to student direct Sondheim.

Cheryl has mediated this conversation before and wants it to go smoothly. Cheryl reminds Georgia that she and Carter want Georgia to set herself up for success after graduation. Though Georgia insists she can do that focusing on theater, Carter doesn't want to hear it anymore and tells her they won't help her pay for school if she doesn't switch her major and just do theater as a hobby. Cheryl wants Carter to back off a little, and she reminds Georgia that Georgia's AP chemistry and biology credits transferred from high school. It wouldn't be too difficult for Georgia to do a STEM major and still have time for theater. Georgia wants to talk them down to a minor, but they ultimately settle on a double major. Even though that means her thesis will now somehow have to combine theater and biology.

7. EXT. GLENSHEE QUAD - DAY - DAYDREAM

The wind out of her sails, Georgia slumps back through the confetti and streamers mess of her musical number while a crew clears away the sets, like this moment of joy never existed. She has to go to her paid job on campus, scene shop student assistant.

END DAYDREAM.

8. INT. BIXBY THEATER - DAY

Georgia walks through the theater doors and immediately hears crashes, commotion, and shouting coming from the scene shop. The sounds of imminent catastrophe means she's home. If there's a theater-related problem to solve, Georgia's pumped to make it work. The pep back in her step, she marches to the back of the theater eager to confront the disaster. This is where she belongs.

END OF TEASER

ACT ONE

9. INT. BIXBY THEATER SCENE SHOP - DAY

Victor has been waiting for Georgia. He wants her to handle the unpleasant situation that is currently destroying the scene shop. Georgia insists on taking over the training of the new FRESHMAN SHOP RECRUITS, huddled terrified in a corner, from the scene shop supervisor, ZLATKA, who is more of a yeller than a teacher. Because of the wide array of power tools present, it's a job with the potential for danger. Even so, Georgia still wants the shop trainees to think it's a fun.

IRIS WILLIAMS, 21, statuesque and very chic, is the senior student costume shop supervisor. She strolls into the scene shop with the air of someone who owns every room she enters. She wants to enlist some of the freshmen to work for her in the costume shop, where "it's safe and there's glitter." Georgia wants Iris to enlighten her as to why Iris can't simply post for freshmen assistants like everyone else. Georgia would prefer that Iris dispense with this dramatic spectacle. Iris feels there's no fun in that for her, and that she gets a special joy from liberating the poor, unsuspecting freshmen from the cold, harsh world of the scene shop. Iris takes almost half the students and leaves.

10. INT. COSTUME SHOP – DAY

After putting them to work, Iris surveys her new employees. She's extremely proud of the work she's done in costumes, and she wants to find a new recruit with potential to groom to take over for her when she graduates. And also to do her bidding. Her last "minion" was a disappointment, and she won't repeat her mistakes a second time. Iris takes a shine to BRANDON, a young man who knows his way around a needle and chiffon. He wants to impress her.

11. INT. SCENE SHOP – DAY

HAROLD HARMAN, late 30s, dressed all in blacks like a cartoon director, enters excitedly. He wants everyone to come out to the theater for the department meeting and show announcement. Harold can barely contain himself, wanting everyone to share in his excitement for his big surprise. He seems like he's about to spill the beans, but then just bursts out for everyone to join him in the theater. Georgia actually is as excited as Harold wants his whole department to be, and she runs out after him to tell him...

12. INT. STAGE HALLWAY – CONTINUOUS

...that Georgia already knows what he's going to say. Georgia wants to thank him so much for the opportunity to work on such an amazing show by someone who is such a gift to the world of American musical theater. This is exactly what she needed after the challenging morning she had with her parents. She can't wait to see his presentation. Harold is surprised, but he is incredibly flattered by the outpouring of support from Georgia. Harold wasn't sure how she'd feel about his choice.

It's clear they are thinking two very different things. Georgia is so focused on her belief that Sondheim is about to happen that she doesn't notice. Assuring Harold she loves the idea, Georgia follows Harold into the theater.

13. INT. BIXBY THEATER STAGE – MOMENTS LATER

The students file in from the scene and costume shops. The ACTORS are already in the seats. Harold announces that he worked all summer on a musical adaptation of the movie *Witness*, called *Witness! The Musical.*

Harold was inspired by the local Amish population and wanted to "pay homage to their beautiful heritage with some deeply respectful and yet thrillingly bodice-ripping musical numbers."

Harold wants PAUL, 20, star actor of the department who is handsome and knows it, to perform one of the numbers Harold wrote so everyone can get a feel for the tone of the play.

As Paul sings, Georgia's rage at being denied the opportunity to direct an actual, good show once again because of Harold's idiocy builds to a boil. She wants to let it all out...

13. INT. BIXBY THEATER STAGE – DAYDREAM
Georgia bursts from her seat to give what essentially builds to the "I'm mad as hell, and I'm not gonna take it anymore!" speech from *Network*. Georgia climbs up on stage, pacing around Paul as he sings.

She snaps out of the daydream as Paul sings the final note of the song.

END DAYDREAM.

14. INT. BIXBY THEATER STAGE – RESUME
Harold wants to know what everyone thinks and gets crickets. Georgia stands, says, "I quit" and exits the theater.

END OF ACT ONE

ACT TWO

15. EXT. GLENSHEE QUAD – DAY
Victor chases after Georgia. He wants her to stop and come back to the theater. She's angry at him and demands to know where he heard it was Sondheim. Victor dodges the question and tells her he had no idea Harold was going to do this. Victor wants Georgia to go back and talk Harold out of this awful-sounding show. Victor wants to avoid at all costs being stuck for another production making Harold's terrible set designs.

Georgia demands once again to know who told him it was Sondheim. Victor wants to keep that information to himself. For lack of a better option, Victor just stands there, gesturing hopefully for her to come back with him to the theater. Georgia says if he won't tell her, she's done with him, too. Georgia stalks off back to her dorm.

16. INT. GEORGIA AND SPIN'S DORM ROOM – DAY

Georgia paces frantically in the three feet of space between her bed and Spin's bed. In full panic-mode, Georgia wants to vent what has just happened with both her parents and the theater department: "I feel like my whole life and everything I ever knew to be true has just completely exploded!"

STEPHANIE "SPIN" PIN, 20, petite, cute, and a true original in terms of style, playfully tells Georgia she's being dramatic. Spin sprays something on a small collection of marijuana plants in her closet. She wants to help Georgia, so she calmly and reasonably finds the silver linings to both of Georgia's clouds. Georgia isn't bad at biology, and the play could at least be funny. It just depends on how Georgia chooses to look at it.

But Georgia doesn't have time to think about it now, because she and Spin have to go to bio class.

17. EXT. GLENSHEE QUAD – DAY

Georgia and Spin head to the bio building. Paul quickly walks up next to Georgia as they reach the center of the quad. Paul wants to talk to Georgia about what happened that morning. Georgia wants Paul to tell her how long he knew about the show. Despite his obvious involvement, he wants to maintain his innocence. He bemoans how it was supposed to be a surprise, and he hadn't known that she wanted to do Sondheim. Paul really doesn't want Georgia to be angry with him. He's worried about the tonal direction of Harold's show. He tries to get Georgia's input. She snaps at him that she wants to be left alone. Georgia wants to put Harold and his crap behind her and move on with her life to a nice, consistent academic career in the physical sciences. She's working hard to convince herself.

18. INT. BIOLOGY BUILDING – DAY
Georgia tries to pay attention in biology class. She doodles in her notebook as the professor drones on.

19. INT. BIOLOGY BUILDING – DAY – DAYDREAM
Suddenly inspired, Georgia raises her hand and directs the professor on ways to make his lecture more interesting. She suggests blocking, and she wants him to communicate the passion that he has for teaching. The class becomes a musical performance about the scintillating field of microbiology.

END DAYDREAM.

20. INT. BIOLOGY BUILDING – RESUME
Georgia is brought back to reality when the professor asks her a question. She gets it right but doesn't seem satisfied. Despite everything, she wants to go back to the theater.

END OF ACT TWO

ACT THREE

21. INT. COSTUME CLOSET – DAY
Victor pulls Iris into the costume closet. He demands to know why she told him last night in his room that she'd heard from Harold they were doing Sondheim. Iris claims she knew he'd tell Georgia. She's over Georgia's controlling attitude and wants her taken down a peg.

Iris had mentored Georgia when Georgia was a freshman, and Georgia had abandoned costumes for directing after the first semester. Georgia was Iris' "disappointment." Victor is pissed at Iris for being petty. He leaves her in the closet. Iris is conflicted over her feelings for him and her intense dislike of Georgia.

<u>22. EXT. BACK OF BIO BUILDING – DAY</u>

It's a beautiful fall day. Spin and Georgia are lying out in the sun after class. Spin pulls out a one-hitter and asks Georgia if she wants to try some of the new weed she's been working on. Georgia says "no" but takes a hit anyway. She wants to ruminate on her future.

Spin wants Georgia to just try to enjoy college for what it is, because her life will never be like this again. Georgia tries to come up with ideas for a joint biology/theater thesis. Dissecting Harold moves to the top of the list. Spin says she thought Georgia wanted to quit theater.

Caught, and a little stoned, Georgia pauses to carefully consider what she wants to say:

"I want...a burrito."

<u>23. INT. COSTUME SHOP – DAY</u>

Iris works on sketches for the musical. She sighs at the drab Amish costumes, but she's dedicated to accuracy. Victor, still upset with her, enters and drops off drawings of dresses strippers might wear if they wanted to go with an "Amish" theme. These are Harold's costume concept drawings.

Horrified, Iris demands that Victor take them back to Harold and explain that Iris has been given total control over all production costumes. It's been this way since she was a sophomore. Victor declines, wanting Iris to understand that the only person Harold ever even sometimes listened to was Georgia. If Iris wants things back the way they were, she's going to have to clean up her own mess.

24. INT. TINY CAMPUS CAFE – DAY

Georgia and Spin are eating enormous burritos. Iris, judging them for consuming these head-sized burritos, approaches. Georgia asks what she wants, then decides she doesn't care and takes a big bite. It's clearly painful for Iris, but she asks for Georgia's help with the costume situation. Georgia can't help herself. Even though this is not even a little bit the show she was hoping for, Georgia wants every play that comes out of Bixby during her time in school to be the best that it can be.

Spin wants to know if Iris will make her one of Harold's dresses.

END OF ACT THREE

ACT FOUR

25. INT. HAROLD'S OFFICE – NIGHT

Georgia wants to get her student directing job back. Harold wants her to know how hurt he is that she abandoned him after the show announcement. She's honest with him that she had hoped they were going to do Sondheim, as they'd discussed last year. She knows how to handle Harold's personality, so though he is being petty and difficult, she gives him what he wants.

After giving it some thought, she says, she thinks *Witness! The Musical* could be the high point of Harold's legacy at Glenshee. But that's not all. Georgia also thinks that, if they get it just right, *Witness!* might be the show that finally gains the theater department entry into the Kennedy Theater Arts Festival in Washington, D.C. Though all his prior attempts have been just as terribly misguided, this is the rabbit Harold has been chasing since he started working at the school. Georgia wants to communicate to him her ideas on how to get them to the festival. She gets her student directing job back.

26. INT. SCENE SHOP – NIGHT

Georgia is back in control and wants to survey the damage. Victor, as repentant as he gets, wants Georgia to know that he's glad she's back. Their friendship runs deep and, wanting to get back to work, Georgia lightly brushes it off with, "What? I just went to get some lunch. Don't cry about it."

Georgia, expecting the worst, wants to see Harold's scenic sketches. Zlatka and Victor hate the sketches tremendously, and it's easy to see why. They look like they were drawn by a four-year-old…is that a spaceship? Stopping Zlatka from marching back to Harold's office to throttle him, Georgia relays her plan.

Everything the department has seen of this play so far is a generally offensive jumble of Amish-themed nonsense. With a little focus and actual direction, Georgia thinks it could go one of two ways. Georgia wants to get Harold to take *Witness!* as seriously as possible. No skanky Amish dresses, no Beatles *Yellow Submarine* sets. That way, if it's just as hilariously terrible as they fear it will be, it will be so on its on merits. On the other hand, if they pull it off…Georgia has started to believe her own hype. She wants to believe there's a way she could bring this trash heap of a musical up from the dump and straight to that arts festival.

Zlatka and Victor worry Georgia has lost her mind.

27. INT. BIXBY THEATER – NIGHT

Georgia wants to begin the first table read of *Witness! The Musical.* It is patently wretched, and everyone knows it. Georgia wants to be there, though she knows this production is going to be an uphill climb of Sisyphean proportions. She wants to make this play work.

END OF PILOT

ENDNOTES

Introduction

[1] [T]he explosion of TV shows—a record 412 original, scripted TV series in 2015...
Littleton, Cynthia. "FX's John Landgraf on Competition For TV Talent: 'It's Moneyball'." *Variety.* January 16, 2016.
http://variety.com/2016/tv/news/john-landgraf-fx-moneyball-tca-1201681533/ (Retrieved January 16, 2016.)

[2] For example, Mickey Fisher's career hit the stratosphere...
Weinstein, Shelli. "How a Contest led First-Time Creator Mickey Fisher to Spielberg." *Variety.* July 1, 2014.
http://variety.com/2014/tv/news/extant-how-a-contest-led-creator-mickey-fisher-to-spielberg-1201254597/ (Retrieved July 14, 2015.)

Andreeva, Nellie. "Sci-Fi Drama From Novice Writer Sparks Major Bidding War in Broadcast & Cable." Deadline Hollywood. August 2, 1013. http://deadline.com/2013/08/sci-fi-drama-from-novice-writer-sparks-major-bidding-war-in-broadcast-cable-555490/ (Retrieved July 14, 2015)

Chapter 1

[3] *Glee* – At a time when the studio and network had to spend more, the ratings dropped and the show lost viewers.
"Glee Season Four Ratings." TVseriesfinale. May 23, 2012.
http://tvseriesfinale.com/tv-show/glee-ratings-2011-2012/

May 14, 2013 http://tvseriesfinale.com/tv-show/glee-season-four-ratings-24348/ (Retrieved July 14, 2015)

[4] NBC president Bob Greenblatt talked about *Parenthood...*
Gonzalez, Sandra. "With Parenthood signing off, a look at the future of family dramas." Mashable. January 29, 2015.
http://mashable.com/2015/01/29/parenthood-family-dramas/
(Retrieved July 14, 2015)

[5] *Empire* premiered with 9.8 million viewers with a 3.7 rating...
"Empire Season One Ratings." TVseriesfinale.
http://tvseriesfinale.com/tv-show/empire-season-one-ratings-35198/
(Retrieved July 14, 2015)

[6] *Empire* – For its freshman season finale...
"Empire Season One Ratings." TVseriesfinale.
http://tvseriesfinale.com/tv-show/empire-season-one-ratings-35198/
(Retrieved July 14, 2015)

[7] *Sons of Anarchy* – The seventh season of "Hamlet set in a motorcycle gang..."
Littleton, Cynthia. "'Sons of Anarchy' Finale Rides off with 9.2 Million Viewers." *Variety.* December 15, 2014.
http://variety.com/2014/tv/news/sons-of-anarchy-finale-rides-off-with-9-2-million-viewers-1201380072/ (Retrieved July 14, 2015)

[8] *The Millers* and *The McCarthys* had tough competition at the Eye.
Andreeva, Nellie. "'The Millers' Cancelled by CBS." Deadline Hollywood. November 14, 2014. http://deadline.com/2014/11/the-millers-cancelled-cbs-1201284943/ (Retrieved July 14, 2015)

[9] *Jane the Virgin* is adapted from a Venezuelan telenovela...
Stanley, Alessandra. "Jane the Virgin Ends a Strong First Season."
The New York Times. May 10, 2015.
http://www.nytimes.com/2015/05/11/arts/television/jane-the-virgin-ends-a-strong-first-season.html (Retrieved July 15, 2015)

[10] *Jane the Virgin* has charmed the critics...
"Jane The Virgin Season One Ratings." TVseriesfinale. May 13, 2015. http://tvseriesfinale.com/tv-show/jane-the-virgin-season-one-ratings-34349/ (Retrieved July 15, 2015) (Retrieved July 15, 2015)

[11] *Marry Me, Selfie, A to Z, Manhattan Love Story,* and *Weird Loners* didn't make it past a first season.
Staff, Deadshirt. "Cancelled TV Postmortem – Sitcoms We Lost This Season." Deadshirt. May 21, 2015.
http://deadshirt.net/2015/05/21/cancelled-tv-shows-2015/ (Retrieved July 15, 2015)

"Weird Loners TV show on FOX: canceled, no season 2." TVseriesfinale. May 9, 2015. http://tvseriesfinale.com/tv-show/weird-loners-fox-comedy-cancelled-after-six-episodes-36572/ (Retrieved July 15, 2015)

[12] Hulu picked up *The Mindy Project...*
Spangler, Todd. "'The Mindy Project' Moving to Hulu for Season 4 after Fox cancellation." *Variety.* May 15, 2015.
http://variety.com/2015/digital/news/the-mindy-project-moving-to-hulu-for-season-4-after-fox-cancellation-1201497556/ (Retrieved July 15, 2015)

[13] Aaron Sorkin's *Newsroom* and *Sports Night* both struggled to gain...
de Moreas, Lisa. "'The Newsroom' Logs Season High in Swan Song." Deadline Hollywood. December 16, 2014.
http://deadline.com/2014/12/newsroom-finale-season-high-ratings-hbo-aaron-sorkin-canceled-1201325945/ (Retrieved July 15, 2015)

Atkinson, Katie. "Sports Night: An oral history, starring Aaron Sorkin and his cast." *Entertainment Weekly.* November 6, 2014.
http://www.ew.com/article/2014/11/06/sports-night-oral-history (Retrieved July 15, 2015)

[14] Fox's *Back to You* created by *Modern Family*'s Christopher Lloyd and Steven Levitan…
"Back to You cancelled, No season two?" TVseriesfinale. May 27, 2008. http://tvseriesfinale.com/tv-show/back-to-you-why-was-it-cancelled-is-it-gone-for-good/

[15] With *American Horror Story, True Detective,* and *Fargo…*
Cwik, Greg. "Fargo and the New Approach to Anthology TV." Cheatsheet. May 10, 2014. http://www.cheatsheet.com/entertainment/fargo-and-the-new-approach-to-anthology-tv.html/?a=viewall (Retrieved July 15, 2015)

Chapter 2

[16] But show bibles are part of the WGA minimum basic agreement…
WGA "Schedule of Minimums: 2014 Theatrical and Television Basic Agreement." WGA. May 25, 2015.
http://www.wga.org/uploadedFiles/writers_resources/contracts/min2014.pdf (Retrieved July 15, 2015)

[17] *Gotham* – The season finale brought in a 1.7 rating…
"Gotham Season One Ratings." TVseriesfinale. May 5, 2015.
http://tvseriesfinale.com/tv-show/gotham-season-one-ratings-33994/ (Retrieved July 15, 2015)

[18] Game of Thrones – It's based, in part, on the War of the Roses.
Gendler, Alex. "The wars that inspired Game of Thrones." Online video. TED Ed, n.d. http://ed.ted.com/lessons/the-wars-that-inspired-game-of-thrones-alex-gendler (Retrieved July 15, 2015)

Martin, George R.R. "George R.R. Martin Webchat transcript." Re: "Qhorinmate says: I have read that Westeros is 'sort of based on medieval Britain.'" *Empire*, n.d.
http://www.empireonline.com/interviews/interview.asp?IID=1496 (Retrieved July 15, 2015)

[19] We'd understand that a decade-long summer is ending...
Martin, George R. R. *A Clash of Kings.* New York, Bantam Books. 1999. Prologue.

"Westeros – A Wiki of Ice and Fire"
http://awoiaf.westeros.org/index.php/Westeros (Retrieved July 15, 2015)

[20] For example, both *Gotham* and *Marvel's Agents of S.H.I.E.L.D.* are...
Outlaw, Kofi. "Gotham Premiere Rating Solid; Can't Outdo Agents of S.H.I.E.L.D." September 23, 2014. http://screenrant.com/gotham-premeire-ratings-vs-agents-shield/ (Retrieved July 15, 2015)

Gonzales, David. Gotham and Agents of S.H.I.E.L.D. Forbes. September 30, 2014. (Retrieved July 15, 2015)
http://www.forbes.com/sites/davegonzales/2014/09/30/gotham-and-agents-of-s-h-i-e-l-d-similar-ratings-similar-goals/

"Gotham Season One Ratings." TVseriesfinale. May 5, 2015.
http://tvseriesfinale.com/tv-show/gotham-season-one-ratings-33994/ (Retrieved July 15, 2015)

"Marvel's Agents of S.H.I.E.L.D. TV show on ABC: latest ratings" TVseriesfinale. May 13, 2015. http://tvseriesfinale.com/tv-show/marvels-agents-of-shield-season-two-ratings-34016/ (Retrieved July 15, 2015)

[21] After landing the role of an SVU detective, Mariska...
Horst, Carol. "Mariska Hargitay: Joyful Heart Foundation Helps Rape Survivors." *Variety.* November 8, 2013.
http://variety.com/2013/biz/news/mariska-hargitay-helps-survivors-of-rape-and-violence-find-hope-1200806915/ (Retrieved July 15, 2015)

[22] In his 1946 book *The Art of Dramatic Writing...*
Egri, Lagos. *The Art of Dramatic Writing.* 1946. November 5, 2007. Rockville, MD: Wildside Press. Pg. 36-37.

[23] He modeled House on Sir Arthur Conan Doyle's character Sherlock Holmes.
Foreman, Richard. "House, MD." *Los Angeles Times.* n. d. http://www.latimes.com/entertainment/lat-sherlock-md_l3rgqmnc20111101161710-photo.html (Retrieved July 15, 2015)

David Shore talks about casting Hugh Laurie
Shore, David. "David Shore Interview: David Shore on Casting Hugh Laurie as Gregory House." Online video. Archive of American Television. The Television Academy Foundation. n.d. http://www.emmytvlegends.org/interviews/people/david-shore# (Retrieved July 15, 2015)

[24] Hugh Laurie – He was nominated for six Primetime Emmys...
"Hugh Laurie – Awards." IMDB. n. d. http://www.imdb.com/name/nm0491402/awards?ref_=nm_awd (Retrieved July 15, 2015)

[25] Other actors Dennis Leary, Rob Morrow, and Patrick Dempsey...
Challen, Paul. *The House that Hugh Laurie Built: An Unauthorized Biography and Episode Guide.* Toronto, ECW Press. 2007. Pg. 39.

[26] David Shore said he had been familiar with Hugh Laurie's comedic...
Ibid.

[27] Here are Lajos Egri's attributes for his character-bone structure.
Egri, Lagos. *The Art of Dramatic Writing.* 1946. November 5, 2007. Rockville, MD: Wildside Press. Pg. 36-37.

[28] ...Aristotle with the idea of negative character traits.
Propp, Vladimir. *On the Comic and Laughter.* Edited and translated by J. P. Debbéche and P. Perron. Toronto: University of Toronto Press Incorporated, 2009. Pg. 105

[29] Here's exactly how Steven Levitan and Christopher Lloyd described the main characters in the *Modern Family* pilot...
Levitan, Steven and Christopher Lloyd. *My American Family.* 20th Century Fox. December 9, 2008.

[30] *Dig* – It averaged 0.32 in the demo with 1.21 million viewers.
"Dig Season One Ratings." TVseriesfinale. July 1, 2015.
http://tvseriesfinale.com/tv-show/dig-season-one-ratings-35954/
(Retrieved July 15, 2015)

[31] *Complications,* a dark drama about a doctor...
"Complications Season One Ratings." TVseriesfinale. July 11, 2015.
http://tvseriesfinale.com/tv-show/complications-season-one-ratings-37173/ (Retrieved July 15, 2015)

[32] USA has already cancelled a previous dark drama about a doctor, *Rush*...It averaged a 0.4..."
"Rush: cancelled by USA, No Season 2." TVseriesfinale. October 2, 2014.
http://tvseriesfinale.com/tv-show/rush-cancelled-by-usa-no-season-two-34195/ (Retrieved July 15, 2015)

[33] *Mr. Robot's* series premiere garnered about 3 million views across multiple non-linear platforms.
Kissell, Rick. "USA Rookie Drama Mr. Robot Surges in Week Two." *Variety.* July 6, 2015.

[34] Every pilot pitching season the broadcast networks hear approximately 400 full-on, in-person pitches...
Miller, Kam. "Upfronts with NBC Development Executive Joey Chavez." kammiller.com May 15, 2012.
http://kammiller.com/2012/05/15/upfronts-with-nbc-development-executive-joey-chavez/ (Retrieved May 15, 2015)

[35] Amy Chozick. "The Math of a Hit TV Show." *The Wall Street Journal.* May 12, 2011.
http://www.wsj.com/articles/SB10001424052748703864204576315240324571266 (Retrieved May 15, 2015)

[36] *Transparent* – Creator Jill Soloway's parent made this transition.
Grow, Kory. "Transparent Creator Jill Soloway on Making the World Safer for Trans People." *Rolling Stone.* October 20, 2014.
www.rollingstone.com/tv/features/transparent-jill-soloway-20141020#ixzz3g0bKzQsJ (Retrieved July 15, 2015)

[37] After saying "Movies don't matter anymore" and retiring from feature filmmaking, Steven Soderbergh...
Child, Ben. "Steven Soderbergh retires from film: Movies Don't Matter Anymore." *The Guardian.* January 30, 2013.
http://www.theguardian.com/film/2013/jan/30/steven-soderbergh-retires-from-film (Retrieved July 15, 2015)

[38] *The Knick* drew 1.7 million viewers...
Kissell, Rick. "The Knick Draws Gross Audience of 1.7 Million for Cinemax, HBO Weekend Plays." *Variety.* August 11, 2014.
http://variety.com/2014/data/ratings/the-knick-draws-gross-audience-of-1-7-million-for-cinemax-hbo-weekend-plays-1201280247/ (Retrieved July 15, 2015)

[39] The *Banshee* season 2 finale demolished Cinemax's ratings record (591K viewers) when it drew 733K viewers for the 10PM airing.
"Banshee Season Finale Sets Ratings Record for Cinemax." The Deadline Team. DeadlineHollywood.com. March 17, 2014.
http://deadline.com/2014/03/banshee-season-finale-cinemax-record-700371/ (Retrieved July 15, 2015)

[40] *Banshee* – Their season three numbers weren't quite up to this level with an average of 580K viewers for the season.
"Banshee Season Three Ratings." TVseriesfinale. March 16, 2015.
http://tvseriesfinale.com/tv-show/banshee-season-three-ratings-35323/ (Retrieved July 15, 2015)

[41] *The Hollywood Reporter* featured an admiring 25th-anniversary retrospective about *Star Trek: The Next Generation*'s pivotal story arc "The Best of Both Worlds Part 1 and Part 2."
Crouch, Aaron. "Star Trek: The Story of the Most Daring Cliffhanger in Next Generation History." *The Hollywood Reporter*. June 20, 2015.
http://www.hollywoodreporter.com/heat-vision/star-trek-story-daring-cliffhanger-803642 (Retrieved July 15, 2015)

[42] Sadly, Michael Piller had died in 2005 after a battle with cancer.
Robinson, Ben. "Re: Interview with Michael Piller." on "Star Trek: The Unlikely Story Behind the Cliffhanger that made Next Generation Cool." *The Hollywood Reporter* – Disqus. June 20, 2015.
http://www.hollywoodreporter.com/heat-vision/star-trek-story-daring-cliffhanger-803642 (Retrieved July 15, 2015)

Chapter 3

[43] In his work *Poetics,* Aristotle didn't refer to acts *per se,* but he proposed the very simple idea...
Aristotle. *Poetics.* Section 1450b. from Aristotle. *Aristotle in 23 Volumes,* Vol. 23, Trans. W.H. Fyfe. Cambridge, MA, Harvard University Press; London, William Heinemann Ltd. 1932.
http://www.perseus.tufts.edu/hopper/text?doc=Aristot.+Poet.+1450b&redirect=true (Retrieved July 15, 2015)

[44] While Indy *loses* the ark (again), he has Marion on his arm (thanks to Marcia Lucas)...
Pollock, Dale. *Skywalking: The Life And Films of George Lucas, Updated Edition.* 2009. Boston, MA: Da Capo Press. Pg. 228.

Chapter 4

[45] Tatiana must hit her marks precisely and execute her performance exactly the same way.
Loofbourow, Lili. "The Many Faces of Tatiana Maslany." *The New York Times.* April 2, 2015.
http://www.nytimes.com/2015/04/05/magazine/the-many-faces-of-tatiana-maslany.html?_r=0 (Retrieved August 5, 2015)

[46] Lee Daniels and Danny Strong are very talented writers. They've had successful, lauded, and varied writing careers.
"Lee Daniels – Awards." IMDb. n. d.
http://www.imdb.com/name/nm0200005/awards?ref_=nm_awd (Retrieved July 15, 2015)

"Danny Strong – Awards" IMDb n.d.
http://www.imdb.com/name/nm0834960/awards?ref_=nm_awd (Retrieved July 15, 2015)

[47] After sharing some of their own families' stories...
Smith, Patrick. "Modern Family series 2: creator Christopher Lloyd on why it won an Emmy." *The Telegraph*. October 02, 2010. http://www.telegraph.co.uk/culture/tvandradio/8032812/Modern-Family-series-2-creator-Christopher-Lloyd-on-why-it-won-an-Emmy.html (Retrieved August 5, 2015)

[48] Actor-writer-producer Rob McElhenney developed the show with Glenn Howerton. Rob, Glen, and Charlie Day shot a pilot on a borrowed digicam recorder and shopped the show around town.
Blitz, Stefan. "The $85 TV Pilot: The Origins of IT'S ALWAYS SUNNY IN PHILADELPHIA." Indigoprod. http://www.indigoprod.com/nyc-video-production-blog/2014/06/the-85-tv-pilot-the-origins-of-its-always-sunny-in-philadelphia/ (Retrieved August 5, 2015)

[49] *Sunny* is the longest running comedy in cable history and the second longest running sitcom in television history. According to Deadline Hollywood, the trio signed a deal in 2014 that is said to surpass their previous $50 million 3-year deal with FX, which they signed in 2011.

Andreeva, Nellie. "Rob McElhenney, Glenn Howerton & Charlie Day Ink Big New 3-Year Deal With FX Prods. That Includes 2-Year Renewal Of 'It's Always Sunny In Philadelphia', Series Pickup Of Tracy Morgan Comedy, Pilot & Script Orders." Deadline Hollywood. April 4, 2014. http://deadline.com/2014/04/rob-mcelhenney-glenn-howerton-charlie-day-ink-big-new-3-year-deal-with-fx-prods-that-includes-2-year-renewal-of-its-always-sunny-in-philadelphia-series-pickup-of-tracy-morgan-comedy-pilot-709797/ (Retrieved August 5, 2015)

Chapter 5

[50] It bowed to record ratings (5.35 million viewers with a 2.7 rating in the 18-49 demographic) for the network...
Seidman, Robert. "Sunday Cable Ratings: The Walking Dead Kills; Boardwalk Empire steady; +Swamp People, Dexter, Ghost Hunters Live,

and Much More." TVbythenumbers. November 02, 2010. http://tvbythenumbers.zap2it.com/2010/11/02/sunday-cable-ratings-the-walking-dead-kills-boardwalk-empire-steady-swamp-people-dexter-ghost-hunters-live-much-more/70585/ (Retrieved August 5, 2015)

[51] The 90-minute fifth season finale averaged an 8.2 rating in adults 18-49 and 15.8 million viewers overall.
Bibel, Sara. "Sunday Cable Ratings: 'The Walking Dead' Tops the Night, 'Talking Dead,' 'Real Housewives of Atlanta,' 'Going Clear,' 'Killing Jesus,' & More." TVbythenumbers. March 31, 2015. http://tvbythenumbers.zap2it.com/2015/03/31/sunday-cable-ratings-the-walking-dead-tops-night-talking-dead-real-housewives-of-atlanta-going-clear-killing-jesus-more/382018/ (Retrieved August 5, 2015)

[52] Based on the Robert Kirkman graphic novels, *The Walking Dead* had been in development for five years before Frank took it to AMC.
Jeffery, Morgan. "Darabont: 'NBC turned down Walking Dead.'" Digital Spy. July 6, 2010. http://www.digitalspy.com/tv/s135/the-walking-dead/news/a239038/darabont-nbc-turned-down-walking-dead.html#~pkxF3cYNhDY5lW (Retrieved August 5, 2015)

[53] In an interview with Steve Barton for DreadCentral, Frank said "I'd gotten turned down enough times, which is no reflection on the material, but no matter what you're trying to sell in Hollywood, you're Willy Loman and it's Death of a Salesman. You're out there trying to sell shit that nobody wants. Even if it's good shit."
Barton, Steve. "'The Walking Dead' Set Visit Part I: Bringing Kirkman's 'Walking Dead' to Life." DreadCentral. August 05, 2010. http://www.dreadcentral.com/news/18773/the-walking-dead-set-visit-part-i-bringing-kirkman-s-walking-dead-to-life/ (Retrieved August 5, 2015)

[54] He paired up with Gale Anne Hurd at Valhalla. Together, they took it to AMC.
McIntrye, Gina. "'Walking Dead' creator Frank Darabont explains the need for 'the occasional ripping flesh.'" *Los Angeles Times*. October 29, 2010. http://herocomplex.latimes.com/tv/walking-dead-creator-frank-darabont-explains-the-need-for-the-occasional-ripping-flesh/ (Retrieved August 5, 2015)

[55] The series, based on the mega-hit *New York Times* best-selling novels by Diana Gabaldon, set the highest rated multi-platform premiere in Starz' history with approximately 2.3 million viewers. It's estimated that roughly 51% of those viewers are women.

[56] Kissell, Rick. "'Outlander' Sets Starz Ratings Record for Multi-Platform Viewing." *Variety*. August 11, 2014.
http://variety.com/2014/tv/news/outlander-sets-starz-ratings-record-for-multi-platform-viewing-1201280319/ (Retrieved August 5, 2015)

[57] *Transparent*'s creator Jill Soloway...was the executive producer of *The United States of Tara*.

"Jill Soloway." IMDB. n.d.
http://www.imdb.com/name/nm0813561/?ref_=fn_al_nm_1 (Retrieved August 5, 2015)

[58] She has written several plays, including *The Miss Vagina Pageant* and *Not Without my Nipples*.
Godfrey, Alex. "My Movie Makes Men Uncomfortable." *The Guardian*. March 31, 2014. http://www.theguardian.com/film/2014/mar/31/jill-soloway-afternoon-delight (Retrieved August 5, 2015)

[59] Alan Ball read her short story "Courtney Cox's Asshole"
Miller, Danny. "Confessions of a Masturgoogler." Chicago Reader. September 15, 2006. http://www.chicagoreader.com/chicago/confessions-of-a-masturgoogler/Content?oid=919916 (Retrieved August 5, 2015)

[60] For several years, Jill, along with Maggie Rowe and Jaclyn Lafer, has produced Sit 'n Spin, which is an open mic/variety show for to working comedy writers in LA. "Sit 'N Spin – People reading things that are funny, dirty, and sad, twice a month in Los Angeles."
Lafer, Jaclyn, Maggie Rowe, Maggie, and Soloway, Jill. Sit 'N Spin, 2015. http://www.sitnspin.org (Retrieved August 5, 2015)

[61] Jill shared part of her experience in a *Rolling Stone* article. She said, "It just immediately hit me as this is the show I've been waiting my whole life to write."
Grow, Kory. "'Transparent' Creator Jill Soloway on Making the World Safer for Trans People." *Rolling Stone* October 20, 2014. http://www.rollingstone.com/tv/features/transparent-jill-soloway-20141020#ixzz3eqiYbVEL (Retrieved August 5, 2015)

Chapter 6

[62] The *Transformers* features franchise has adopted the TV writers room model...
Fleming, Mike. "Akiva Goldsman Explains 'Transformers' Writers Room as Paramount adds Scribe Pair." Deadline Hollywood. June 4, 2015. http://deadline.com/2015/06/transformers-akiva-goldsman-writers-room-michael-bay-paramount-1201438017/ (Retrieved August 6, 2015)

Chapter 9

[63] "For me and most other writers I know, writing is not rapturous. In fact, the only way I can get anything written at all is to write really, really shitty first drafts."
Lamott, Anne. *Bird by Bird.* New York, NY: Anchor Books, 1995.

[64] We don't see Professor Keating's face...
"Pilot." *How to Get Away with Murder.* Writ. Peter Norwalk. Dir. Michael Offer. Walt Disney Studios, 2014. Streaming video.

ABOUT THE AUTHOR

Kam Miller is a TV writer who has created pilots for Fox, CBS, 20th Century Fox, Paramount Television, and Universal Cable Productions. She wrote for Fox's *Killer Instinct* as well as the long-running NBC show *Law & Order: SVU.* Her first feature, *The Iris Effect,* was produced while she was at the USC School of Cinematic Arts.

Kam has taught TV writing at the USC School of Cinematic Arts and Boston University's Film and Television department. She is a graduate of the WGA Showrunners Training Program.

Kam is developing several TV projects and writing her second novel. Kam's first novel, *Myth of Crime,* is a crime-suspense thriller. *Myth of Crime* introduces Victims Assistance Center psychologist Dr. Erika Harlow and rookie homicide detective Carter Hunt. Kam joined with other women TV writers for a short-story anthology, *Empower: Fight Like a Girl,* benefiting the non-profit Lupus Foundation of America. *Empower: Fight Like a Girl* contains the short story "Dangerous Stars," featuring Erika and Carter; it's available on Amazon.

For more about Kam and her upcoming projects,
visit **kammiller.com** and
follow **@kammotion** on Twitter.